A *WESTERN HORSEMAN* BOOK

UNDERSTANDING LAMENESS

Examining Equine Lameness from Diagnosis to Prognosis

By Terry Swanson, DVM, with Heidi Nyland, MS
Research Assistance by Jennifer Paulson

Edited by
Fran Devereux Smith and Cathy Martindale

Photography by
Heidi Nyland
John Brasseaux
Littleton Equine Medical Center
Terry Swanson
John Bell
Sddita Fradette
Dr. Chris Pollitt/Hoofcare & Lameness Journal:
Keila Rooney

Illustrations by
Roy Dean Swanson
Dwayne Brech

Understanding Lameness

Published by
WESTERN HORSEMAN magazine
3850 North Nevada Ave.
Box 7980
Colorado Springs, CO 80933-7980
800-877-5278

www.westernhorseman.com

Design, Typography, and Production
Western Horseman
Fort Worth, Texas

Front and Back Cover Photos by
Heidi Nyland

Printing
Branch Smith
Fort Worth, Texas

Manufactured in the United States of America

First Printing: February 2009

ISBN 978-0-911647-74-7

DEDICATION

This book is dedicated to all the horses—past, present and future—that perform the tasks we ask of them as willing and enthusiastic partners.

ACKNOWLEDGMENTS

It's a great privilege to present this information about equine lameness. This book represents an accumulation of my clinical experiences. More important, it is a compilation of the influence that my professional colleagues have had on my interpretation of those experiences and in helping me understand what I was seeing. It's fortunate that equine veterinarians are so generous in sharing their experiences and knowledge with all who are interested.

Therefore, I'm especially grateful for my partners and associates at Littleton (Colo.) Equine Medical Center, once known as Littleton Large Animal Clinic. We gather weekly to go over case rounds and discuss interesting and difficult lameness issues. These open and frank discussions provide a great forum for progressive thought processes. Likewise, local, national and international equine veterinary colleagues, not competitors, gather to exchange ideas and help each other for the good of the horse. This makes me proud to be a part of equine veterinary medicine.

The credit for the collection of the material in this book goes to Jennifer Baron Paulson for her great research and to Heidi Nyland, who did the writing. Their patience and understanding of a veterinarian's work style made it all come together.

Photographs are very helpful in most learning situations. I want to thank Heidi for her excellent work and also express gratitude to John Brasseaux for his photographs of horses doing amazing things with their bodies.

I also appreciate the confidence of *Western Horseman* and of the book editor, Fran Smith, for helping me to do this.

To my wife, Peachie Elaine, and my son, Roy Dean: I'm so grateful for your support, patience and understanding while I have taken the time to look at one more horse.

I'm proud to say the sketches, which add another dimension to the understanding of the written words, are the products of Roy Dean Swanson.

My original partners, Dr. G. Marvin Beeman and Dr. Charlie D. Vail, fostered an environment in which we all developed a desire and an appreciation for learning more about the horse. I appreciate their guidance and professionalism, as well as their friendship. Of the many values I learned from them, one stands out regarding lame horses: There is no substitute for an accurate and thorough physical exam.

To the many clients who patiently have worked through their horses' problems with me, I say, "Thank you."

We are all fortunate to be living in this time of the resurgence of the horse.

—Terry Swanson, DVM

Many thanks to friends and family who provided help and support during the writing process. I must thank my supportive editor, Fran Smith, who knew just when to send a friendly e-mail. Thanks, also, to my mom, Carolyn Nyland, and dear friend Pam Federer for help during long brainstorming sessions to create "worst-case scenarios" and for answering late-night phone calls to discuss how to portray veterinary terms in easy language. Federer also modeled therapy and take-home care with her registered Paint Horse, Mister Rhythm. To my cohorts at *Western Horseman* and my many friends in the equine publishing industry, thanks for your patience and constant can-do attitudes.

—Heidi Nyland, MS

PREFACE

Lameness is the most common infirmity of the horse. It's rarely a life-threatening issue when compared with other problems, such as colic or major fractures, but it often causes pain, resulting in an alteration of the horse's gait.

A veterinarian must perform many steps to successfully determine the site of lameness. First, he asks the owner for a history of the cause of concern, such as a gait alteration, performance decline or other indicators. The well-informed owner can provide information that the veterinarian might not otherwise know, specifically about how the horse's current behavior differs from his normal attitude. Then, the veterinarian can proceed with the diagnostic exam to pinpoint the lameness.

Terry Swanson, DVM, has compiled this book to provide horse owners and riders a tool to better understand conditions that produce lameness in their horses. This understanding will enhance the owners' and riders' abilities to provide thorough and meaningful information that will be helpful in solving their horses' problems. In addition, by better understanding the conditions Swanson so aptly describes in this book, owners are more likely to detect problems earlier in their development, allowing for more satisfactory resolutions of those problems.

The abilities to detect lameness and determine the site of pain require astute, trained observational capabilities, both visually and through palpation. These abilities don't come without considerable time and effort that focus on discerning as much information as possible in a rapid manner. Simply said, it's a matter of the veterinarian learning to see what he or she is looking at. Swanson has certainly learned to see what he's looking at.

Swanson was a student of the lame horse before becoming a veterinarian because he was first a horseman. Throughout his professional career, Swanson has improved his ability to evaluate and detect lameness through the use of advanced diagnostic methods and by learning from educational opportunities in the United States and abroad. Swanson also continually shares opinions and seeks advice from his associates at Littleton Equine Medical Center in Littleton, Colo. His involvement has been a major factor in the clinic's ability to obtain and utilize sophisticated diagnostic equipment that can verify the sites of pain and, therefore, lameness. Additionally, he rides horses and is very aware of the various jobs his equine patients perform. An educated veterinarian and a sensitive rider has a very deep understanding of a horse's problems.

These credentials have provided Swanson with the materials to produce a very useful book on the lame horse. I hope you'll gather information from this work and apply it in such a way that your horse's health and welfare will improve.

G. Marvin Beeman, DVM
Littleton Equine Medical Center

CONTENTS

1

IS YOUR HORSE LAME?

**Work closely with your trusted veterinarian to identify
and treat your horse's lameness problems.**

You've invested much time and money in your favorite horse. You've bought everything possible to keep him safe and injury-free. He has a cushioned, mat-lined stall, guards to keep him from being cast and boots to wear when you ride and while he's on the trailer. Your feed room door always is closed, and your horse's stall has a special latch to ensure that he doesn't escape to look for founder-causing treats. His regimented workout routine keeps his muscles and bones strong.

Still, you can't help but worry about what might happen. In your thoughts, a hypothetical scene plays again and again—you walk to your barn, head to your horse's stall and find him standing on three legs. At first glance, you might imagine the worst—that your horse is permanently lame

and won't be able to continue his usual training or daily workouts. Your thoughts continue to spin. Just what can be done if your horse is lame? How can you tell how bad the injury or lameness really is? What will become of your horse if he hurts himself or simply turns up lame one day?

In books and movies, lame horses typically don't have long or bright prospects; in those works, lameness is synonymous with "the end." Now, for many causes of lameness, new technology and advanced diagnosis methods can help identify and treat lameness. Many horses can be healthy again, returning to their previous workloads after proper healing time. However, some accidents can cause enough damage to significantly alter your horse's future performance prospects and even affect his long-term health.

Your horse is your trusted partner, and you do your best to keep him in top shape. But you worry that he might be injured and become too lame to maintain his steady pace.

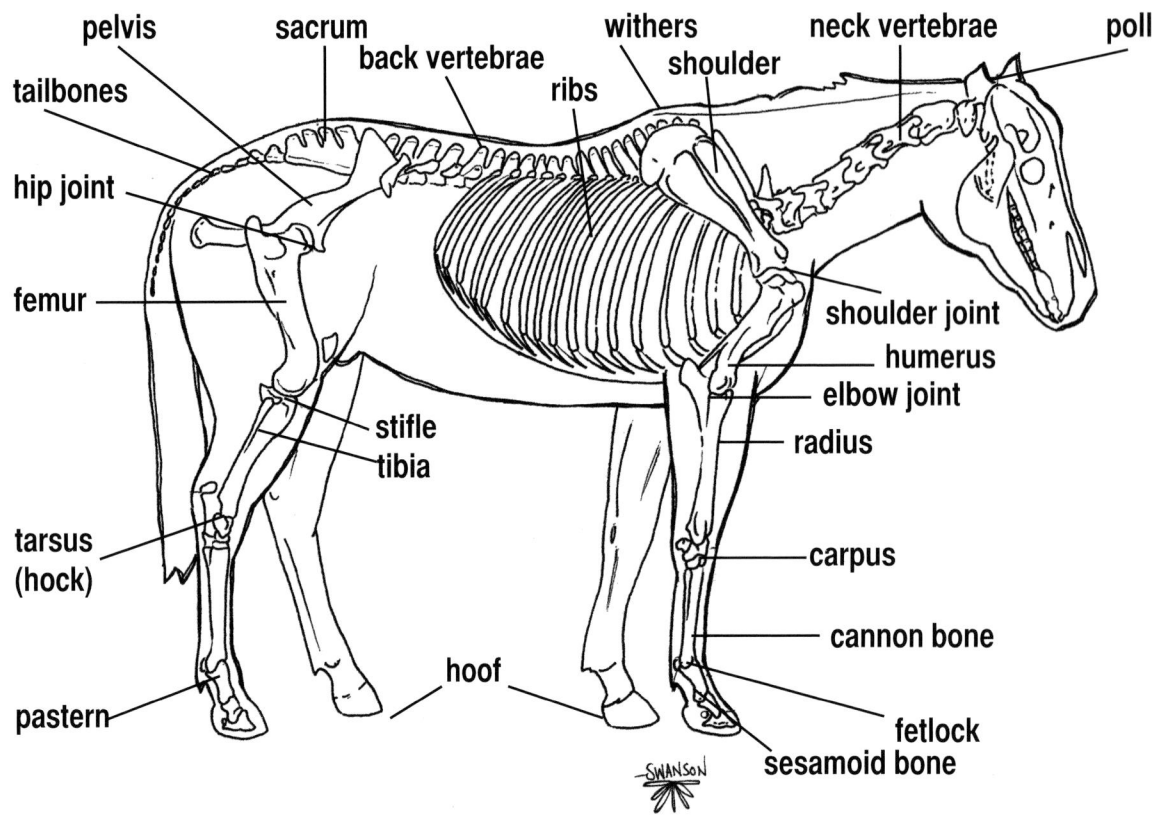

pelvis sacrum withers neck vertebrae poll
tailbones back vertebrae shoulder
ribs
hip joint
femur shoulder joint
humerus
elbow joint
stifle radius
tibia
tarsus carpus
(hock)
cannon bone
hoof
pastern fetlock
sesamoid bone

Learn about each part of your horse's body that can incur an injury resulting in lameness. Use this book as a guide to help identify potential problems with all parts of your horse—from the ground up.

As a responsible horse owner, it's up to you to watch for the first signs of lameness and know when to seek help. By training your eye to see even the most subtle changes in movement—or by learning to constantly check your horse's body for soreness, heat and swelling—you might help prevent further damage or identify problems before they become severe.

Use this book as your field guide to help you understand different degrees of lameness and the effects different injuries can have on your horse's future health. Relax and take a breath. With guidance from Terry Swanson, DVM and partner at the internationally respected Littleton Equine Medical Center (formerly known as Littleton Large Animal Clinic), you can understand every part of your horse's structure that impacts his ability to move soundly and with cadence. Swanson guides you through each part of your horse's structural anatomy—starting with the foot, as your veterinarian most likely will during any lameness exam. Swanson then travels up the front legs, analyzes the hindquarters and stifle, and finishes with soft-tissue and spinal problems that can lead to lameness.

For each problem in each part of the body, you learn how your horse might incur injury. Too, you learn what symptoms and signs to watch before delving into the details and learning what's really going on in your horse's body, as well as how he might heal. Keep in mind that this book's goal is to discuss common lameness problems. Complex fractures and traumatic injuries are outside the scope of this book.

Read on to find out how veterinarians define lameness. Understand how to describe levels of lameness to your veterinarian if you must report a common problem. Find out what a lameness exam involves—what your veterinarian considers and what tools he might use to pinpoint your horse's lameness.

A Working Definition

If your horse is lame, he doesn't move as smoothly as usual. His gait might be obviously different, or he might just seem stiff and "off." Pain prevents your horse from maintaining an evenly cadenced gait. Pain also might limit your horse's range of motion. How much his gait changes depends on how much pain he feels and the extent to which an injury or internal problem has impacted his internal structures. Your horse might move differently because of anatomical, mechanical or neurological issues. Terms such as "off," "a little short," "not free," or "choppy" are interchangeable with "lameness." The phrases are subjective, but can be helpful to describe your horse's altered movement to your veterinarian.

You've probably also heard the terms "sound" and "unsound." The words aren't descriptive and don't provide the details your veterinarian needs to fully understand how a horse moves. When speaking with your veterinarian, "sound" refers to your horse's ability to complete a suitable job willingly and as asked. "Unsound" means your horse isn't able to complete a job willingly and safely.

These definitions depend on what a horse is being asked to do. If your horse shows some lameness, but is still able to do the work as you ask, he might be considered "serviceably sound." For example, a horse with arthritis might not have the flat-kneed action desirable for Western pleasure showing, but he might do a great job as a children's therapy horse that walks in soft footing twice a week while carrying a light load. He's sound for that given job. On the other hand, the same horse would be unsound for high-level Western pleasure classes. A horse only slightly lame might be completely unsound for a specific job. For a more black-and-white description, use the phrase "free of lameness" to describe a horse that's totally sound, no matter what job he's asked to perform.

JOHN BRASSEAUX

The same horse that isn't sound enough for demanding performance classes might be sound for other, less intense work.

Pay close attention to your horse's stance and movements. You know his habits better than anyone and will be the first to notice when he doesn't stand or move correctly.

Seem confusing? Think of the terms applied to a professional football player. The linebacker's body is most likely beaten and bruised from continuous practice and high-intensity games. When a doctor examines the player, he might find swollen knuckles and ugly bruises. Still, the player says he feels fine, and the doctor clears him for the next day's game. The player is sound for his job of running straight ahead and plowing through the competitor's formations. But if that same battered football player was expected to perform a complex and refined gymnastic floor routine, his body might not be healthy enough to perform. The bruises and swollen joints would stop him from bending and flexing as required in gymnastics.

A veterinarian's job is slightly different from the team doctor's for one huge reason—the football player can express if and where he feels pain. A veterinarian, however, must assess his equine patient and determine the source of pain without discussion. The veterinarian also must decide if the horse can safely continue his job without exacerbating the lameness.

Recognizing Lameness

Depending on how much pain he feels, your horse might exhibit different levels of lameness. And just as with humans, different horses respond differently to the same amount of pain. One horse refuses to move his injured foot, but another horse with the same injury might try to do what's asked of him. Different horses have different pain tolerances.

It's up to you to learn about your horse's personality and how he responds to the slightest changes. If your horse is suddenly unwilling or reluctant to perform, that could indicate low-grade lameness. You also might notice that your usually cooperative horse suddenly has problems with lead changes or doesn't move as well when tracking to the right as when tracking left. Watch your horse to make sure that he doesn't rest the same leg consistently, point one foot in front of the other or constantly shift his weight from side to side. All these signs point to a low-grade lameness issue.

If your horse has a more pronounced lameness issue, he might limp, especially at the trot, where each leg must bear weight independently. Watch your horse's movement at

LAMENESS Q&A

What role does behavior play in diagnosing lameness?

Some lameness cases involve the horse's behavior. A horse that kicks out during lead changes, charges or rushes through obstacles or maneuvers, fusses with his head position, or refuses to move forward might be responding to pain in some part of his body. This is an area where the veterinarian and owner must be astute to sort out these issues. Dental problems might be part of this complex picture.

I've seen a horse react inappropriately in the roping box. The horse didn't want to settle in the box and tried to charge out and whirl around. A horse may act out in those ways because he anticipates being uncomfortable. He might have subtle lameness when he's working in the arena—when he stops and turns the steer—or he might have discomfort when his rider pulls back and the bit touches the horse's mouth in the wrong place. It's important for the horse's owner, rider, veterinarian and farrier to work together to determine the cause of the behavior and find a way to alleviate it.

How do I know when to call a veterinarian? Are there certain steps I can take to "test" my horse a bit before I call?

If you work closely with your horse, you often can detect lameness before anyone else. You know when your horse isn't performing as well as he can. Here are some steps you can take if you're not certain it's time to call your veterinarian. The information you gather helps your veterinarian know how quickly you need an appointment:

- If your horse experienced an injury or is obviously lame, don't bother with the tests. Place a call immediately.

- Walk your horse on a firm, flat surface and notice if your horse's cadence seems rhythmic or uneven. Then turn him to see if he's more lame as you turn or round a corner.

- You also can feel your horse's lower leg for a digital pulse. Touch just above your horse's heel bulb along the tendons of the pastern and feel for a pronounced pulse. When your horse is healthy, you won't easily find a pulse.

- Put your hands on the outside of your horse's hoof to feel for heat. Compare temperatures by feeling his unaffected hoof, too.

the trot, and you might easily determine if one or multiple legs are affected.

For a more telling observation, walk and trot your horse in a small circle on a hard, even surface. Not every lameness issue shows up while your horse moves in a circle, but the circle test often is an easy way to tell which leg or legs are hurting. Usually your horse bobs his head and struggles more when his lame leg is on the inside of the circle. So if

MAKING THE GRADE
Lameness Categories as Defined by the American Association of Equine Practitioners (www.aaep.org)

Grade 1: Your horse's lameness is difficult to observe; it isn't consistently apparent, even when the horse carries weight or works on an incline or hard surface.

Grade 2: Your horse's lameness is difficult to observe when he moves at a walk or trot in a straight line. However, the lameness is consistently apparent when he carries weight, circles and/or works on an incline or hard surface.

Grade 3: At this stage, your horse's lameness is always observable at a trot.

Grade 4: Your horse is obviously lame. He nods his head, shortens his stride and/or moves with obvious pain.

Grade 5: Your horse doesn't want to move—or isn't able to do so. He bears no weight on his affected leg.

your horse's left front leg is lame, he limps or bobs his head more when tracking left. This general rule has several exceptions. Some lameness issues are more obvious when the affected leg is on the outside of the circle. Your veterinarian can help you see the gait changes as your horse moves.

If, as he evaluates your horse's movement, your veterinarian asks you to lead your horse, make sure you do so on a smooth, flat surface. If possible, lead your horse to an asphalt driveway or parking lot surface. Be prepared to lead your horse at a consistent speed. Look ahead and walk or jog rhythmically. Your vet-

erinarian might ask you to lead your horse at a walk or trot in a straight line, or circle your horse to the left and right.

As you lead your horse, your veterinarian watches for specific movements and avoidance behavior. By altering his gait, your horse is trying to minimize the pain he feels when the sore limb connects with the hard ground. Your horse also might swing his leg strangely in an attempt to reduce pain or to avoid touching down and bearing weight. If your horse has a weight-bearing lameness, which means he doesn't want to put weight on one or more legs, he raises his shoulder

After interviewing you about your horse's habits, your veterinarian begins his exam by evaluating your horse's stance, posture and conformation.

and head in a nodding or bobbing motion when his affected leg hits the ground. Again, he attempts to hold up his body and minimize the amount of weight placed on the injured leg. When your horse's opposite leg hits the ground, he allows his body weight to land much harder. He drops his head as the sound leg lands, creating more pressure on the healthy side. The sound of your horse's hooves on the ground, if you listen closely, supports your observations. When your horse's affected leg hits the ground, it sounds softer than the healthy leg when it hits the ground. Sometimes, an injured horse might shorten his diagonal hind leg's stride to take additional body weight if his front leg is sore.

If one of your horse's hind legs is in pain, he might lower his head to help pull his body weight forward. When your horse's lame hind leg hits the ground, he lowers his head to shift weight onto his front legs. By using his neck and head, the horse can transfer weight forward or backward, depending on his selected position. With many hind-leg lameness scenarios, your horse shortens his length of stride as the pained leg moves forward, and he doesn't reach as far forward with that leg as usual.

If your horse has "swinging-leg" lameness, he makes a labored effort to pull his injured leg forward by swinging it forward from his shoulder or hip. Your horse might swing forward if his shoulder or forearm muscles are injured. He labors to move the limb forward, and you see pronounced shoulder or hip movement.

Keep in mind that you often see a relationship between your horse's lame leg and the diagonal front or hind leg. When your horse works so hard to avoid placing pressure on a leg, he stresses the diagonal leg. If he's been lame for some time, he might have a secondary lameness in the leg diagonal to the initially injured leg.

Making the Grade

As you already have learned, much of the language used to describe a lame horse's condition is vague. To create a more precise way to communicate, the American Association of Equine Practitioners developed guidelines to define and classify levels of lameness. Knowing the guidelines can help you use specific and telling language when talking with your veterinarian. The lameness levels also

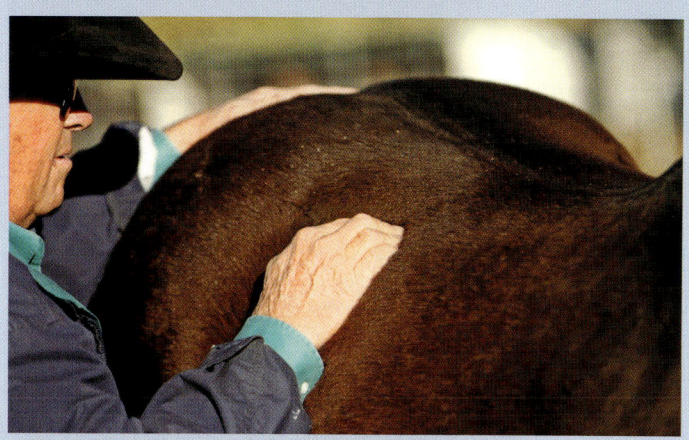

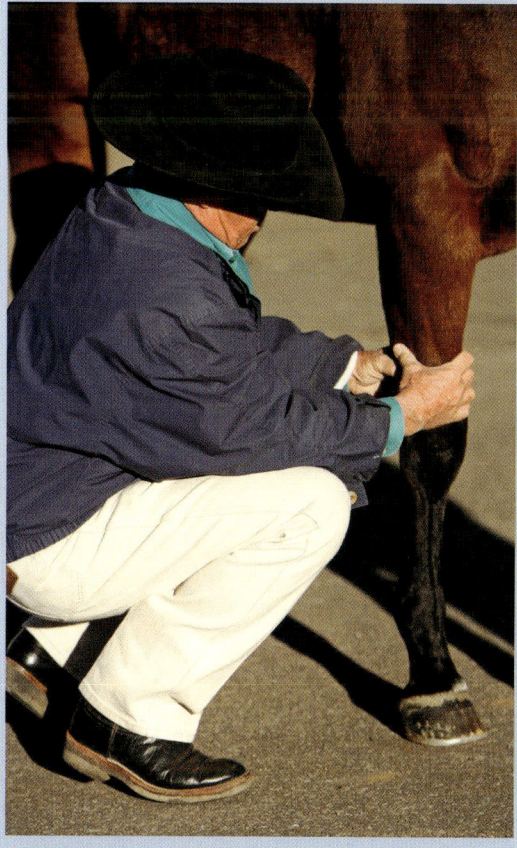

Your veterinarian then feels your horse's neck, back and legs to detect pain and sensitivity.

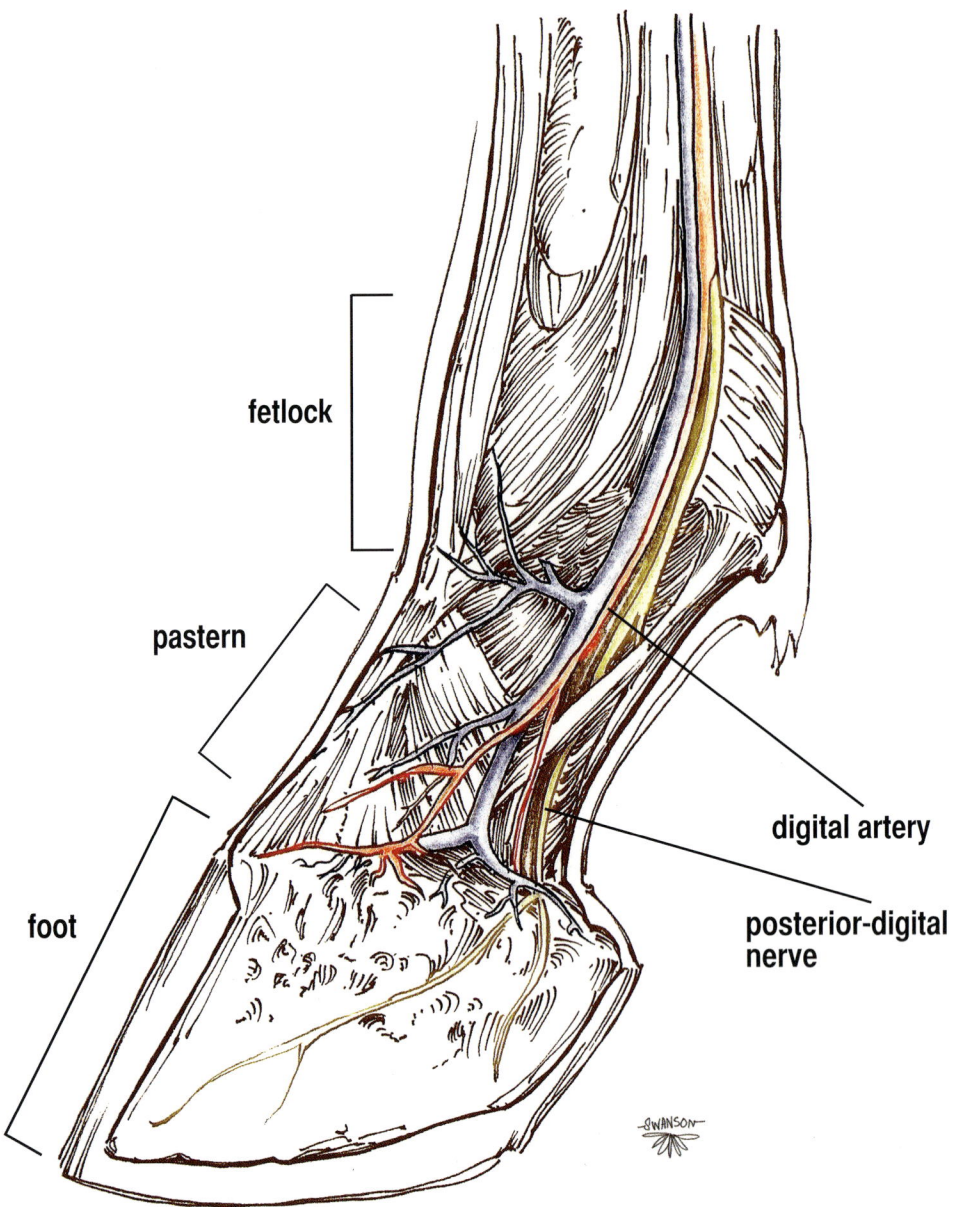

fetlock

pastern

foot

digital artery

posterior-digital nerve

SWANSON

The red area shows the artery; you feel your horse's digital pulse as blood in the artery passes through the fetlock or pastern. The yellow area is the posterior digital nerve—the first nerve addressed in diagnostic nerve blocking. The blue area shows the horse's vein as it removes blood from the foot.

help veterinarians talk with each other about specific cases.

Your veterinarian grades your horse with one number when he completes his lameness examination, but he also grades each stage of the evaluation, which helps him to track changes throughout the exam. Your horse might receive a Grade 1 lameness rating during a flexion test and a Grade 3 while he circles on the asphalt. Refer to the scale to see if your horse rates a 1, 2, 3, 4, or 5. Grade 1 lameness is minor; Grade 5 is severe.

Your Horse's Lameness Exam

If you and your horse compete in any sport at any level, you want to work with your veterinarian to ensure your horse's constant health and ability to keep competing. With proper care, you might help your performance horse maintain or even extend his career. You want your veterinarian to know how your horse moves usually, when there is no problem. Then you and your veterinarian can work together to notice problems quickly should anything change. The veterinarian can help you decide if your horse is up to the tasks you're asking him to perform.

During a lameness exam, your veterinarian wants to gather as much information as possible about your horse's orthopedic problems. The cause of your horse's lameness might be obvious and straightforward to heal; some lameness problems are complex and even obscure. Your horse's symptoms might result from an underlying, nagging issue that hasn't been apparent until it began to affect other body parts.

Your veterinarian interviews you to find out what you've noticed in your horse's movement as you've led and ridden him. Think about what language most clearly portrays your horse's change in motion. Also make notes about any behavioral changes that occurred in your horse at the same time the physical symptoms emerged. Your veterinarian also needs a list of all your horse's past veterinary issues, as well as past treatments. Make sure to have a current list of all your horse's medications and supplements. Don't feel pressured to diagnose your horse's lameness before your veterinarian arrives, just have as much data as possible ready and available to help.

On-site, your veterinarian observes your horse's stance, posture and conformation. The veterinarian palpates your horse's neck, back and legs, noting any soreness or heat that could be the root or symptom of the lameness. Your veterinarian feels your horse's lower leg to check for any increase in digital pulse, a throbbing, detectable pulse on your horse's lower leg, just above the heel bulb, along the tendons at the back of his pastern. By feeling your horse's muscles and structures, your veterinarian can understand more about your horse, become familiar with the horse's usual movements and learn how your horse responds to touch.

Next, your veterinarian observes your horse in motion. Your veterinarian watches from both the front and rear as your horse tracks in a straight line and also watches your horse circle in both directions. The veterinarian also might ask that your horse work on a longe line in soft, arena footing, while watching closely for any gait irregularities when your horse transitions between a walk, trot and canter or lope. The veterinarian also might longe your horse on a harder surface to note any changes. Depending on what he notices in your horse, you also could be

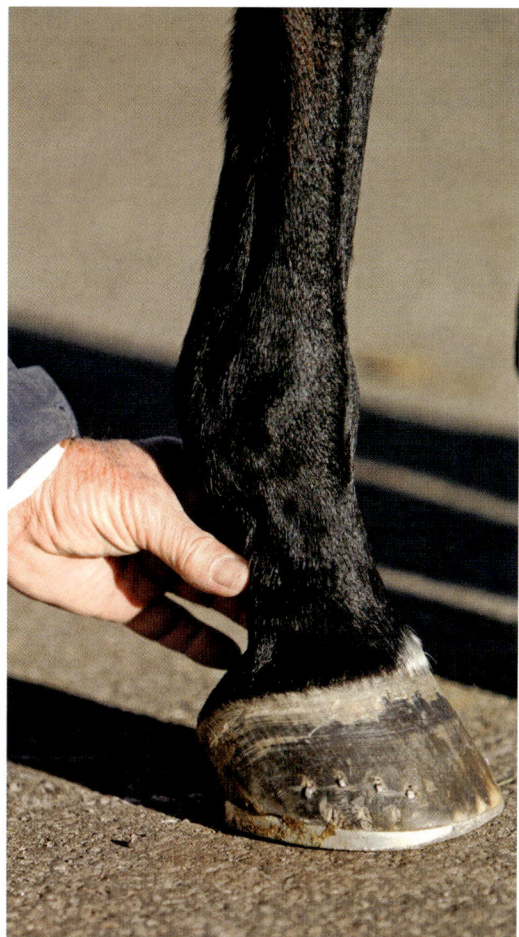

Next, your veterinarian feels your horse's lower leg to check for a digital pulse.

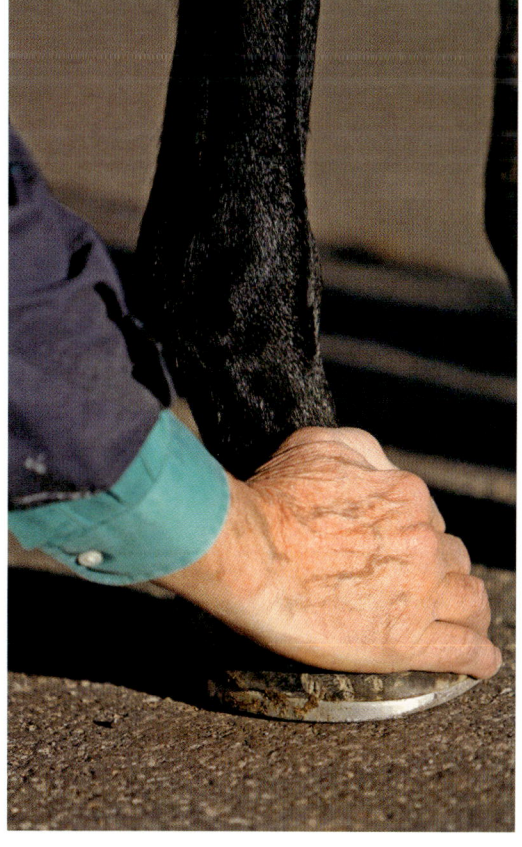

Feeling the outside of the hoof capsule helps your veterinarian detect any heat—a sign of pain and internal inflammation.

As your horse travels in a straight line, first at a walk and then at a trot, your veterinarian evaluates the horse's movement.

The veterinarian also wants to see your horse move in circles, both clockwise and counterclockwise.

asked to ride your horse to demonstrate his movement. Watching you ride can help your veterinarian see any problems related to specific athletic movements, such as sliding stops, side-passes, or intricate dressage maneuvers.

Back on the ground, your veterinarian most likely uses hoof-testers to evaluate your horse's foot for soreness—especially if the veterinarian believes the soreness begins at the horse's lower leg. Your veterinarian compares your horse's hooves, evaluating the hoof on the sore leg and comparing your horse's response with testing on the opposite leg.

Then your veterinarian checks for joint stress by performing flexion tests. He bends your horse's leg and holds it in position for about a minute and a half. After this flexion, a handler trots your horse, so your veterinarian can see if the lameness worsens. If flexing your horse's leg makes the lameness worse, the flexed joint can be the source or a part of the lameness problem. Flexion tests on your horse's back legs don't show joint problems quite as specifically as testing on his front legs. When flexing the back legs, it's more difficult to decipher which joint is most affected by your veterinarian's hold. The stifle, hock and fetlock joints all move together because of the tendons' and ligaments' reciprocal-apparatus arrangement. (See Chapter 12 for more about the reciprocal apparatus.) However, the information your veterinarian gathers from the back leg flexions still can be helpful.

If your veterinarian senses several body parts are involved in your horse's lameness, or if the veterinarian is unsure where the lameness is, he might choose to perform diagnostic blocking, sometimes called nerve blocking or a nerve block. To block your horse, the veterinarian injects a local anesthetic close to a nerve or directly into your horse's joint. The horse becomes numb in the blocked area and distal areas away from or lower than the blocked area. Intra-articular blocks affect only the joint injected, but not the leg below that joint. If your horse moves freely when an area is blocked, your veterinarian can pinpoint the lameness source since your horse's pain derives from the blocked area. Your veterinarian begins blocks at the bottom of your horse's leg and works up, blocking the leg until the lameness is located.

If your horse's lameness is complicated, your veterinarian might have to make several blocks—including more than one leg—before determining the cause. Make sure you schedule ample time to allow for multiple blocks, as well as the waiting time between each of them. Be aware: Not all horses can tolerate multiple blocks. Your horse might become too sensitive to needle pain.

Your veterinarian chooses not to perform blocks if your horse has an acute or severe injury. Blocking a non-displaced fracture, or a cracked bone that isn't separated, causes your horse to feel better, because he no longer can feel the pain. He might make the injury worse because now he is willing to place additional weight on an injury that needs pain's protection. In these acute lameness cases, your veterinarian most likely uses radiographic (X-ray) technology in an attempt to rule out a fracture.

Advanced Diagnostic Techniques

Ever-changing technology is helping veterinarians be more and more precise when diagnosing lameness issues. If your horse's lameness is unidentifiable, or if your veterinarian wants to gather more detail, he might perform diagnostic procedures known as radiography, ultrasound, magnetic resonance imaging (MRI), nuclear scintigraphy and/or computer tomographic radiography (CT scan).

Radiography: Also called an X-ray, this diagnostic uses gamma rays to form detailed images of your horse's bones. Your veterinarian can see pathology, or any condition that deviates from normal, on and within the bones. He also might see soft-tissue problems related to tendons and ligaments.

Your veterinarian might have a mobile radiograph machine, or you might have to transport your horse to a clinic for a radiographic diagnosis. Veterinary staff wear lead vests and use techniques to avoid overexposure to radiation.

Older or "wet" forms of radiographs must be processed and analyzed by looking at the image in front of a light box. The new technology, digital radiography, allows your veterinarian to see extra details—from the horse's skin to the inner layers of the bone. Your veterinarian also can "process" the image on screen, allowing him to darken and lighten specific areas to see different structures more clearly. Your veterinarian can easily upload radiographs in the digital

Your veterinarian might want to evaluate your horse's motion on soft footing as he works on a longe line.

The veterinarian might use hoof-testers to determine if your horse has soreness in the foot or hoof capsule.

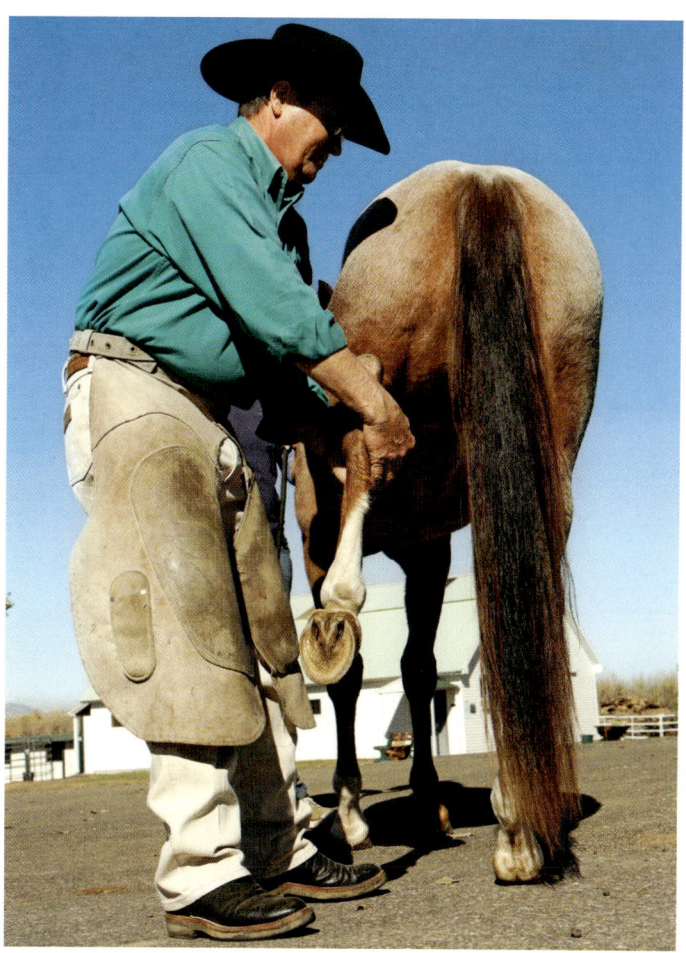

Your veterinarian also might hold your horse's limbs to perform flexion tests and then watch your horse move, noting any differences after the intense stretch.

format to a server for storage or archiving, and can e-mail images to specialists for consultation. You or other selected parties also can view radiographs on the Internet. The images can be printed on photographic paper or on film similar to conventional radiographs, if necessary.

Currently, veterinarians use two forms of digital radiographs to aid in equine medicine. Each has its advantages. CR, or computer radiography, works best in clinic settings. CR offers excellent image details and the flexibility to gather images of large areas, such as the horse's head, neck and back. DR, or direct radiography, provides a portable system with instantly available images anywhere, which can be stored on a computer. All new digital radiography requires fewer retakes than traditional radiography. That's a bonus for the veterinary crew's health, as well as that of your horse. As with any radiation, it's best to limit exposure.

Ultrasound: Sometimes called sonography, an ultrasound bounces sound waves off internal structures to create a view of soft-tissue structures underneath the skin. Your veterinarian can see if tissues or fibers within your horse's tendons, ligaments or muscles are affected or causing lameness, and also is able to assess the soft tissues' attachments to

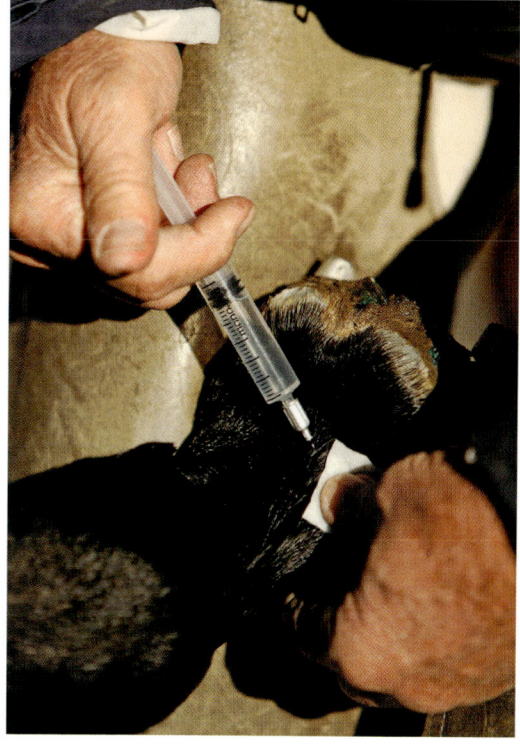

If the cause of lameness isn't evident, diagnostic blocking often helps to pinpoint the pain source.

19

the bone. Ultrasound can evaluate some bony surfaces, but not internal bone structure.

To prepare for an ultrasound, your veterinarian might clip your horse's hair and spread gel on your horse's leg or other area to be viewed. Ultrasound equipment is portable and offers a versatile and safe image. There are no known long-term repercussions from using ultrasound as a diagnostic tool for horses.

Magnetic Resonance Imaging: With an MRI, your veterinarian examines both bone and soft tissue in a specific area of your horse's leg and also can see physiological changes

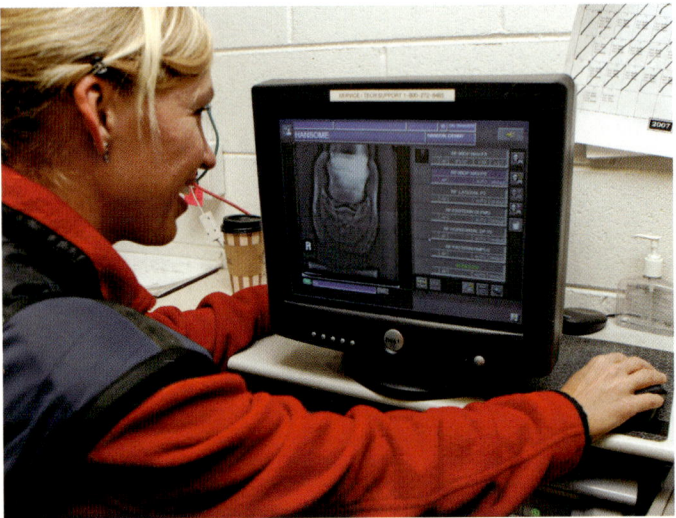

With today's digital radiographs, your veterinarian can see and evaluate your horse's images almost immediately.

within the structures. This diagnostic tool is helpful when ultrasounds and radiographs fail to reveal lameness causes. An MRI can show more detailed information about your horse's internal structures than most any other diagnostic. This quality imaging is especially helpful when your veterinarian looks inside your horse's foot or hoof capsule.

The MRI process is identical to the technology used in human medicine. Presently your veterinarian can view your horse's leg only from the knee and hock down because of how the machine is built. It's difficult to create a magnet and case large enough to surround your horse's midsection.

To create images, a strong magnetic field surrounds your horse's injured leg. A computer captures the temporary ionic changes and creates images of your horse's internal structures. These images are captured as a series of parallel slices through the target area. The collective images are called a sequence. For each target area, your veterinarian captures several sequences—creating several hundred images that must be evaluated—so it might take a few days for your veterinarian to report his final findings.

Note: Your veterinarian must remove your horse's shoes before an MRI, or risk his metal shoes snapping to the magnet. There are two forms of the technology—high- and low-power magnets. If your horse is scheduled for

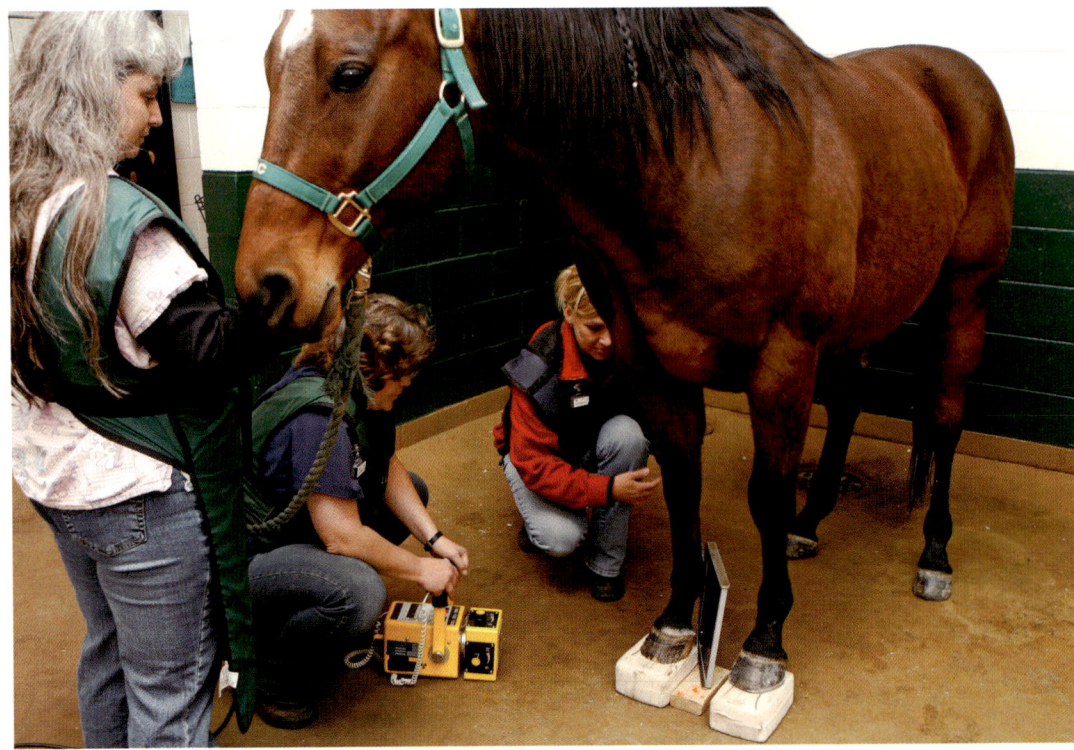

A radiograph, commonly known as an X-ray, helps your veterinarian see your horse's solid internal structures.

a high-power MRI, he needs general anesthesia for the exam; the low-power magnet exam requires only that your horse be sedated. Your veterinarian can identify the specific area causing your horse's lameness before scheduling an MRI. Because so many images are collected, he wants to ensure that only the affected area is evaluated.

Nuclear Scintigraphy: Your veterinarian uses this diagnostic tool to locate bone pathology and sometimes to see your horse's soft-tissue pathology.

To begin, your veterinarian injects a radioactive isotope into your horse's blood. The small particles emit radiation—sending a message that's picked up by a sensor or scanner held over your horse's affected leg or other body part. The injected isotopes accumulate in your horse's bones, grouping excessively in areas with bone pathology.

The image produced includes a series of dots. More dots indicate a high concentration of radiation ions. That concentrated group of dots shows your veterinarian where your horse's problem is. If your horse has an unusual concentration of radioactive ions at his cannon, your veterinarian suspects a fissure or hairline fracture, in which the crack extends only to the outer bone layer—not completely through the bone.

Scintigraphy examines only a structure's physiology—internal structure and function at the moment. Most other diagnostics show anatomical changes, in other words, how a bone has changed or how cartilage has disintegrated. Scintigraphy shows where your horse is experiencing bone changes in his body.

By looking at scintigraphy dot groupings, your veterinarian can see older, nearly healed sites that aren't the source of your horse's lameness. Your veterinarian combines his findings during the clinical exam and correlates those results with the nuclear scintigraphy patterns. But he needs to follow with ultrasound, radiography or MRI technology for a complete diagnosis.

Note: Your horse needs to stand quietly during the information-gathering process. The isotopes stay in your horse's system for only about a day, and your horse is scanned for safety before being released. The process is deemed extremely safe for your horse and the technicians performing the exam. The radiation emitted is less than the radiation exposure when taking a set of radiographs.

Computed Tomography: CT scans provide a three-dimensional image of bones and soft tissues when multiple radiograph exposures pass through your horse's affected areas in a 360-degree pattern. A computer interprets the group of radiographs and sends high-resolution images to the screen. A CT scan might show soft-tissue lesions and fractures not seen

An ultrasound bounces sound waves off internal structures to create a picture of your horse's soft tissues.

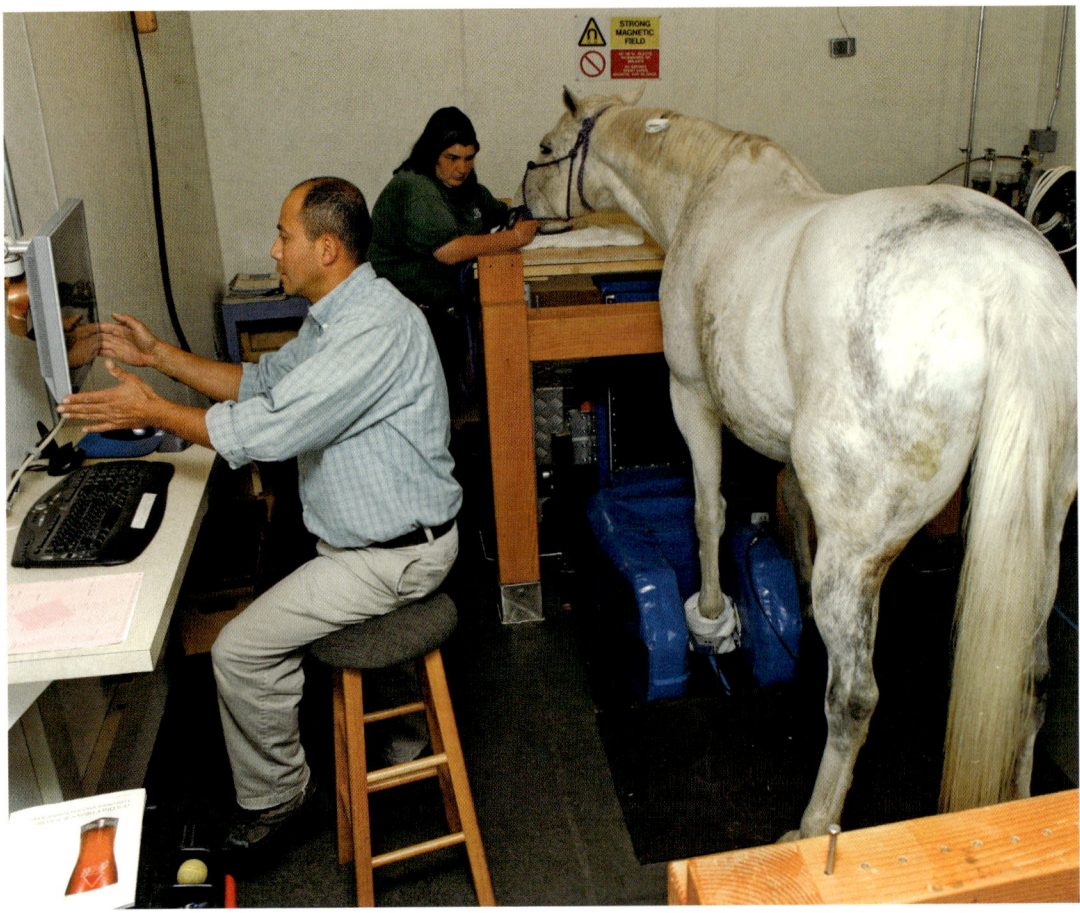

With an MRI, your veterinarian sees bone and soft tissue after your horse enters a specially designed room with the large, image-capturing magnet.

with traditional radiographs. As with scintigraphy and MRI, your veterinarian must evaluate multiple images after he collects data.

Note: Your horse must have general anesthesia and be in a hospital setting. His head, neck or lower legs are directed into the large scanning canal. Caveat: The equipment is expensive and requires your veterinarian to have a hospital location.

Myelogram: In this radiology technique, your veterinarian looks for areas of pathology in or along your horse's spinal cord—usually at the neck. For this procedure, your horse is anesthetized. Your veterinarian injects a radiological opaque material, which shows up on radiographs, into the space surrounding the spinal chord and then takes radiographs. If growths or other areas of pathology occupy space or put pressure on the spinal cord, your veterinarian sees the problems with this diagnostic. This procedure is performed on horses that demonstrate neurological lameness.

Treatment and Prognosis

Once your veterinarian gathers all the information needed to identify your horse's lameness source, it's time to begin treatment and announce a prognosis. You can read more about treatments for specific problems to specific body parts in the following chapters, as well as more about the usual prognosis for each lameness issue.

Here's a rundown of your veterinarian's labels that describe healing time and the possibility of a horse's future work:

Favorable: A horse with a favorable prognosis most likely recovers completely after care and with proper management.

Guarded: A horse has a good chance to recover, but recovery isn't certain. You must commit to constant care and continued treatment to achieve the desired outcome. Your horse needs rest and continual management.

Unfavorable: In this worst-case scenario, a horse isn't likely to recover fully—no matter how much care you provide and rest he receives. The "unfavorable" horse still should be treated in an effort to cure the problem, but the odds are not in his favor.

Your veterinarian might say your horse is in between two of these categories. Your horse might have a favorable–to-guarded prognosis, or a guarded-to-unfavorable one.

Horseman's Dictionary

blocking: injecting anesthetic along a horse's nerve or into a joint to block pain in an attempt to locate the lameness source.

digital pulse: a pronounced pulse in an area where a horse's pulse isn't usually easy to detect—just above the heel bulb, along the tendon sides in the pastern area.

fissure fracture: a bone crack that extends only partway through the bone with no displacement of the parts; also known as a hairline fracture.

lameness: a deviation from the horse's normal gait or posture due to pain or mechanical dysfunction.

orthopedic: relating to the bones, joints, ligaments or muscles.

serviceably sound: a horse's ability to complete a suitable job willingly as asked.

swinging-leg lameness: the action in which a horse swings his entire limb in a labored movement, as opposed to limping when weight is placed on the affected leg.

tracking: moving a horse, usually in hand, in straight lines or circles to the right or left to observe his way of going.

unsound: injured or unsuited to perform a task because of lameness.

The categories can be subjective, and prognoses can change throughout the treatment and healing processes.

Your Horse's Future

No matter how much attention and care your horse receives from you and your veterinarian, it's important to realize that not all lameness issues are curable. In some cases, managing lameness and working to keep your equine friend as comfortable as possible are the only answers.

Keep in mind that not all horses must be free of lameness to perform their jobs. A change in your horse's movement might not be painful. Your veterinarian can help you decide which lameness is harmful to his health and career and what gait changes don't affect his everyday work. As long as your horse's lameness management doesn't go against his best interests and impede his long-term health, it's possible for him to have a long and rewarding career.

Also keep in mind that each lame horse is an individual. The way one horse reacts to pain differs from another horse's reaction. Two horses with the same health issue can have different prognoses, depending on how each horse reacts and what job he usually does. As you read scenarios about horses that have the same lameness issue as your horse, remember that your horse's outcome might be very different.

Make sure you're open and honest with your veterinarian; talk freely about your horse's ability and willingness to perform after an initial lameness problem. Only with honesty can you and your veterinarian work together to make important decisions about your horse's recovery and welfare. You also need to be honest about your safety as a rider by making sure your bond with your horse doesn't blind you to possible risks.

2

THE FOOT—
THE HOOF CAPSULE

Your veterinarian first examines your horse's foot, a complex, yet small structure that must support your horse's total weight.

You've probably heard the expression "no hoof, no horse." In actuality, no individual part of a horse's leg or foot is any more important than another. However, your horse's hoof, or foot as it's commonly called, has many small, intricate parts positioned under his large, heavy body. So much weight adds pressure to any pain your horse might feel in his hoof.

Injury or pain in your horse's foot might prove an easy fix, or might threaten your horse's long-term health and rideability. Whatever the eventual outcome, many horses are lame because of foot problems. That's why your veterinarian begins a lameness exam by analyzing your horse's feet.

Here, we start discussing your horse's complex, ground-impacting feet by detailing hoof-related problems—pain and ailments working in from the outside. In Chapter 3, we look inside the hoof wall, then discuss diseases and problems that impact all hoof structures in Chapters 4 and 5.

Abscess

You rode your horse last night and he seemed fine. Now, just 12 hours later, you walk to the paddock and see him standing with his right front foot pointed forward. His weight is shifted onto his back legs. You put on his halter and ask him to walk toward the barn. He doesn't want to

Each of your horse's hooves must absorb the full weight of his body during athletic moves. Notice that only one foot supports the horse's weight.

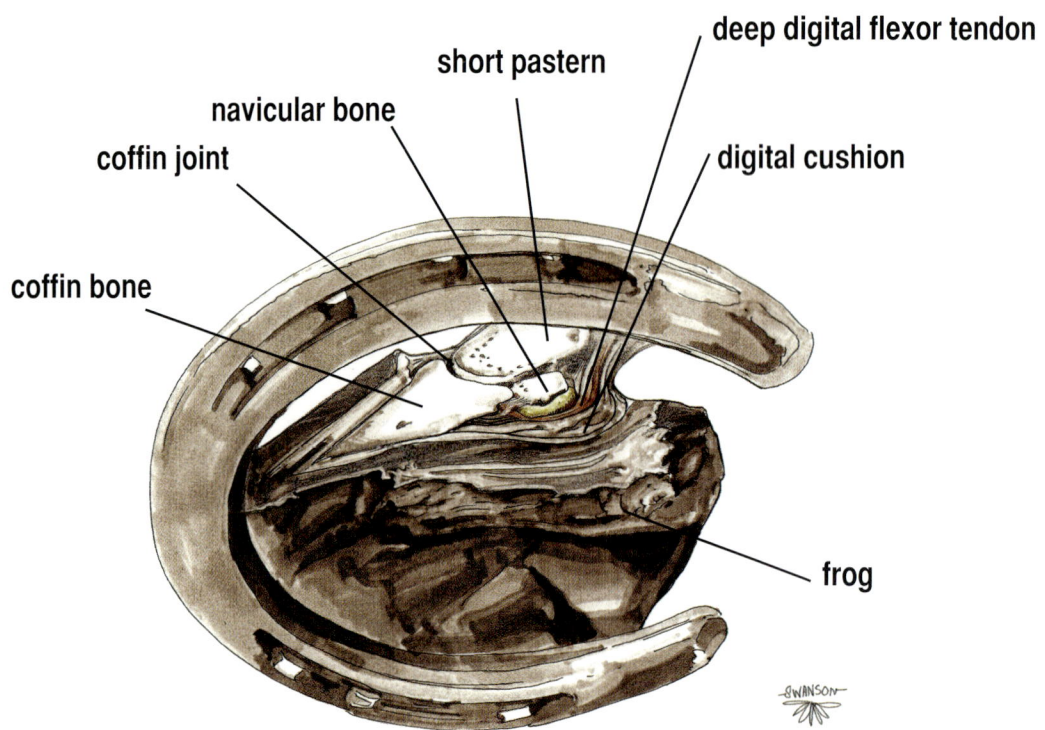

Your horse's hoof capsule—partially covered here by a shoe—protects his internal foot structures. The hoof capsule includes the hoof wall, the sole, the bars and the frog. When the hoof capsule is compromised, the sensitive internal support structures can cause your horse pain.

bear any weight on his right front. Stopping, you pick up his foot and feel heat radiating from the hoof wall; the area around his pastern is swollen. As you palpate around his coronary band, he quickly pulls away.

What might be happening: If your horse has an abscess, he's probably trapped debris inside his hoof capsule, the hard structure encasing his foot's soft, sensitive tissue. This capsule is a breeding ground for bacteria, which thrive and produce gas and liquid byproducts. When the gases and liquids, trapped by the confining hoof capsule, can't escape, pressure builds. The pressure creates a painful abscess, a pus-filled cavity formed by inflammation and complicated by bacteria. When your horse must bear weight on the infected foot, the pain multiplies.

Your horse also might form an abscess after bruising his sole. The bruise can cause blood to pool between his soft sole and the restrictive hoof wall. Stagnant blood is another perfect environment for bacteria. Bacteria can enter the bruise's pooled blood through the horse's bloodstream or, if the bruise was caused by a puncture, through the wound. Bruises and abscesses can form if your farrier inadvertently drives a nail into your horse's sensitive sole or wall, bruising the sensitive part of the foot, and the open puncture space might allow bacteria to enter. An abscess also can form when a nail is too close to the sensitive portion of your horse's hoof. The nail might not penetrate the live tissue, but the pressure can cause pain and bruising with time, opening the way for an abscess to form.

What you notice: If your horse has an abscess, he might be fine one day, then suddenly show symptoms. The onset is fast, and symptoms sometimes appear all at once. You see a Grade 3 to Grade 5 lameness with such symptoms as:

- An abrupt and significant change in movement. Your horse might seem "off" at the trot, or have more obvious, head-nodding lameness. He might appear to move with a "hitch," as if there's a start and stop to his movement or as if a rusty hinge is stuck. At worst, your horse might not want to bear any weight on the affected foot; he might refuse to move.

- A strong digital pulse in your horse's foot when you pick it up.

- Heat in the hoof wall.

- Swelling or edema, swelling caused by body tissue fluid, in the pastern area.

- Reluctance to bear weight on the affected foot. Your horse might place the painful foot forward or to the side to avoid pressure.

- Sensitivity to your touch when you apply pressure to a specific area of the coronary band or heel bulb. Initially, the lameness might be severe enough to confuse with a bone fracture.

What you do: Look for the listed symptoms by picking up and cleaning your horse's foot. Feel for heat and palpate around your horse's heel and coronary band. Notice any throbbing or swelling. If your horse has many of the symptoms listed, call your veterinarian.

What your veterinarian does: Your veterinarian uses clamp-like hoof-testers to help locate the painful area. Once he locates your horse's abscess, the veterinarian opens and drains it by cutting a hole through your horse's sole to the abscess site. Caution: Only a veterinarian should attempt to open the abscess. Done incorrectly, draining it might damage other sensitive and vital foot structures.

Your veterinarian flushes the abscess site with disinfectant; the type used depends on the nearby foot structures. If the abscess is near the hoof wall or sole, a hydrogen peroxide and 2 percent iodine flush works best. If the abscess site is near bony structures or other vital structures, a flush with mild disinfectants and antibiotics is in order. Your veterinarian then packs the abscess cavity with cotton and bandages your horse's foot to prevent further contamination from soil and manure. He also might recommend soaking the injured foot in a solution of warm water, Epsom salts and disinfectants to increase your horse's local blood circulation and expedite healing.

If your veterinarian is unable to locate the abscess's site, he might soak your horse's foot and use a warm, moist poultice, or dressing, to ease pain, improve circulation, and expedite the time it takes for the

abscess to mature. With heat and prompting, the abscess expands so it can be located and drained; in some cases it breaks and drains on its own.

The healing process: Your horse might receive a round of antibiotics to reduce the risk that abscess bacteria infect vital or vital structures. Your veterinarian decides if antibiotics are necessary; the treatment is required only if the abscess formed in close proximity to vital structures.

Down the road: Once treated, your horse should feel better within 24 to 48 hours, depending on the abscess's magnitude. As he heals, it's important to keep the drainage hole clean and protected with bandages. If dirt

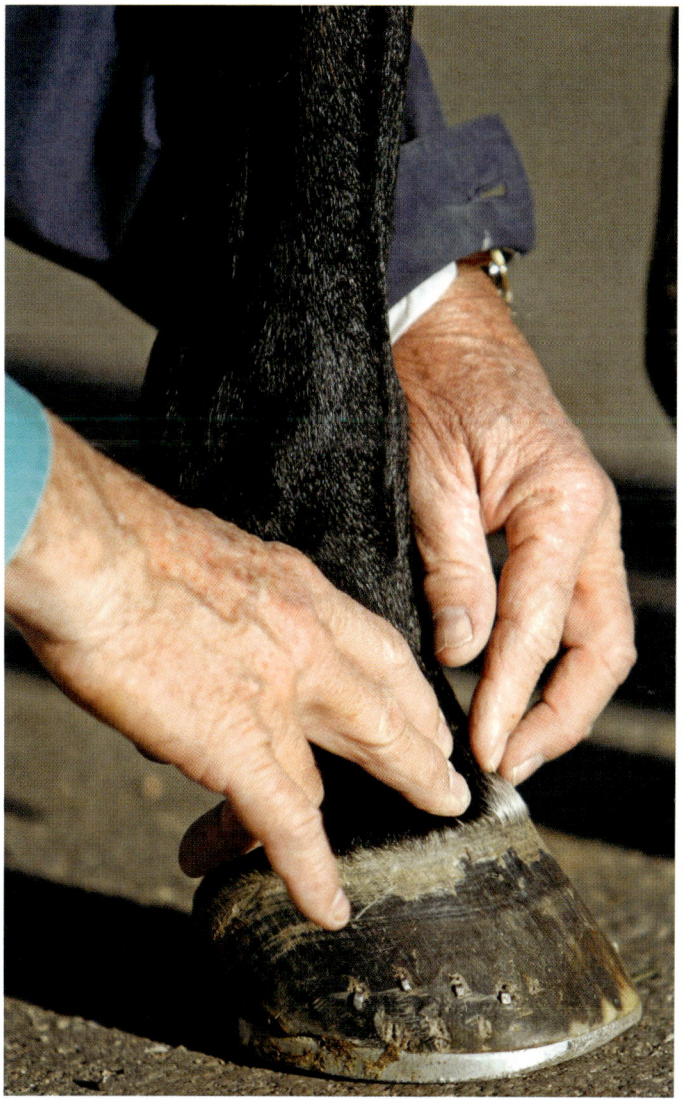

If you suspect your horse has an abscess, palpate the coronary band and note any sensitive areas. An abscess creates pressure that can migrate up to the coronary band.

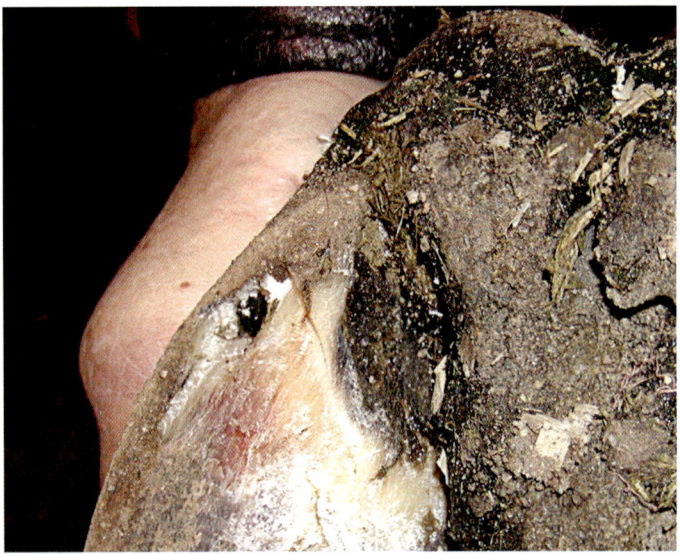

The black substance—seen here just inside the hoof wall—is pus draining from an abscessed corn.

and manure leach into the drainage hole, the abscess can redevelop.

Once the abscess cavity is dry and fully drained, your veterinarian might recommend placing a pad between your horse's sole and shoe to further protect the site. You might keep the protective pad in place until the hoof-capsule defect, where the abscess has been, grows out completely.

In the worst scenarios, your veterinarian might attach a removable plate to the bottom of the horse's shoe. This medication plate, attached with screws, allows easy access to the site and keeps the site clean. Your veterinarian also might recommend using a hoof boot, children's diaper or cotton plug to protect the site as it heals.

Once the abscess drains and heals, your horse should have a favorable prognosis as

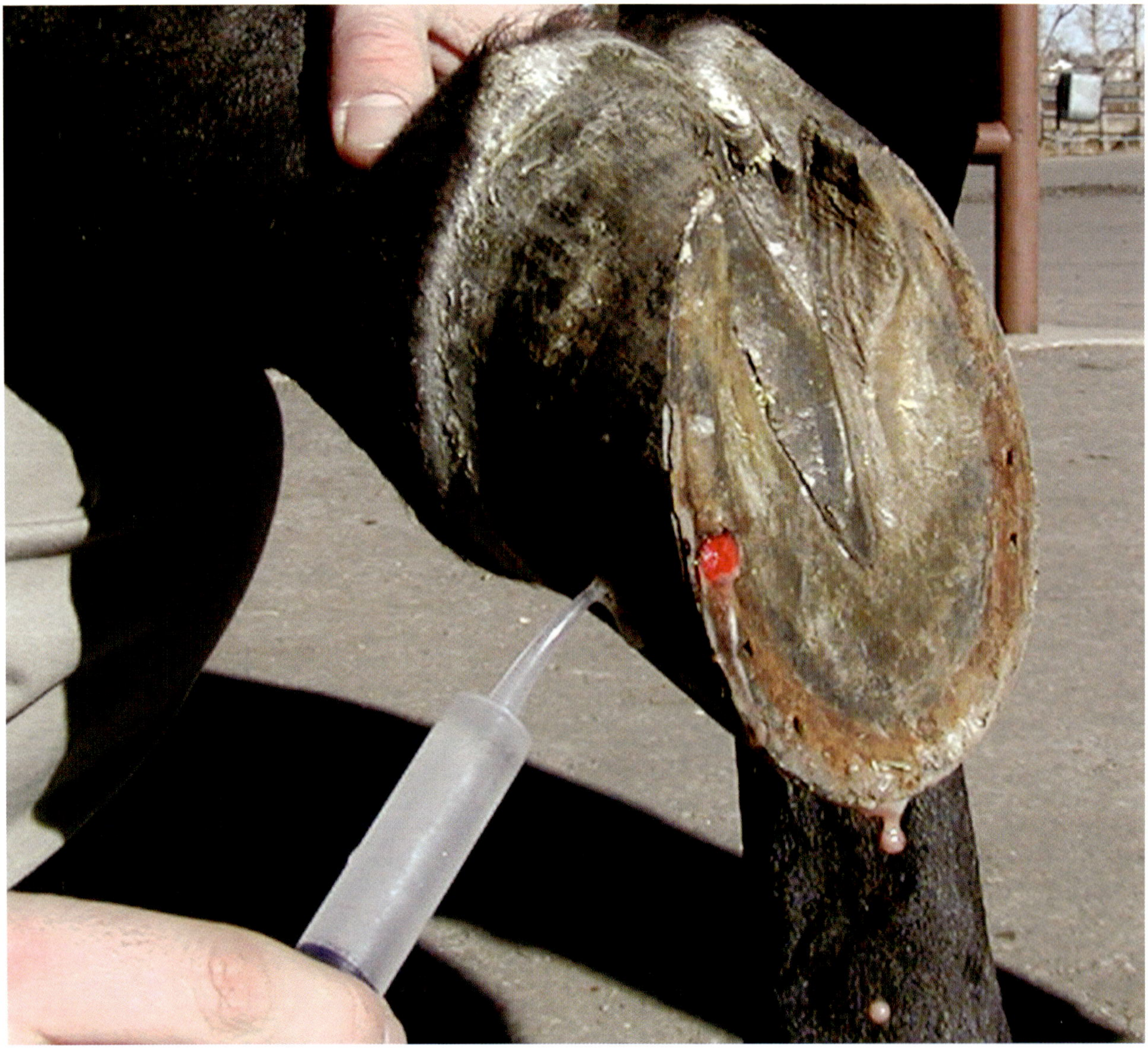

Your veterinarian flushes your horse's abscess with a disinfectant.

long as vital structures aren't affected. Your horse might be able to return to work once the abscess is dry and protected, usually within 48 hours.

Puncture Wound

You just finished constructing your new barn. Excited to move your horse into his new home, you don't take time to examine the barn floor and scout for fallen nails. Just after moving your horse into the barn, you take him from his shaving-filled stall and walk him to your tie rail. As he turns the corner, you notice that his stride is short; he's also nodding his head. At the rail, you check his feet and see the culprit—a nail embedded in his left front foot, with the point protruding from his heel bulb. You can't see how

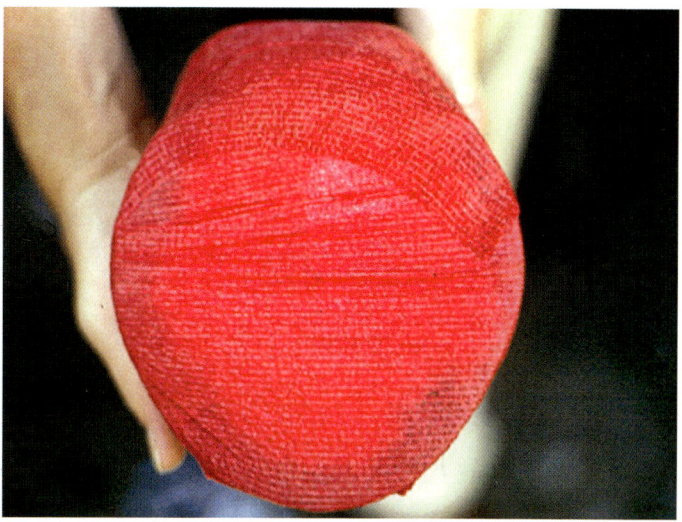

If you see a puncture wound in your horse's sole, clean his foot and apply a protective bandage to keep out further contamination.

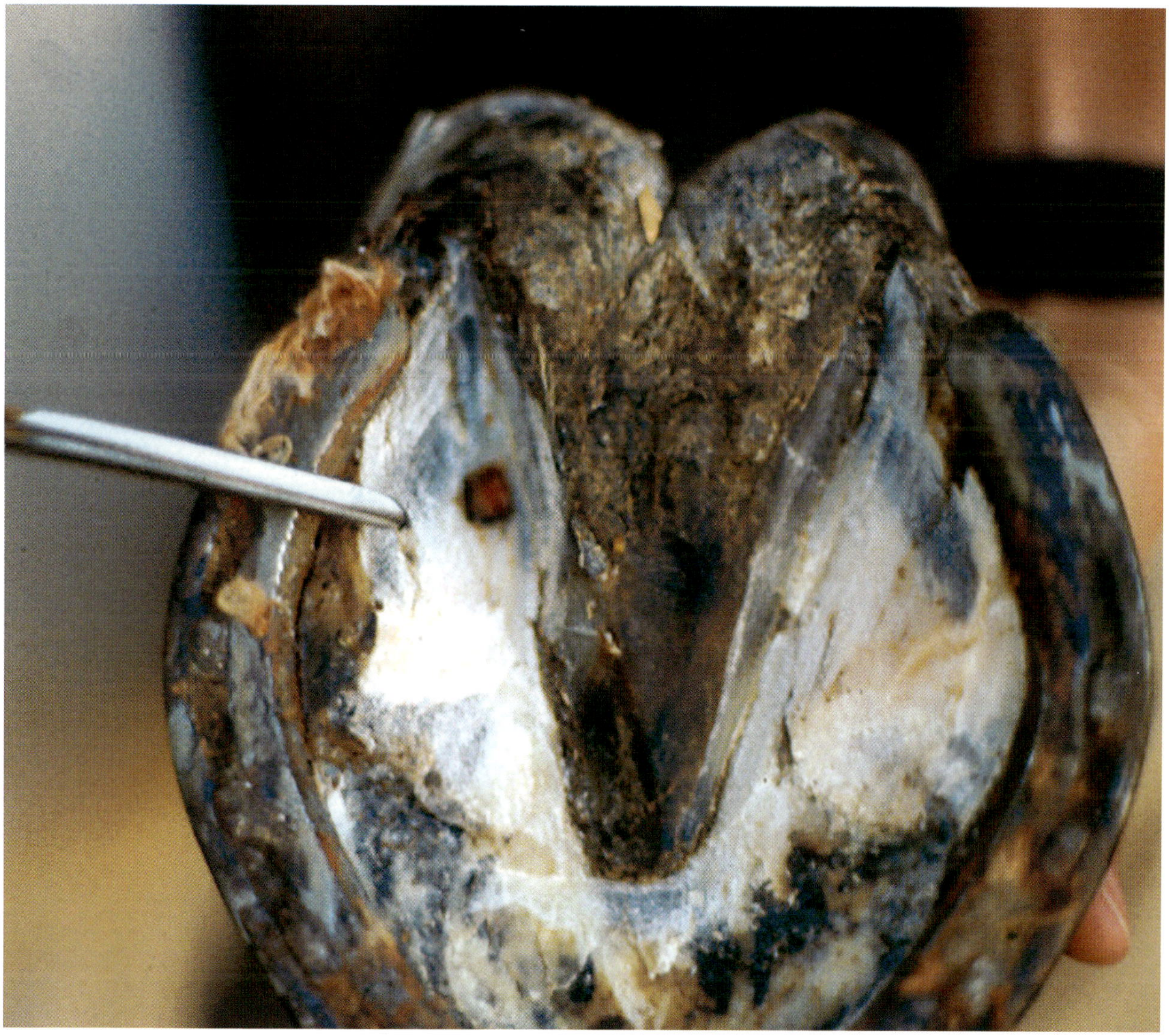

Although a puncture might appear small from the outside, the internal damage can be extensive. Here, a nail made a small, but lengthy wound reaching to the navicular bursa.

much damage the nail has made, but realize the problem could be serious.

What might be happening: Simply put, a foreign object has punctured your horse's foot and penetrated the soft part of his hoof capsule. Most punctures enter through the bottom of the foot although the entrance sometimes is through the heel bulb. The injury can be significant, no matter what part of the foot is affected. The injury is serious when a foreign object impales the center foot between the lateral, or outside, and medial, or inside, sulci, or depressions in the central region of the frog, where crucial structures usually are safe deep within the hoof wall, an area sometimes called the red zone. An abscess might form following a puncture wound if bacteria can travel into the hoof from the puncture or if bacteria are introduced by the foreign body. If bacteria enter your horse's bone, tendon sheath, tendon, or joint, your veterinarian considers your horse's injury to be serious.

What you notice: Many symptoms are the same as those previously listed for an abscess. You also see a Grade 2 to Grade 5 lameness as you notice a visible foreign body in your horse's hoof capsule.

What you do: Clean your horse's hoof to analyze the entire sole including the sulci, or depressions alongside the frog and in the frog's center line and frog. If you find a puncture hole or foreign body, call your veterinarian immediately. Your veterinarian considers a puncture wound an emergency until he can determine which of the foot's structures have been affected. While on the phone with your veterinarian, describe the wound and ask his advice before removing any impaling objects. In most cases, it's best to remove the foreign body to stop it from pushing farther into your horse's hoof as he walks.

Before removing the foreign object, if instructed to do so by your veterinarian, clean the entire affected foot with a chlorhexidine or povidone-iodine disinfectant solution and a scrub brush. Carefully remember where the object penetrated the foot or take a photo using your digital camera. Remove the object with your fingers or with pliers, if necessary. Then cover the bottom of your horse's foot with antibiotic ointment and cotton. Use duct tape to keep the cotton in place and to protect the foot from dirt and debris.

What your veterinarian does: When your veterinarian arrives, he investigates the extent of the puncture. He might take radiographs to help pinpoint the structures impacted. He also might flush the wound and fill it with a radiopaque substance that blocks radiation and clearly shows the wound's depth on a radiograph.

The healing process: Your horse's healing time varies, depending on the punctured structures. Initially, if your veterinarian can't isolate the puncture's path, he assumes that vital structures—the deep flexor tendon, navicular bursa, navicular bone, impar ligament, coffin bone and coffin joint—are affected. He administers broad-spectrum antibiotics and might infuse liquid antibiotic at the wound site. Your veterinarian follows up with diagnostic procedures to ensure the coffin joint and navicular bursa aren't impacted; otherwise, your horse might require surgery to drain and flush the synovial structures.

You continue to protect the site from contamination by applying a bandage, a protective boot, a shoe with a medication plate or a combination of safeguarding tools.

Down the road: Your horse's ability to heal quickly depends on how many vital structures the puncture has affected. You might be able to treat your horse at home if the injury is minor. If more internal structures are impacted, your veterinarian might want to keep your horse in a hospital setting. Throughout the healing process, someone must keep the wound clean and contaminants away from the horse's injured sole.

Most horses with puncture wounds are given favorable prognoses—as long as vital structures aren't seriously compromised and therapy is initiated promptly. It's usually possible to control infection. If infection spreads, your horse might have secondary, even life-threatening ailments. If the navicular bone has been struck, a horse's prognosis and future soundness can be guarded.

Bruises to the Hoof Wall, Sole or Frog

On a beautiful day for a trail ride, you and your horse masterfully negotiate a rocky patch of trail; your horse seems confident and places his feet in just the right spots. Then one misplaced foot lands on a sharp, loose rock. Your horse stumbles slightly before beginning to limp. You jump off and lead him a few steps forward. He doesn't limp quite as much as when you're mounted, but the limp is still there. You decide to lead him to the trailhead, load him and head home. Back home, you feel his injured foot and immediately sense heat in the hoof capsule. There's a slight digital pulse. Now, your horse doesn't want to bear any weight on his bruised hoof.

What might be happening: When any surface of the horse's foot receives a blunt trauma, blood can leak from vessels inside the hoof capsule. The result is a hematoma, a collection of blood resulting from a hemorrhage or internal bleeding. The blood leakage causes pressure inside your horse's hoof, making it painful for your horse to put more pressure on the injured foot. Because rigid structures hold the foot together, it can't accommodate swelling. Swelling and blood build-up create constant pressure on the hoof wall, causing great pain.

What you notice: Signs of a bruise might vary depending upon which part of the sole or internal structure was injured and the degree of injury. You see a Grade 1 to 5 lameness and notice:

- Heat in the hoof capsule.

- An increased digital pulse.

- Your horse's reluctance to bear weight on the affected foot.

- Blood visible through the hoof wall if your horse has nonpigmented feet, or white hoof walls.

What you do: Call your veterinarian.

What your veterinarian does: Your veterinarian uses hoof-testers to locate the sensitive areas of your horse's foot and examines the sole, frog, bars, hoof wall and every combination of the structures. Your horse doesn't respond quite as sensitively as when hoof-testers are used to explore an abscess, but pain might be noticeable.

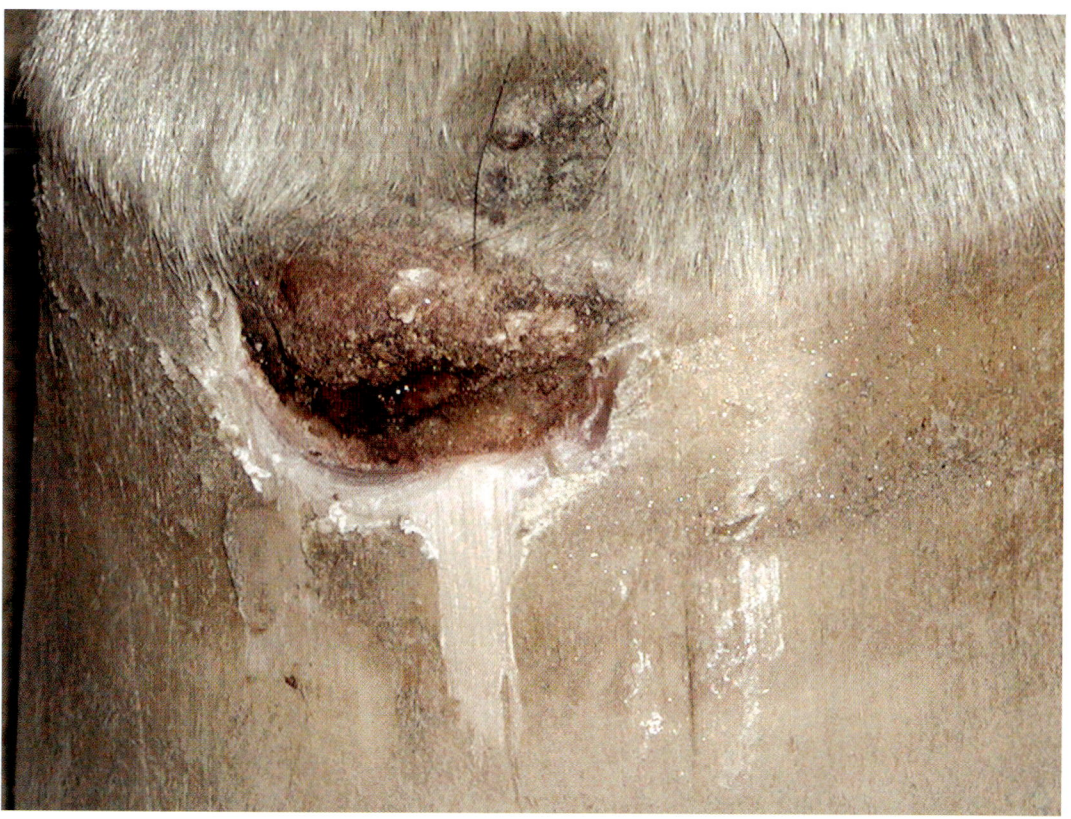

If your horse injures his foot as this horse did—creating a bruise on the line between the hoof wall and the coronary band—your veterinarian might trim the top of the hoof wall to relieve pressure from swelling tissues.

Your veterinarian probably takes radiographs to rule out coffin-bone or navicular-bone fractures, which might have occurred at the same time as a bruise.

The healing process: Your veterinarian most likely prescribes anti-inflammatory firocoxib or phenylbutazone medications to help reduce swelling and lessen your horse's pain.

The veterinarian also might ask that you provide cold water and ice therapy for the first 48 hours after the injury occurred, to reduce the hemorrhage or bleeding. You might cool your horse's leg with cold hose water or invest in special gel wraps designed to chill the legs. Your veterinarian tells you how long to keep ice or cold water on your horse's foot, but a good rule of thumb is to apply in 20-minute intervals two to three times per day.

Your veterinarian might ask that you apply the fragrant-yet-helpful dimethyl sulfoxide, a wood-pulp byproduct commonly known as DMSO, as a poultice to help reduce swelling. A topical, antibacterial nitrofurozone solution used to treat infections in wounds and burns also can help resist infection and aid in healing.

You also might soak your horse's foot in hot water to stimulate blood circulation after the initial two-day healing time. These treatments can be helpful if you apply them right after the initial injury. Make sure not to pack DMSO or nitrofurazone under plastic or a bandage. The combination of poultice and heat under a wrap might cause more bleeding initially.

If your veterinarian doesn't think the pressure within your horse's hoof is relieved after a few days' time, he might need to open the hoof capsule or sole to release pressure. No matter the treatment, continue to rest your horse to ensure his healing.

Down the road: Some horses' bruises don't respond to therapy as quickly as others. It might take an extensive rest period to help your horse fully recover. This extra healing time is especially crucial if your horse has damaged a large area of his hoof wall; the bruise might have affected his hoof wall laminae, which bonds and supports structures between the coffin bone and the hoof wall.

When your horse puts weight on his affected foot and shows no pronounced lameness, he

Your veterinarian uses hoof-testers to squeeze your horse's hoof capsule, detecting sensitivity and looking for a bruise.

probably can return to work. Monitor him for any signs of reinjury, including lameness, heat in his hoof or increased digital pulse. Most bruised horses have favorable prognoses and return to work at their original levels.

Corn

On Independence Day weekend your tried-and-true horse participates in several long parades routed down your city's paved and hard-surfaced streets. After the last parade or the next day, your horse seems a bit stiff and sore, which you first dismiss as signs of fatigue. A few days later, he shows more signs of lameness. He short-strides with his left front leg, and his head nods as he grazes across your pasture. When you check his feet, you feel heat in one hoof capsule and a throbbing digital pulse. You might even see swelling in his pastern.

What might be happening: A corn is a bruise to deep, sensitive structures at the angle of the sole, that part of the sole at your horse's heel, which is the triangular area between the bar and the hoof wall. The attachments between the sole's sensi-tive laminar areas and the hoof capsule tear or weaken, causing a hematoma and soreness. The torn tissue and pooled blood often develop into an abscess. From the outside, you notice a corn's redness.

Corns are most frequently caused by use trauma, and are common in the front feet of horses that do repetitive work on hard ground. The general consensus is that corns develop in the front feet because there's often more pressure pounding down there, especially when a horse is heavy on his forehand. Corns are seldom found in horses' back feet. Some especially pigeon-toed horses are predisposed to having corns. A pigeon-toed horse has more twisting interaction with the ground as his foot lands, bears weight, and leaves the ground, and often is flat-footed and doesn't grow solid heels. If the heels are crushed down by repetitive hits on hard surfaces, more sensitive tissues within the foot might bruise. As the corn matures, or if the affected area is trimmed, bruising reddens the sole at the heel.

Corns also can form when the horse's hooves grow too long between shoeing sessions or if the heels are left long in an attempt

A corn forms when deep tissue in your horse's foot tears and causes bleeding. This horse's corn—near his heel, between the hoof wall and the bar—appears small, but the internal damage might be extensive.

Your veterinarian trims your horse's foot to remove damaged tissue surrounding a corn. The trimming might cause bleeding. Cotton and iodine keep the newly trimmed area clean.

to give the flat foot more heel. Longer heels aren't always solid and tend to crush or roll under force, and bruising is inevitable.

What you notice: The symptoms of a corn are similar to those of an abscess and bruise—in the corn's early stages. At the onset, you see Grade 2 lameness and Grade 3 to Grade 4 lameness if the corn develops into an abscess. You also notice some or all of the following:

- An increased digital pulse in your horse's hoof.

- Heat in the hoof capsule.

- Swelling in the pastern above your horse's affected hoof.

What you do: Call your veterinarian.

What your veterinarian does: Your veterinarian finds the sensitive part of your horse's hoof by using hoof-testers. If the corn is new, you might not be able to see it on the outside of your horse's sole. In this case, your veterinarian might take a radiograph to rule out a coffin-bone fracture and make a more precise

diagnosis. The signs of a coffin-bone fracture and a corn can be quite similar.

If you can see the corn, you probably see redness. That's blood from a previous bruising, which now is growing out with the damaged sole tissue. It's possible to see only redness, which might be the limit of the corn's progress. If that's the case, your veterinarian performs an extensive lameness exam to locate the true pain source, since your horse could have sole redness from previous bruising without that causing his current soreness.

The healing process: Your veterinarian wants to relieve the pressure that causes your horse pain and avoid further damage to sensitive hoof structures. The veterinarian trims bruised tissue from your horse's foot, and might ask that you apply a DMSO and nitrofurazone poultice to help reduce swelling and pain in the affected area.

Your veterinarian works with your farrier, outlining a trimming plan that helps your horse walk pain-free. The two professionals want to reduce heel concussion with trimming and special shoeing. Your horse might benefit from an egg-bar shoe or a pad placed between his shoe and sole. Your farrier also might use a tongue-bar or frog-support pad to transfer weight to your horse's frog. Your veterinarian and farrier choose the best shoe and pad combination to aid your horse's specific needs. No matter the choice, the two work to allow your horse to build solid heel structure. If squishy, unstable heel material remains, your horse crushes it when he returns to work, causing the corn to continue. If your horse develops an abscess of his corn, he requires extra treatment.

Down the road: Once corns have been a problem, be sure to work closely with your veterinarian and a qualified farrier. Proper hoof care and shoeing, and hoof-strengthening supplements can help your horse resist future problems.

If your horse's corns developed because of his conformation, the problem likely recurs. Your horse needs constant attention and care to limit the painful formations.

If poor trimming—or lack thereof—causes your horse's corns, he has a good prognosis. With a few consistent trimming sessions, he can bear weight in the correct locations, and the damaged corn tissue grows out of his foot. If your horse has been treated with aggressive caulks or borium patches to limit slipping on ice, he can be predisposed to corns. There's a delicate balance between supplying your horse with enough traction and providing too much. Too much traction can aggravate his sole, as well as other structures in the foot and pastern.

Hoof-Wall Cracks

You recently have switched farriers; your longtime shoer moved, and you had to find a replacement in a pinch. While you shop around for a new professional and knowledgeable trim, your horse has had several trims by different folks. One farrier suggests trimming your horse's hooves in a way that changes the angles—in an effort to correct the horse's pigeon-toed stance. The idea backfires. Now you see a vertical crack in your horse's hoof—angling down from the coronary band. It doesn't bother your horse at first, but now he's seems a bit sore. And there's a small amount of blood at the top of the crack at the coronary band, and you worry an abscess might be behind the crack.

What might be happening: Significant hoof cracks can show up at your horse's hoof quar-

ters—inside, outside or at the toe. The crack's shape and depth determine how much your horse suffers during the healing process and how long the healing process takes. Many horses in dry climates have shallow vertical wall cracks all around their hoof walls, which don't develop into clinical problems.

Your horse's hoof wall grows down from the coronary band just as your fingernails grow from your cuticle area. The coronary band is made of soft tissue—comparable to your cuticle structures. If that soft tissue is cut or torn, a hoof-wall crack or defect can form at the coronary band and eventually extend to the ground surface. A crack that extends through the entire hoof—from the outside wall toward the foot's inner structures—can result in soft tissue damage and causes your horse pain. Vertical hoof cracks perpendicular to the ground are most threatening. When a crack begins at your horse's hairline and follows the hoof tubule lines to the ground, the two hoof wall sections might split, creating pain in the underlying laminar tissues. If cracks aren't complicated and the horse has adequate care and attention, the cracks can travel downward and eventually grow out.

The hoof quarter is the area forward from the heel and just behind the foot's widest part. Here, the hoof wall tends to be thinner than in other places around the foot. The quarters aren't supported by the coffin bone's rigid structure, which appears to be the hinge area for hoof expansion during weight-bearing. The area can give a bit, but tears and cracks under excess stress. If your horse's leg confor-

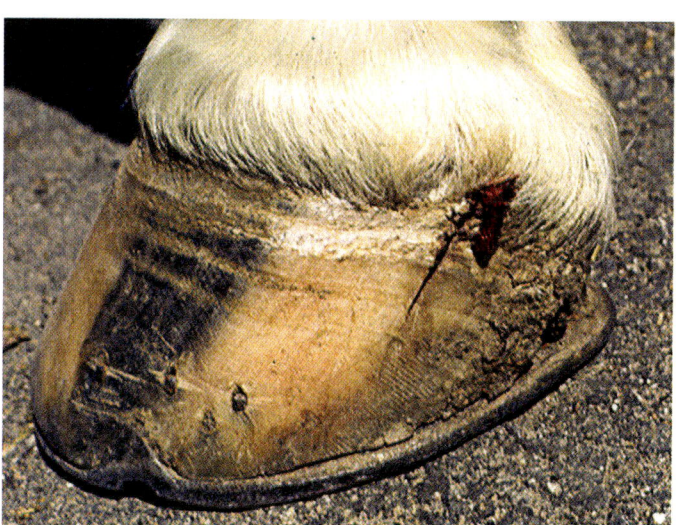

You might see blood when your horse's hoof first cracks and tears the attached tissue. Tearing tissue is a sign that it's time to address the balance of your horse's foot.

35

If your horse is prone to quarter cracks, ask your veterinarian to work with your farrier to ensure that your horse's hooves are properly balanced.

mation creates an unbalanced foot, he might be predisposed to quarter cracks. Hooves also can crack if he hasn't been trimmed in a timely manner or if the trim isn't a balanced one. If your horse's hoof doesn't bear weight as designed, the hoof might crack.

If your horse has naturally thin hoof walls, the walls might crack more easily with any repetitive pressure. In some cases, an abnormally shaped coffin bone inadequately supports the hoof wall, and cracks develop.

Horizontal cracks develop after your horse bruises his coronary band. These cracks might be unsightly, but usually aren't troublesome. They usually don't cause lameness unless bacteria become trapped inside and an abscess develops.

A hoof-wall crack might develop as a secondary problem after an acute, or quick-onset, coronary band injury. Your horse might cause a hoof crack if he clips the coronary band with his opposite hoof. If your horse cuts his coronary band, catching it under a fence or alongside a barn, permanent damage to the coronary band's germinal cells, which initiate growth, can result in a permanent defect.

What you notice: You might not see any lameness symptoms. In more severe cases, you see a Grade 1 to Grade 3 lameness and notice:

- A small crack beginning at the hairline above your horse's hoof.

- A vertical tear or wound at the coronary band, accompanied by bleeding.

What you do: If your horse's hoof crack causes pain or a change in his motion, call your veterinarian.

What your veterinarian does: Your veterinarian most likely uses hoof-testers to determine if the crack is the primary lameness cause, or perhaps if an underlying problem might have caused the crack, which would then be a secondary problem. Since your horse might be sensitive to coronary-band pressure, your veterinarian palpates the top of your horse's hoof and notes his reaction. If your horse reacts or pulls away, the coronary band might be affected, resulting in a more severe diagnosis. Your veterinarian might take radiographs to assess your horse's overall hoof structure and balance.

The healing process: You must work with your veterinarian and farrier to balance your horse's hooves so that future cracks don't develop and current cracks can grow out without further damage. Your horse's hooves must be balanced from side to side and front to back, all trimmed within a precise ratio for perfect balance. Rely on a trained, professional farrier to create and maintain the proper hoof, sole and heel proportions. For many hoof cracks, proper trimming and foot maintenance is the only required treatment.

If your horse's hoof crack is deep or bleeding, your veterinarian might open and clean it to prevent trapping dirt and blood beneath the surface, which could lead to an abscess. In some cases it's important to trim away the hoof wall to relieve pressure on underlying soft tissue. For cosmetic reasons, your veterinarian can cover the crack with an acrylic patch. The crack area must be dry and free from blood, serum drainage or pus before being covered; otherwise, bacteria buried within the hoof cause more problems.

For more severe cracks, your veterinarian might stabilize your horse's hoof to ensure that the crack can begin to grow together at the coronary band. If the hoof wall on one side of the crack moves independently from the wall on the other side, coronary band tissue can continue to tear. The defect then has no chance to heal and grow together to eliminate the crack. For stability, your veterinarian might lace stainless-steel wires across the crack, drilling small holes in a

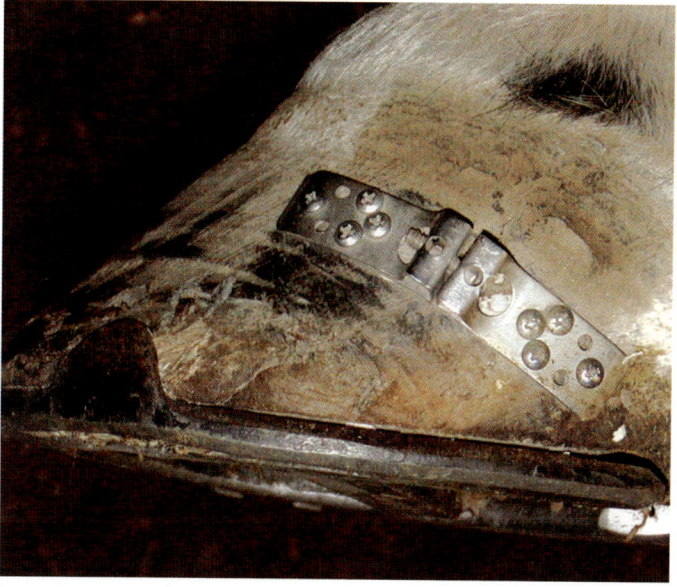

This quarter crack is stabilized by a clamp and screws, which allow the hoof to grow together.

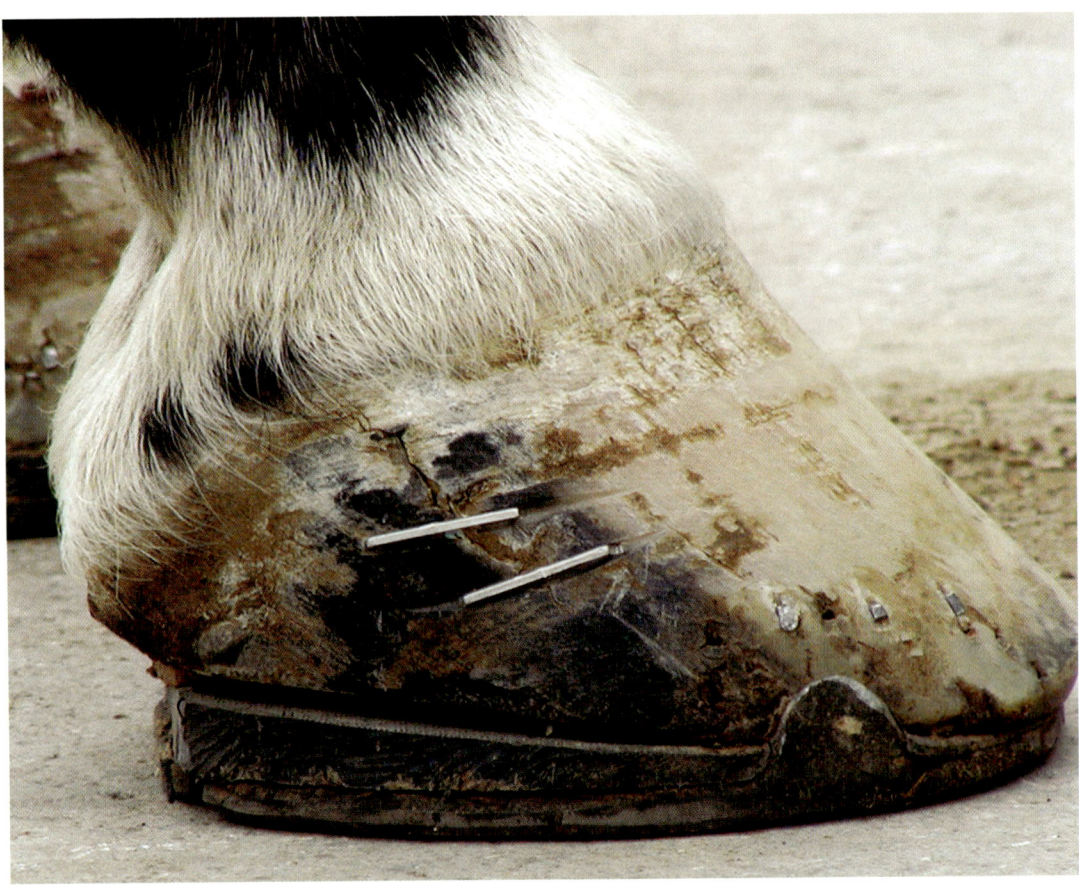

Here, a specially designed staple stabilizes a quarter crack. It's your farrier's choice to use a clamp or staple.

Your veterinarian or farrier might make a horizontal groove just below your horse's coronary band to relieve stress on the hoof wall near a crack.

strong hoof wall portion on each side of the crack to accommodate the wire. Special staples, clamps or patches also can inhibit hoof crack movement. Acrylic patches alone don't always provide the necessary support, but can protect the area, keep it clean, and improve the crack's appearance. Your veterinarian also might ask your farrier to shoe your horse with diagonal bars or other special shoes to "unload" the wall affected by the crack.

Above all, have a qualified farrier balance your horse's foot. Achieving balance might be a difficult—or even elusive—task if your horse has poor lower-leg conformation.

When the hoof cracks in the front toe area, anterior-to-posterior foot balance is critical. Radiographs might help your veterinarian evaluate this critical balance. Supporting a toe crack isn't as difficult as working with a quarter crack because a toe crack separates when the hoof is unloaded. Conversely, a quarter crack separates when the hoof bears weight.

Down the road: Proper hoof care and scheduled trimmings must be top priorities if your horse has a cracked hoof wall. Continual hoof maintenance is the best plan for any horse. But if your horse has conformation faults that predispose him to cracks, schedule your farrier regularly. New cracks might form quickly with out-of-balance hooves. Although no special shoe can correct every problem, work closely with your veterinarian and farrier to keep your horse in the best, balanced shape.

Talk with your veterinarian about providing your horse with hoof supplements and applying topical dressings to reduce the risk of future cracks.

Depending upon the location and severity of your horse's hoof crack, prognoses range from guarded to favorable. If a small crack responds quickly to treatment, your horse might be back to work fairly quickly. However, many hoof cracks require a great deal of attention from the owner and farrier. When cracks are caused by conformation or poor hoof structure, there's a good chance the hooves crack again. Following treatment for a more severe crack, your horse probably can return to work when his crack begins to close and grow out. Some veterinarians ask that a horse return to work only after the normal hoof wall grows more than three-quarters of an inch.

If your horse's crack results from a coronary band wound, he'll always have a hoof defect, which you need to manage with proper and timely hoof care, shoeing, and, in some cases, mechanical crack stabilization.

Thrush

It has rained for days, and your paddock is boggy with mud. You do your best to keep your horse's feet clean, but there's no way to keep them dry. While grooming, you pick out your horse's feet and see a dark tar and smell a foul odor.

What might be happening: Your horse's frog and the deep sulci, or grooves along the frog, provide a home for thrush bacteria to grow. These anaerobic organisms don't require oxygen to thrive, especially when a hoof is caked in mud. Mud packs into the sole, creating the dark, air-free environment thrush loves. A dirty stall with standing urine and feces also can cause sludge to pack into a horse's hoof. Bacteria that is allowed to live there eventually might eat away the frog tissue. Layers of sensitive tissue under the frog's horny cover become exposed, and your horse becomes sore. Although most thrush cases don't evolve to this level, thrush, left untreated, can cause lameness.

Some horses develop thrush following another lameness problem. If your horse has a bruise or other injury, and isn't comfortable placing weight on his foot—in a full weight-bearing, heel-to-toe walking motion—structures within his sore foot might not expand and clean as well as they should. Your horse's foot isn't used as intended, so doesn't create the callus and form with the strength it should. Just as you must place weight on your bones to keep them healthy, your horse must put weight on his bones and hoof structures to keep them strong. When hoof structures are weak, they're permeable, and bacteria can easily enter. When your horse's hoof works properly—moving in a balanced way beneath his weight—the frog and soft tissues "pump" and expand the hoof. This keeps the hoof clean. Without the pressure and the movement, bacteria and debris accumulate, and thrush thrives.

You might notice thrush problems more frequently if you live in a moist region. The problem is common in the South, Northeast, Northwest and Midwest, although conditions can be right for thrush in any geographic area.

What you notice: You might see no lameness or see lameness up to a Grade 2. You also notice:

- A foul odor, especially evident as you clean the sulci, or depressions alongside the frog.

- A black discharge, the byproduct of the anaerobic, thrush-causing bacteria.
- Your horse pulls away when you attempt to pick out the frog's sulci. The area might be pressure-sensitive without the protection of healthy frog tissue.

What you do: Clean your horse's hooves as often as possible, allowing air to access areas around the frog. If possible, move your horse to a dry area, where he doesn't stand constantly in mud. Clean out stalls and paddocks to ensure your horse doesn't stand in urine and waste.

The healing process: Work with your veterinarian and farrier to make sure your horse's sulci are clean. Have your farrier trim away diseased frog tissue. As soon as air reaches the active bacteria, it stops harming your horse. Pack affected areas with cotton soaked in a disinfectant solution. Ask your veterinarian what treatment he prefers, for example, a 2 percent iodine solution or a commercial thrush-treatment product. The cotton keeps dirt from entering the affected area. The solution protects against bacteria and limits reinfection, allowing normal tissue growth. Your veterinarian might ask you to soak the cotton in disinfectant and reapply daily or weekly. You might use a bandage, protective boot or duct tape to hold the cotton and medication in place, if necessary.

Down the road: Your horse most likely has a favorable prognosis. Make sure to keep his feet clean. Also treat any other lameness problems with care so that thrush doesn't develop as a secondary issue.

White-Line Disease

You show your horse on Florida's A Circuit every year. Off-season, he continues his high-level work with his Southern-based trainer. This show season, your horse has missed several events, and your trainer says he's "off." Your farrier notices a white, mealy, dry sub-

Thrush bacteria break down the horse's cornified frog tissue, exposing the sensitive frog. The frog here shows degeneration that's painful for your horse.

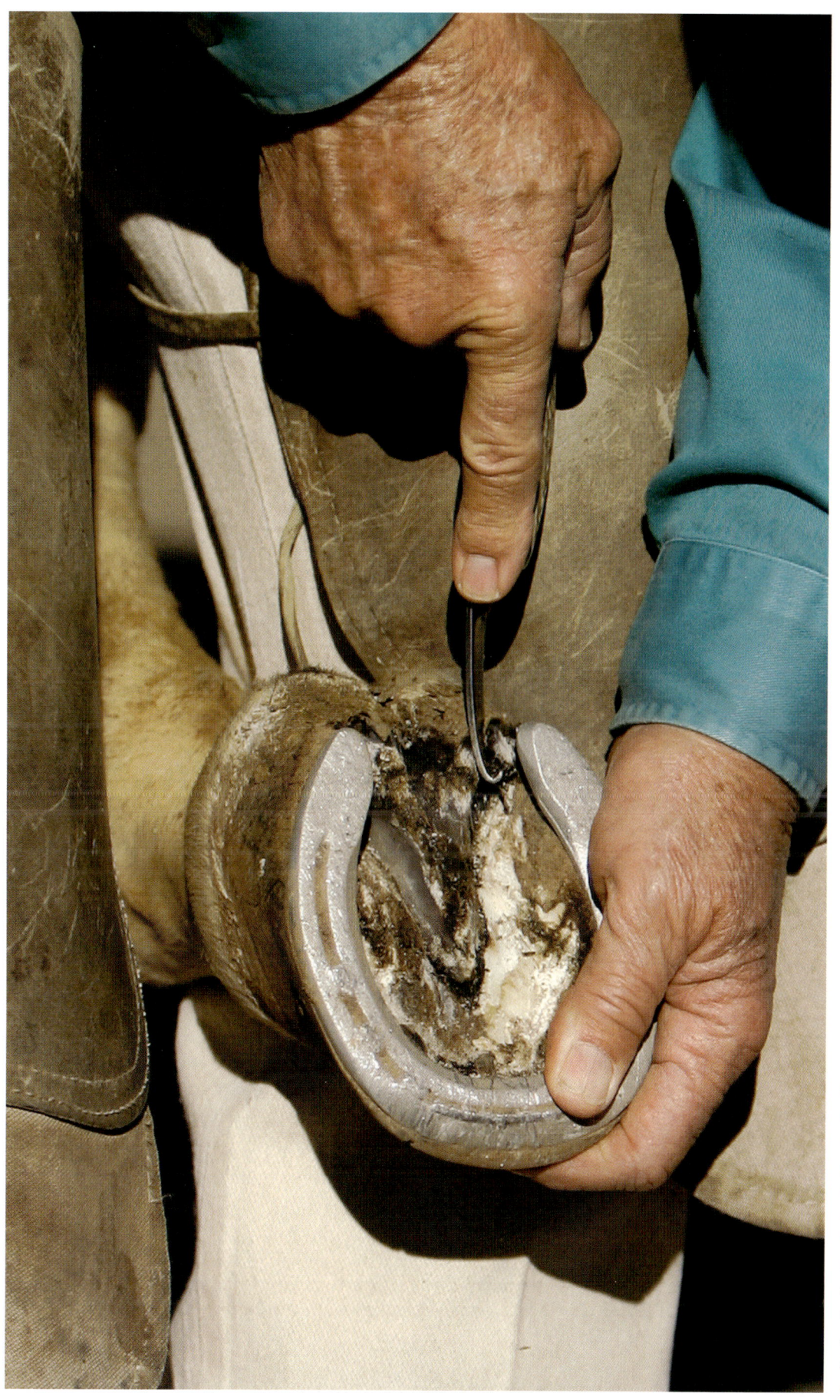

Prevent thrush by cleaning your horse's hooves regularly. When the hoof is clean and air circulates, anaerobic bacteria can't grow.

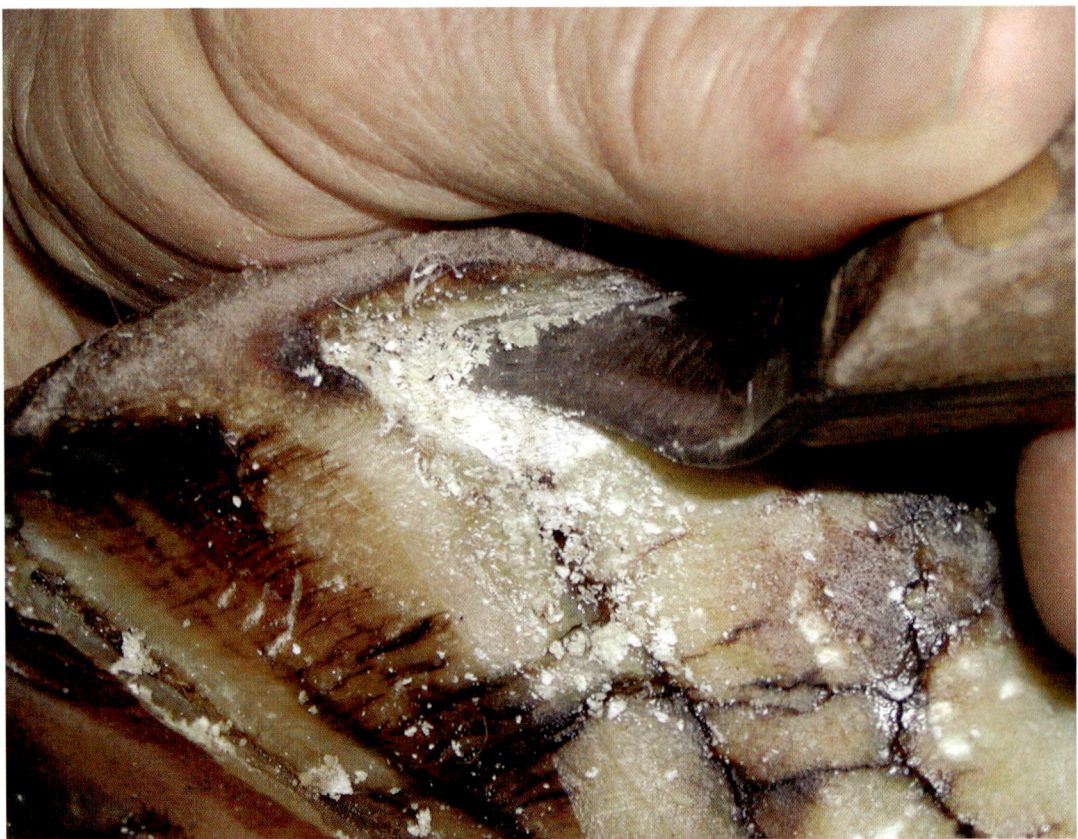

If your horse has white-line disease, you see a mealy white substance inside the hoof wall, along the hoof's white line.

stance along your horse's white line, the white layer of the hoof wall, and suggests calling your veterinarian immediately.

What might be happening: If your horse has white-line disease, a degeneration, or disease process causing gradual deterioration of a body part's structure, has occurred in the white line, the inner hoof wall layer adjoining the laminar layer. Bacteria or fungus (yet to be determined) causes the white layer to degenerate, leaving behind white, mealy, dry material. Degeneration generally progresses upward from the sole area, undermining the support of the coffin bone. White-line disease, unlike laminitis, which involves the horse's entire physiology, affects only the foot. With white-line disease, the basement membrane portion of the lamina isn't harmed.

Your horse feels pain when the disease progresses to affect the coffin bone's support, resulting in stress to the supporting laminae. When the sole must bear weight intended for the hoof wall, your horse feels intense pressure, which can become painful.

White-line disease often is considered a regional condition; more horses in warm, moist climates have the mealy, white residue under a portion of their hoof walls.

What you notice: You see a Grade 1 to 4 lameness. You might not notice other obvious signs because a shoe often covers the affected part of the hoof.

What you do: White-line disease isn't as much an emergency as laminitis. However, identify the problem as early as possible to limit further degeneration.

What your veterinarian does: Your veterinarian removes your horse's shoe or shoes to investigate the white line's integrity. In a healthy hoof, the white line is an obvious, but firm and stationary layer. However, even a healthy hoof might not be completely attached around the sole perimeter. Your veterinarian probes the line with a hoof knife to see if the wall is adequately attached to the sole.

Radiographs show if your horse's hoof has white-line disease. Your veterinarian sees a darkened, vertical streak parallel to the hoof wall, which represents the inner hoof wall degeneration.

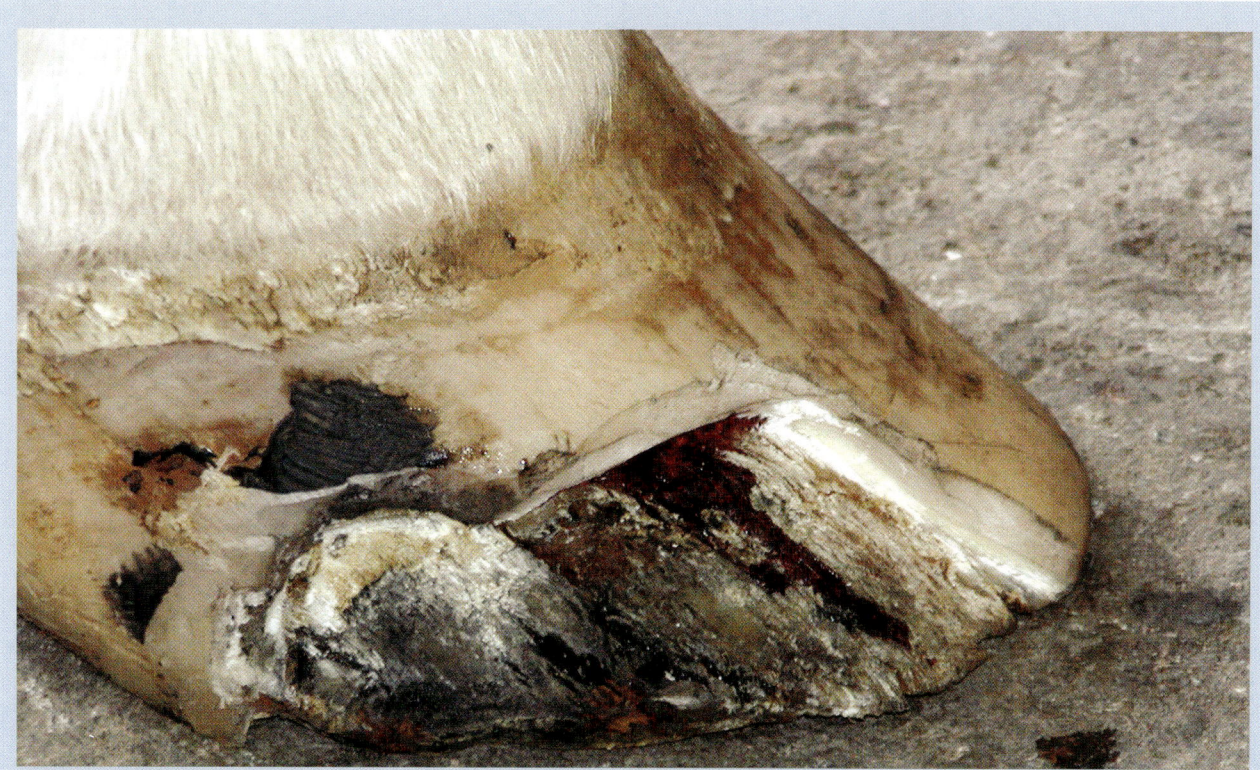

White-line disease, which eats away a horse's hoof and breaks down the hoof wall, has weakened this horse's hoof so extensively that the veterinarian removed a section to apply needed disinfectants.

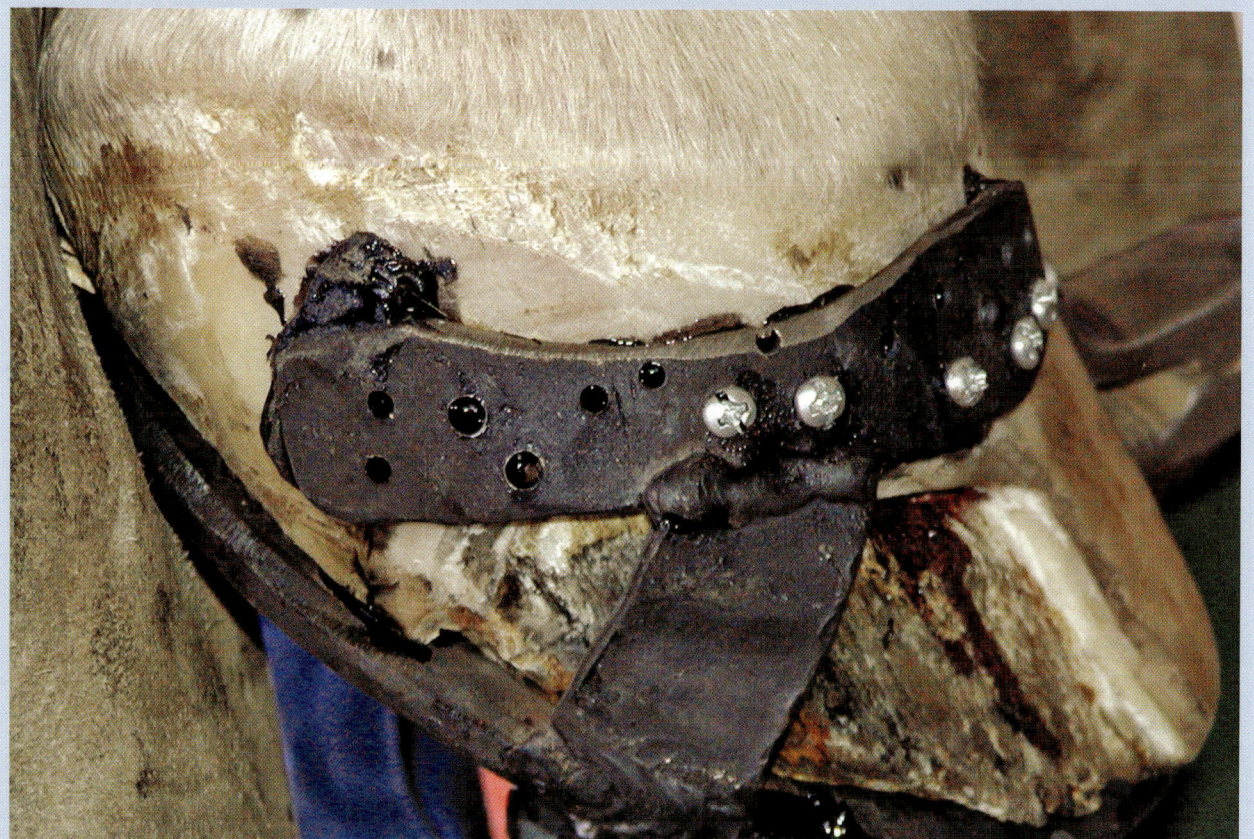

If white-line disease affects a significant part of the hoof wall, your horse might need support, such as a bridge shoe shown here, for his frog and internal foot structures.

LAMENESS Q&A

When it's time to purchase a horse, make sure he has strong hooves to withstand the load and pressure in any sport in which you compete.

What foot qualities should be considered when purchasing a horse?

The major internal structures obviously aren't visible to the naked eye; however you can make evaluations based on the foot's external qualities. Consider the following elements:

- **Quality hoof wall.** The hoof wall should look smooth and strong, not flaky.

- **Foot depth.** A deep foot, from the coronary band to the ground, offers greater protection to the sensitive inner tissues and structures than does a shallow foot.

- **Heel characteristics.** Look for a defined heel, not one that's compressed or underslung. Your horse's heels should not be too long, and they should be relatively symmetrical, the left being the same length as the right

- **Healthy sole.** A firm, uniform sole offers greater protection to vital structures.

- **Healthy frog.** The frog should meet the ground and look healthy and robust, not dry or shriveled.

- **Overall evaluation.** There's no perfect size or depth when evaluating a horse's feet. They should be proportionate to the horse's body size.

What medication is best for flushing foot structures?

It depends on the wound site. If an abscess is in the hoof wall or sole—and sensitive lamellar tissue isn't involved—strong medications, such as 2 percent iodine work well. If vital structures, such as joint capsule, coffin bones or tendon sheaths are involved, isotonic and buffered antibiotic solutions are best. Avoid medication that can destroy tissue, such as hydrogen peroxide or undiluted iodine.

The healing process: Once your veterinarian makes a white-line disease diagnosis, he needs to remove the unattached hoof wall. This exposes the affected portion to air and allows him to clean and treat the area with a disinfectant solution, which inhibits the disease's progression. All of the affected hoof wall must be removed to ensure adequate treatment and to ensure that no more infection remains.

Next, your veterinarian cleans the hoof to make sure all mealy debris is gone. You then continue the cleaning process, disinfecting the affected hoof every day for up to two weeks.

Your veterinarian might recommend special shoeing to support your horse's hoof, especially if the degenerative process has compromised a large portion of hoof wall. Your veterinarian works with your farrier to choose the most helpful shoe, usually a frog-support shoe of some degree, to reduce the laminar stress and support the coffin bone. Your horse might be fitted with a combination of heart-bar or egg-bar shoes and pads, depending upon the amount of damage and the wall portion affected. The shoeing goal is to support the coffin bone while the hoof wall grows back.

Down the road: Your horse should be able to return to work as soon as his hoof is adequately supported. Some horses take a few months to heal, especially if a large chunk of hoof wall needs to grow. With management, most horses should have favorable prognoses. Watch for white-line disease each time your farrier removes and replaces your horse's shoes. Since your horse has had the problem before, he might develop the mealy white line again.

Case Study: The Hoof Capsule

Puncture wounds in horses' feet occur as accidents—even in the best-managed stables. A recently shod Warmblood stood near a fence as his aggressive stable mate charged the fence line. As "Romeo" moved quickly from the fence and the aggressor, Romeo's left forefoot stepped on the edge of his right front shoe. His right front shoe pulled loose and twisted to one side—but remained attached. As the horse stepped down with his right front foot, he landed on two nails still in the now-dangling shoe—and pointing upward.

Horseman's Dictionary

abscess: a pus-filled cavity formed during the inflammation process, often caused by bacterial infection.

acute: sudden onset often sparked by an injury.

corn: a bruise to deep, sensitive structures at the angle of the sole, the triangular area between the bar and the hoof wall.

degeneration: a disease process causing gradual deterioration of a body part's structure, to the point the structure might lose ability to function.

edema: swelling caused by fluid in the horse's body tissues, outside of the blood vessels.

hematoma: a collection of blood resulting from a hemorrhage or bleeding into tissue.

hitch: a descriptive word for lameness having different meanings depending upon geographic regions. Avoid using.

hoof capsule: the cornified portion of the foot that encases the foot's sensitive structures. The hoof capsule includes the hoof wall, sole, bars, heel buttress and frog.

hoof-testers: a clamp-like device used to evaluate your horse's foot. A horse pulls away when sensitive to pressure from the metal testers.

laminae: vertical, leaf-like projections between the coffin bone and the hoof wall.

lateral: outside or away from your horse's midline.

medial: inside, closest to your horse's midline.

poultice: a moist, hydroscopic dressing applied to painful and swollen body parts.

radiopaque: anything that doesn't allow radiation to penetrate; can be a liquid or metal.

red zone: the most critical hoof area because it includes vital structures: the central portion of the frog, the deep flexor tendon, the navicular bone, the impar ligament and the coffin joint.

sulci: depressions alongside the frog and in the frog's centerline.

thrush: frog degeneration caused by anaerobic bacteria that thrive when trapped in the area. Untreated, the bacteria can eat away the frog and expose the foot's soft tissue.

These two nails penetrated the sole of the foot to the sensitive tissues. Romeo's owner immediately removed the dangling shoe and placed the injured foot in a protective bandage to prevent further contamination. The veterinarian blocked the foot to allow proper opening, draining and flushing of the punctures. Radiographs were taken to assess any damage to the coffin bone.

In this case, the coffin bone had been spared. Romeo had an uneventful recovery. The wounds were packed with antibiotic ointment and kept bandaged for two weeks, and then Romeo was shod with a protective pad. He also received systemic antibiotics for 10 days and soon showed improvement.

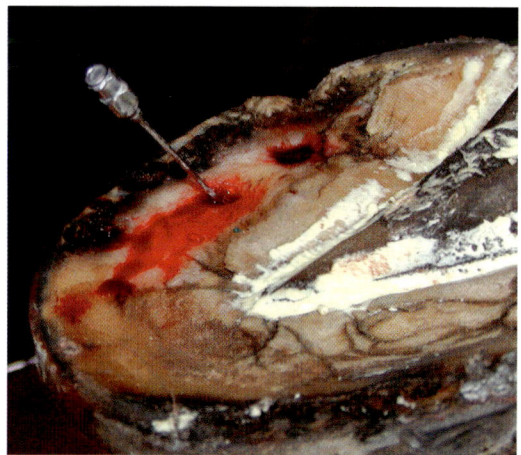

This close-up of Romeo's foot shows the two punctures after they were opened for drainage and flushing. The special blunt-ended needle seen here was used to flush antibiotics into the deep punctures.

3

THE FOOT—INTERNAL STRUCTURES

Although the inside of your horse's foot has been designed with protection, injuries and impact can harm the sensitive structures found within the hoof.

Although your horse's hooves are healthy and hard, the internal structures are never far from the ground and its potential impact. Here, we look inside the hoof wall to find out what can happen to delicate internal structures if your horse experiences sudden impact, poor and moist footing conditions, or suffers from constant-use trauma. Read on to find out what you can do to keep your horse comfortable and when it's time to call for veterinary help.

Coffin-Bone Fracture

Your barrel-racing horse was at full steam—charging around the course. Soon after your money-earning run, you lead him back to the stall row and notice he's suddenly lame. He touches the toe of his left hind and avoids pressure. You feel moderate digital pulse in his pastern area. Then you realize that he misstepped just before the finish line.

What might be happening: Your horse can fracture his coffin bone if he hits something; hitting a jump or even landing strangely on a rock can result in a direct blow to his hoof capsule. He also can fracture the coffin bone during an athletic event, for example, when turning while barrel racing. Horses running free and playing also can fracture their coffin bones if they twist and land in strange ways. A coffin-bone fracture can

An equine athlete stresses internal foot structures when he strikes the ground and twists his lower leg. This horse's left front foot supports his weight during impact and must continue to support his entire body and the rider throughout the turn.

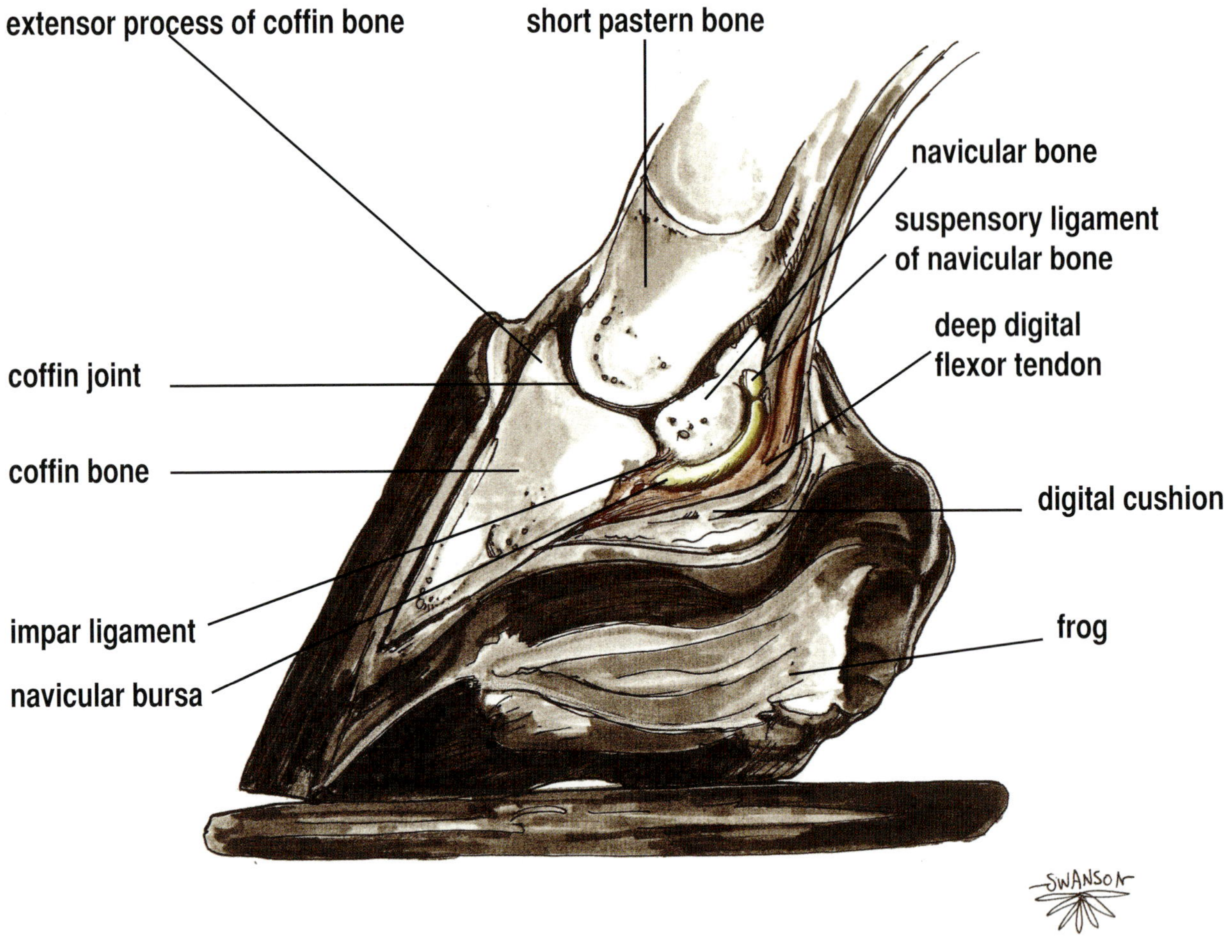

extensor process of coffin bone

short pastern bone

navicular bone

suspensory ligament of navicular bone

deep digital flexor tendon

coffin joint

coffin bone

digital cushion

impar ligament

navicular bursa

frog

—SWANSON—

This side view of a horse's internal hoof anatomy, seen from the side closest to your horse's midline, reveals your horse's delicate foot structures.

This cross-section model of a horse's leg shows internal foot structures in true-to-life style.

be significant because the bone is a primary support for your horse's entire weight. Worse, if the fracture involves the coffin joint, your horse might suffer permanent joint damage. Your horse most likely displays coffin-bone fracture symptoms soon after or during a performance session. The fracture does not always involve the coffin joint. When the coffin bone alone is fractured, your horse's prognosis is better than if he's injured his joint.

What you notice: You see Grade 2 to 5 lameness. Some horses don't show specific outward signs, but suddenly appear "off." You also might notice:

- Your horse pointing his injured foot.

- An increased digital pulse.

- Heat in the hoof wall.

- More obvious lameness when your horse turns in the direction of the affected foot.

What you do: Call your veterinarian whenever your horse shows acute lameness.

What your veterinarian does: Your veterinarian wants to find the exact cause of lameness and uses hoof-testers, radiographs and nerve blocks to locate and diagnose the problem. Note: If your veterinarian suspects a fracture, he might take radiographs before any blocking procedures. A nondisplaced fracture could be worsened if your horse continues to move on the limb and doesn't feel pain. Your veterinarian also might employ other diagnostic technology, such as an MRI, to see the total extent of damage to the bone and joint.

The healing process: Once the diagnosis is made, your veterinarian wants to immobilize your horse's coffin bone to allow the fracture to heal. The veterinarian works with your farrier to shoe your horse in an egg-bar shoe with a flat, hard aluminum pad. Silicone between the pad and your horse's sole helps immobilize and protect the bone while it heals. Even with his foot immobilized with special shoeing, your horse needs stall rest and confinement for a minimum of 90 days. You can hand-walk your horse a minimum amount for stall-cleaning and grooming.

If your horse's coffin joint has been affected, your veterinarian most likely medicates the

Your veterinarian can work with your farrier to place an egg-bar shoe and pad to support a fractured coffin bone.

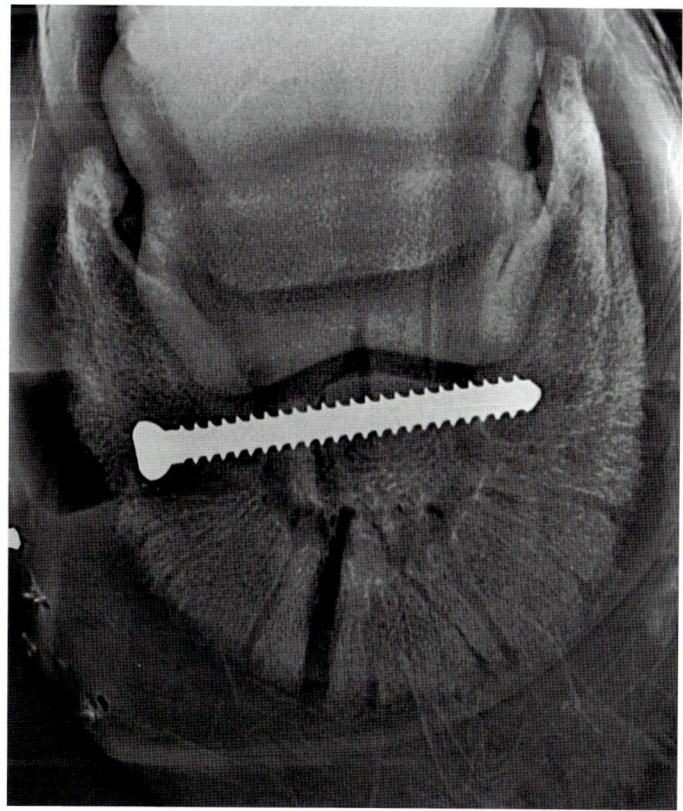

This radiograph shows the screw placed to stabilize a horse's fractured coffin bone, allowing it to heal.

LAMENESS Q&A

Your veterinarian uses hoof-testers to locate the pain's source and to interpret your horse's pain tolerance level.

What are hoof-testers?

Hoof-testers are tools that function as extensions of your veterinarian's fingers. The tool gives your veterinarian mechanical leverage to check for sites of specific foot soreness. He feels for a reaction from your horse when the hoof-testers place pressure on usually insensitive areas of the sole and hoof wall.

Your veterinarian interprets the horse's tolerance level and measures and evaluates the horse's response by testing a sound hoof to establish a control. If an area of your horse's hoof shows sensitivity once, but not upon immediate re-examination, the reaction probably isn't significant.

A side note: A horse's sensitivity to hoof-testers can be influenced by the climate in which the horse lives. For example, a horse in an arid climate has hard feet, so it's more difficult to elicit a response with hoof-testers. However, a horse whose feet absorb environmental moisture from, for example, a lush meadow, usually presents a stronger sensitivity to hoof-testers.

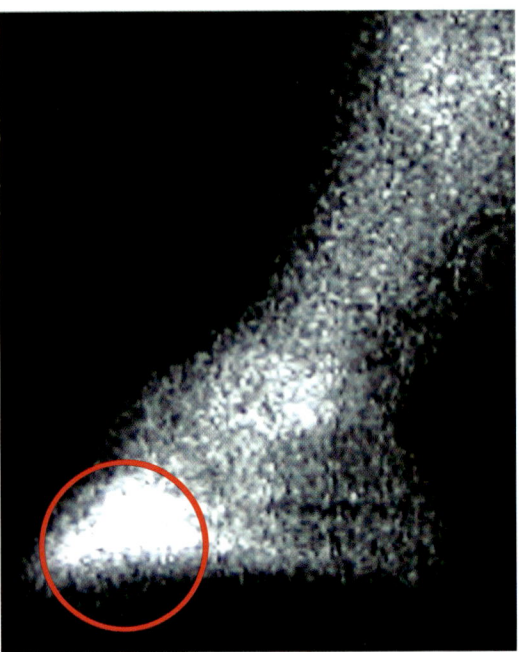

Nuclear scintigraphy is used to demonstrate bone injuries. In this case, the radioactive chemical has accumulated in the coffin bone, creating the bright spot seen above.

horse to keep your horse's coffin bone supported for a year or longer to avoid reinjury.

Generally speaking, horses with coffin-bone fractures have favorable prognoses—as long as only the bone is affected. If your horse's coffin joint also is affected, the prognosis might differ. Your horse's coffin bone fracture might be evident on radiographs for years to come, but it should heal well enough to allow your horse to return to work after the initial healing time of four to six months.

Reinjury is possible. Make sure you analyze ground conditions before you work your horse. Avoid hard and rocky ground, especially if your horse moves fast during the work session or if you're practicing for performance events. Hard or rocky ground might pound against your horse's foot and cause the fracture to split once again.

joint with hyaluronate and other anti-inflammatory medications to reduce inflammation. If the fracture splits the coffin bone through the middle, from the direction of your horse's toe to his heel, your veterinarian might need to surgically place a screw to immobilize the bone and facilitate healing.

Down the road: Your veterinarian most likely recommends protective shoeing for your

Coffin-Bone Extensor Process Fracture

Your amateur show hunter mare has performed very well until this week. The right lead canter is not quite as smooth as usual, and she takes her right lead, but with some reluctance. She still does her job, but not as comfortably. While reviewing last weekend's ride, you recall the mare hit a rail pretty hard with her right front foot.

What might be happening: It is possible your mare fractured the extensor process of her coffin bone (P3). The extensor process is just inside the hoof capsule and just below the coronary band. The common digital extensor tendon attaches to this process and pulls up the toe, and then extends the foot prior to it landing on the ground. An impact on the vulnerable coronary band can fracture a portion of the process. The fractured piece can be a small fragment or a larger significant portion of the process. This fracture causes an inflammatory response in the coffin joint, resulting in pain and lameness. The degree of lameness usually is related to the size of the fragment and to the amount of direct trauma to the hoof capsule.

What you notice: The degree of lameness ranges from barely perceptible to an obvious lameness. Lameness varies from Grade 1 to Grade 4, depending on the extent of the fracture and the amount of bruising to the hoof-capsule structures.

What you do: Your examination of an affected leg can reveal increased fluid in the coffin joint, just above the coronary band at the front. You can feel heat in the hoof capsule in the acute phase. In some cases, an old fracture has not been clinically evident until that area has been reinjured. In such a case, the fracture healed, and the fragment has been stable until affected by the new trauma.

What your veterinarian does: With signs of lameness, your veterinarian, in many cases, bases the diagnosis on clinical signs and confirms it with radiographs. In less obvious cases, he might rely on diagnostic blocks to locate the source of pain and lameness. In chronic cases, the foot can become somewhat triangular, or snow-plow-shaped, at the coronary band.

Surgical removal is the preferred treatment for this fracture. The fragment is best removed with arthroscopic procedures, which can be difficult if the fragment or chip is large. Because the coffin bone is behind the hoof wall, reaching the fragments with a regular surgical incision usually is more difficult.

The healing process: Once the fracture fragment has been removed, inflammation within the joint subsides, and the lameness is resolved. The recovery time ranges from six weeks to four months, depending on the bone

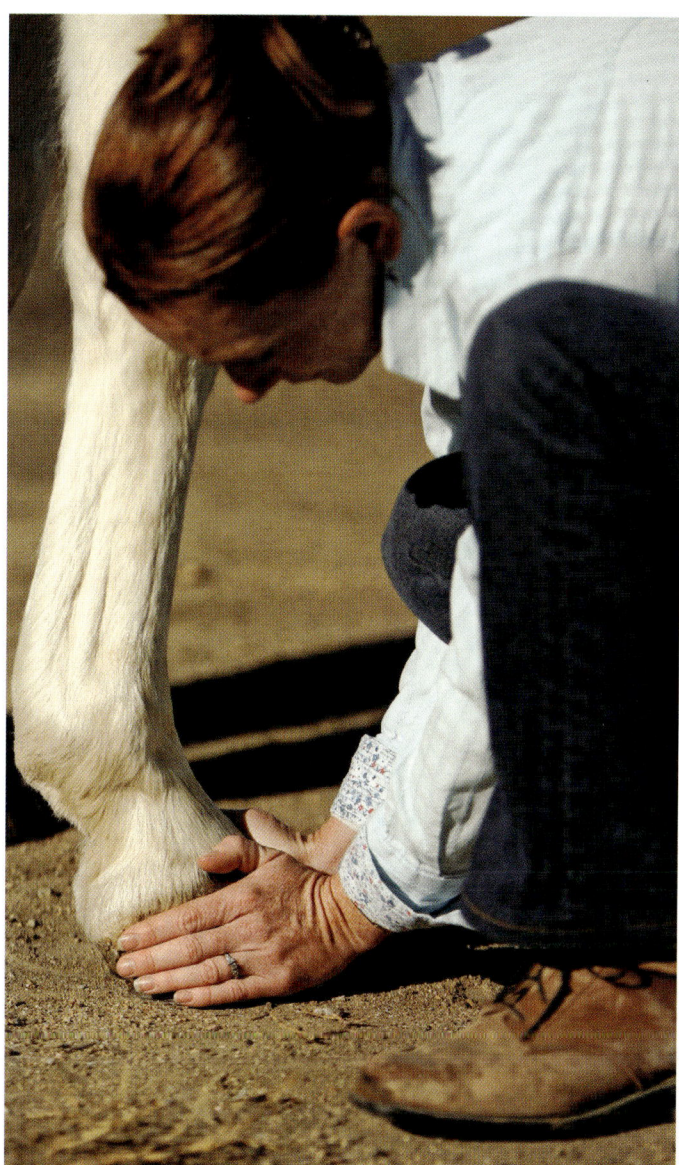

If your horse has an acute fracture to the coffin-bone extensor process, you can feel heat around his hoof capsule.

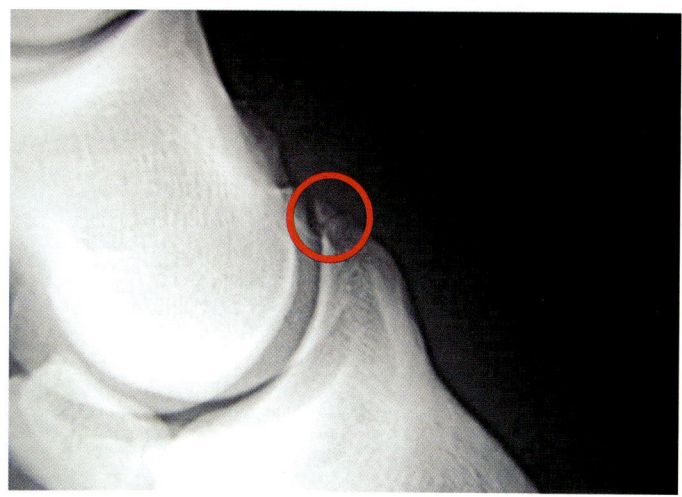

This radiograph, showing a side view of a horse's foot, reveals the horse's fractured coffin-bone extensor process.

fragment's size and the amount of damage to the cartilage surface in the coffin joint. In some cases your veterinarian might want to augment the healing process with intra-articular medications (injections). However, most cases receive oral, systemic joint supplementation.

Down the road: Most horses have a favorable outcome for this problem and return to the original level of performance. That is a favorable prognosis. If the fragment is small to moderate in size, there are no restrictions on the level of use.

There are circumstances in which the extensor process fragments are large and can be a result of improper bone development, a type of developmental orthopedic disease. Many times these cases are bilateral and involve both front coffin bones. These large fragments result in some coffin-joint instability and eventually lameness, and in some cases, these fragments can be too large to successfully remove.

Coffin-Bone Rim Fracture

Your veterinarian and farrier have told you that your horse's soles are thin—it's best to keep shoes on him throughout the year. Your horse doesn't agree. He throws a shoe in the dry, hard-packed pasture and runs around without it all day before you arrive home to feed. While you're out searching for the shoe, your horse trots by you—with a shortened, unrhythmic stride. He bobs his head in discomfort. You stop him, analyze his shoeless hoof and feel a strong digital pulse.

What might be happening: Rim fractures occur most often when a horse's thin sole is traumatized. Your horse's coffin-bone perimeter tapers to a thin edge and lies close to the bottom of your horse's foot. If your horse has thin soles, he might be prone to coffin-bone trauma, specifically trauma to the thin "rim" of the coffin bone. Small fractures or stress fractures at the edge of the coffin bone cause your horse to feel pain each time he steps on the affected foot. Stress fractures are breaks caused by continuous repetitive stress or an acute incident, and are not evident from the outside of the hoof. However, a rim fracture isn't as severe as a coffin-bone fracture that stretches into the body of the bone. Still, your horse isn't comfortable. He feels more pain as more pressure pounds down onto his sole.

What you notice: Your horse might show signs of injury all at once, or symptoms might appear gradually. You see Grade 1 to 3 lameness, as well as notice:

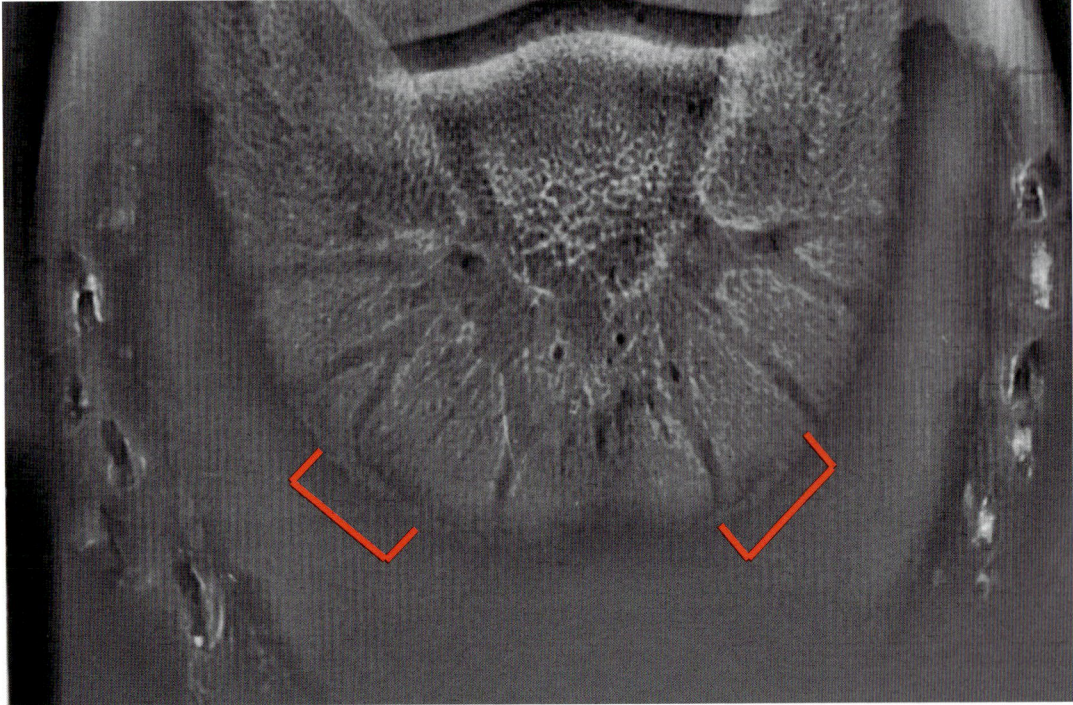

This radiograph shows a dorsal view of the coffin bone and two small fractures along the bone's rim, which aren't as severe as a coffin-bone fracture that reaches into the body of the bone.

As with most coffin-bone injuries, your veterinarian recommends special shoes to relieve pressure as your horse stands and moves. A custom shoe or one with a wedge or special support might be required.

- More lameness when your horse is barefoot.

- An increased digital pulse.

- Lameness exacerbated by hard ground.

- Soreness after shoeing.

What you do: You probably notice your horse is "off" and call your veterinarian.

What your veterinarian does: He uses hoof-testers to find out what part of your horse's hoof is most affected. If your horse jerks away when the hoof-testers are placed near the perimeter of his coffin bone, your veterinarian suspects a rim fracture and takes radiographs to confirm the diagnosis.

The healing process: As when dealing with other coffin-bone fractures, your veterinarian suggests special shoes as the first treatment step. For rim fractures, your veterinarian works with your farrier to fit a shoe that relieves pressure on the fractured area. Your farrier places a flat pad trimmed to the shape of the shoe, known as a rim pad, beneath your horse's foot. He also places a regular flat pad below the rim pad, with silicone or soft acrylic between the flat pad and the sole. This helps minimize pressure to your horse's coffin bone as he stands and walks.

Your veterinarian prescribes systemic anti-inflammatory medications immediately after the diagnosis. At home, make sure your horse rests, keeping pressure off his injury. You also must make sure his special shoeing treatment continues.

Down the road: Your horse might be cleared to continue his performance career soon after or even during the healing process. Most horses with rim fractures have favorable prognoses—as long as owners are willing to keep up with special shoeing treatments.

Degenerative Coffin-Joint Disease

Your favorite reining mount is a bit "toed-in," but has a desire to please. He obeys every turnaround cue—stepping across with as much grace as his build allows. In time, you notice he doesn't respond as willingly or turn as quickly. Now, you notice a small bump above his coronary band, just in front of the pastern.

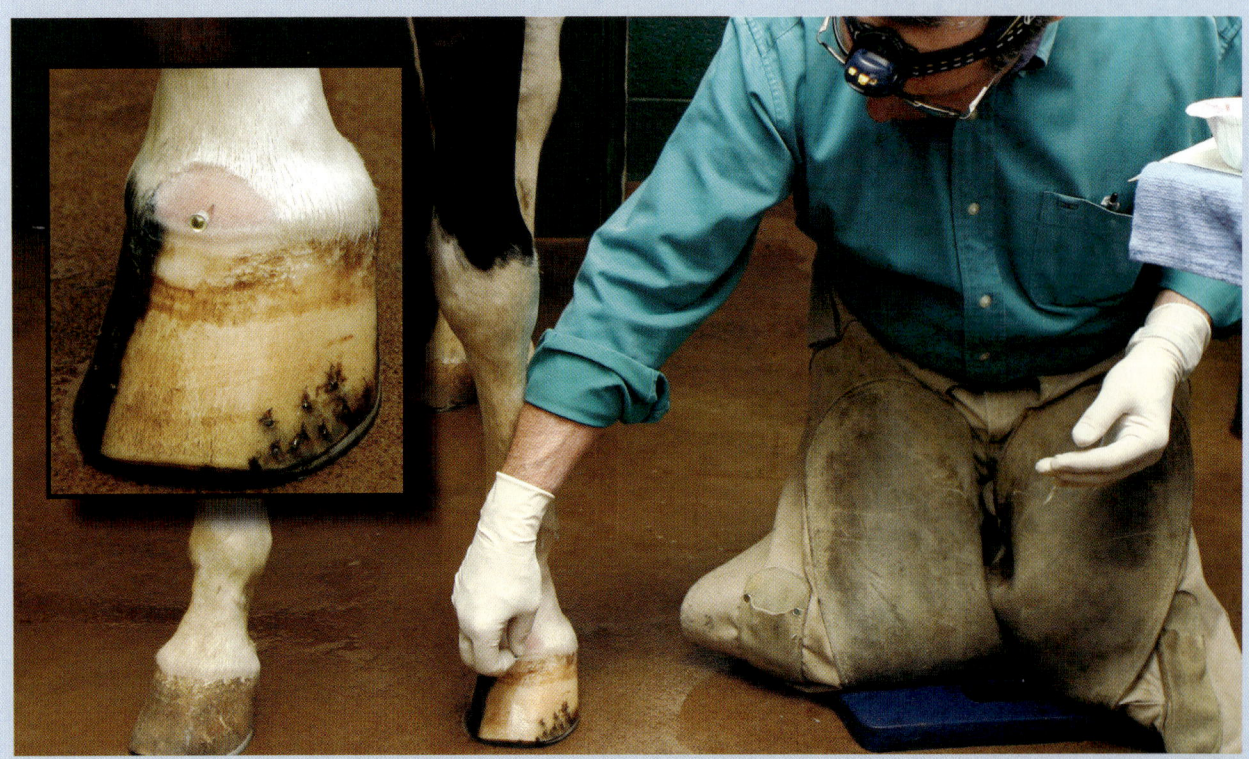

A horse with degenerative coffin-joint disease is a candidate for coffin-joint injections. After cleaning and shaving the horse's leg, Dr. Swanson inserts the needle.

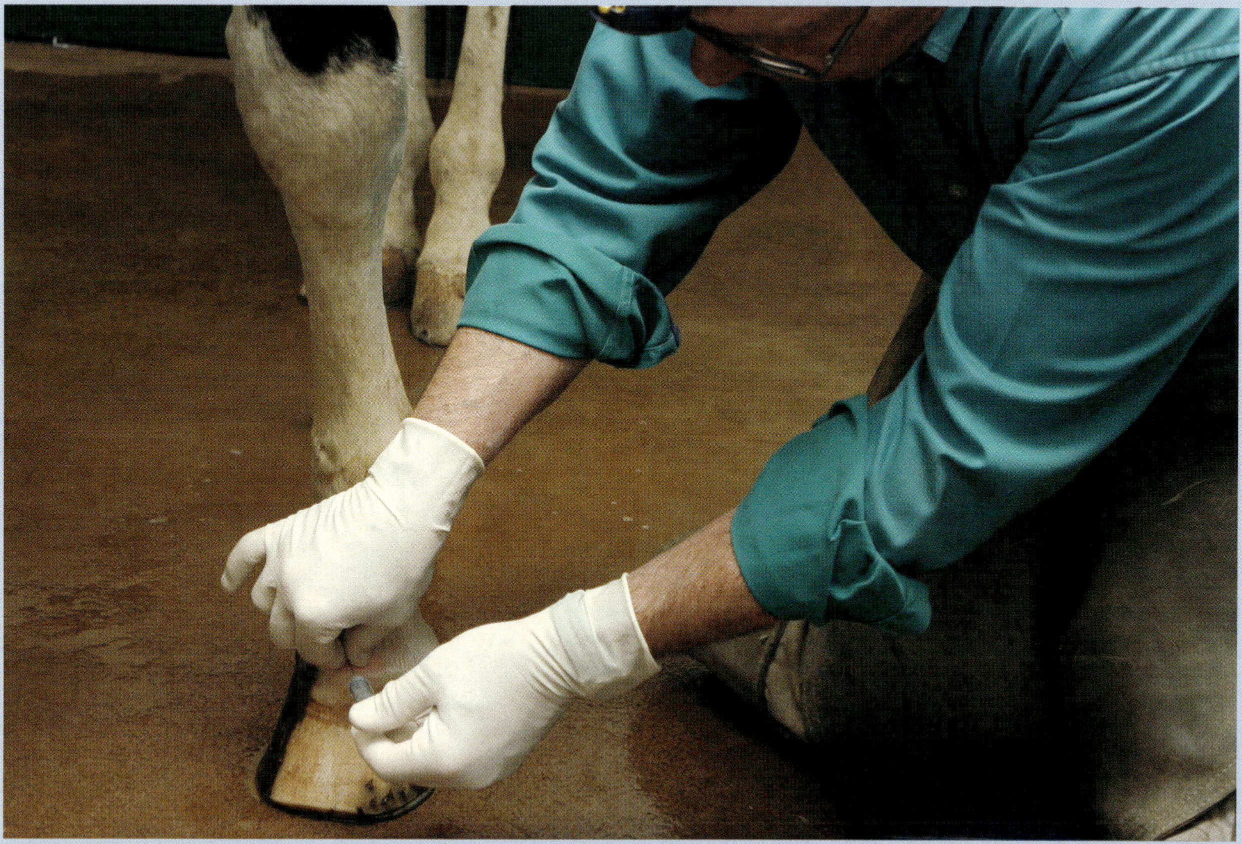

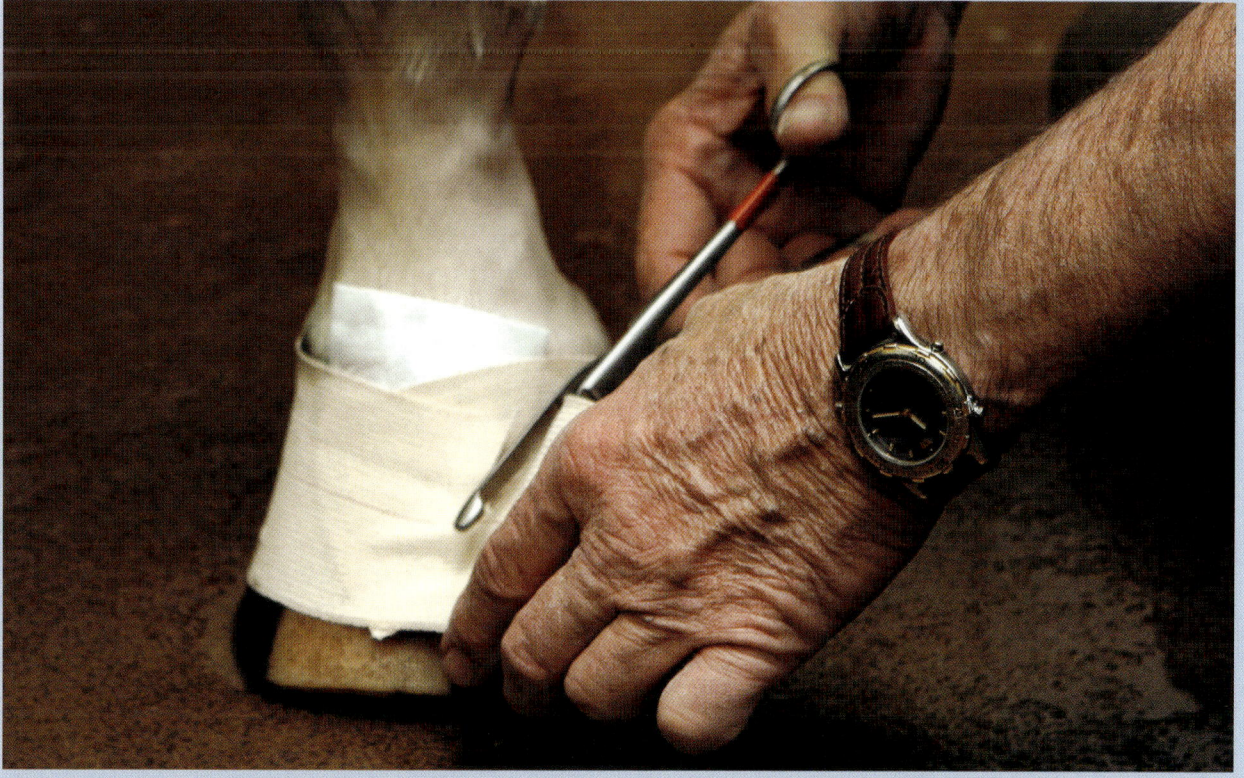

He then attaches the syringe and injects interleukin-1 receptor antagonist protein or "IRAP" into the coffin joint to help reduce joint inflammation.

Following the injection, Dr. Swanson dresses and wraps the site to keep out bacteria and dirt.

What might be happening: Your horse can develop degenerative joint disease (DJD) or arthritis of the coffin joint following a previous coffin-bone injury. The coffin joint is the articulation between the short pastern bone and the coffin bone. If your horse has injured or fractured his coffin bone in the past, by twisting or jamming it and impacting the entire coffin joint, the inflammatory process can wreak havoc on the joint. Eventually inflammation causes your horse's recognizable lameness.

DJD also might appear if your horse continuously performs twisting motions, especially if his leg conformation isn't straight or correct. Repetitive movements resulting in lameness are referred to as use trauma. Bone cysts that develop adjacent to joint surfaces can also cause DJD.

Once your horse's coffin joint is damaged in any way, it might not heal completely. Instead, cartilage wears away and causes your horse to feel pain as bone rubs against bone. DJD gets its name because the joint has been injured previously, then shows signs of breaking down, causing a progressive ailment and degeneration.

What you notice: You see Grade 1 to 4 lameness and:

- A bump just above your horse's coronary band, on the front side of the pastern. The bump, a wind puff, is soft to touch and is filled with excess coffin-joint fluid.

- More severe lameness when your horse pivots on his affected foot while bearing weight. A shuffling gait if both your horse's feet are involved.

What you do: Keep your veterinarian informed about any changes in your horse's once-fractured or injured foot, especially if you see a wind puff.

What your veterinarian does: Your veterinarian uses hoof-testers to identify the sensitive area of your horse's foot, and relates to your horse's prior coffin-joint injury. Radiographs rule out a coffin-bone fracture and might display signs of DJD. Your veterinarian sees changes in your horse's bone along the coffin joint's perimeter, especially at the extensor process. However, DJD might not be entirely detectable on radiographs. Diagnostic blocking helps confirm the DJD diagnosis. MRI evaluation also can be helpful to establish the diagnosis and prognosis.

The healing process: Your horse needs rest and controlled exercise to heal after diagnosis and treatment. The amount of time off he requires depends on how much damage your veterinarian sees in the coffin joint. He prescribes intra-articular medication administered via an injection into your horse's coffin joint. Medications might include hyaluronate and short-acting cortisone or "IRAP." Scientifically known as interleukin-1 receptor antagonist protein, IRAP is processed blood plasmatherapy that combats osteoarthritis, to help reduce joint inflammation. Your veterinarian also might recommend shockwave therapy to calm the joint components.

Down the road: Once your horse recovers, you need to monitor and possibly modify his workload. Check ground conditions before riding. You don't want to risk compounding your horse's injuries by riding or working him on hard, uneven or frozen ground.

Most horses with DJD have guarded–to-unfavorable prognoses; the label depends on the extent of joint damage. With constant care, you might be able to successfully manage your horse's DJD. However, the disease is progressive and can be career-limiting.

Coffin-Joint Collateral-Ligament Injury

Your reining horse has been "off" for more than a month, but you can't seem to target the source of his stiff movement. You don't feel heat or a pulse on any foot. Still, something's not right.

What might be happening: Your horse's collateral ligaments hold the coffin joints together and are attached to the coffin bones and the short pastern bones. The ligaments can be abused continuously as your horse twists and turns, or if your horse often performs movements during which he jams his feet into the ground. With constant wear and after twists and turns, the ligaments can tear. Though stress to the ligaments is continuous in everyday life—and especially during strenuous performances—coffin-joint collateral-ligament injury, or CJCLI, isn't too common.

What you notice: This injury doesn't have specific or consistent signs and requires your veterinarian's diagnosis. Nonetheless, the following signs might lead to a CJCLI diagnosis. You notice a Grade 1 to Grade 3 lameness and also might notice:

- An enlarged, firm, soft-tissue structure just above your horse's coronary band, at the front corners of the pastern. This presentation is linked to the collateral ligaments, but doesn't always form when a horse has the injury and might be present without lameness.

- A bruise or specific trauma to the front corner of the pastern, just above the coronary band, which can lead to collateral ligament injury.

- More evident lameness when turning or circling, as with most lower leg injuries.

What you do: Though your horse's lameness might not be easily identifiable by sight alone,

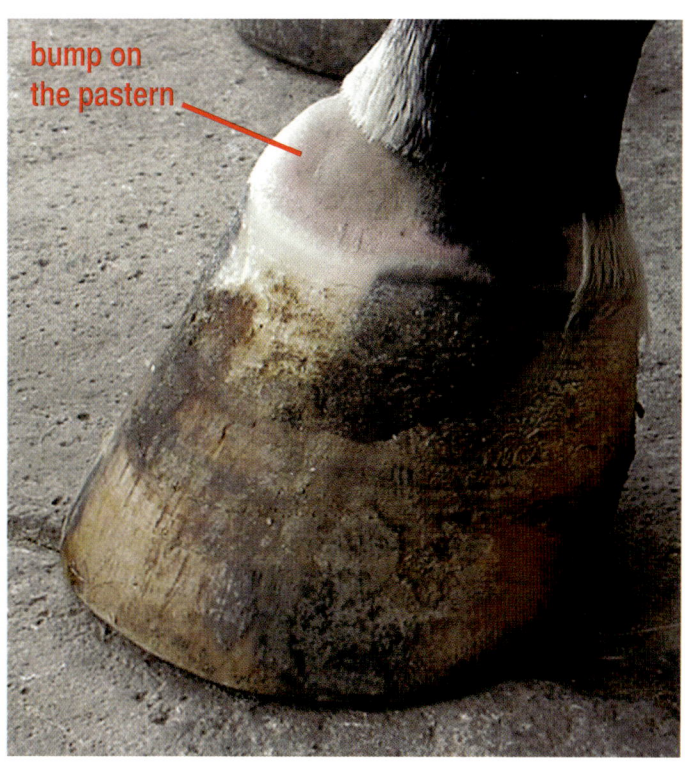

bump on the pastern

Soft tissues surrounding an injured collateral ligament of the coffin joint might swell and be evident from the outside.

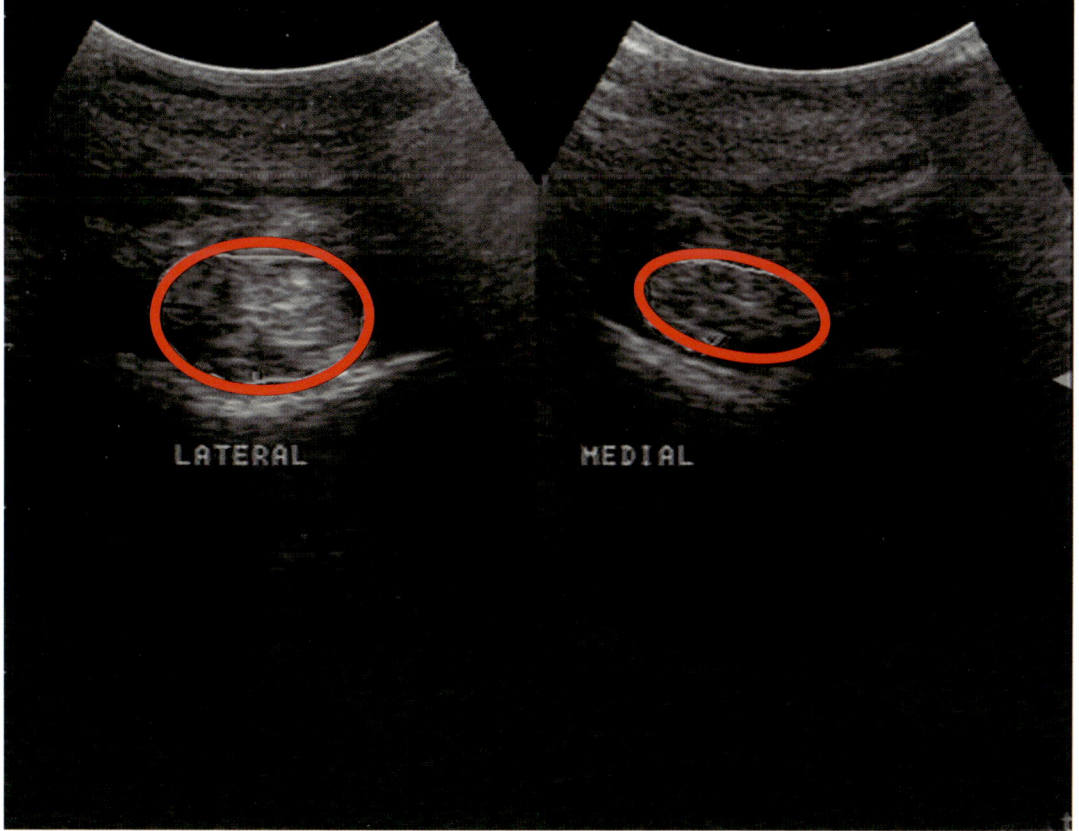

LATERAL   MEDIAL

The ultrasound image on the left shows the enlarged collateral ligament of the coffin joint, as compared to the normal-size ligament shown at right. This can be detected only with an ultrasound or MRI. Because this injury is near and above the coronet band, an ultrasound was used; only an MRI can help with diagnosis if the injury is inside the hoof wall.

you can sense when something isn't right. CJCLI is better treated and your horse might have a more favorable prognosis if you catch the problem early. So, call your veterinarian as soon as you sense a problem.

What your veterinarian does: Your veterinarian uses diagnostic blocking to pinpoint your horse's pain. An ultrasound can show the soft structures involved in some cases and help confirm the diagnosis. Your veterinarian recommends an MRI evaluation to help him make a complete and accurate diagnosis. Nuclear scintigraphy sometimes aids in your veterinarian's diagnosis. The injury can involve other structures within the foot.

The healing process: You must confine your horse and strictly control his exercise—hand-walking him for at least a month and usually longer after the initial injury. CJCLI can take four to six months to heal.

During the healing time, your veterinarian might recommend shockwave therapy for your horse. Your veterinarian also might work with your farrier to fit your horse with a shoe that supports the affected side of the joint.

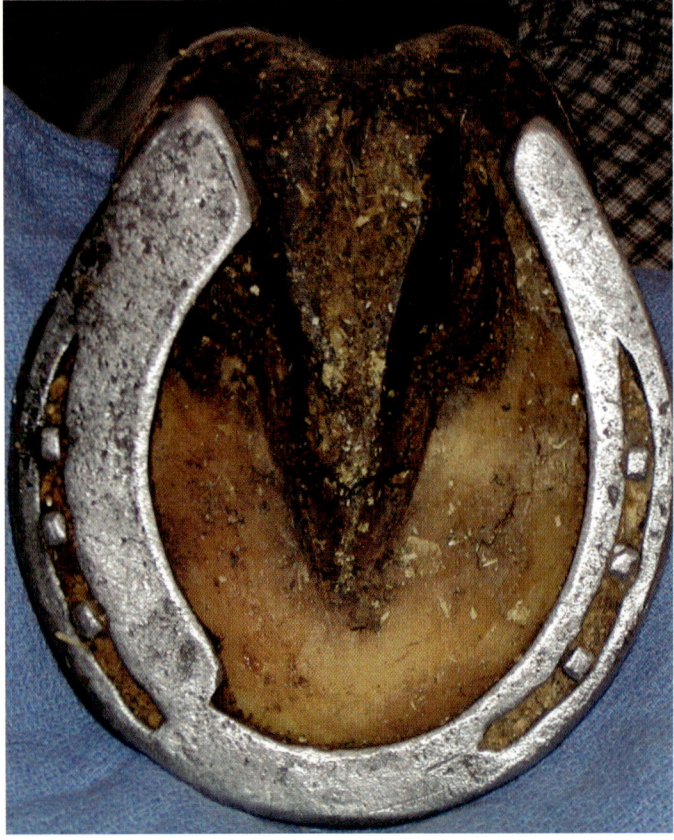

This shoe has a wide branch to support the injured collateral ligament of the coffin joint.

If your horse has coffin-joint damage as well as CJCLI, your veterinarian might inject hyaluronate, short-acting cortisone or IRAP by intra-articular administration to reduce joint inflammation.

Down the road: Your horse's prognosis might range from guarded to unfavorable. Make sure to follow your veterinarian's precise healing-time directions. You must monitor ground conditions before you begin leading or riding your horse; working on hard or uneven ground can cause reinjury. Be sure to continue your horse's special shoeing protocol.

Some horses with CJCLI can return to work. However, many don't respond well despite treatment and must retire. Early detection is the key to a more favorable prognosis.

Deep Digital Flexor Tendon Trauma Affecting the Foot

You work hard to keep the varmints out of your pasture, but prairie dogs have invaded the tract's north corner. Your horses are turned out, but don't often venture to the property's north border. From your kitchen window, you watch as your horse makes a beeline for the prairie dog corner. There's no stopping him. You see him take a strange step—catching his toe on level ground as his heel sinks down into the varmint's burrow, and your horse stretches his heel abnormally. After a few days of rest, he doesn't walk heel-to-toe on the affected foot.

What might be happening: Your horse's deep flexor tendon travels down the back of his leg through the pastern region and then enters his foot. The tendon ends in the attachment on the bottom of the coffin bone. Your horse's distal or palmar annular ligament (DDAL) runs down the backside of the deep flexor tendon, ranging from the pastern area to the coffin bone.

This ligament and the deep digital flexor tendon (DDFT) are susceptible to stretching injuries when your horse's toe overextends—just what happens if he steps in a hole and catches the edge with his toe. As his heel falls into the hole and bears weight, the ligament and the tendon stretch more than they should.

The DDFT and the DDAL also are susceptible to injuries incurred from the ground up. If your horse punctures his foot through the sole, frog or heel bulb, the injury can impact these structures within the foot. Navicular bone and navicular bursa injuries also can impact the deep flexor tendon.

What you notice: You see Grade 1 to 5 lameness as well as:

- Quick or slow onset of lameness symptoms.

- Thickness at the back of your horse's pastern—the line along the deep flexor tendon as it enters the hoof capsule.

- Pointing of his affected foot to avoid weight-bearing.

- Lameness recurrence with the return to work following a rest, signifying a mild case.

- In severe cases, avoidance of walking on his heel so as not to bear weight on the fetlock.

What you do: A prompt and accurate diagnosis might mean a faster or more full recovery

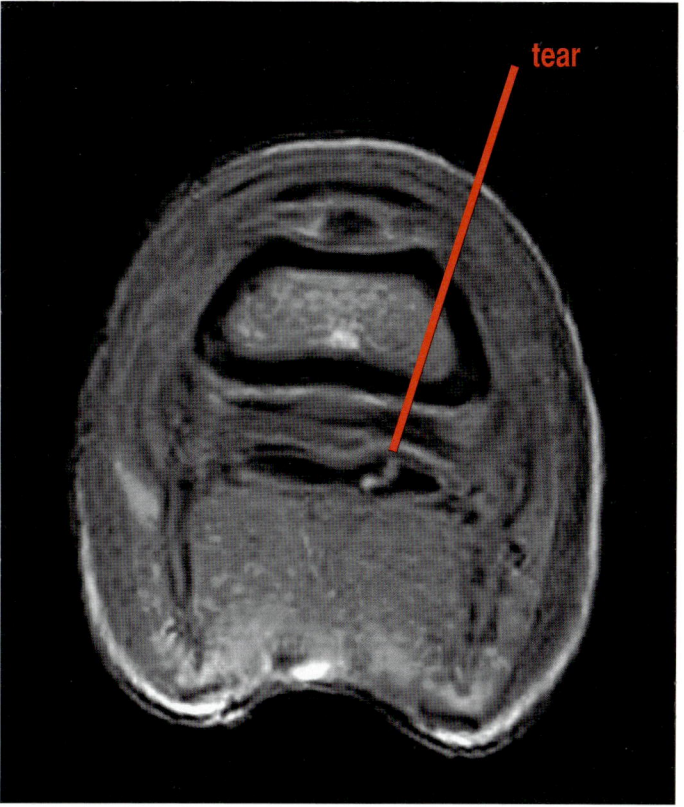

This MRI reveals an angled line across the deep flexor tendon, the dark area in the hoof's center, and indicates a tendon tear.

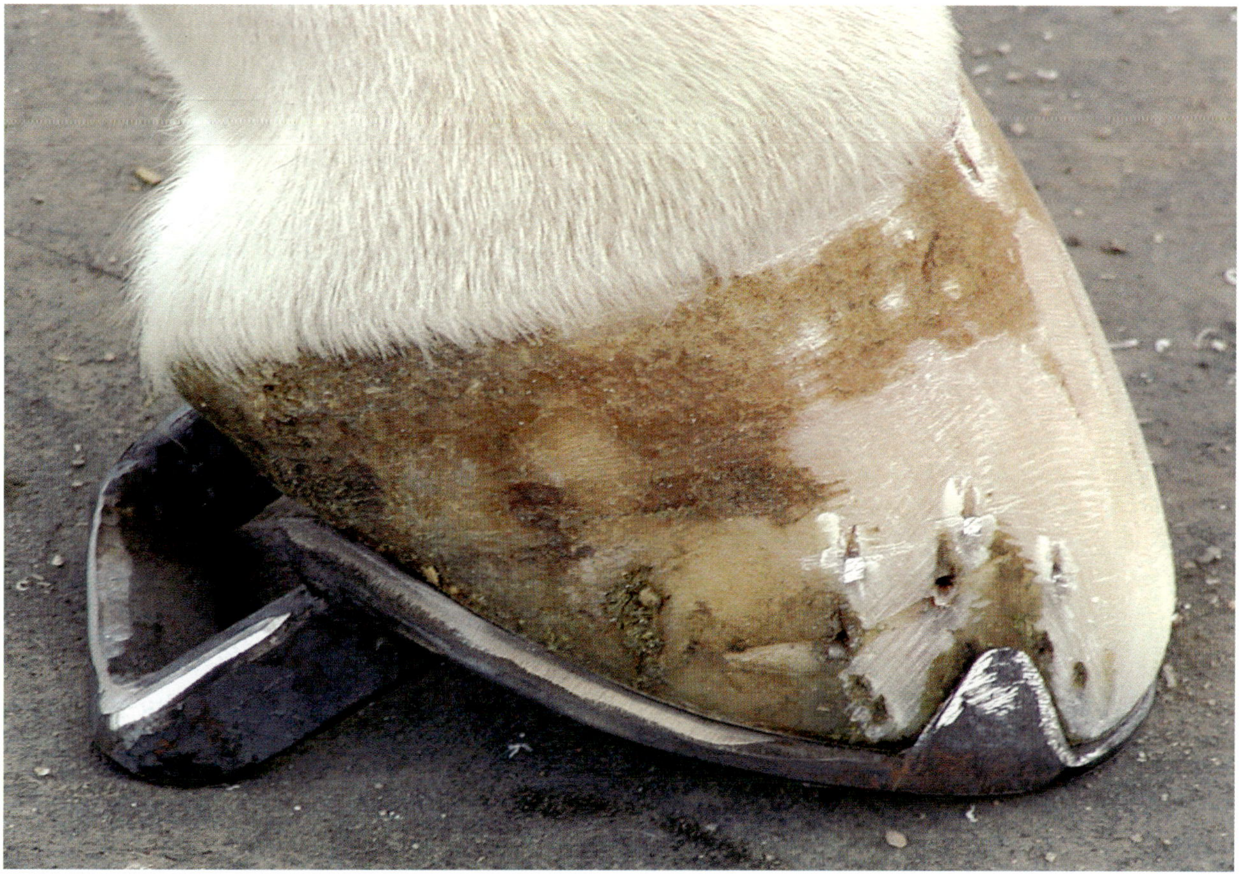

Your veterinarian might outfit your horse with a Patton shoe to relieve pressure on the deep flexor tendon.

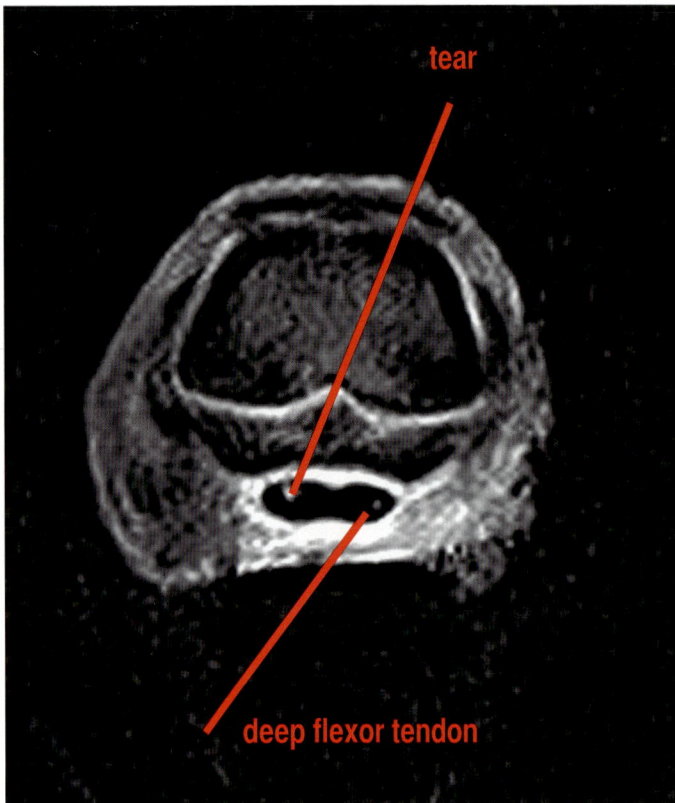

The dark, peanut-shaped structure is a cross-section view of the deep digital flexor tendon; the white dots in each section of the peanut represent tears in the deep digital flexor tendon fibers, which can be seen only with an MRI.

for your horse. So call your veterinarian if you suspect tendon or ligament problems. If you see the stretching accident happen or your horse develops lameness after working in a soft or deep arena, you can begin therapy before your veterinarian arrives. Begin by icing your horse's lower leg and foot for 20 minutes.

What your veterinarian does: Your veterinarian likely begins his lameness exam by using hoof-testers to locate your horse's pain. The veterinarian also evaluates your horse's response to fingertip pressure on the deep flexor tendon and the distal digital annular ligament—along the line where both the tendon and ligament enter the foot between your horse's heel bulbs.

If your horse seems sensitive, your veterinarian might use ultrasound technology to examine your horse's lower leg, specifically where the tendon passes from the pastern into the foot at the heel level. Your veterinarian also can use an ultrasound to view the tendon from another angle—up through your horse's frog. To see into the hoof through

your horse's thick frog, your veterinarian might need to trim the sole extensively. Trimming might be counterproductive to your horse's overall soundness in the near future. Your horse needs the cushion and "pump" that the frog provides to maintain other structures in the foot. Before performing an ultrasound, your veterinarian makes a judgment call, considering your horse's overall well-being. Be sure to discuss the pros and cons of frog-trimming before you allow an invasive trim.

An MRI shows the tendon, other soft tissue structures and bone structures, but requires no trimming. An MRI evaluation is the definitive answer to the diagnosis of DDFT injury. This procedure shows your veterinarian the lesion, as well as if the problem is a reinjury or new injury. Your veterinarian also wants to take radiographs to rule out a fracture, especially if your horse hurts because of an acute injury.

The healing process: After seeing and treating your horse, the veterinarian might ask you to continue the previously described cold therapy. You could be asked to ice or apply cold water to your horse's injured leg four or five times each day—keeping the affected area cold for 20 minutes during each treatment.

Your horse needs strict stall rest for two to four months, followed by controlled exercise for another two-month period. During the healing time, your veterinarian might perform shockwave therapy and provide your horse with anti-inflammatory medication to speed the process. Some cases benefit from injecting therapeutic medications, including stem cells, IRAP or platelet-enriched plasma, directly into the tendon lesion.

Your veterinarian also might work with the farrier to develop a shoeing plan to help your horse keep pressure off the affected tendon. Your horse's heel might be raised dramatically with a Patton shoe combined with a flat pad. The shoe heels are elevated 1¼ to 1¾ inches, depending on the size of the horse's foot. This shoe is handmade for your horse. As the tendon heals, your farrier lowers the Patton shoe heel, beginning the third month of confinement for most horses. In six to eight months your farrier switches to a wedge pad. With serious injuries, initially your veterinarian might outfit your horse with a Kimzey splint, a large aluminum brace that keeps

Horseman's Dictionary

intra-articular: administered via injection into a horse's joint.

IRAP: scientifically known as interleukin-1 receptor antagonist protein, IRAP is a collection of blood factors that combats osteoarthritis.

Kimzey splint: a large aluminum brace that keeps your horse's hoof angled down so the ligaments and flexor tendons of the lower leg aren't weighted.

Patton shoe: a shoe that raises your horse's heel dramatically.

pointing: a horse's stance when he places one front foot forward to relieve pressure from his body weight.

stress fracture: a break caused by continuous repetitive stress or an acute incident. The bone break is not evident from the outside, creating a narrow fracture line within nondisplaced bone fragments. Scintigraphy, MRI or CT can be the only diagnostic tools to demonstrate this pathology.

toed-in: a conformational fault causing a horse's hooves to angle toward one another at the toe and thus appear pigeon-toed.

wind puff: A soft-to-the-touch bump near a horse's joint and filled with joint fluid.

---

your horse's hoof angled down so the tendon isn't stretched.

Your horse's total healing time might last for four months or up to a year. Schedule regular visits with your veterinarian to ensure your horse's continued healing. Be sure to find and develop a solid working relationship with a qualified farrier, who can help you and your veterinarian implement special shoeing strategies.

Down the road: Your horse has sustained a dramatic and often complex injury. If the tendon or ligament is merely challenged, his recovery chances improve significantly.

If your horse ruptures his tendon, his future is grim. His prognosis most likely is guarded to unfavorable. If your horse has been a top performer in the past, he might not be sound for that job again. If your horse has a lower-impact job, he might be able to return to work.

When and if your horse is cleared to work, make sure his workouts aren't excessive or strenuous. Be sure to work him on level, soft footing, not deep, heavy footing.

Case Study: Internal Structures

During a prepurchase exam with radiographs, a veterinarian noted that Buddy, an amateur hunter, had a small right front extensor process fracture. The fracture wasn't significantly displaced, and Buddy didn't show obvious lameness signs. Buddy was sound when led in hand on a hard surface and showed no lameness under saddle. The prospective owners decided to purchase Buddy and continued to show him in hunter classes. Several years later, Buddy seemed slightly uncomfortable when cantering on the right lead, but he still performed in an acceptable manner. Then Buddy sustained an injury to his left front fetlock and required surgery. While he was under anesthesia for his left front fetlock injury, veterinarians decided to remove the small extensor process fragment from the right front coffin bone, the original fracture seen in the prepurchase exam. When Buddy recovered from both surgeries, he returned to the previous level of work and was much more comfortable cantering in his right lead.

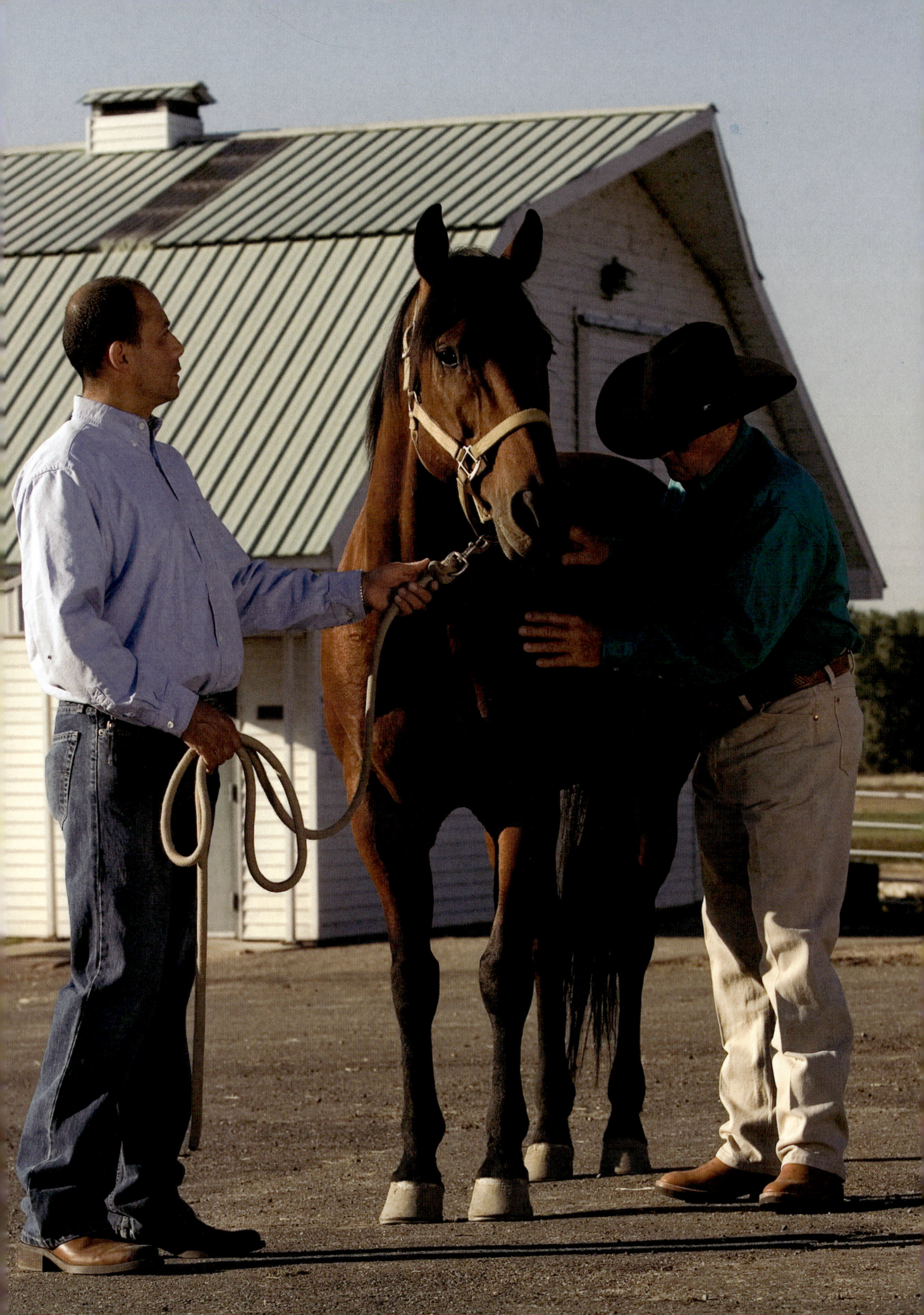

4

THE FOOT—NAVICULAR PROBLEMS/SYNDROME

When the navicular bone complex, an integral part of the foot, is compromised by injury, your horse can be in constant pain.

It's a diagnosis most horse owners are afraid to hear. Navicular problems—often affecting both of a horse's front feet—are seen in horses that work hard and often. These problems also can arise because of a horse's conformation and build; horses with small feet and large bodies or horses with unusually straight shoulders might be more susceptible to this pain. When the injured navicular bone is compressed as a horse moves, the horse feels sharp pain. Read on to find out how to prevent, identify and help a horse with navicular problems.

Navicular Problems/Syndrome

You've been shopping for a horse that your husband can ride—a strong, gentle type with enough size to support a grown man's weight. You found a horse nearby and rode him in the seller's soft arena footing. You enjoyed your ride. At home for a week-long trial, the large-bodied horse seems stiff when you begin to ride him, then "warms" out of it and seems smooth. Later in the week, he again seems sore and favors his right front leg when you take him on a short jaunt down your packed-dirt road. By the end of the week, both small, front feet seem to be affected, causing him to trot with a short, shuffling gait.

What might be happening: Your horse's navicular bone sits deep within the confines of his foot and is

A horse's navicular bone is compressed with every step as he propels his body forward. When you shop for a new horse or worry that your horse is sore after constant work, have your mount evaluated by a knowledgeable veterinarian.

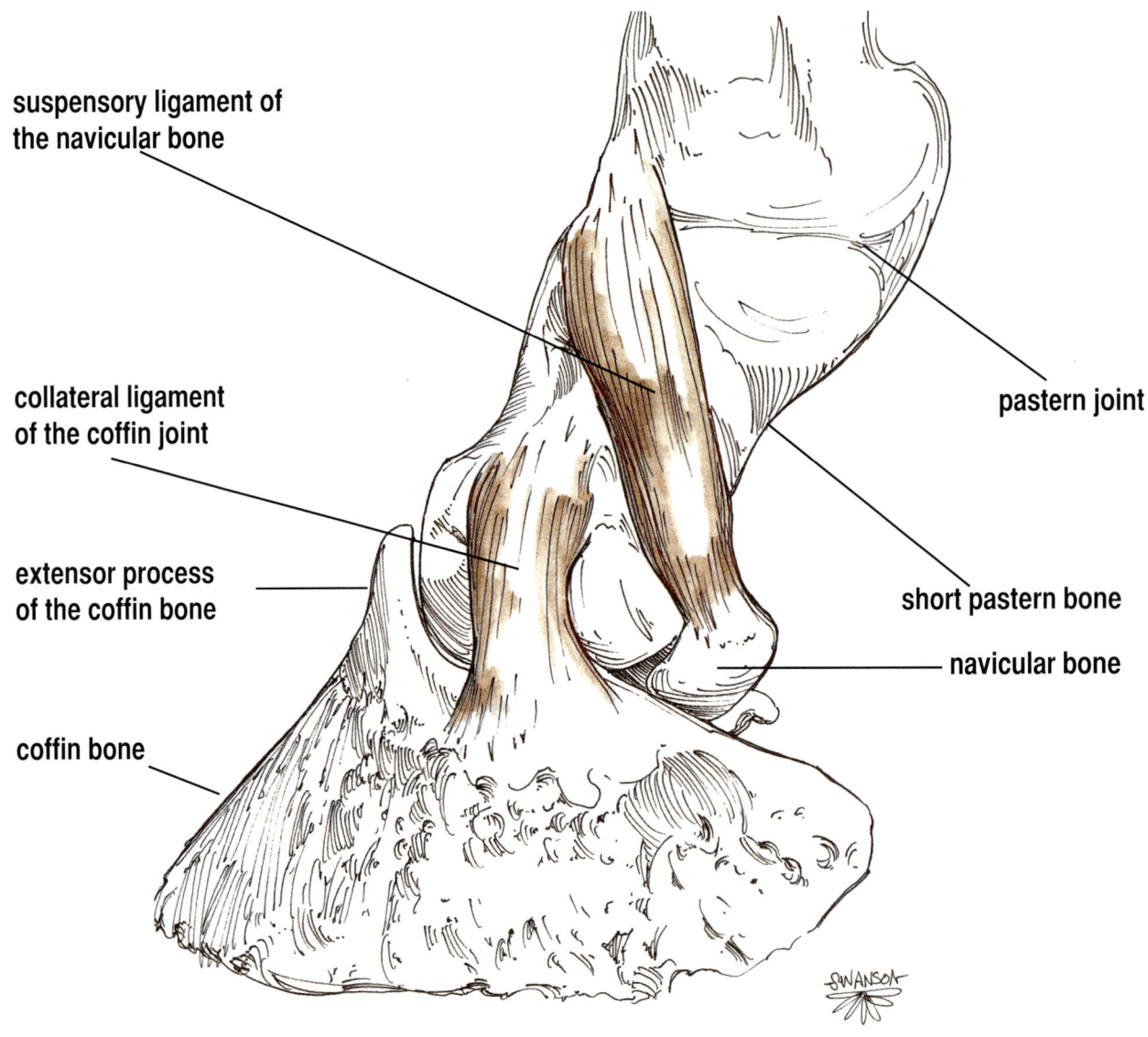

suspensory ligament of
the navicular bone

collateral ligament
of the coffin joint

extensor process
of the coffin bone

coffin bone

pastern joint

short pastern bone

navicular bone

Knowing the anatomy involved in navicular problems can help you talk with your veterinarian. Here, you see a longer suspensory ligament of the navicular bone and the shorter collateral ligament of the coffin bone.

actively involved in each step he takes. When your horse takes a step, the navicular bone supports the lower end of the short pastern bone and functions as part of the complex coffin joint between the short pastern bone and the coffin bone. The navicular also forms a fulcrum. The deep flexor tendon uses a navicular bone as a fulcrum to pull on the coffin bone as the upper leg and body advance forward. If your horse has inflammation in any of the structures associated with the navicular bone, he likely feels pain. Your horse has more pain as the inflammation increases. The navicular bone is compressed when your horse takes a step to propel his body, meaning he's in constant pain when bearing weight and moving forward.

If your horse has navicular syndrome, a group of signs and symptoms that together characterize a specific disease or disorder, several structures in this small yet vital area might be affected. The painful problem might involve one or all of the structures—the coffin bone, short pastern bone, coffin joint, navicular bone, suspensory ligament of that same bone, impar ligament, navicular bursa, deep flexor tendon and, in some cases, the digital cushion, a firm fibrous pad located in the bottom of the foot between the deep flexor tendon and the frog.

Navicular syndrome doesn't always appear because a horse has a specific type of accident or because he participates in a specific sport. Your horse might show signs of navicular if he's an athlete or pasture companion. All breeds are at risk. Though many types of horses can have navicular syndrome, some conformation faults, accidents, and even geographic regions might predispose your horse to the condition. Ask yourself, does your horse have or has he had:

- A large body and small feet?

- Navicular-bone conformational defects, such as excessive angular and rotational conformation defects of the lower leg?

- An injury that bruised his central frog, or acute trauma, such as stepping on a rock and bruising the central frog?

- Poor navicular-bone quality as noted in radiographs?

- Trauma from constant, repetitive use on hard surfaces, such as a feedlot horse sorting cattle on concrete alleys?

- A short, choppy gait?

- A tendency to land toe first?

- A tendency to stumble with his front legs?

- Slow-developing lameness that bothers both front feet, but one more than the other?

- A tendency to warm out of lameness as seen in its early stages?

- A tendency to become sound with rest and then lame when he starts back to work?

When your horse is diagnosed with navicular syndrome, he might be experiencing one change or a combination of changes to his navicular bone and the attached ligaments and tendons. Changes might include:

- Degeneration of the navicular bone.

- Enlargement of the navicular canals along the bottom of the navicular bone.

- Cystic development in the navicular bone or along the back, or palmar, border.

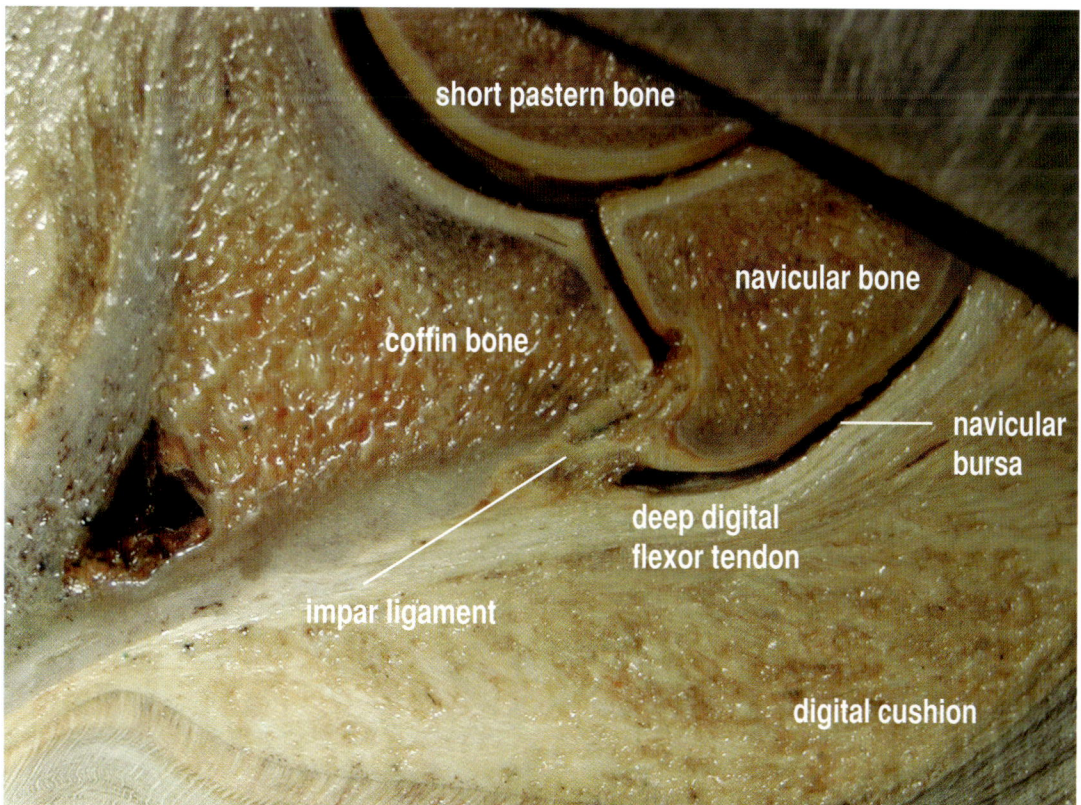

A photograph of the internal foot structures shows the anatomy within the foot: the coffin bone, navicular bone, short pastern bone, impar ligament, deep digital flexor tendon and digital cushion.

- Spur development on the ends of the navicular bone.

- Small bone fragments along the navicular bone's distal, or far, border.

- An altered attachment between the deep flexor tendon and the coffin bone.

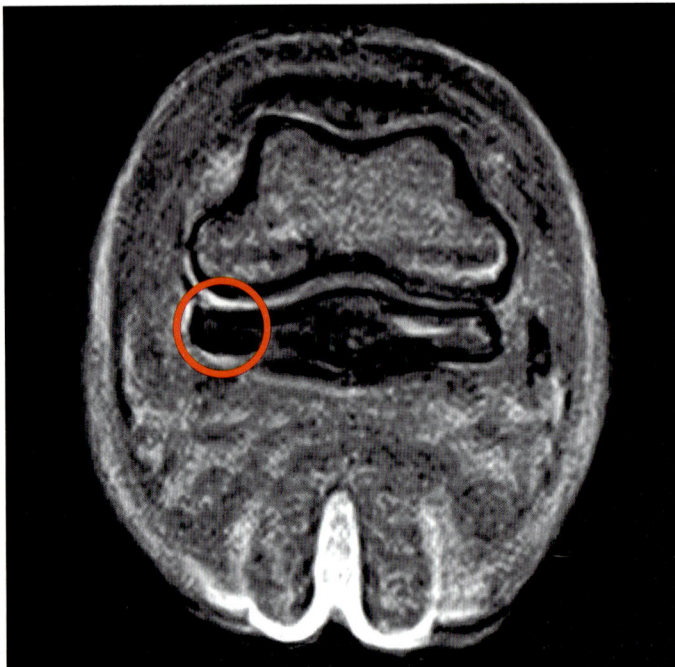

Here, the navicular bone has degeneration on the palmar side, or back part of the front leg. Changes to the palmar surface are not always noted on a radiograph, so an MRI, as shown here, can be useful.

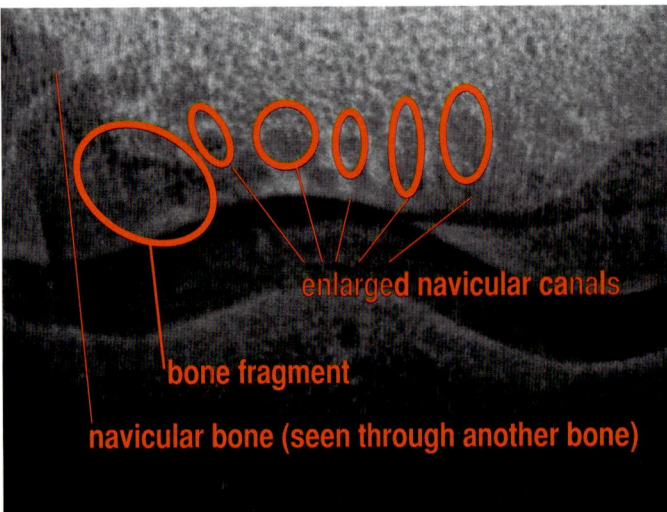

enlarged **navicular canals**

bone fragment

navicular bone (seen through another bone)

The radiograph shows an advanced case of navicular syndrome as seen through the short pastern bone. Within the navicular bone, the horse has several enlarged navicular canals and a distal border bone fragment. With these pathological changes, this horse will be difficult to maintain as a sport horse.

- Coffin bone changes at the point where the navicular bone interacts, or articulates, with it.

- Degeneration of the navicular bursa.

- Tears and adhesions, or scarring that causes structures to become attached together.

- Alteration of the navicular bone's suspensory ligaments.

- Alteration of the navicular bone's blood supply.

What you notice: You see Grade 1 to Grade 4 lameness, as well as notice a combination of symptoms such as:

- An acute- or gradual-onset lameness in one or both front feet. Your horse might warm out of minor lameness and seem fine after a short period of exercise, but be lame again after a rest period.

- Your horse points the foot most affected.

- Your horse's most affected foot has a long heel and is small in diameter at the coronary band. You can tell a difference when comparing the lame hoof to your horse's opposite foot.

- Your horse is more noticeably lame when working on hard surfaces and while turning on his affected leg.

What you do: If you suspect your horse has navicular syndrome, contact your veterinarian and work with him to properly diagnose the problem.

What your veterinarian does: Your veterinarian most likely begins his exam by watching your horse move to characterize his way of going. Your veterinarian also uses hoof-testers to identify which parts of your horse's foot are sore and looks for sensitivity within the center of your horse's frog. That area links to the navicular bone area.

Your veterinarian also performs diagnostic nerve blocks and takes radiographs to pinpoint and analyze your horse's foot structures. Diagnostic blocks can isolate the problem and help your veterinarian make a navicular syndrome diagnosis. The posterior digital nerve block, or PDN, anesthetizes the navicular bone and its related ligaments, your horse's sole and frog, heel bulbs, the lower portion of the deep digital flexor tendon, most of the coffin joint, a portion of the pastern joint, a large portion of the coffin bone, and the lower portion of the collateral ligaments of the coffin joint. Your veterinarian locates the sites for this block in the back of the pastern—in the lowest portion next to the collateral cartilage and also along the edge of the deep digital flexor tendon. He blocks both the medial, or inside, and lateral, or outside, posterior nerves.

Because the PDN block numbs many structures, your veterinarian works to rule out other potential problems before he confirms navicular syndrome as the lameness cause. It is possible to block only your horse's navicular bursa—a block directly related to your horse's navicular structures. However, many veterinarians choose not to perform this block routinely because of its risks. Blocking this area potentially could damage the area, and the potential risk often outweighs the diagnostic help.

Radiographs show changes in the navicular area. However, the technology doesn't always show every change. Your horse's navicular bone might not show radiographic changes during the syndrome's early stages. Bone edema and ligament damage can't be seen in radiographs. If your veterinarian suspects navicular disease or syndrome, he also might see an enlargement of the navicular canals along the bottom of the navicular bone when looking at radiographs. Research shows that this enlargement correlates with chronic inflammation in the navicular area. Radiographs also might show if cysts have developed in the navicular bone's main body or along the bone's back, or palmar, border. Your veterinarian might see that fragments have broken off the bone's lower border. What else can a radiograph show? Changes to the navicular bone's shape or spurs developing along the bone end also might be visible.

Your veterinarian might perform an ultrasound to show changes in your horse's deep flexor tendon, the navicular bursa and impar ligament. Ultrasound data might be helpful, but the technology can't see all the involved structures clearly and might not show enough information to prove navicular problems. The sound waves don't travel through keratinized tissue found in the hoof wall, which has become horn-like in consistency.

In order to "see" into your horse's hoof, your veterinarian aims the ultrasound up through your horse's softer thinned frog area. Since sound waves can't travel through your horse's dense hoof capsule, your veterinarian must make a "viewing portal" by soak-

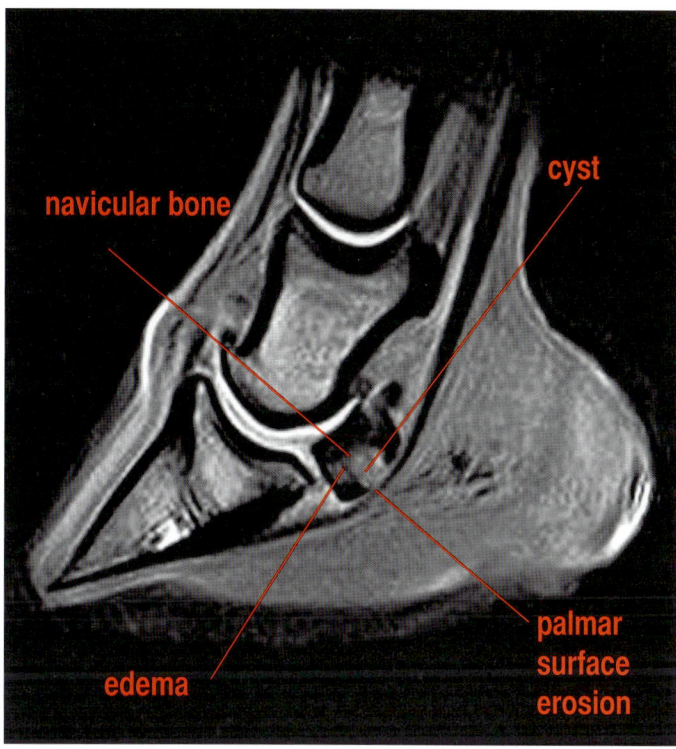

A horse diagnosed with navicular syndrome might experience a combination of changes to his navicular bone. This MRI shows a fluid cyst in the navicular bone and edema within the navicular bone, evident only with an MRI.

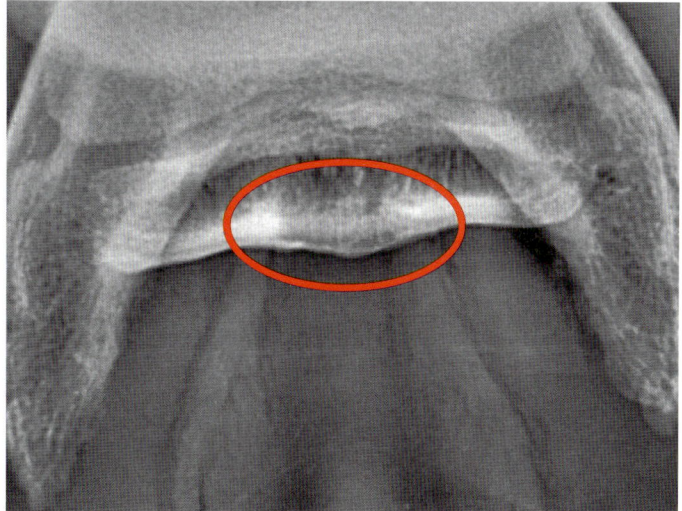

This radiograph shows degeneration of the palmar border of the navicular bone. A healthy horse's radiograph shows a solid white line at the bone edge, rather than the change evident here by a change in color.

Your veterinarian works with your farrier to plan a corrective shoeing strategy tailored to your horse, who might need wedge shoes or pads to reduce pain.

ing your horse's foot and trimming the frog to a shallow thickness to create a less dense route for ultrasound waves. Even with intense preparation, ultrasound views often are limited and not always worth the effort. Most veterinarians reserve this technique for special or complicated cases. Trimming the frog can help for the ultrasound, but might impact your horse's later movement and hoof function, nullifying the diagnostic benefits.

MRI technology clearly demonstrates signs of navicular syndrome. As MRI machines become more available to veterinarians throughout the United States, diagnosis of this complex syndrome becomes more accurate. MRIs show bony and soft tissue—offering a more detailed view of all the parts involved in navicular syndrome. With an MRI, your veterinarian might clearly see edema in the navicular bone, tears or defects in the navicular ligaments and the deep digital flexor tendon tissues, inflammation in the navicular bursa and changes in cartilage quality. An MRI also shows your veterinarian if your horse has adhesions, or scars that cause structures to adhere together, between the navicular bone, as well as the deep digital flexor tendon, navicular bursa and the navicular ligaments. In some cases, the MRI's clear images can help your veterinarian estimate the age of the lesion or change, which helps him make a proper prognosis. All of the additional information gained with the high-tech MRI helps your veterinarian plan a successful healing and management course based on your horse's precise needs. Your veterinarian recommends MRI evaluation if conventional management and therapy is not successful.

The healing process: If your horse is diagnosed with navicular syndrome, he requires ongoing management throughout his life. Your veterinarian considers all of your horse's lameness issues before forming a treatment plan. Many "navicular horses" also have conformational faults or injuries affecting their movement in multiple ways.

Your veterinarian works with your farrier to plan a corrective shoeing strategy tailored for your horse. Your farrier might move back the foot's break-over point, the most forward point on the ground surface of your horse's foot or shoe, which acts as a fulcrum as he moves forward and his heel leaves the ground. Your veterinarian also might ask your farrier to put a pad on your horse's navicular-affected

foot, adding cushion. An egg-bar shoe might help distribute concussion, relieving pressure on your horse's navicular bone. A wedge pad or shoe can raise your horse's heel to reduce stress in the navicular area. The farrier and veterinarian need to work together to find the best shoeing option for your horse.

Your veterinarian might prescribe the drug isoxsuprine, a vasodilator that dilates or opens blood vessels, to help increase circulation to the navicular bone. Research scientists haven't been able to measure the blood circulation through the navicular area; therefore, at press time there's no specific evidence to show isoxsuprine's effect on a horse's navicular area. However, many veterinarians and horse trainers—through experience—favorably support use of the drug and look forward to more specific testing. The drug's effects are cumulative; it takes two to three weeks to become fully active. Your veterinarian also prescribes anti-inflammatory medication, such as firocoxib or phenylbutazone to help settle the inflammation in your horse's feet.

Shockwave treatment can help your horse feel more comfortable. Other pain-reducing treatments include posterior digital neurectomy surgery, commonly referred to as nerving. In this procedure, your veterinarian removes two to three inches of the two posterior digital nerves, which removes the sensation of pain. The removed nerves are designed only for sensory input, so there's no interference with lower leg function.

If your horse is nerved, you can expect his performance to return to normal, providing there aren't other significant lameness issues. In most cases, nerved horses are safer to ride than they were before the surgery. They use their feet correctly and don't stumble. The procedure helps your horse continue his career without pain. The benefits last for two years for most horses, and some horses go much longer without feeling pain.

Nerving isn't an option if your horse has coffin-joint secondary degenerative joint disease (see Chapter 3), a damaged deep flexor tendon, laminitis or other significant lameness issues, in addition to navicular syndrome. If your horse has multiple lameness issues on the same foot as his navicular syndrome, the other lameness issues can worsen with nerving surgery.

There are possible complications of nerving surgery. An inflammatory reaction on the

Hoof-testers can be a valuable asset in pinpointing the source of navicular pain within the foot.

areas of the navicular-syndrome foot, which happen over a long period of time.

Scientists are now studying tiludronate, a new navicular-management medication developed in France, to review its benefits. Clinically, the drug has shown some benefit when administered intravenously. Ask your veterinarian about the drug's ongoing research findings; current anecdotal reports have been encouraging.

Along with the management techniques discussed above, your horse needs regular, low-impact exercise to help keep blood flowing to the navicular bone and to keep all his feet healthy. Make sure your horse has daily low-intensity workouts instead of sporadic and intense training sessions. Jarring movement might make your horse uncomfortable and set back his overall healing.

Down the Road: If your veterinarian labels your horse with navicular syndrome, you have a lifetime of pain-reducing management. The diagnosis can have a favorable prognosis, but only with proper and judicious management. Your horse can move with ease after rest periods or periods of light work. Then he appears lame again if returned to a heavy workload. In most cases he can return to work if you're willing to manage his shoeing, medications and workload. If many structures around the navicular bone are affected, your horse might have a guarded-to-unfavorable prognosis.

Case Study: Navicular Problems

A 10-year-old Quarter Horse has been trained in dressage and has competed often. However, he has had intermittent, significant lameness in his front feet. His owner noticed a problem for more than four years, but couldn't find a conclusive answer. Now, the horse's left front foot is noticeably lamer than his right foot. Both seem to hurt him.

At the veterinary clinic, initial diagnostics indicate navicular syndrome. When prodded with hoof-testers, the horse has significant pain around the central third of his frog. A digital nerve block at the back of his lower leg temporarily alleviates his lameness. However, radiographs don't show significant changes to the navicular bone.

He responds well to corrective shoeing to move his toe back for an easier break-over. With continued corrective shoeing, the horse seems better and returns to competition for

cut end of the nerve can make your horse lame. This occurs in about 10 percent of surgical cases and is most likely to happen in the first few weeks after the surgery. The inflammation can be managed if recognized early. Other complications include regrowth of the once-trimmed nerves and problems in other

Horseman's Dictionary

adhesions: scarring that causes structures to adhere together.

break-over point: the most forward place on the ground surface of your horse's foot or shoe, which acts as a fulcrum as he moves forward and his heel leaves the ground.

keratinized: becoming horn-like in consistency.

palmar: describing the backside of a horse's front leg.

plantar: describing the backside of a horse's hind leg.

posterior digital neurectomy: commonly referred to as nerving; permanently removing a portion of the posterior digital nerves to relieve pain in a portion of the horse's foot.

syndrome: a group of signs and symptoms that together characterize a specific disease or disorder.

a while. Even with monitored exercise and proper care, the horse's owner notices lameness again. This time, the episodes are more frequent and severe.

Back at the clinic, the veterinarian orders MRIs for both of the horse's front feet. He wants to see boney structures, as well as soft tissue—especially because radiographs, which show only boney matter, don't show a significant problem. The MRI shows a significant tear in the horse's deep digital flexor tendon, close to the navicular bone. This foot area can't be palpated or seen with an ultrasound, which can't see through the cornified structures to the soft tissue beneath. MRI and computed tomographic radiology, or CT, are the only noninvasive methods to expose this lesion.

With proper diagnosis, the horse is resting in confinement—wearing a Patton shoe to relieve the deep digital flexor tendon. His owner walks him a few minutes each day. His prognosis is guarded to favorable, making it possible for him to return to dressage performance if he has proper care and uninterrupted healing time.

5

THE FOOT—LAMINITIS

Your horse's laminae can weaken and detach for many reasons—a sudden eating binge, geography, a drug reaction or other complex reasons.

Your horse's laminae, vertical, leaf-like projections between the face of the coffin bone and the inside of the hoof wall, bond together to hold the coffin bone tight against the inside of the hoof wall, keeping all the crucial and intricate parts in place. When the delicate laminae become damaged—or worse, detach—your horse feels pain. When your horse's coffin bone drops and rotates because the laminae can no longer hold it, your horse feels constant pain while supporting his body weight. Here, we detail the many causes and stages of laminitis, or founder, as it's commonly known to many people.

Laminitis (Founder)

Your first—and still favorite—pony is now a cresty-necked retiree who'll always have a home with you. He's an easy keeper, and you know to be careful about how often and long he's turned out on grass. When you head out of town for a reunion, you ask your teenage neighbor to check the horses at bedtime. Though you carefully outline his duties, the teen forgets to snap the chain on your pony's stall door. Of course, Old Mr. Magic unlatches the stall himself and heads straight for the grain barrel. When you arrive home two days later, your pony is standing still as a statue with both front feet parked to the front and his weight settled back in his hindquarters. You feel hot hoof walls and see that his pasterns are swollen.

What might be happening: Laminitis, or founder, means the laminae in your horse's hooves have started to detach. The laminae bind the coffin bone

Many laminitis cases are associated with equine digestive-tract changes, which might be initiated by changed or excessive food intake, changes in intestinal bacterial flora or formation of other triggering agents within the gut.

to the inside of your horse's hoof wall, and their detachment impacts many structures within the foot. The layer of cells called the basement membrane lines the coffin-bone side of the attachment and provides the physiological basis for this attachment. The coffin bone, basement membrane, and hoof wall must all work together to provide support for each of your horse's legs. Here's a more advanced look at what's going on inside each of your horse's hooves.

The hoof wall rim and the frog, not the sole, are the major weight-bearing structures in the foot. The leg's bony column is supported by the coffin bone, which attaches to the hoof wall's inner surface. That connection makes the hoof wall the major support structure. So, keeping the hoof wall—the support structure—attached to the coffin bone is a crucial connection. The laminae's role is to sustain that connection.

Laminae extending from the face or surface of the coffin bone dovetail with laminae originating from the hoof wall's inner surface to create the important attachment between the coffin bone and the hoof wall. When disease damages the laminae, the connection between the hoof wall and coffin bone weakens. When this disease progresses, the laminae sometimes completely separate. When the laminae can't maintain the attachment, the coffin bone rotates or begins to sink under the horse's weight. Instead of the hoof wall acting as the support structure, the small coffin bone now bears all the body's weight and presses onto the horse's sole. The new support arrangement interferes with blood circulation to hoof structures and causes great pain. The horse's weight is no longer supported in a way to protect the structures inside the hoof capsule.

It's also important to remember that the basement membrane is a thin layer of cells associated with the coffin-bone laminae. These cells are crucial to keeping the two layers of laminae connected. However, the basement membrane is weakened and damaged by laminitis' triggering factors, several yet-to-be-identified factors that can cause your horse's foot structures to change. Laminitis researchers soon will know exactly what happens after your horse eats too many carbohydrates and before his feet pathologically change. Researchers do know that laminar structures weaken if the area doesn't receive enough glucose or oxygen. If the basement membrane weakens or disintegrates, the hoof wall and coffin bone can permanently separate, which results in rotation or sinking of the coffin bone.

If the disease process is discovered in time, your veterinarian can minimize or stop your horse's coffin-bone rotation, and can potentially reverse the rotation with the help of your farrier in some cases. The ability to recover most likely is related to the amount of damage to the basement membrane cell layer. However, by the time most horse owners see clinical laminitis signs, the disease process, including the early separation of the laminae, already is under way. *For that reason, laminitis always should be treated as a medical emergency to achieve the best outcome.*

Your horse's systemic or whole-body blood circulation also impacts the pathology of his hoof structures. Blood seems to deliver triggering factors that eventually alter the hoof's laminae. Scientists continue to study circulation and the connection to laminitis.

Your horse has four hooves—all with the components that can create healthy structures or the laminitis disease. Although you've probably heard that your horse's front feet are more susceptible to laminitis, all four are subject to the problem. The front feet often are more affected because the front legs bear more weight than the hind legs, which causes added trauma from concussion after the laminae are compromised and have started to separate. One foot might be more affected than all the others, but make sure to watch and notice changes in all his hooves.

Your horse might develop laminitis for a variety of reasons. Some horses are predisposed to the disease. Abrupt changes to your horse's physiology, or internal makeup, can predispose him to future bouts of the disease. Laminitis is not yet fully understood, but the following causes have been linked to the disease. The list isn't exhaustive, but helps you understand the many risk factors that can contribute to laminitis:

- **High-carbohydrate grass.** Rapidly growing cool-weather grass, as seen in the spring and fall, has a high concentration of the carbohydrate fructan. The increased fructan level causes physiological reactions within a horse's gut that can cause laminitis.

- **Grain overload.** Excess carbohydrates in a horse's digestive tract—from consuming too much grain—can alter the gut's dynamics.

A horse accidentally accessing the grain barrel is a common cause of laminitis, but not the only one.

- **Trauma.** Working your horse on hard ground can cause foot trauma, also known as road founder. The constant pounding can alter the coffin-bone and hoof-wall connection and lead to laminitis.

- **Excessive trimming.** When a horse's hooves are trimmed too short—in toward the crucial structures—the feet don't have adequate protection. Without protection, a horse's feet might become inflamed, leading to laminitis.

- **Physiological predisposition.** A cresty-necked, easy-keeper horse has the stereotypical look telling you that he might be prone to laminitis—even without a specific, triggering event, such as getting into a grain bin or eating too much rich grass. A horse with Cushing's disease or subclinical Cushing's disease is a prime candidate for developing laminitis. Cushing's is a hormonal disorder caused by a benign pituitary gland tumor, which, in turn, causes horses to have excess corticosteroids in their system. This causes the horses to store fat and prevents them from shedding hair. A horse with insulin resistance also is at risk for developing laminitis.

- **Toxic buildup.** An infection, bout with colic or a retained placenta in a mare can cause toxins to build in a horse's body. When the toxins reach the blood, triggering factors can cause pathological changes to the laminae's fine structures.

- **Injuries or lameness.** When a horse is injured on one leg and must bear more weight than usual on the opposite healthy leg, the normal leg can be overtaxed. The "good" hoof's laminae weaken from constantly supporting the additional weight, which ultimately led to the racehorse Barbaro's euthanization.

- **Geography.** A horse's environment might predispose him to the disease. Geographic factors are not fully understood, but more horses in specific areas of the country often develop the disease. The reason might link to specific bacteria common to the region's horses' intestinal flora, the range of bacteria normally present in the horse's large intestine. Changes to horses' bacterial flora might instigate or trigger laminitis.

- **Drug Reaction.** Secondary to some drugs, including medications and vaccinations, a reaction also can trigger a case of laminitis.

- **Stress.** Horses under excess stress are more likely to suffer from laminitis. It's difficult to pinpoint and define what causes horses stress, but any undue stress might predispose horses to laminitis.

What you notice: You see Grade 1 to 5 lameness that can appear quickly, or during a period of days after a specific founder-causing event. Your horse doesn't feel pain until his laminae are damaged to some extent. You also notice all or some of these signs:

- Your horse's reluctance to move.

- Your horse stretching his front feet forward, in front of his body, to distribute weight to his heels in an attempt to ease pain. However, if your horse's coffin bone is sinking straight down, rather than rotating, his stance might appear normal.

- Your horse walking forward with relative ease, but showing soreness when turning stresses his laminae.

- Your horse's swollen pasterns.

- An increased digital pulse.

- Heat in your horse's hoof wall(s).

What you do: Call your veterinarian immediately if you see any signs of laminitis, or if you know your horse has eaten too much or experienced any of the events that can cause the disease. Laminitis should be considered an emergency condition. Your veterinarian might suggest icing your horse's legs before he arrives. Scientific research shows constantly icing the horse's legs, from the knee and hock down to and including the foot, for 72 hours after a precipitating event can prevent laminitis. The caveat: Icing, known as cryotherapy, must begin before there is significant laminae damage, and horses do not show clinical signs before the laminae begin to have pathological changes.

What your veterinarian does: Your veterinarian begins his exam by feeling your horse's digital pulse and applying pressure with hoof-testers to locate where your horse feels pain. For laminitis, your horse might show sensitivity in his coffin-bone area of the sole, but the area also might be so numb that he doesn't respond to testing. Because hoof-testing can't provide a full answer, your veterinarian also recommends radiographs. By looking at the coffin bone's position, he can see how the disease has progressed and if the coffin bone has rotated or is sinking.

After your horse has recovered from his initial laminitis emergency, your veterinarian might take blood tests to rule out metabolic diseases. If your horse tests positive for Cushing's, his treatment differs from typical laminitis therapies. He needs a specific diet and medication for Cushing's. However, your veterinarian doesn't want to test for Cushing's when your horse is inflamed with a laminitis episode, as there's potential for the test to aggravate the laminitis condition.

The healing process: You need to treat the hoof that's currently hurting while remembering that your horse's laminitis pain stems from a full-body ailment. Caring for the injured hoof or hooves is your top priority, but sometimes even the best care can't fix the larger problem—and sometimes the larger problem isn't fully understood.

To treat the affected hoof, your veterinarian works with your farrier to support the coffin bone and reduce pressure on your horse's laminae with corrective shoeing. As an emergency treatment, applying a foam cushion to the hoof bottom provides the needed protection and support. Foam building insulation shaped to the foot and attached with duct tape is quick and effective.

Attention to support of the frog is important. Shoeing options depend on the stage and severity of the disease process in the horse's foot. In the acute phase, removing or changing the current shoes could add additional trauma to the compromised laminae. Adding support to the frog and back half of the foot without pulling the shoe can be adequate initially. Shoeing goals are to support the coffin bone by using pressure on the back, or posterior, half of the foot, including the frog. Avoid any sole pressure in front of your horse's frog, and ease his dorsal or front laminar stress by rolling the toe of the shoe and setting the shoe back to ease break-over. Ease his lateral/medial, or side-to-side, laminar stress by using rails along the inside edge

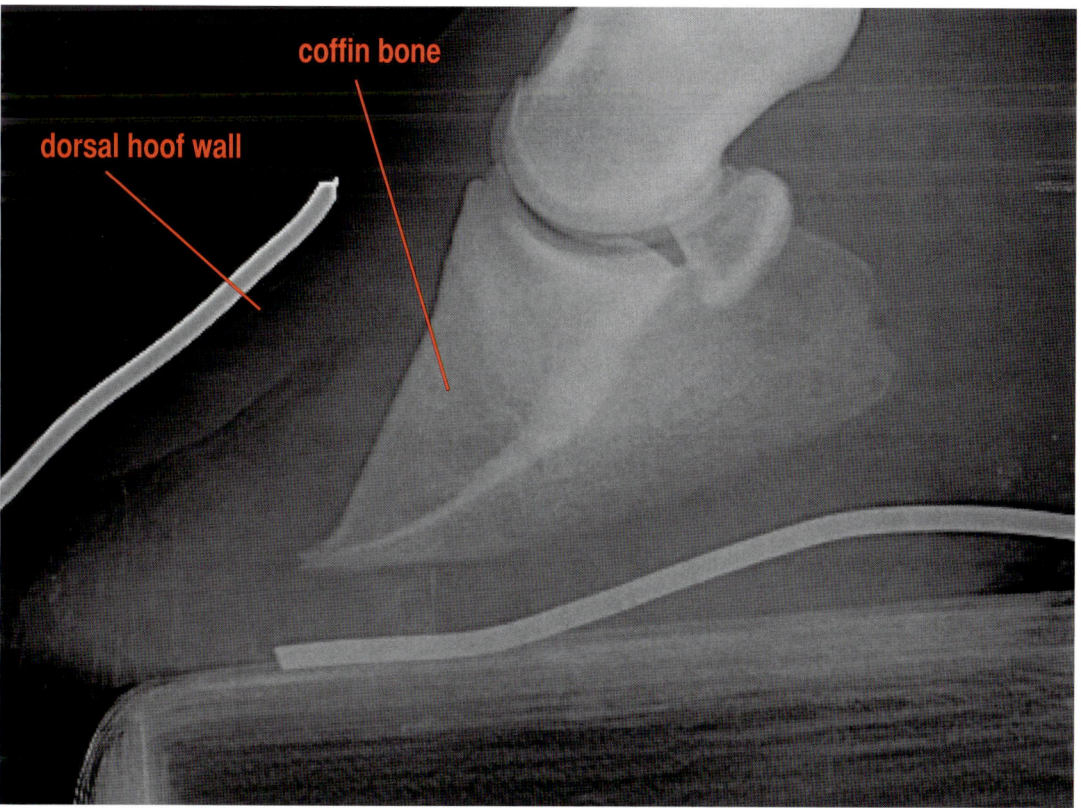

This radiograph clearly shows the coffin-bone rotation. A healthy horse's coffin bone is parallel to the hoof wall. Here, a wire placed next to the dorsal hoof wall emphasizes the drastic rotation.

A horse with laminitis stands with his front feet "camped-out" to the front in an effort to relieve pressure on the hoof laminae.

of the shoe branches. Dome-shaped metal or wooden shoes can achieve these same goals. The use of wedge pads is debated in the veterinary and farrier professions. The need for wedges or heel support can change with the stage of the disease process, as can the need for lateral support. Radiographs can help determine where the support is needed, from side to side as well as from front to back.

Plaster hoof casts also are used to support the inside of the foot. This process is technical and reserved for practitioners with experience. Remember: The goal of shoeing is to save the foot to save the horse. Shoeing does not cure the initiating cause of the disease.

Your veterinarian might prescribe anti-inflammatory medications to help minimize the effects of toxins and to control pain. Too much pain relief allows the horse to overuse his compromised laminae. In contrast, pain will enhance laminitis. Your veterinarian focuses on the whole horse in managing this disease.

While your horse is being treated, minimize his movement. Provide soft footing to cushion your horse's walking space and encourage him to lie down as much as possible. Don't force your horse to exercise when he's on pain medication; pain is a natural sign that tells your horse when to stop moving. Without pain as a signal, your horse might overuse his affected foot, harming it more.

If carbohydrate overload prompted your horse's laminitis, make sure he doesn't ingest a dangerous amount again. Be sure your grain bins have lids and that your feed room has a lock or sturdy latch. Also make sure anyone who helps at your barn knows to double-check every gate and chain. If your horse has Cushing's, provide him with the daily medication. Talk with your veterinarian to develop a menu that keeps your horse healthy and reduces the potential for future laminitis episodes.

Down the road: If your horse has laminitis once, he's at risk for future bouts. The sensitive foot structures already might have some permanent damage, weakening the laminae and making them susceptible to future damage. Be alert and initiate therapy immediately with any indication that there is a recurrence of laminitis. You must be determined and committed to help your horse to heal and to avoid future problems.

Your horse's prognosis hinges on how much laminar damage and basement-membrane damage has occurred. The prognosis also depends upon when during the course of the disease you noticed and got help for your

Horseman's Dictionary

Cushing's disease: a hormonal disorder caused by a benign pituitary gland tumor that causes horses to store fat and keep from shedding. The disease also is linked to horses that are predisposed to laminitis.

fructan: a carbohydrate found in grass and hay that, in excess, can cause physiological changes in a horse's gut and trigger effects in the hoof's laminae.

insulin resistance: failure of tissues to respond appropriately to insulin, which results in high insulin levels and contributes to the metabolic causes of laminitis. Insulin levels in the blood can be tested.

road founder: a breakdown in a horse's laminae following work on hard surfaces. Such constant pounding can initiate the complex set of events that causes laminitis or founder.

horse's problem. Work closely with the veterinarian and farrier. Especially for severe cases, the successful outcome depends upon a committed team: farrier, veterinarian and particularly the owner. There is no good diagnostic procedure to find out how much your horse's internal structures have been affected; treatment must be initiated. Your horse's response to treatment provides the information to help establish a prognosis. A committed team then devises a plan about what can be done to bring your horse back to health.

Note: If your horse's coffin bone has rotated, he might need several months of rehabilitation—if he can actually overcome the disease. If your horse's case is severe, he might not perform again. No one can guarantee your horse's future health or guarantee against setbacks. Early in the disease process, have a frank discussion with your veterinarian about your horse's prognosis. This discussion should be reviewed during any setback. Euthanasia is an honorable end for any horse with severe laminitis.

Case Study: Laminitis

Blue, a 14-year-old Quarter Horse gelding used as a heading horse in team roping, developed acute signs of laminitis.

He consistently ate the same food and never accessed grain or overate. He was reluctant to move, turning was painful and he had a significantly increased digital pulse. Immediate treatment consisted of supporting the frog and back half of the foot, administering anti-inflammatory medication and adding extra bedding to his pen to encourage him to lie down. There were no known precipitating factors. Although an easy keeper, Blue had tested negative for Cushing's disease prior to the development of laminitis. Initial radiographs didn't show any coffin-bone rotation. In spite of the good husbandry, veterinary care and hoof care, the disease continued to progress. There were periods of improvement, but the setbacks became more dramatic. After three months, the coffin-bone rotation was severe. The veterinarian decided the damage to the basement membrane cell layer was irreversible, and the prognosis was unfavorable. In Blue's best interest, the veterinarian and owner agreed that euthanasia was an honorable course of action. The precipitating trigger factors were never identified for Blue. It would be presumed that they were due to a complex or multiple of metabolic conditions, including insulin resistance.

6

THE PASTERN

The bones of the pastern area connect your horse's

fetlock to his foot and are subject to concussion and rotational injuries.

The pastern bones connect your horse's fetlock and foot. When a friend or your veterinarian says your horse has stiffness or lameness in his pastern, that person is referring to the area that includes the long and short pastern bones, also known as the first phalanx, or P1, and second phalanx, or P2, as well as the pastern joint, the proximal interphalangeal joint, or PIP joint. The pastern also includes the soft-tissue structures discussed more in a later chapter. The pastern joint has a relatively small range of motion when compared to your horse's coffin joint and fetlock joint.

Your horse's pastern is prone to chronic and repetitive injuries if he performs circles on hard ground or especially if he has a toed-in conformation. Arthritis is a common diagnosis in this lower

joint. When repetitive motions, hard ground conditions and conformation faults compound trauma to the pastern joint, arthritis may be inevitable. Add a lower-leg-twisting injury and your horse's pastern most likely can cause lameness problems.

There is good news: Your horse might not be prone to arthritis of the pastern just because he's a hard worker or because he performs in events requiring circles. Barrel-racing and reining horses aren't necessarily prone to pastern problems because these sport horses often work in cushioned footing. Plus, it's a standing and twisting motion—not the stepping across movement necessary for a spin—that is difficult for horses with arthritis in the pastern.

Performance horses can develop lameness in the pastern area after acute trauma, for example, an

Many associate arthritis and ringbone with hard-working horses, and if your horse performs on hard ground, he will be more susceptible. But he might not be prone to the disease just because he's a performance horse. Barrel racing and reining horses often avoid pastern problems because the sports promote cushioned footing.

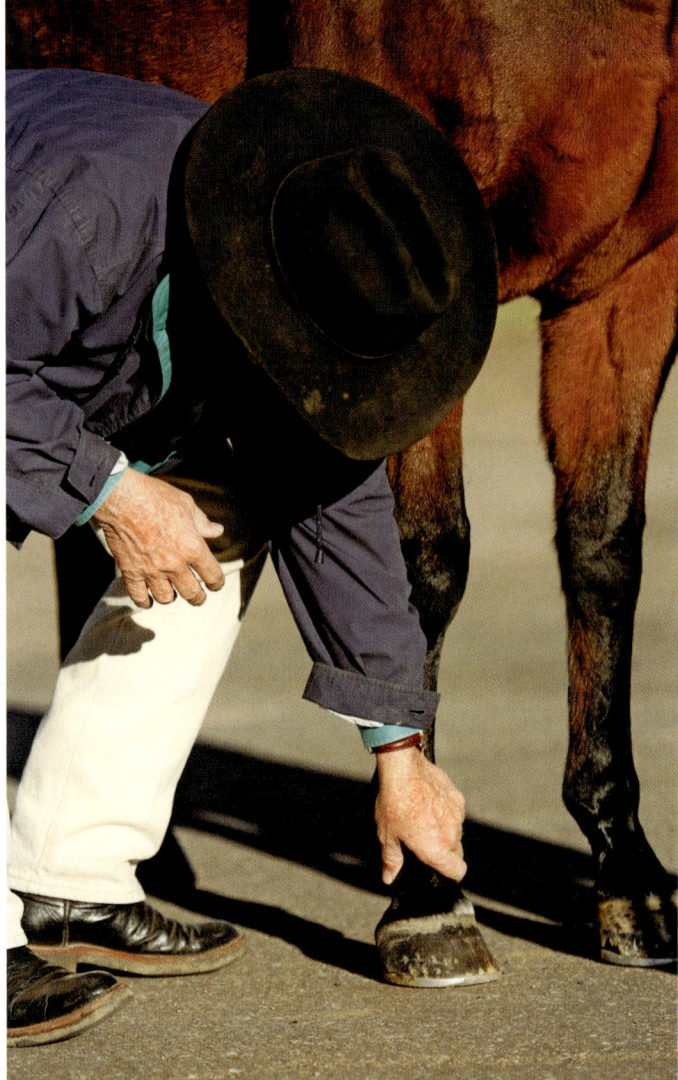

If your horse has inflammation in his pastern—a warning sign of arthritis—you feel heat in his leg. In advanced cases of ringbone, you feel the bony enlargements as you scan your horse's lower leg.

accident where a horse falls and twists the joint, or with continuous-use trauma, which impacts the joint with a twisting motion, such as jumping horses in a schooling environment might experience when they go over fences and then always are asked to circle sharply. These traumas can lead to pastern osteoarthritis, also known as ringbone.

The pastern bones also can fracture as the result of an acute injury, resulting in severe lameness. Read on for more specifics about pastern lameness.

Pastern Osteoarthritis (Ringbone)

You allow your trainer to use your slightly pigeon-toed pleasure horse for riding lessons whenever possible. Your old gelding is retired from the show ring, but loves having a job. Day after day, he rounds the arena at a trot as advanced youths and amateurs learn from his longtime training. Lately, he's been "off," especially while rounding corners. He seems fine when working the long side of the arena, but bobs his head slightly while turning, especially when a heavier student is mounted. The trainer stopped the riding lesson and felt your horse's leg. He noticed heat in the pastern and suggested you call your veterinarian.

What might be happening: Your horse might have ringbone because of consistent-use trauma or following a specific, twisting injury. Your horse's conformation also can predispose him to the joint-pain disease. If he's toed-in, or is pigeon-toed, or has steep pasterns, his conformation forces more stress on the pastern joints each time he moves. If your horse works on hard or frozen ground for long time periods, he also might develop ringbone. Hard ground doesn't provide "give" when your horse steps on it. Instead, your horse's joints are jarred and must absorb the concussion and rotation.

Chances are, you notice the stiffness in your horse's front limbs, where a larger percentage of his weight lands. However, your horse can develop ringbone in his hind legs. One leg is more affected than the other three legs.

No matter how your horse's ringbone develops, the disease is progressive and never totally goes away.

What you notice: Ringbone can onset after a specific injury or as the result of use trauma, which is the progressive and accumulative effect normal work has on an anatomical structure, such as a joint. Conformational problems, some types of work and even the work environment can enhance use trauma. If you suspect ringbone, you see Grade 1 to Grade 4 lameness as you also notice:

• A decline in your horse's performance.

• Heat in the pastern area.

• Enlargement of your horse's affected pastern, a change in the pastern's shape and size, as compared to his other legs. Change is evident when looking at the affected pastern from the side or at an angle, and, in some cases, when looking at the pastern from the front.

- An effect on your horse when turning in either direction of of the affected leg, and often more than one limb is affected.

- Some lameness at the start of a ride, but more easy movement once your horse warms up, with stiffness and soreness recurring routinely after rest periods with no movement.

- Thickness above your horse's coronary band, especially on the front "corners" of the pastern area in more advanced cases.

What you do: Early detection is key. You have a better chance of managing pastern osteoarthritis if you pay close attention to your horse and contact your veterinarian at the first signs of a problem. If your horse has suffered a twisting leg injury or if his conformation or past work experience makes him a ringbone candidate, keep a close eye on his lower legs. When ringbone advances without treatment, it can be career-ending for your horse.

What your veterinarian does: When ringbone is suspected, your veterinarian takes radiographic images to identify the telling signs. He sees a bony proliferation around your horse's joint, and the bone outline looks fuzzy, instead of smooth and defined. Your veterinarian might notice more changes in your horse's motion than in the radiographs. That's common, but doesn't change a diagnosis. In some cases your veterinarian expects the radiographic or bone changes because he already has seen your horse's degree of lameness. Bone cysts, also associated with the pastern joint, might be evident on the radiographs, and the cysts are another underlying cause of ringbone.

Your veterinarian uses the radiographic images to evaluate the thickness of cartilage in the pastern joint. If your horse has severe ringbone, his joint space has narrowed because of joint cartilage degeneration. The narrowed cartilage, which, in its normal state, keeps bones from touching, no longer protects the joint as it once did.

Diagnostic nerve blocking can confirm a ringbone diagnosis. If your veterinarian blocks below the pastern joint, but doesn't see a difference in your horse, he continues blocking

LAMENESS Q&A

Why is osteoarthritis of the pastern referred to as ringbone?

In advanced stages of development, this disease causes bony proliferations to develop. Externally, the growths make a ridge around the pastern just above the coronary band—prompting the term "ringbone."

nerves farther up your horse's leg. If your veterinarian blocks above the pastern joint and sees a difference in your horse's movement—specifically your horse's ability to turn with ease—ringbone likely would be the pain-causing culprit. Your veterinarian also might use an intra-articular injection of anesthetic solution to diagnose pastern joint pain.

He also might recommend an MRI of your horse's leg, which helps the veterinarian see the soft tissues, in addition to the bone changes evident in a radiograph. An MRI can back up the radiograph report or add soft-tissue details not seen before. The MRI shows the collateral ligaments of the pastern joint, the distal sesamoidian ligaments and the flexor tendons. Each could cause your horse pain in the pastern area, but can't be seen with radiographs. Plus, an MRI might show bone cysts in the pastern.

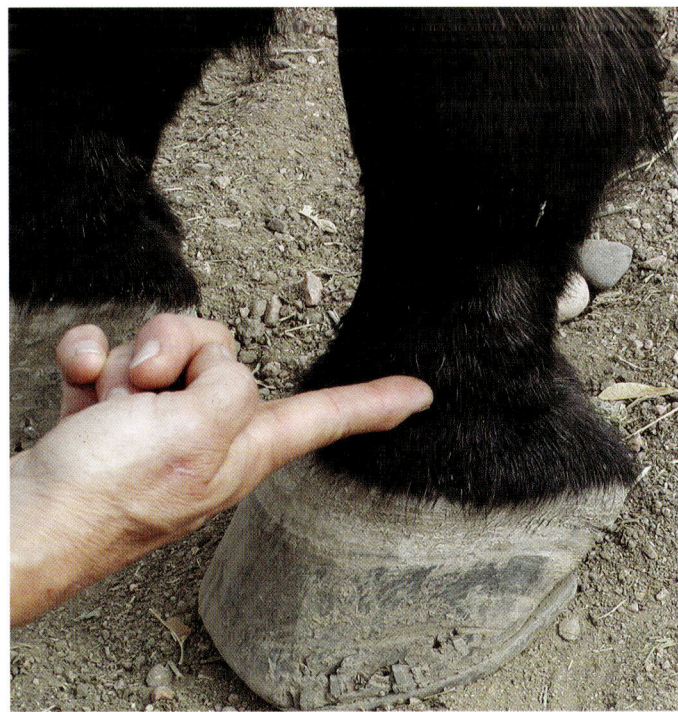

If your horse has severe arthritis and develops an extreme case of ringbone, you see a ring-shaped enlargement on his pastern, hence the name "ringbone."

The healing process: If your horse has ringbone, your veterinarian works to reduce pastern joint inflammation and limit the disease's progression. Your horse needs confinement and controlled exercise as treatment continues. You could be asked to give your horse anti-inflammatory medication—both systemically and locally on the pastern area. Your veterinarian also may recommend shockwave treatment to help calm the affected joint. Intra-articular injections can help relieve

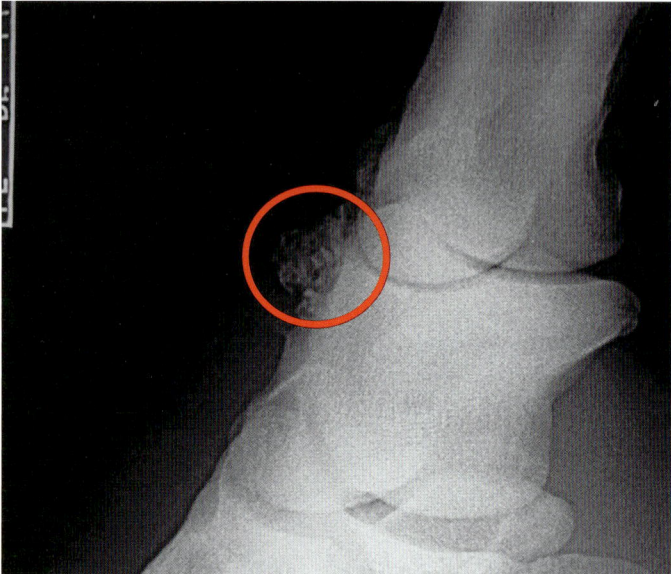

As your horse's ringbone progresses, radiographs show drastic changes to the pastern bones. Here, above and below the horse's joint, you can see the sharp crystal-like formations, which can cause your horse significant pain.

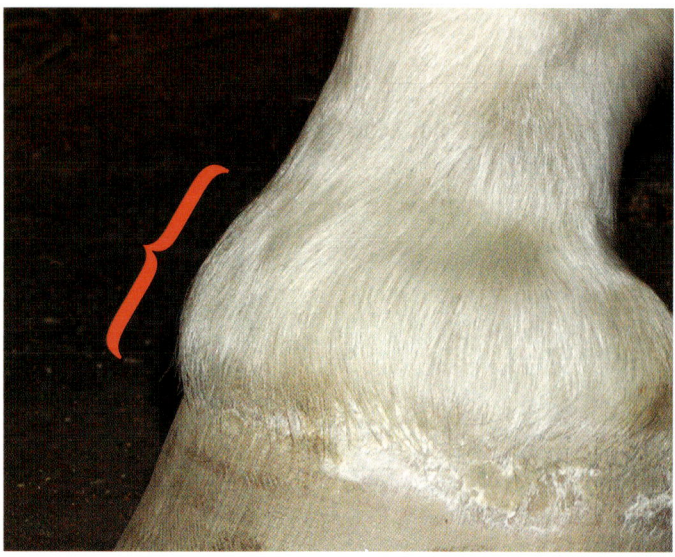

You can see the ring-like changes in your horse's pastern without a radiograph when the crystal-like formation grows excessively. Here, the ridge, or "ring" above the coronary band shows the new bone growth.

joint inflammation and pain, but the results can be temporary and need to be repeated.

Your veterinarian works with your farrier to change your horse's break-over point, moving it back in an attempt to reduce the amount of stress the pastern joint must endure. Your farrier might place lightweight shoes on your horse to further reduce stress, and also might install a dome-shaped pad or metal plate to help the heel roll forward easily toward the toe, again reducing the amount of pastern stress. Extreme corrective shoeing might not be an option for high-level performance horses, but such techniques can keep horses with chronic ringbone sounder for such activities as light trail and pleasure riding. However, some shoes can be dangerous on slick footing or during fast-paced performances. Be sure to discuss your horse's workout and show schedule with your veterinarian and farrier before shoeing your horse.

If your horse's ringbone is advanced, or conservative therapies haven't been effective, your veterinarian might recommend surgically fusing the joint to help ease your horse's pain and extend his working life. If the joint cartilage is significantly compromised, surgical joint fusion might be the only option to help make your horse serviceably sound. In this complex procedure, the veterinarian removes your horse's existing joint cartilage and compresses the lower end of P1, his long pastern bone, and the upper end of the shorter P2 together, using a metal plate and bone screws. In a few months the bones fuse together. Your veterinarian recommends this joint fusion only if your horse is younger than 14 and has no secondary lameness issues. After surgery, your horse might not move as smoothly as he once did, but he's free of pain.

Down the road: When your horse is cleared to return to work, make sure to ride and work him in soft footing. Stay away from frozen, uneven and rocky ground—and any footing that might cause him to twist or torque his lower leg. You also want to plan and monitor your horse's workload. Carefully choose the events in which you'd like your horse to compete, and be sure not to overwork him. If you have a big team penning competition in a week, for example, allow your horse to rest; don't practice at warp speed every day leading up to the event.

Ringbone is a progressive disease that can reactivate—even if your horse seems fine at

Horseman's Dictionary

long pastern bone: also known as the first phalanx, or P1.

pastern joint: also known as the proximal interphalangeal joint, or PIP joint, the joint between P1 and P2, the long and short pastern bones.

ringbone: osteoarthritis in the horse's pastern joint.

short pastern bone: also known as the second phalanx, or P2.

surgical joint fusion: a surgical process to end joint pain by stopping the joint's ability to move and wear. After removing the joint cartilage, the joint bones are screwed together, causing them to fuse in the healing process, much as a fracture heals.

use trauma: a progressive and accumulative trauma occurring to an anatomical structure, such as a joint, with normal work. Use trauma might be enhanced due to conformational problems, some types of work and the work environment.

the moment. Keep an eye on your horse and guard his activities so he's rested and ready for your best days.

Your veterinarian must consider many factors, such as the amount of degeneration, your horse's age and weight and his intended use, when labeling your horse with a prognosis. Keep in mind that your horse's disease is progressive and his prognosis can change at any time, or if any further injury occurs.

Case Study: Pastern

Alex, a 14-year-old Warmblood gelding who competed in hunter shows, began showing intermittent lameness under saddle. His owner said Alex was perfect at some shows, but notably off at other events, and he became somewhat reluctant to perform his job. His owner knew it was time to get help and consulted her veterinarian.

At the veterinary hospital, a lameness exam demonstrated Alex had a consistent Grade 3 lameness of his right front leg when he traveled to the right on a hard surface. On a soft surface, he exhibited only light Grade 2 lameness on the same leg. When the veterinarian examined Alex's right front leg, he didn't find specific lesions. However, diagnostic nerve blocks localized his lameness to the pastern area. The veterinarian's radiographs showed mild-to-moderate bone proliferation around the front half of the pastern joint.

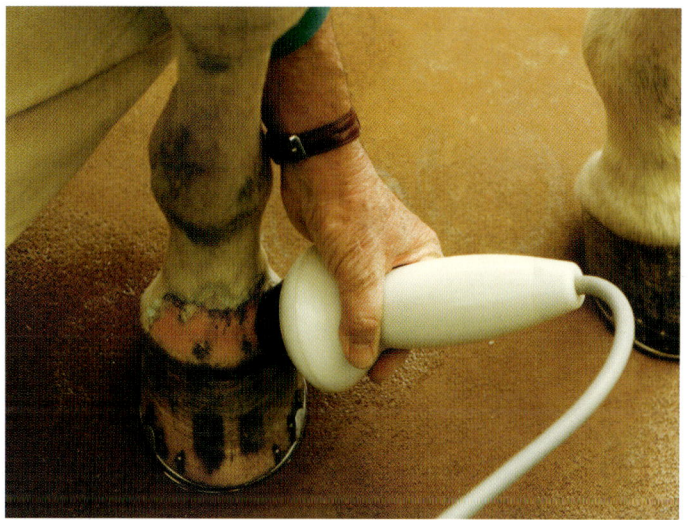

Shockwave therapy can help reduce pain if your horse is diagnosed with arthritis or ringbone. If your horse improves after the series of treatments, they might be repeated every six to 12 months, or as needed.

Alex's therapy consisted of stall rest and controlled exercise with daily walks under saddle, three sessions of extracorporeal shockwave therapy, with two weeks between sessions, and 10 days of topical anti-inflammatory medication applied twice daily, between shockwave treatments, to the front pastern area.

After eight weeks of careful attention, Alex began his show preparation and conditioning. He was ready to go back to work and performed successfully on the hunter circuits for the next three years.

7

THE FETLOCK

As your horse's "shock absorber," the fetlock with its bones, ligaments and tendons helps cushion the impact each time your horse takes a step.

You might refer to your horse's fetlock joint as his "ankle." You've probably seen how your horse's fetlock settles down toward the ground each time he takes a step.

This complex structure—combining bones, ligaments and tendons—is your horse's shock absorber. The fetlock cushions impact to your horse's entire leg each time his foot hits the ground.

Here's how the complex joint works. The lower end of the cannon bone and the top of the long pastern bone (P1) meet to form the joint. Two small sesamoid bones lie at the back of the joint. The suspensory ligament's lower end attaches to the top of the two sesamoid bones. The distal sesamoidian ligaments connect to the bottom of the sesamoid bones and extend down to attach to the back of the

pastern. All together, the small bones and ligaments support the fetlock. The sesamoid bones also cradle two flexor tendons, which further support the fetlock joint as they pass into the pastern.

Your horse's shock-absorbing fetlock can be overtaxed. When your horse's muscles, ligaments and tendons become fatigued, the structures risk injury. If your horse works to the point of exhaustion, his fetlock may be at risk. Endurance horses and racehorses often incur fetlock injuries. Your horse also might have fetlock trouble if he makes quick athletic movements on hard or uneven ground. A one-time incident or a lifetime of continuous working stress can cause havoc to your horse's fetlock. Here's a rundown of the most common fetlock problems.

This horse's extended right front leg is about to hit the ground, and the horse's body weight must be absorbed by the fetlock.

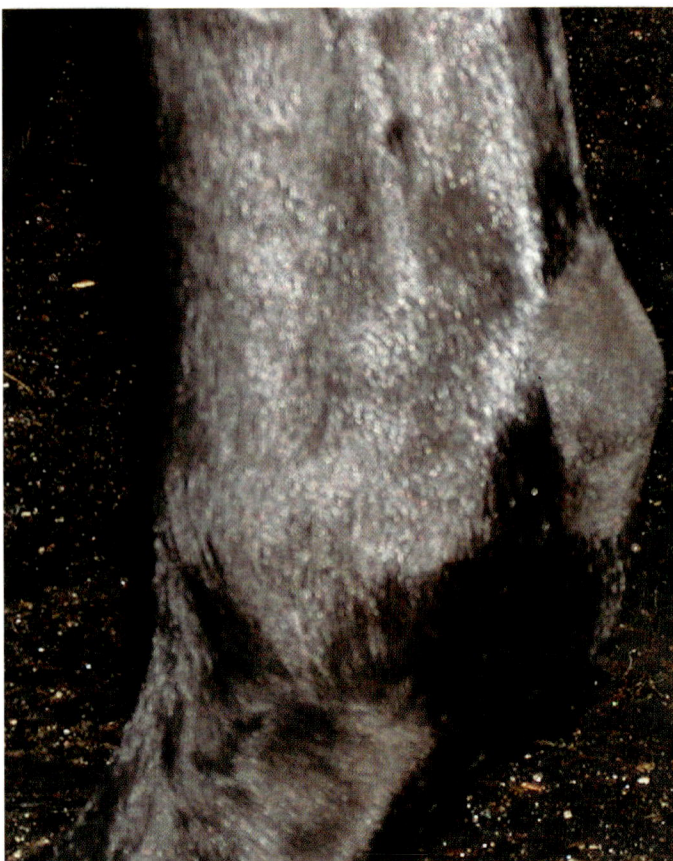

This horse overreached with a hind leg and seriously tore structures surrounding his fetlock, resulting in the obvious swelling. The fetlock is vulnerable to accidents and injuries that can cause your horse significant lameness problems.

Fetlock Osteoarthritis

Your Arabian is a stellar endurance competitor—he takes most any obstacle in stride and powers on to every checkpoint. When preparing for your last race, you felt like your mount had the heart to push on, but his body wasn't quite as eager. When you called your veterinarian to clear your horse for the race, the veterinarian found a wind puff just above your horse's fetlock joint. When your veterinarian performed a flexion test, your horse was noticeably agitated.

What might be happening: Your horse's articular cartilage and subchondral bone, the bone that lies directly under the cartilage to support it, can degenerate after repetitive use or specific injury. Although the stress may be minor each time you ride your horse, cartilage can become damaged and lose its cushioning properties. This lack of cushion adds to the cycle of inflammation and degeneration. With time, the continued stress wears away at your horse's joint and causes clinically

observed inflammation and lameness. When the joint is inflamed, it produces excess synovial fluid. That excess joint fluid—which in normal quantities lubricates and protects your horse's joint—creates the wind puff you can see on the outside of your horse's leg.

If your horse has had an injury to his fetlock joint, a piece of bone might have chipped from the top end of the long pastern bone. Or, your horse might have an avulsion fracture of a sesamoid bone, in which a fragment has pulled away from the bone. With chips in the joint, your horse's anticipated recovery time might increase.

What you notice: You see a Grade 2 to Grade 4 lameness as you also notice:

- Varying degrees of heat and swelling around your horse's fetlock joint.

- Your horse in pain after his fetlock joint is flexed.

- A wind puff showing there's increased synovial fluid in your horse's fetlock joint.

What you do: Call your veterinarian any time you see swelling or feel heat, and especially if you see a new wind puff associated with lameness.

What your veterinarian does: With all of those symptoms—plus a flexion test of the fetlock revealing pain—your veterinarian diagnoses a fetlock problem and pursues other further diagnostics for confirmation. He might perform diagnostic blocks to help solidify his findings.

Radiographs help evaluate the fetlock and confirm fetlock osteoarthritis. Your veterinarian sees if cartilage has deteriorated and if your horse's bones are close to touching in advanced stages. The images also show if there are any chip fractures or if there's damage to the bone under your horse's joint cartilage.

Your veterinarian may also perform synovial centisis to assess joint fluid quality. Using surgical techniques and a syringe and needle, your veterinarian draws synovial fluid from within the joint capsule. He then evaluates the fluid, looking for signs of infection or hemorrhaging. This procedure usually isn't a part of a routine lameness exam, but can aid your veterinarian in diagnosing and treating more advanced degeneration.

Your veterinarian also might recommend using MRI technology to examine your horse's fetlock. Because radiographs see only bone, and soft tissues help make up the joint, the MRI can help your veterinarian see everything he needs to see to make a thorough diagnosis.

The healing process: Your veterinarian might ask you to treat your horse's joint with cold water and ice during his initial healing time. The veterinarian also provides you with systemic anti-inflammatory medication to help reduce swelling and pain. Your horse needs controlled exercise and support bandages while healing. In the future, protective bandages can be useful when working your horse.

If your horse's fetlock injury proves severe, he might require an intra-articular injection of anti-inflammatory medications, such as short-acting cortisone and sodium hyaluronate. Your veterinarian also might recommend that you provide your horse with an intravenous (systemic) injection of hyaluronate, which becomes concentrated in your horse's inflamed joint capsule and helps reduce inflammation. A form of glucosamine, an important protein in joint cartilage, can be injected intramuscularly or directly into the joint to improve its health. IRAP (interleukin-1 receptor antagonist protein) is another intra-articular therapy that your veterinarian might recommend to help reduce joint inflammation.

If radiographs show that your horse has bony chips and fragments in the joint, your horse might require surgery. The chips can cause continued inflammation if they aren't removed. If necessary, your veterinarian can perform arthroscopic surgery. Afterward, your horse needs two to six months of rest, depending upon how much cartilage damage has been done.

In some cases your veterinarian may think the small chips are not a source of inflammation, so doesn't recommend surgery.

Down the road: Your horse's ability to return to work depends on what damage your veterinarian sees on radiographs, MRI scans or during arthroscopic surgery. If your horse's fetlock responds to therapy after an injury—and radiographs don't show a significant change—he should be able to return to his previous workload. If your horse's joint cartilage is worn thin from continued use

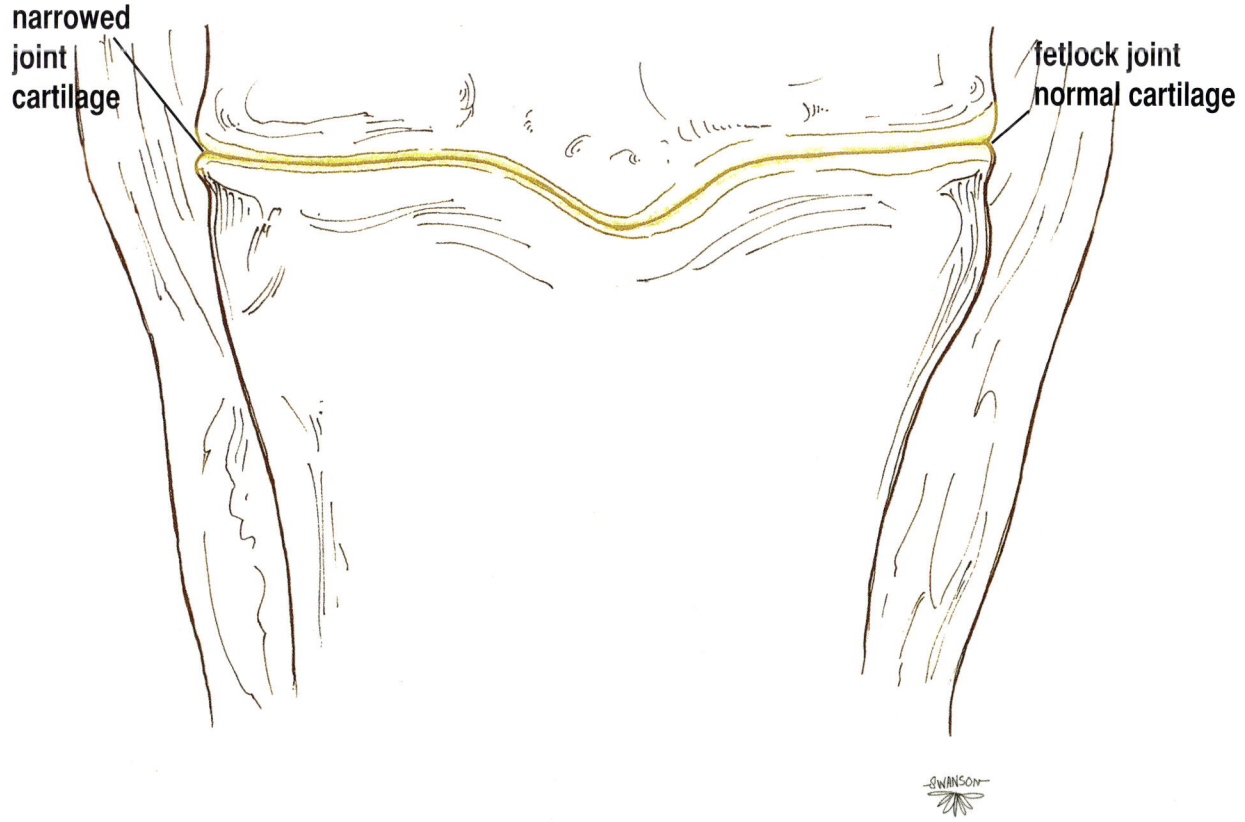

narrowed
joint
cartilage

fetlock joint
normal cartilage

SWANSON

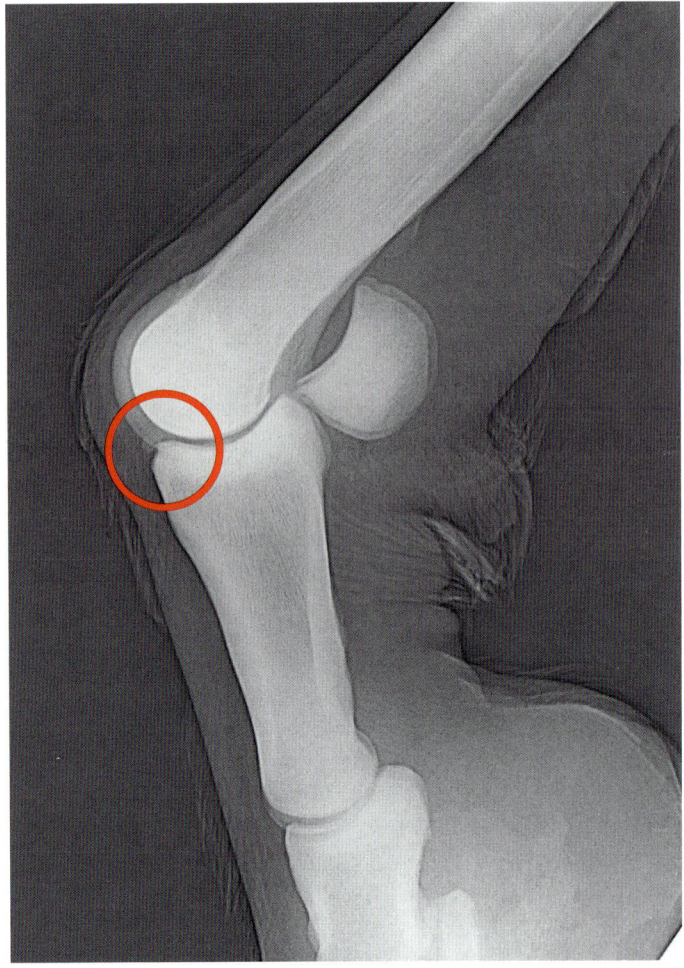

This radiograph shows a bone fragment in the fetlock joint. With constant wear and irritation, the fragment might prompt a horse to develop osteoarthritis in his fetlock, but removing the chip helps the horse avoid future discomfort.

What might be happening: Your horse's sesamoid bones are held in place by the suspensory ligaments, collateral ligaments and the distal sesamoidian ligaments. Working together, the small bones and ligaments form a semi-rigid structure that supports your horse's fetlock joint and provides the elastic, shock-absorbing action when your horse takes a step.

Your horse can fracture his sesamoid bone in several ways. First, he might nick his opposite leg while moving quickly. The inside sesamoid bone on either leg and closest to the middle of your horse's body is most vulnerable to this striking or interfering injury. When your horse hits one leg with his opposite hoof, he can severely bruise or fracture the small sesamoid bone.

Your horse also can stress his joint during heavy work; his ligaments can pull away from his sesamoid bones and pull away a piece of connected bone. When the ligaments pull away from the attached bones, breaking off a bone fragment, your horse has an avulsion fracture of the sesamoid bone.

If both of your horse's sesamoid bones in one leg fracture, the fetlock joint loses all its support. Your horse is in great pain from a catastrophic injury more common in racehorses, but unusual in non-racehorses.

What you notice: You usually see a Grade 3 lameness as you also notice:

- Increased fluid in your horse's fetlock joint—a wind puff.

- Swelling on the back part of your horse's fetlock joint.

- Your horse's resistance and pain when he flexes his fetlock.

What you do: Call your veterinarian when your horse is obviously lame or when you've witnessed a leg injury caused by your horse being kicked or kicking at another horse.

What your veterinarian does: Your veterinarian palpates your horse's lower leg and the area around the sesamoid bones. He also takes radiographs to confirm a fracture. He could suggest ultrasound or MRI scans to evaluate both your horse's bones and soft-tissue structures, to totally establish the extent of damage.

and you didn't catch the osteoarthritis in time, his prognosis is less favorable. In some cases, equine cartilage is damaged beyond the body's ability to repair, even with the medications available.

Sesamoid-Bone Fracture

Your favorite Paint horse always wears protective boots when turned outside. His lower leg conformation predisposes him to hit the inside of his fetlock with his opposite foot as he runs and plays. While you were away, a friend turned out your horses and forgot to outfit him with his boots. While playing in the pasture, he must have nicked himself once again. When he trots up to greet you at the gate later in the day, you notice he's nodding his head. As you notice his lack of boots, you also notice his lower leg is swollen, and there's an obvious wind puff.

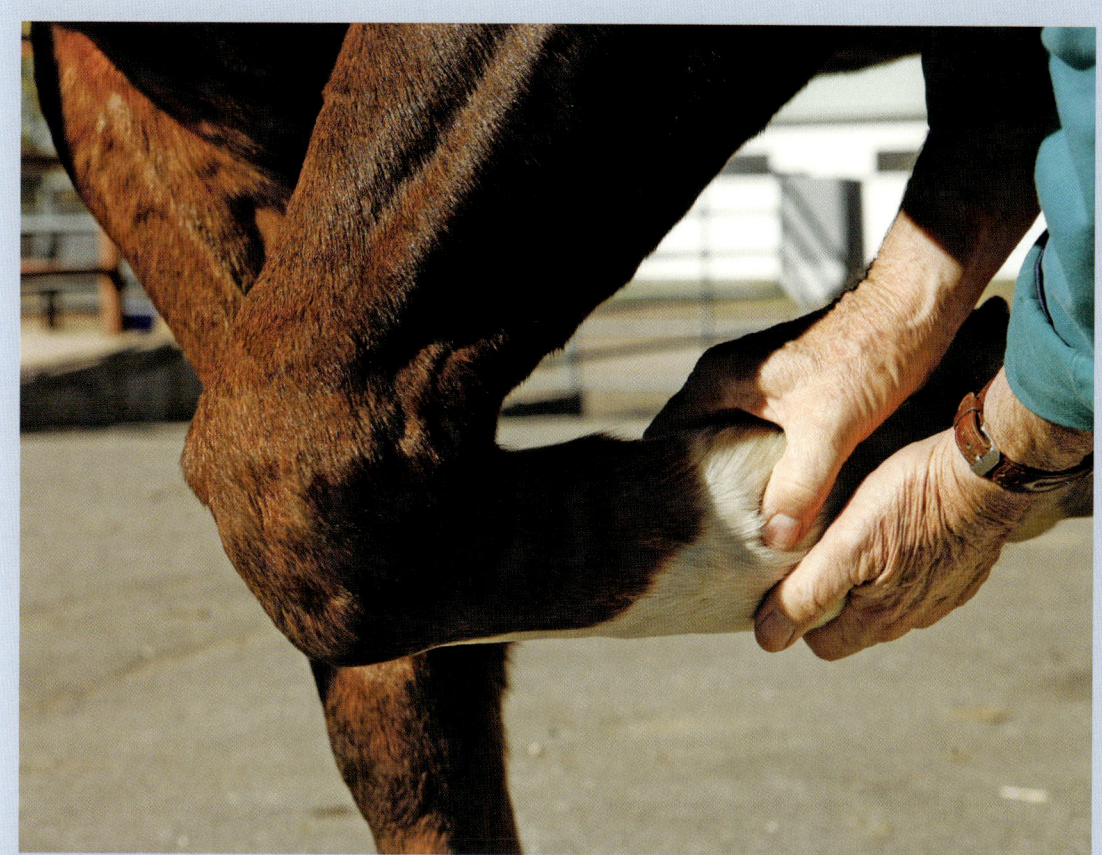

Careful and thorough palpation of the fetlock structures helps your veterinarian detect bone or ligament enlargements, extra joint fluid, and painful areas.

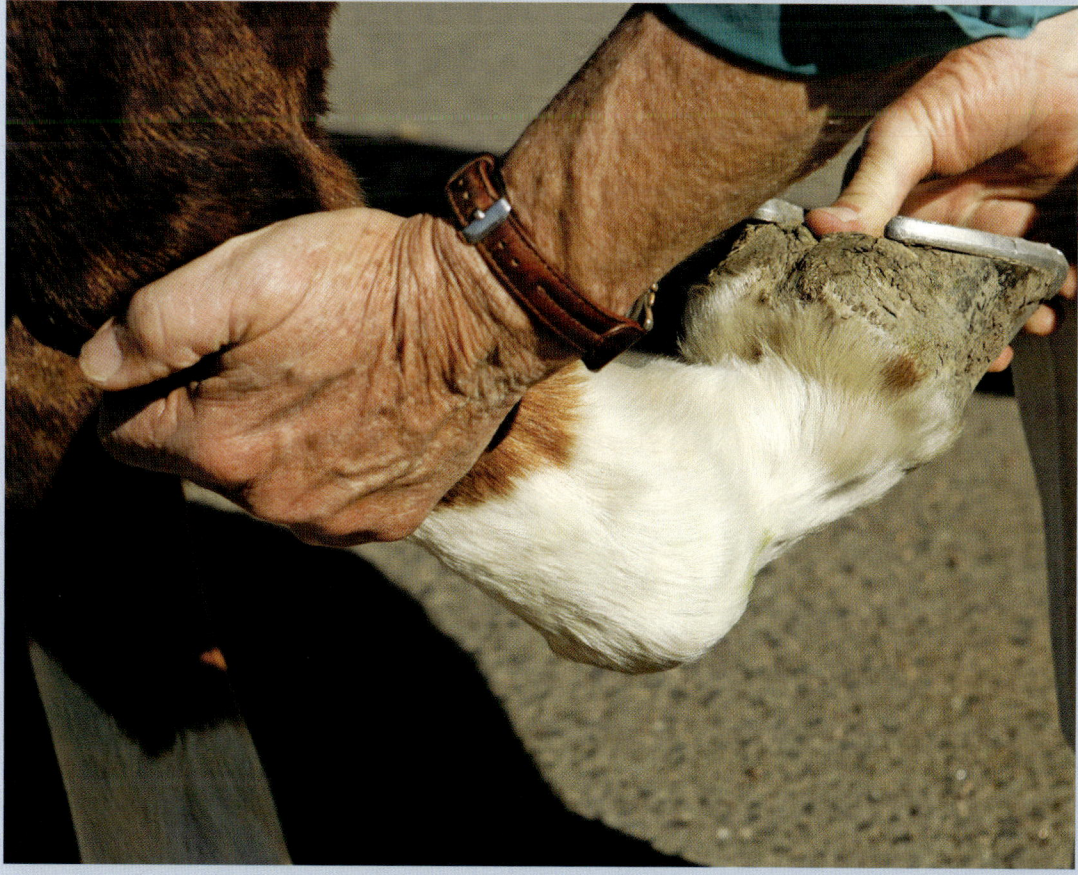

Your veterinarian also performs a fetlock flexion test, forcing the fetlock to flex. Then, after one minute, the veterinarian watches the horse trot and notes any increased lameness.

LAMENESS Q&A

What's a wind puff and what does it look like at my horse's fetlock joint?

A wind puff refers to the increase of synovial fluid within a joint capsule, and develops at a specific site where the joint capsule can stretch. The wind puff is a soft fluid-filled swelling, and the fluid can be pushed down into the joint, only to return when pressure is released.

In the fetlock a wind puff develops just above the bulge of the fetlock joint, on the side behind the edge of the cannon bone and in front of the suspensory ligament, and is seen on both sides of the joint.

A wind puff might be a sign of severe pathology within a joint or merely the result of use-related stress. If a wind puff results from regular use, it dissipates with a support bandage, though it likely develops again once the bandage is removed. Any other signs of joint disease, such as heat, swelling (other than within the joint capsule), pain upon palpation and lameness, are red flags that represents a greater problem within the joint.

The healing process: If stress causes your horse's sesamoid injury and part of his bone has pulled away, your veterinarian can elect to remove the bone fragment through surgery. When healing, your horse could benefit from intra-articular injections and systemic anti-inflammatory medication. He also needs supportive bandages and controlled exercise.

If your horse's sesamoid fracture doesn't involve his joint, he might heal well with a support bandage combined with a gel cast and prolonged rest. If the sesamoid fracture involves one-third to one-half of the bone, your veterinarian surgically stabilizes the fracture with a single screw. Surgical stabilization is not a viable option if your horse has splintered his sesamoid bone into several pieces, instead of one "clean" fracture line.

In extreme cases, when both sesamoid bones on the same leg are affected, your horse can require extensive surgery to fuse his fetlock joint. Your veterinarian surgically connects the lower end of your horse's cannon bone to the top of his long pastern bone and sets the connection with screws, wires and a plate. After such dramatic surgery, your horse is unable to perform again. However, he might be sound and pain-free for companionship or for breeding.

If your horse fractured his sesamoid bone or bones, chances are he also suffered damage to his suspensory ligament. Your veterinarian recommends extra rest and possibly shock-wave treatment to help your horse during his double healing process. As with most soft-tissue injuries, your horse requires extensive confinement and controlled exercise.

Down the road: Your horse should return to work after surgery, rest, and the healing recommendations your veterinarian suggests. Pay special attention to any future lameness. The sensitive soft structures may not bounce back quite the same, and re-injury is common. Use supportive boots for leg protection and to provide support for his soft-tissue structures any time you work your horse.

Your veterinarian gives your horse a favorable prognosis if his fracture is small and his suspensory ligament damage isn't severe. The prognosis is unfavorable if both sesamoid bones fractured at the same time.

Distal Sesamoidian Ligament Injury

Your loyal team-roping mount made a near-perfect run. He rated the steer, tracking perfectly. As he faced the steer your horse took a strange step and stumbled just as your partner dallied. As you trotted from the arena, your roping horse was lame.

What might be happening: When your horse's legs are stressed, fibers within his sesamoidian ligament can tear. Your horse can stress his fetlock during a slip or if he takes an awkward step.

What you notice: You see Grade 2 to Grade 3 lameness as you also notice:

- Swelling—in some cases, minimal and hard to see—just below his fetlock on the back side of your horse's pastern.

- Obvious discomfort when palpating the back of your horse's pastern.

- A lack of easy fetlock movement and a limited range of motion.

What you do: Call your veterinarian when you see a sudden change in your horse's gait—especially after a strange step or abrupt movement during a ride. As with any acute injury, it is usually beneficial to apply cold therapy. Soak your horse's foot in ice water or compress with cold bandages until the injury is evaluated.

Horseman's Dictionary

avulsion fracture: when the ligament pulls away from its attachment and a piece of bone pulls away, as well.

bone-lipping: with chronic joint inflammation, the extra bone the body produces along the bone edge; often called bone-modeling; common in horses with osteoarthritis.

sodium hyaluronate: a long chain protein, which reduces joint inflammation, and an important part of a horse's synovial fluid.

subchondral bone: supportive bone lying directly under the cartilage.

synovial fluid: fluid inside the joint that lubricates and protects, and also provides nutrition to the joint cartilage. Excess fluid creates a soft swelling called a wind puff.

What your veterinarian does: Your veterinarian palpates your horse's legs, then performs flexion tests to assess your horse's range of motion. The veterinarian also might request an ultrasound to examine the sesamoidian ligaments and related structures for pain-causing tears. Radiographs will be taken to rule out fractures.

The healing process: Your horse needs confinement and controlled exercise for two to six months, depending on the extent of ligament damage. Your veterinarian might recommend shockwave treatments to help your horse's internal structures heal as quickly as possible.

Down the road: When your horse is cleared to begin working, carefully consider the type of footing on which he works. Groomed footing helps cushion your horse's steps and relieves pressure from his ligaments. Avoid deep, heavy ground. Your horse most likely earns a favorable prognosis, but keep in mind that some tears, if ragged or large, might not heal well or might tear again.

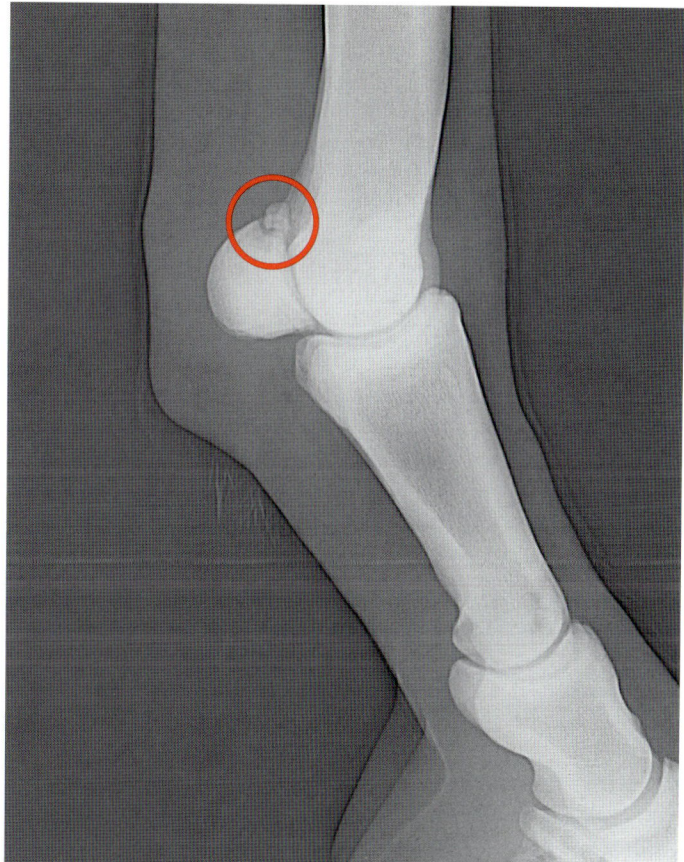

This horse's fractured sesamoid fragment is slightly displaced from the parent bone and appears as an extra bulge on the radiograph. With this type of fracture, the horse's suspensory ligament also can be damaged.

Case Study: Fetlock

A 16-year-old team-roping horse, a beloved competitor, wasn't moving as well as usual and had developed a wind puff. His owner monitored his horse's gait and could see that the right front fetlock didn't settle in the same way the joint on his left front leg did.

After the veterinarian flexed the fetlock joint and asked the horse to trot (a flexion test), the horse was in pain. Radiographs showed that the horse had bone-lipping, or modeling along the top border of the long pastern bone in the fetlock joint, which is common in osteoarthritis.

The veterinarian recommended intra-articular joint medication and systemic anti-inflammatory medications. After two months of rest and treatment, the horse moved with ease, and the veterinarian has cleared him for future competition.

8

THE SPLINT BONE

Your horse's small splint bones serve as vital
weight-bearing structures for his front legs.

Splint bones lie on both sides of your horse's cannon bones. The splint bones help support your horse's knees (carpi) in his front legs and, to a lesser degree, your horse's hocks in his rear legs. If your horse has a splint-bone injury, chances are he's a performance horse or has been injured doing some type of athletic move. Many splint-bone injuries occur after a specific trauma. However, young performance horses might feel splint-bone soreness after repetitive weight-bearing stress.

The good news: Most injuries to these slender, supportive bones heal fairly quickly with good management.

You can tell that your horse's splint bones are hurting if, when you palpate along the sides of his cannon bones, he quickly pulls away. In most cases you also can see swelling or a bump at the same place where your horse is sore.

Keep reading for in-depth discussions about common splint-bone injuries.

Interosseous Ligament Injury or Splint

You just purchased a horse that has been in training for reining. He doesn't work out as a reiner; he just isn't as collected as the trainer wants him to be while working in the deep, well-groomed arena. Still, the horse has speed and shows promise for another event. You're starting him on barrels. The switch in workload or movement seems to have been too much, too soon. When he turns around a barrel—heading to the right—he's obviously sore.

During any athletic movements, your horse risks bumping the inside of one leg with his opposite foot and damaging his splint bone.

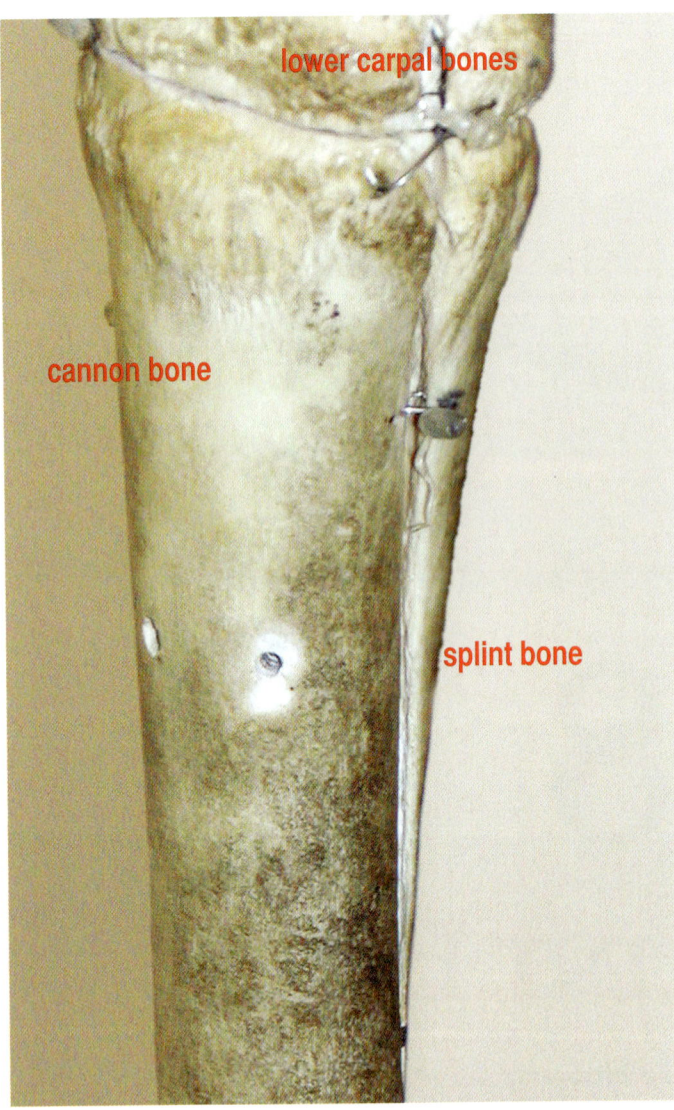

lower carpal bones

cannon bone

splint bone

The "splint bones," a lay term for the long, slender bones on either side of the cannon bones, serve as braces that help the cannon bone support the knee (carpus) or hock joints. This anatomical specimen shows the base of the horse's knee and one of the splint bones adjacent to the large cannon bone.

What might be happening: The word "splint" has two definitions. Anatomically, "splint" is the common name for the long, slender bones that lie on either side of your horse's cannon bone. The splint bones are scientifically known as the second and fourth metacarpal bones in the front legs and the second and fourth metatarsal bones in the hind legs. These bones serve as braces to help the cannon bone support the knee or hock joints. A very short interosseous ligament runs the length of each splint bone and connects that splint bone to the respective cannon bone. As your horse matures, the ligament mineralizes and forms a bony union between the splint bones and the cannon bone.

The second definition of "splint" refers to the firm, soft-tissue enlargement or mineral deposit that can form when the splint-to-cannon bone attachment, or interosseous ligament, is challenged by trauma or stress. The splint bone is susceptible to injury because it bears weight while supporting the carpus, or knee, especially when your horse is turning. Many times, injury occurs when a horse must bear weight and also make a fast turn at the same time.

During the injury-causing compression, the ligament between the splint and cannon bone tears, causing bleeding and swelling in the splint area. The torn tissue turns into bone as your horse's body attempts to heal the injury. You can feel the mineral deposit splint along your horse's splint bone. The deposit feels like a bony knot. The knot can vary in size, but always is easy to see when present. Its bony protrusion obviously sticks out against the cannon bone's usually smooth surface.

If the knot is new or still mineralizing, your horse can feel pain as he works. The amount of pain varies for each horse and each injury. Some horses with splints show extreme signs of lameness, but others can tolerate work.

If you push a young horse during performance training, he might be a candidate for splints. Young bones continue to mature and develop; any extra trauma can have a significant effect on a young horse's splint bone and soft-tissue attachments.

Adult horses, however, can develop splints when they change careers and suddenly perform in an event for which their bones aren't conditioned. Splints form when a horse's bones aren't prepared for the new event, and the pounding and pressure changes.

Another type of splint injury occurs when a horse is kicked or his splint is bruised. If another horse kicks your horse on the splint, the bone's periosteal covering and/or the interosseous ligament tears and forms bone. These injuries also might fracture the splint bone, causing additional complications.

When a splint forms, but your horse hasn't broken a bone, he feels pain for about six to eight weeks. That's the time it takes for the splint to heal. During another six months, the mineralized, bony knot decreases in size. Even though it shrinks from its original form, the splint might be visible for your horse's entire life. Your horse feels no pain unless the splint is reinjured.

Outfit your horse in protective splint boots to prevent injuries to the delicate bones by the same name. Your performance horse should wear boots any time he goes to work, turning and bending.

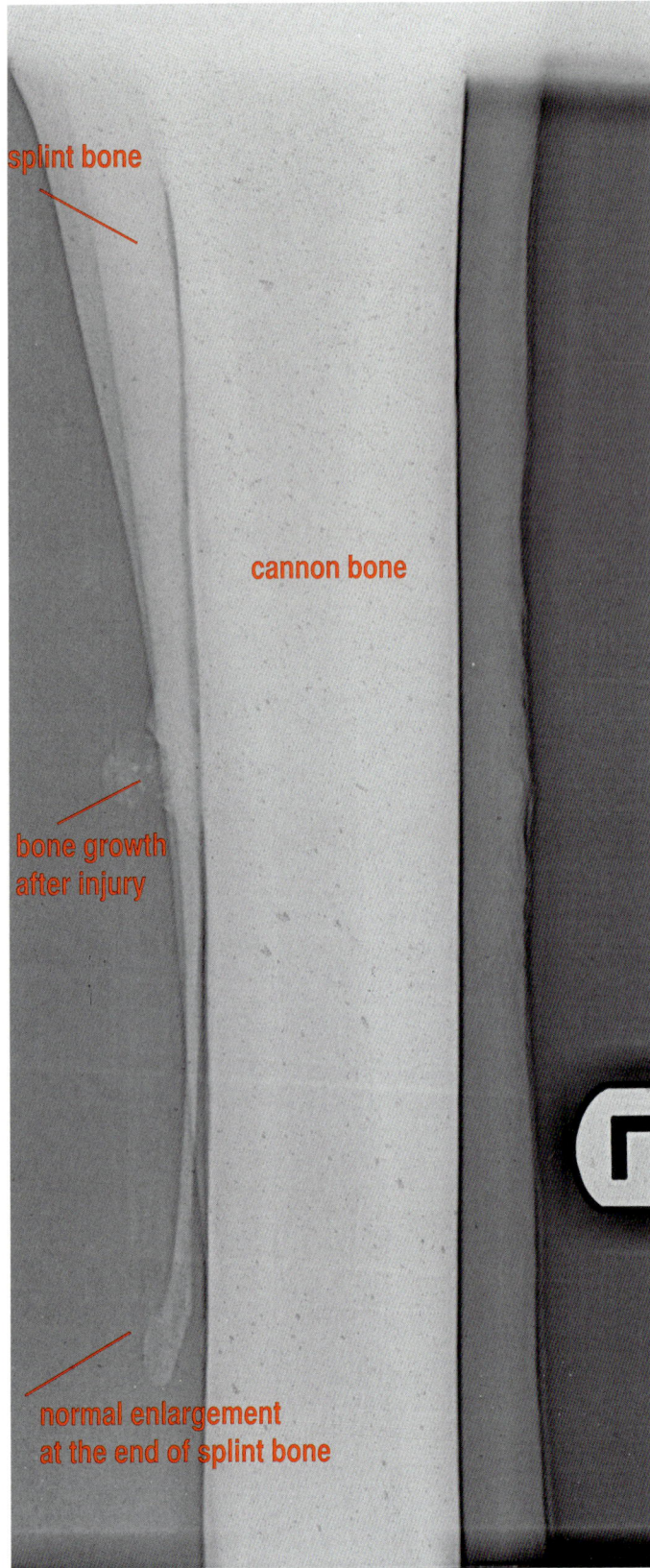

splint bone

cannon bone

bone growth
after injury

normal enlargement
at the end of splint bone

This radiograph shows the horse has sustained an injury to his splint bone, resulting in new bone growth, the round knot on the left side. That new bone growth is what you feel on your horse's leg when he has a splint. However, every horse has a natural enlargement at the splint bone's lower end, as shown.

What you notice: Splints are easy to see on a slick-coated horse and easy to feel during everyday grooming. Compare one of your horse's legs to the matching leg on the opposite side when considering his symptoms. You see Grade 1 to Grade 3 lameness as you also notice:

- A firm, bony-like growth

- That same area is sensitive to your firm finger pressure.

What you do: Notify your veterinarian if your horse is kicked by another horse or if you detect a bony growth. A support bandage and cold therapy are good for most cases.

What your veterinarian does: Your veterinarian palpates your horse's leg and notes if the splint-bone area is sensitive to pressure. He also watches your horse travel to evaluate the lameness the splint might be causing. Afterward, your veterinarian takes radiographs to rule out a fracture and to find out how much bone damage has occurred.

The healing process: Your horse requires rest and controlled exercise to alleviate unnecessary splint-bone stress. Your veterinarian might prescribe anti-inflammatory medication, both topical and systemic, and cold-water therapy to reduce swelling and help your horse heal.

Your veterinarian also might treat your horse's splints with locally injected corticosteroids, manmade drugs that closely resemble cortisol, an anti-inflammatory compound naturally produced by your horse's adrenal glands. Good quality, short-acting steroids reduce inflammation and pain, and can minimize tissue reaction. Before administering local steroids, your veterinarian makes sure your horse doesn't have a fracture. If a bone fractured during the incident, corticosteroids interfere with the healing process.

If the injury is significant, your veterinarian outfits your horse with a gel cast or other type of support bandage to immobilize your horse's affected leg. Your veterinarian replaces the supports in two-week intervals. Your horse's entire treatment should take six to eight weeks.

Down the road: Some horses continue to perform while receiving treatment for their splint bones; others must have total rest. Your

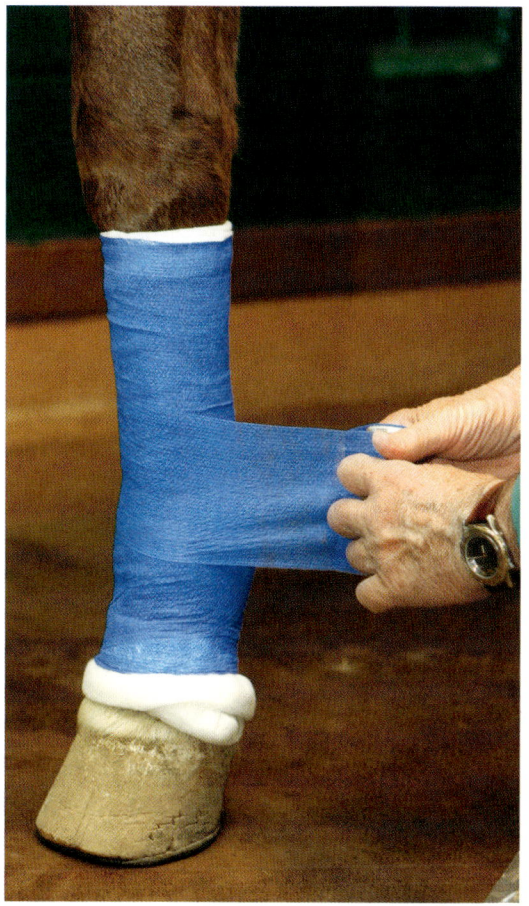

If your horse's injury is significant, your veterinarian immobilizes the affected leg with a gel cast or other support bandage, which is replaced every two weeks until the splint heals.

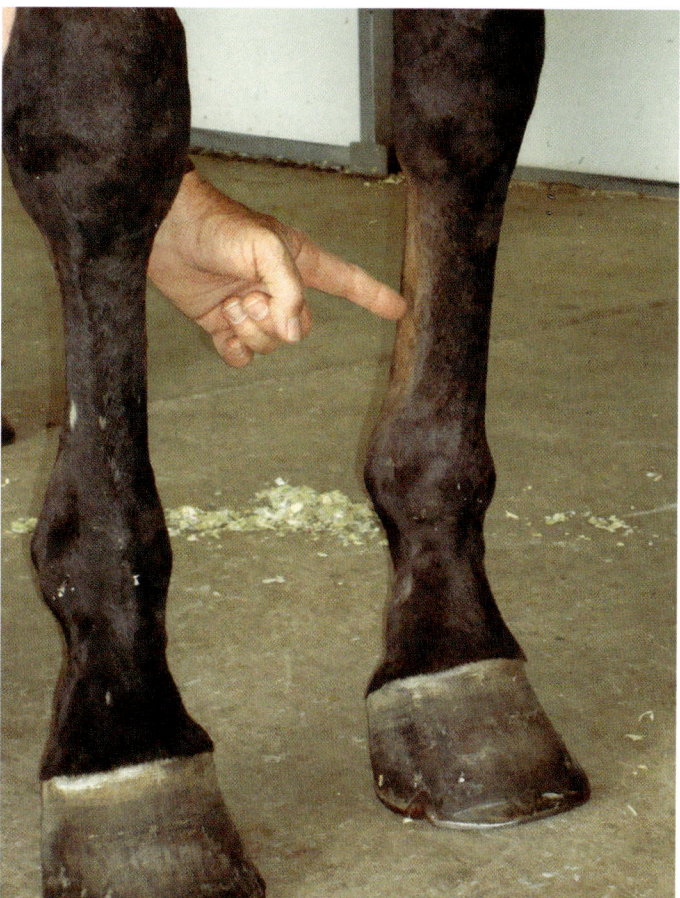

When a splint first forms, it's small and might be noticeable only by careful palpation, and such early detection can reduce your horse's healing time. The small bump midway between this horse's knee and fetlock usually signifies injury to his splint bone.

horse's lameness grade and the quantity of affected structures inside his injured leg dictate how much he should exercise. You can treat your horse with cold-water therapy at the time of injury and again as you reintroduce him to work.

Prevention is key for this ailment. Make sure your horse wears boots to protect his legs from kicks. Use good judgment as you introduce your horse to small-circle work and limit a young horse's circle work during performance training regimens. The unilateral stress places excess weight on your horse's young and still-solidifying medial splint bones. Reinjury is possible for a young horse. New splints usually form just above the site of the original injury.

Splint-Bone Fracture

You just moved your horse to a new facility, where he'll be turned out with other geldings. After his introductory period, when he was allowed to run in a small paddock by himself as his new buddies sniffed him from the other side of the fence, it was his turn to mix with the herd. In the excitement of the introductions, another horse bucked, kicking your horse in the lower leg.

What might be happening: Splint-bone fractures result when your horse nicks his own leg, when another horse kicks him, or when he kicks a solid object, a fence, for example. When your horse's splint bone is fractured, a fragment or fragments break off and attach loosely within the wound.

What you notice: You see Grade 2 to Grade 4 lameness as you also notice:

- Your horse's lameness is most prominent when he travels in the direction of the injured splint.

- You see swelling in the splint-bone area.

99

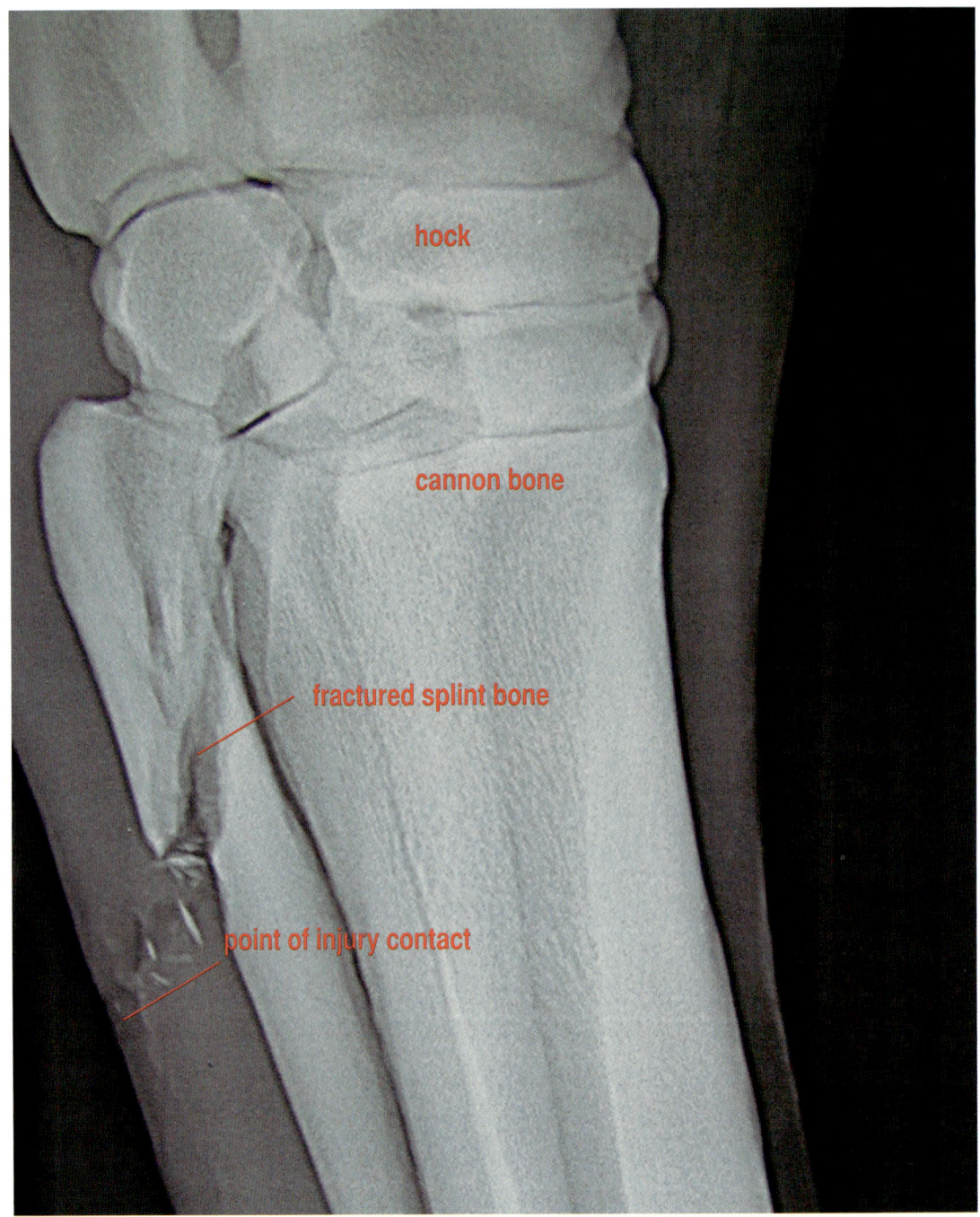

hock

cannon bone

fractured splint bone

point of injury contact

A kick from another horse fractured this splint bone. The radiograph shows the impact site, bone splinters, the fracture and how the kick's force traveled up and toward the horse's hock. This horse healed well with systemic antibiotics to control infection at the wound site, stabilization with a bandage and controlled exercise.

- His splint-bone area is sensitive when pressure is applied.

What you do: Contact your veterinarian as soon as you suspect a fracture.

What your veterinarian does: Your veterinarian takes radiographs to confirm the fracture and identify any loose fragments.

The healing process: In most cases, a splint fracture heals without surgical intervention. Your veterinarian advises you if surgery is needed for your horse's specific case.

Even without surgery, your horse requires rest, controlled exercise, a support bandage or gel cast and anti-inflammatory medication. However, if your horse's bone has chipped and there are loose fragments, your horse might

Horseman's Dictionary

carpus: the knee, or joint between the forearm and the cannon bone.

corticosteroids: manmade drugs that closely resemble cortisol, a hormone naturally produced by your horse's adrenal glands. Given for a short period of time, steroids reduce inflammation and pain and can minimize tissue damage. Administering in excessive amounts intra-articularly can result in cartilage damage. Excessive systemic administration can result in reduced immune function and other physiological changes, including laminitis.

periosteum: the tough, thin tissue layer that covers each bone in your horse's body.

splint: anatomically, the common name for the small, slender bones that lie on either side of your horse's cannon bone. In the front leg these are the metacarpal bones, and in the rear leg they are the metatarsal bones. "Splint" also can refer to the firm, soft-tissue enlargement or mineral deposit that forms when the splint-to-cannon bone attachment is challenged by trauma or stress, or as a result of the periosteal tissue that covers the splint bone being traumatized

require surgery. If not removed, the fragments can delay healing. If your horse needs surgery, the prognosis likely is favorable.

Down the road: Fractures require 10 to 12 weeks to heal. Once healed, your horse shouldn't require any special management. He should have a favorable prognosis following recovery, allowing him to return to his original performance level.

Case Study: Splint

A 4-year-old cutting horse developed a periosteal reaction, or splint, after a long season of practices and competitions. While working a cow, the horse bumped his splint bone with his opposite front leg. At the veterinary clinic, radiographs showed that the left front splint bone still was intact, but the damaged periosteum caused the horse great pain and a Grade 4 lameness.

The owner rested the horse for more than a month, but the lameness didn't improve in that time. When the horse returned to the veterinary clinic for a checkup, the veterinarian recommended another 30-day confinement stint and controlled exercise. He also prescribed anti-inflammatory injections in the splint site. After more rest, the horse showed no lameness and had no pain in the splint area. The follow-up radiographs showed that the splint hadn't grown and was shrinking. The horse returned to his job and now successfully competes as a cutting horse.

9

THE KNEE

Your horse's carpus, or knee, with its seven bones and three major joints, provides a wide range of motion to move your horse forward athletically.

Your horse's knee is a high-motion joint. At the front of his leg, the joint opens completely when it's bent. At the back of your horse's leg, the joint works as a hinge that opens only a little. The bones of the joint are held together with the palmar carpal ligaments, strong ligaments that allow for motion and provide stability for your horse's leg whether the structure is bent or straight. If these crucial ligaments are torn or traumatized, your horse shows signs of lameness. In addition to ligament damage, your horse's knee bones can fracture or the bone edges can chip. When your horse's leg is forced to extend, for example, to support him during a sliding or any abrupt stop, force pounds down on the front edge of the carpal bones. This can prompt a degenerative process on the bone surfaces.

This degeneration results in weakened bones and subjects your horse to fractures along the bones' edges, leaving small broken pieces known as knee chip fractures.

Carpal Degenerative Joint Disease

Your colt is turned out each morning. You watch at the gate as he takes off to play, twisting and turning. As he lands from a final flying leap, his knee twists as he hits the ground. He keeps moving, but hesitates for a few steps. You don't think much of it at the time, but in the weeks to come you notice a bump on the front of his knee, and the entire knee appears to be swollen. You're worried that his innocent accident might have repercussions as he matures.

If your horse performs at speed, his knees are under stress. Reining and performance maneuvers, such as running fast circles, compress the knee's bones and stress the knee's ligaments.

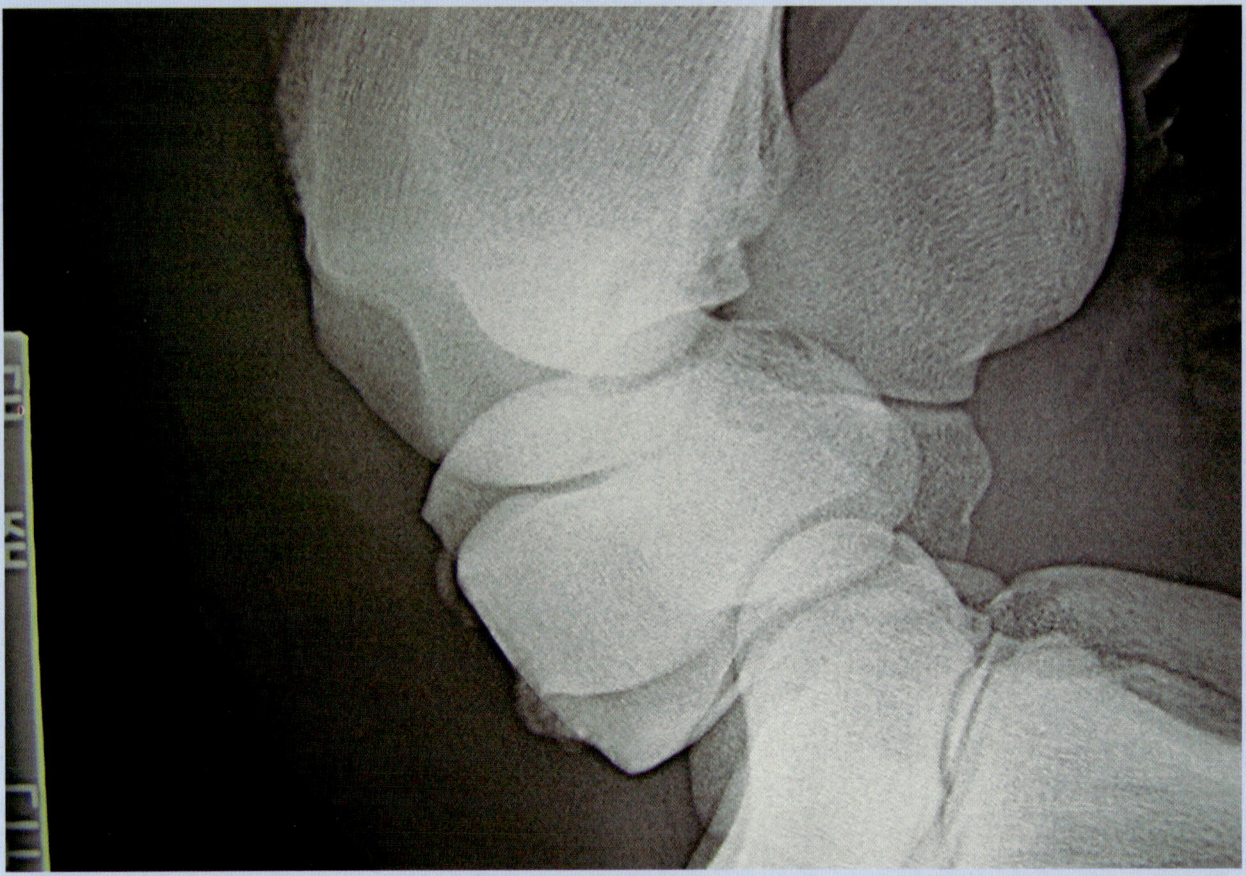

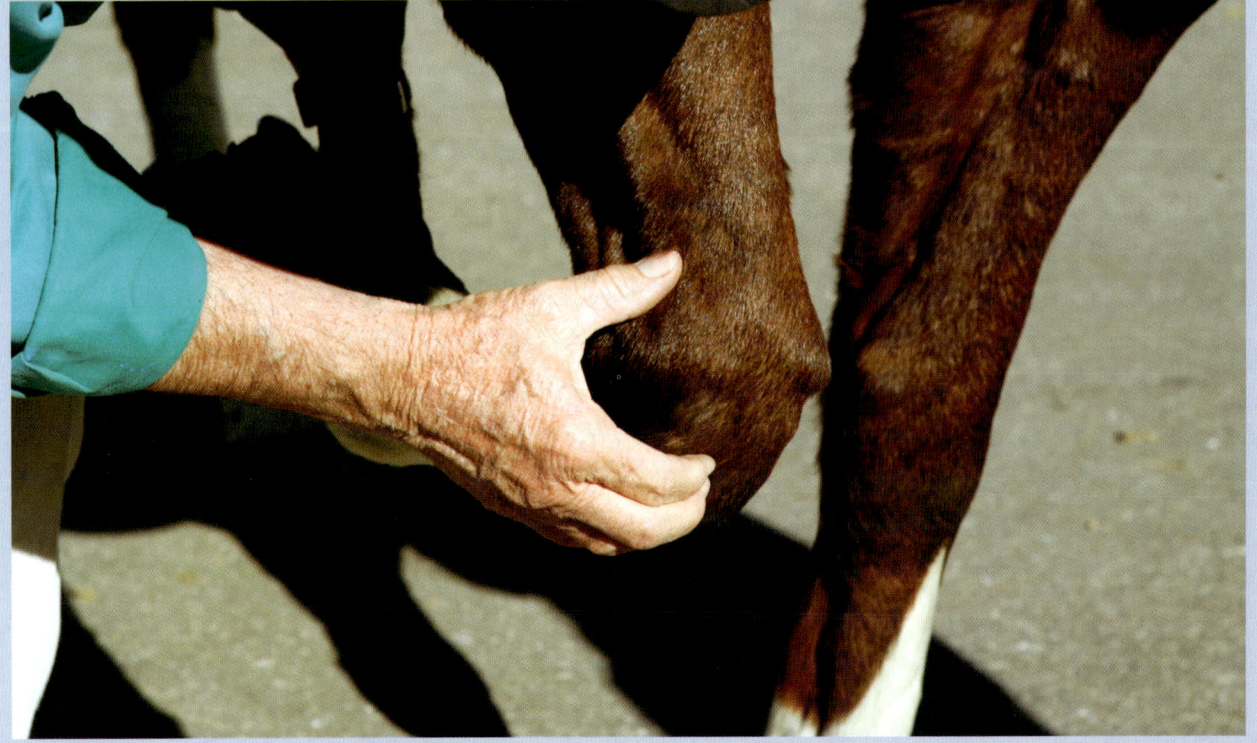

When a horse's knee, or carpus, flexes, the front portion of the joint opens, as seen in this radiograph. The ligament structures in back of the joint allow the knee to flex and then straighten, maintaining the joint's integrity.

When the carpus flexes, the front of the carpal joint opens and allow your veterinarian to palpate individual bones.

What might be happening: Many carpal-joint injuries begin when a horse twists or overextends his knee. The injuries spur the beginning of a degenerative process in the carpus, and the bony and soft-tissue structures can break down. The degeneration can progress slowly or rapidly but eventually leads to lameness. How much lameness your horse exhibits depends on his workload and the severity of the original injury. If his prompting injury was severe or he continues to work at a high-intensity job, carpal degenerative joint disease, or CDJD, might be severe.

If your horse's initial injury involves any carpal palmar ligaments, which connect the carpal bones in the backside of the knee, the CDJD process can be severe. Stressing and tearing these ligaments creates slack in the joint, enhancing the degenerative process. CDJD also is considered severe if your horse shows degeneration or narrowing of the joint cartilage. Knee chips and most any type of joint trauma also can start the disease process.

What you notice: You see a Grade 1 to Grade 4 lameness as you also notice:

- More lameness when your horse circles away from his affected leg.

- A bump on the front of his knee, a fibrous and/or bony reaction to trauma. Many times this bump isn't as medically significant as it appears.

- Increased fluid in your horse's knee joints, causing an enlarged appearance.

- Your horse in pain and unwilling to bear weight after he flexes his knee.

- A noticeably decreased range of motion or ability to flex his knee. You might notice this when you bend your horse's knee to clean his hooves, or your farrier notices it when he shoes your horse.

What you do: Call your veterinarian as soon as you notice a change in your horse's mobility.

What your veterinarian does: Your veterinarian performs a thorough lameness exam, including flexion tests to evaluate your horse's range of motion and/or pain. The veterinarian also watches for gait alterations. Radiographs point out bone problems if your

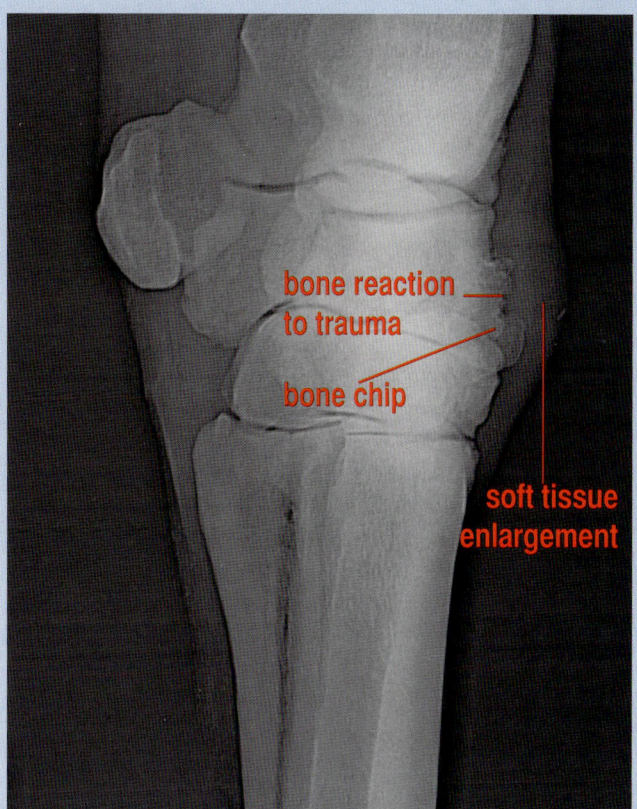

This radiograph shows the joint degeneration associated with chronic carpal degenerative joint disease. Notice the bone chip fragment on the knee's right side, the new bone growth and the soft tissue enlargement—all elements that can cause your horse pain.

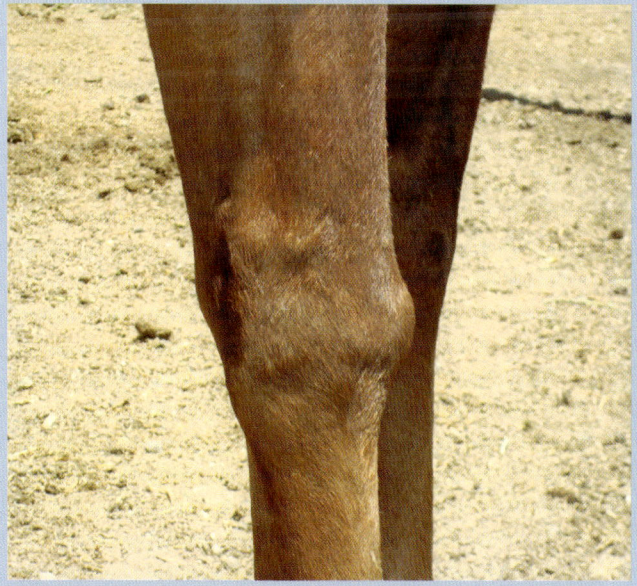

Looking at the same horse from the outside, the bump on the right side of the knee is obvious, but it's impossible to know how severely the knee is damaged without radiographs. Some knee enlargements don't signal significant damage.

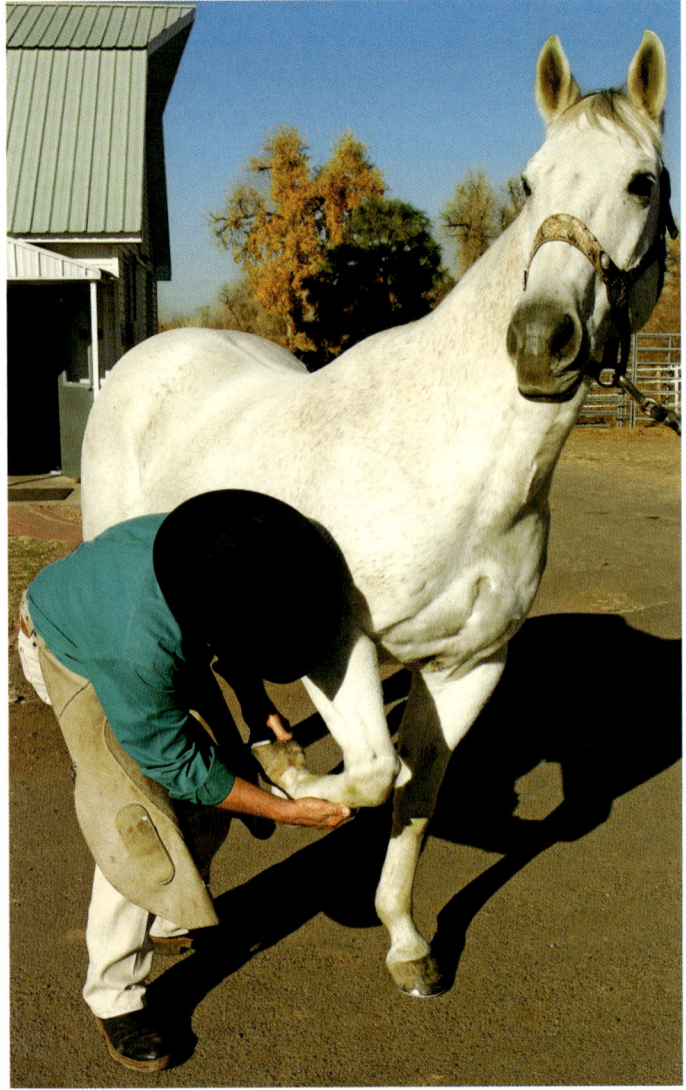

If your horse has an accessory carpal-bone fracture, he experiences pain when your veterinarian flexes the joint.

option to clean and smooth the tissues as with arthroscopic surgery.

If your horse's ligaments or cartilage, but not bones, are injured, your veterinarian might opt to treat your horse with intra-articular medications and rest. However, if ligament injuries are severe, your horse might require arthroscopic evaluation and treatment. Frayed ligament tissue that's only partially disrupted responds positively to surgery and cleaning. Currently there's no treatment for a completely ruptured ligament. Significant cartilage thinning or loss is difficult to reverse. A technique called micro-picking, performed via arthroscopy, can help heal the cartilage.

The healing process: Rest, cold therapy and controlled exercise are important during your horse's initial treatment phases. He needs attention and rest to heal as fast and completely as possible. To aid in healing, your veterinarian might recommend intra-articular injections of high-quality hyaluronate and short-acting cortisone.

Down the road: CDJD in the carpus is usually manageable for performance horses, except when a major fracture or significant ligament or cartilage damage occurs. Intra-articular treatment with IRAP is helpful for many cases. Your horse's condition requires long-term management, but your work and attention can render positive results. You need to evaluate your horse's competition schedule and workload to make sure he has ample rest time between events. Overall, your horse's outcome depends upon the severity of his initial injury, how fast CDJD progresses and the amount of care received. One caveat: If a performance horse completely tears the palmar carpal ligaments, prognosis for recovery is unfavorable.

Accessory Carpal-Bone Fracture

You pull up to your favorite trailhead and begin to unload your mount. As she starts to back down the trailer ramp, she turns her body and steps off the slippery edge. She stumbles, twists and falls. You help her to stand and immediately examine all of her legs. You're heartbroken when you see she's reluctant to put weight on her right front leg. When you feel the back of her knee, you notice an area of pain. She's obviously uncomfortable when you attempt to flex the joint.

veterinarian suspects a chip or spurs, and he also might recommend diagnostic blocking to locate the precise lameness source. Diagnostic blocking helps your veterinarian locate injury to the carpal ligaments, soft structures in the knee that can't be seen with radiographs.

If radiographs and diagnostic blocking show damage to your horse's knee, your veterinarian might opt to investigate the joint more through arthroscopic surgery. Surgery offers diagnostic information, allowing your veterinarian to clearly see what's happened to the joint, as well as a chance to clean the joint and remove any bony fragments or damaged soft tissue that otherwise contributes to the onset of CDJD. An MRI can show your veterinarian exactly what's going on inside the joint. He sees the details within the bones, ligaments and cartilage, but doesn't have the

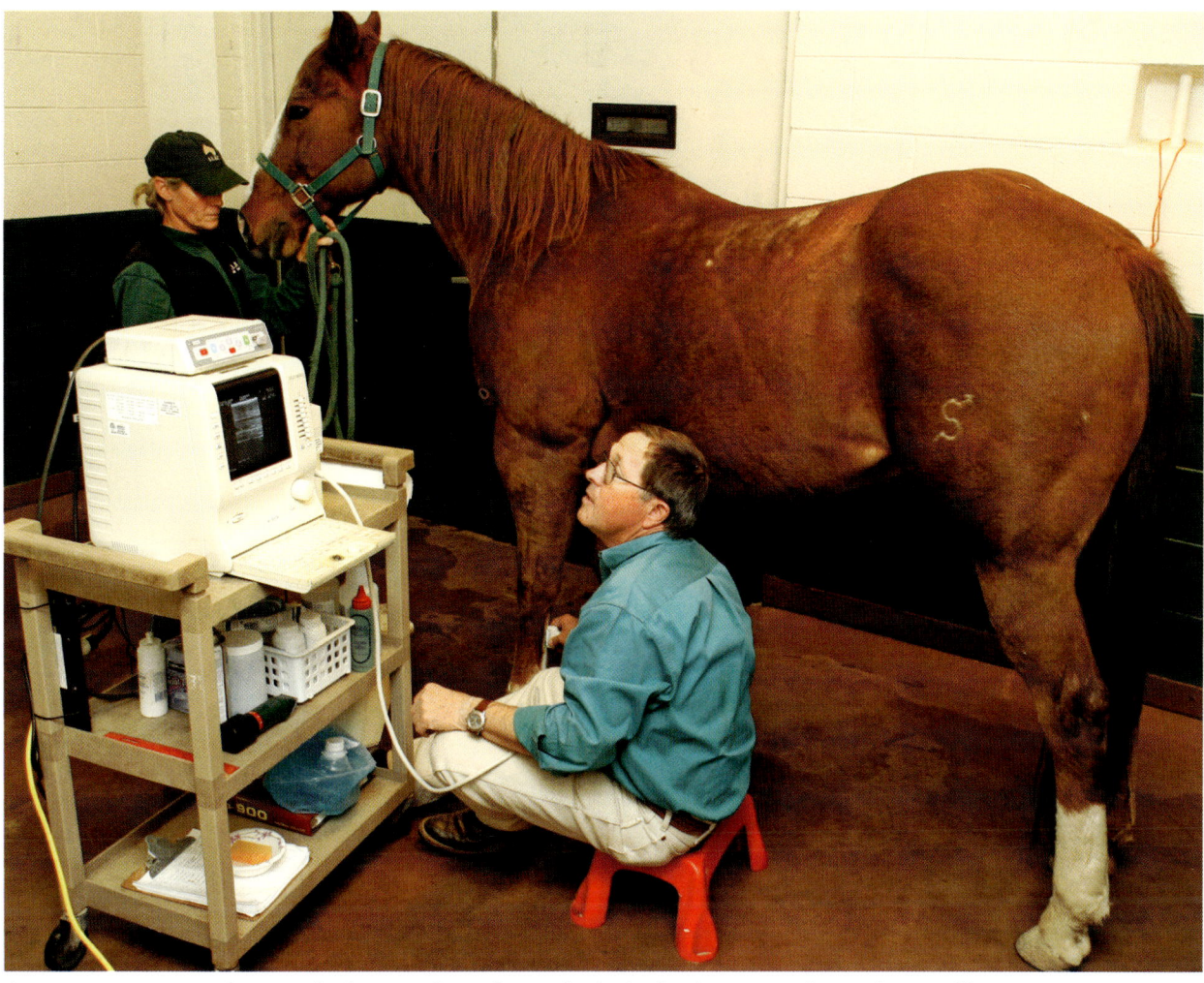

As your veterinarian ultrasounds the carpal canal area, he looks for damage to the tendons and ligaments.

What might be happening: Your horse's accessory carpal bone forms a bump you can feel on the back of the knee. The bones shape the carpal canal, which encases your horse's two flexor tendons as they course down the back of the knee. An accessory carpal bone fracture isn't common, but can occur if your horse if your horse overflexes his leg. The fracture also can occur when your horse falls or steps in a hole and extends his leg in the wrong direction.

What you notice: This injury isn't common, but when it occurs, it can be serious. You see a Grade 2 to Grade 5 lameness as you also notice:

- Immediate lameness.

- Significant pain when your horse flexes his knee.

- Swelling at the back of your horse's knee.

What you do: Call your veterinarian and, while waiting for his arrival, apply cold therapy to the knee.

What your veterinarian does: Your veterinarian looks for accessory carpal bone fracture symptoms, then takes radiographs to identify a fracture. Usual treatment consists of rest, controlled exercise and a large, restrictive support bandage.

If your horse's fracture is severe, he might require internal surgical fixation to make sure that the bones heal correctly. However, the fractured piece must be large enough to accommodate an implanted screw. Your veterinarian also might remove small bone splinters from within the joint capsule during arthroscopy.

The healing process: Your horse needs close attention during his healing process. Secondary degenerative joint disease can be a problem after a horse's initial injury. A horse

107

LAMENESS Q&A

How does cartilage work?

Cartilage is a soft, resilient material that covers bone ends within a joint. Cartilage provides cushioning or shock absorption for the related bone and facilitates bones gliding across each other during motion.

Cartilage has high water content. When weight is placed on a joint during movement, some of the water is squeezed out of the cartilage and onto the cartilage surface to lubricate the friction between the two bones. It's much like putting a wet sponge on a table— it doesn't slide very well until you push down and get a little water out of it to lubricate the surface. Once the water is squeezed out and the weight comes off the cartilage (or sponge), the cartilage regenerates by reabsorbing the water. That process returns water and essential nutrients to the cartilage. The latter function is most important because cartilage doesn't have blood vessels to supply necessary nutrients.

If cartilage is damaged and loses the necessary long chain protein molecules that hold fluid within it, the cartilage can't reabsorb the water as well, and that fuels a progressive degenerative process.

What's the difference between short- and long-acting cortisones?

Short-acting cortisone relieves inflammation and helps maintain cartilage health, but doesn't remain in the joint for a long time period. Long-acting cortisone, on the other hand, initially relieves inflammation, but because it stays in the joint for a long time, can lead to cartilage degeneration. Steroids can have an adverse systemic effect if administered regularly. One negative effect is to suppress the immune system. Before administering local steroids, your veterinarian makes sure your horse doesn't have a fracture. If a bone is fractured, corticosteroid interferes with the physiology of the healing process.

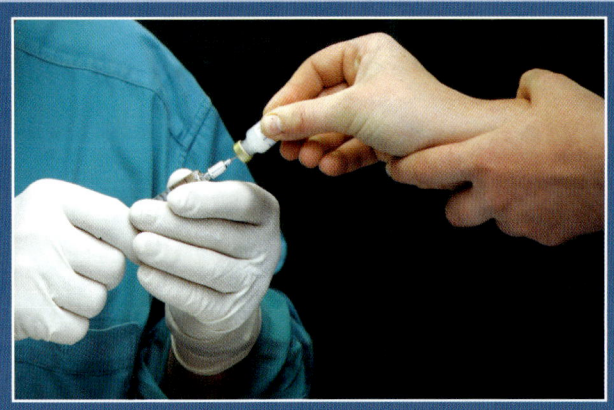

Corticosteroids are powerful anti-inflammatory medications that your veterinarian can inject into your horse's joints. Short-acting corticosteroids protect your horse's cartilage. Long-acting corticosteroids can lead to joint-cartilage degeneration.

also can develop excessive pressure within the carpal canal, which affects the flexor tendons.

Down the road: If your horse shatters his accessory carpal bone, he has an unfavorable prognosis. In most cases, the outlook is guarded at best. The horse might return to some level of performance, but generally can't perform at his previous level. If the fracture heals, you must closely manage your horse's career, monitoring his work intensity and the ground quality where you ride in order to prevent future problems.

Injuries within the Carpal Canal

Your working cow horse has been intermittently "off" for several weeks. One morning, you head out to practice and find him lying down in his stall. When you lead your mount to the crossties, he doesn't want to bear weight on his left front leg. Instead of walking normally, he keeps his affected knee bent and almost "hobbles."

What might be happening: Your horse's superficial and deep flexor tendons are encased in a tendon sheath to keep them lubricated as they pass through the carpal canal at the back of the knee. When the tendons are injured and swell, the swelling places excessive pressure on the nerves and blood vessels that travel through the carpal canal. This pressure develops because the ligament tissues that complete the canal aren't elastic and do not stretch as the tendons swell. Your horse experiences pain when his affected leg is loaded with weight. He feels some relief by lying down and relieving pressure. The scenario is similar to a human's carpal tunnel syndrome.

What you notice: The carpal canal lies at the back of your horse's knee. When the structures that lie within the canal are injured, you see a Grade 2 to Grade 5 lameness as you also notice:

- Extreme lameness when your horse stands after lying down.

- Excessive fluid buildup in the carpal sheath along the backside of the carpus.

- An incompletely weighted leg, with the affected leg buckling forward.

Stall rest and controlled exercise are the most important healing tools after your horse sustains an flexor-tendon injury. Returning to work too quickly could worsen his overall prognosis.

What you do: Call your veterinarian.

What your veterinarian does: Your veterinarian takes radiographs and uses ultrasound images to confirm the diagnosis and quantify the damage level to your horse's tendons. The veterinarian might suggest surgery to relieve pressure on the canal's structures. Anti-inflammatory medication and shock-wave treatment also can be helpful.

The healing process: Forced rest and controlled exercise are very important for a positive recovery. Once the structures heal, your horse can return to work. You must carefully consider the type of job the horse performs to minimize the risk of reinjury.

Down the road: Depending upon the degree of tendon damage, the prognosis can vary from very favorable to very unfavorable.

Extensor-Tendon Injury

At the beginning of the new show season you're excited about your horse's jumping prospects. He's done so well during practice runs. Your countenance changes when your horse hits his knee on a pole as he goes over the first big jump. Your horse doesn't seem to be in great pain, but his right knee is obviously larger than the left. He seems short-strided on the right, and his range of motion is limited.

What might be happening: The extensor tendons crossing the front of your horse's knee are vulnerable to injury, especially if you compete in an event where your horse's knee must bend and "open." For example, when a hunter-jumper horse hits a pole going over a jump, his knee is bent. As the knee bends, the tendons are at the front of the joint and in line to be hit. When these extensor tendons sustain trauma, the tendon sheath surrounding them can fill with fluid. This fluid buildup can cause significant swelling, thereby reducing the range of flexion. If the tendons are severed completely, a rare circumstance, a horse can't extend his leg forward and instead learns to flip it forward in extension.

What you notice: After the initial soreness dissipates, this injury is more mechanical in

109

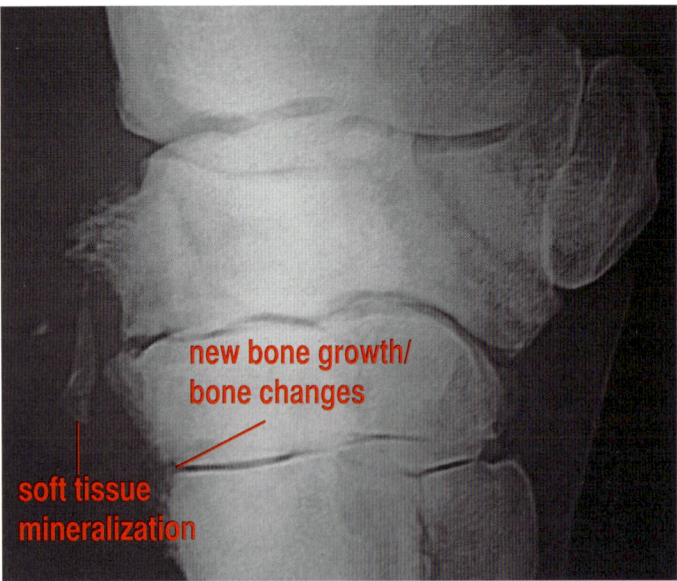

new bone growth/bone changes

soft tissue mineralization

This radiograph shows extensive degenerative joint disease in a horse at the end of his career.

nature than painful. You notice:

- Enlargement at the front of your horse's knee.

- Your horse's decreased range of flexion, with or without pain.

What you do: Immediately begin cold therapy sessions and apply support bandages to the leg, including the knee. If the swelling does not respond within 48 hours, call you veterinarian.

What your veterinarian does: Your veterinarian palpates your horse's joint to evaluate the extent of the damage. Your veterinarian might use ultrasound images to further assess tissue damage and take radiograph images to rule out fractures to the underlying bones. Intra-synovial injections in which medication is injected into the tendon sheath can reduce swelling, allowing your horse's knee to move with greater range of motion. If swelling isn't managed, a significant enlargement can persist, which limits the horse's future range of motion.

The healing process: Your veterinarian rec-

ommends providing your horse with rest, controlled exercise and a restrictive support bandage to help reduce swelling and limit range of motion during the healing process.

Down the road: Consider your horse's range of motion before returning him to a full workload. If your horse can't flex his knee completely, he might risk catching a toe on obstacles and stumbling—leading to another or greater injury. With proper care and rest, your horse's prognosis should be favorable.

Case Study: Knee

A 10-year-old Quarter Horse gelding used for barrel racing at the professional level developed carpitis, or arthritis of the left carpus, following a strain injury. Radiographs showed a small bone chip near the joint surface, and there was extra synovial fluid in the two main carpal joints. The horse's range of motion was reduced, and flexing the carpus increased the lameness. Intra-articular medication dissipated the lameness, and the horse returned to competition. However, six months later the horse was lame again. The veterinarian recommended arthroscopic surgery of the carpus for therapeutic and diagnostic purposes.

Arthroscopic surgery demonstrated damage to the palmar carpal ligament, as well as two chip fractures in the middle carpal joint. The veterinarian removed the two chips and cleaned the frayed ligament area. The horse rested with controlled exercise for five months. The process proved beneficial to the horse's joint function, the inflammation subsided and the cartilage healed. The damaged ligaments were the primary long-term concern, because damaged ligaments can allow some joint looseness, which, with time, results in osteoarthritis.

The owner managed the horse well, using it in selective arenas. The knee received intra-articular medication twice yearly, as well as daily oral joint supplements. This horse competed successfully for the next seven years because of the surgery's success and careful management.

Horseman's Dictionary

carpitis: inflammation of the carpus, or knee.

implant: a screw or plate positioned to hold your horse's bones together for proper healing.

intra-synovial injections: medication injected into the tendon sheath or joint.

knee chip fractures: fragments along the edges of the carpal bone.

micro-picking: a process performed via arthroscopy that can help heal damaged joint cartilage.

palmar carpal ligaments: strong ligaments that aid in motion and provide stability for your horse's knee, whether the structure is bent or straight.

10

THE SHOULDER

Your horse's shoulder, which isn't protected by tack and can't be covered by supportive aids, takes the brunt of the impact when he collides with an object or another horse.

Shoulder lameness often results from improper growth in young horses or an impact injury in any age horse. If your horse hits his shoulder on a barn doorjamb or fence, falls, or is hit by another horse in the pasture or during a performance, he can feel pain in the nerves and muscles surrounding the shoulder. Worse, some shoulder impact results in an obviously catastrophic dislocation and fracture, leaving a horse in pain and with a prognosis much more serious than a typical lameness problem.

In addition to impact injuries, young performance horses can be susceptible to developmental orthopedic disease, or DOD, affecting their shoulders and causing bone and joint problems when cartilage doesn't properly mature to bone. For more about DOD and how it relates to the shoulder, turn to Chapter 16.

Physical Trauma

You and your horse are scheduled to participate in a drill team exhibition before your town's annual rodeo. You participate in the event only once a year, so sometimes your practices are little "rodeos" of their own. During the practice before the exhibition, you canter toward the middle of the arena to the left of your friend and her horse. But your friend's horse isn't listening to cues. She's headed straight at you instead of angling away to follow her planned course. Your friend's horse rams into your horse's shoulder even though you try to turn away and avoid the collision. You ride on toward the arena wall and start to turn your horse. Then you realize he's hurting. He's unbalanced in the turn. You hop down and notice he's having trouble moving his foreleg forward.

Imagine riding toward this drill team horse's exposed right shoulder at top speed. No protective tack guards your horse's shoulder from injury, and what feels like "just a bump" from another horse might cause your horse muscle, nerve or bone damage in his shoulder.

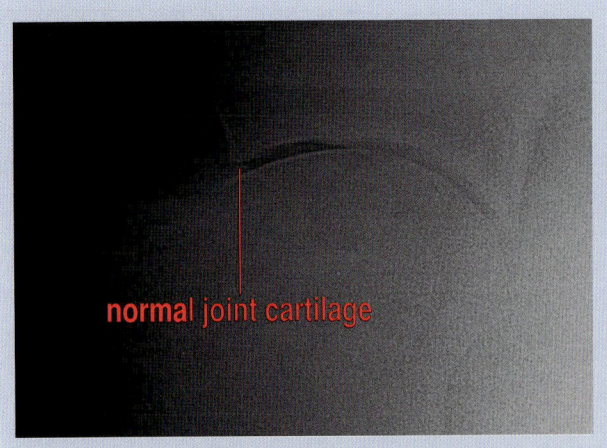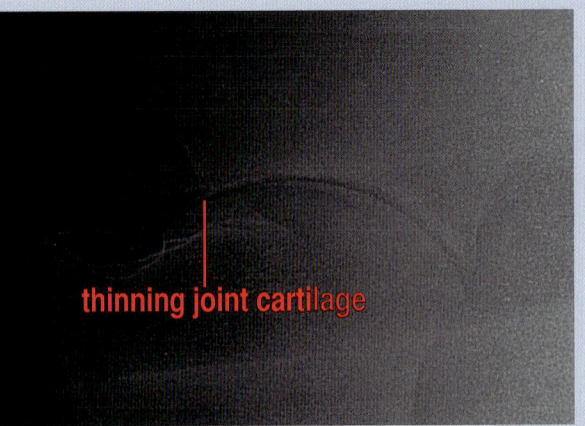

The radiograph at left shows normal joint cartilage thickness, as noted by the thick line between the bones. The radiograph at right shows thinning joint cartilage—a cardinal sign of degenerative joint disease and a possible occurrence after a horse experiences shoulder trauma.

What might be happening: As with any joint in the horse's body, the shoulder is a complex structure combining bones, muscles and nerves in a complex fashion. When the structure receives a blow, many parts of the shoulder can be impacted.

The most prominent, forward portion of the shoulder, the point of the shoulder, reveals the shoulder joint's location. The scapula, or shoulder blade, and humerus bone meet to form this joint. The biceps muscle covers the bones at the point of the shoulder, and a bursa, or fluid-filled sac, lies beneath the biceps. Additionally, the suprascapular nerve runs out and over the scapula's upper edge and provides nerve supply to the major muscles on the scapula's surface.

When a horse hits his shoulder on a doorjamb, gate opening or other solid structure, the injury might be slight or severe, depending upon his speed and angle of impact. The resulting injury might be a simple bruise or could involve significant bone and soft-tissue damage, such as a fracture or severe biceps bursa irritation. In some cases, shoulder-joint osteoarthritis develops as a result of the initial impact.

The suprascapular nerve lies in a vulnerable position along the scapula's upper edge, exposing the nerve to bruising and pinching. The nerve even can become severed from severe trauma, which results in loss of use of the scapular muscles. Once the nerve is severed, the muscles shrink because they're not used. This is referred to as disuse atrophy, and the scapula becomes more prominent, resulting in a visible ridge referred to as "sweeny

shoulder." The sweeny's extent depends on the amount of suprascapular nerve damage.

What you notice: After a horse sustains a shoulder blow, you might see a Grade 2 to Grade 4 lameness as you also notice:

- Apparent labor and pain as your horse attempts to extend his leg forward.

- Swelling and soreness in the shoulder area.

- Greater signs of lameness when his affected leg is on the outside of a circle.

- Muscle atrophy around your horse's shoulder, which he moves in an abnormal way. Atrophy might take several weeks to show up; if you think your horse's shoulder is injured, don't wait for this symptom.

What you do: Call your veterinarian. First-aid treatment should include cold therapy for the shoulder.

What your veterinarian does: Your veterinarian palpates your horse's shoulder, then might take radiographs to evaluate the shoulder bones. Ultrasound images can examine muscle trauma or damage to the shoulder's bursa. In some cases, nuclear scintigraphy can help pinpoint the diagnosis.

Once your veterinarian has a clear picture of your horse's shoulder and the extent of the trauma, he chooses the appropriate treatment. After ruling out a fracture or other serious condition, your veterinarian might recom-

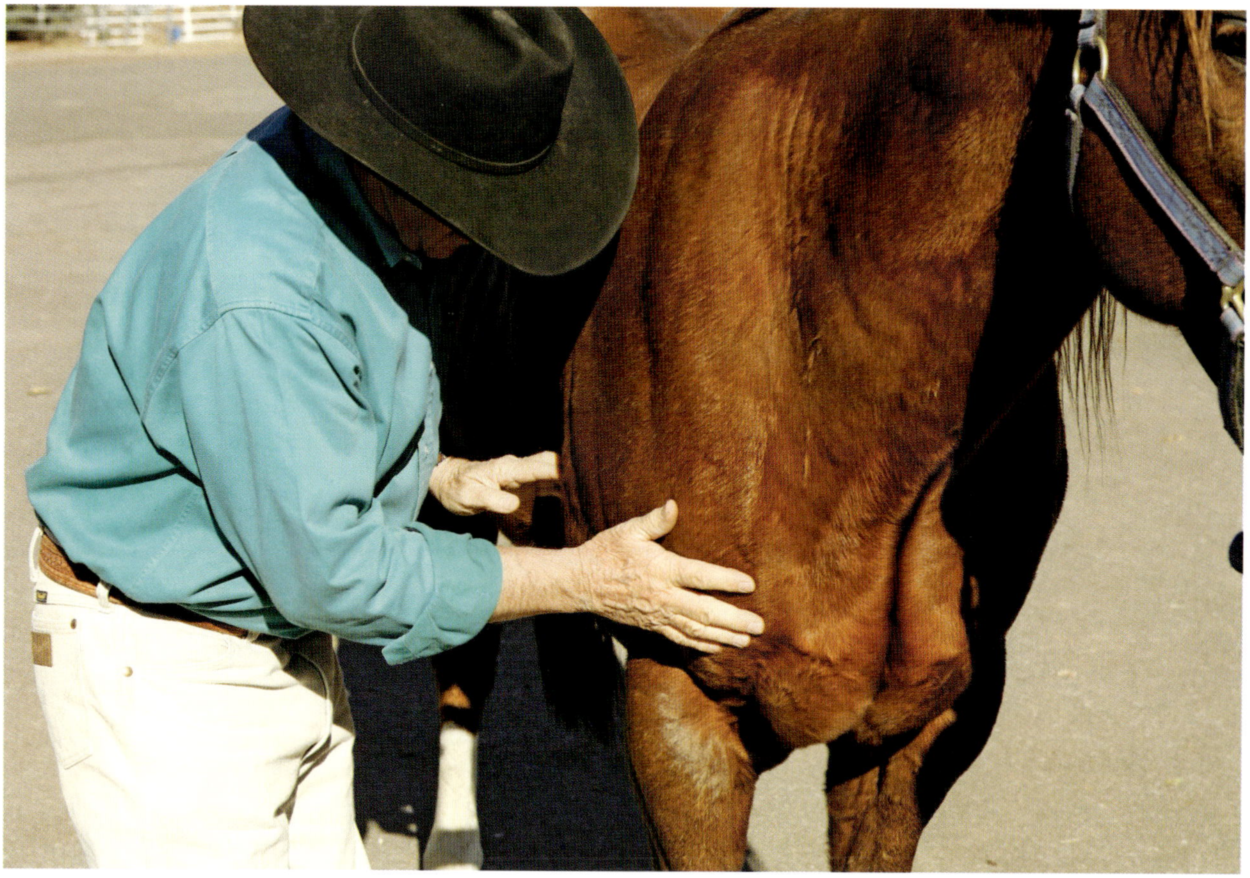

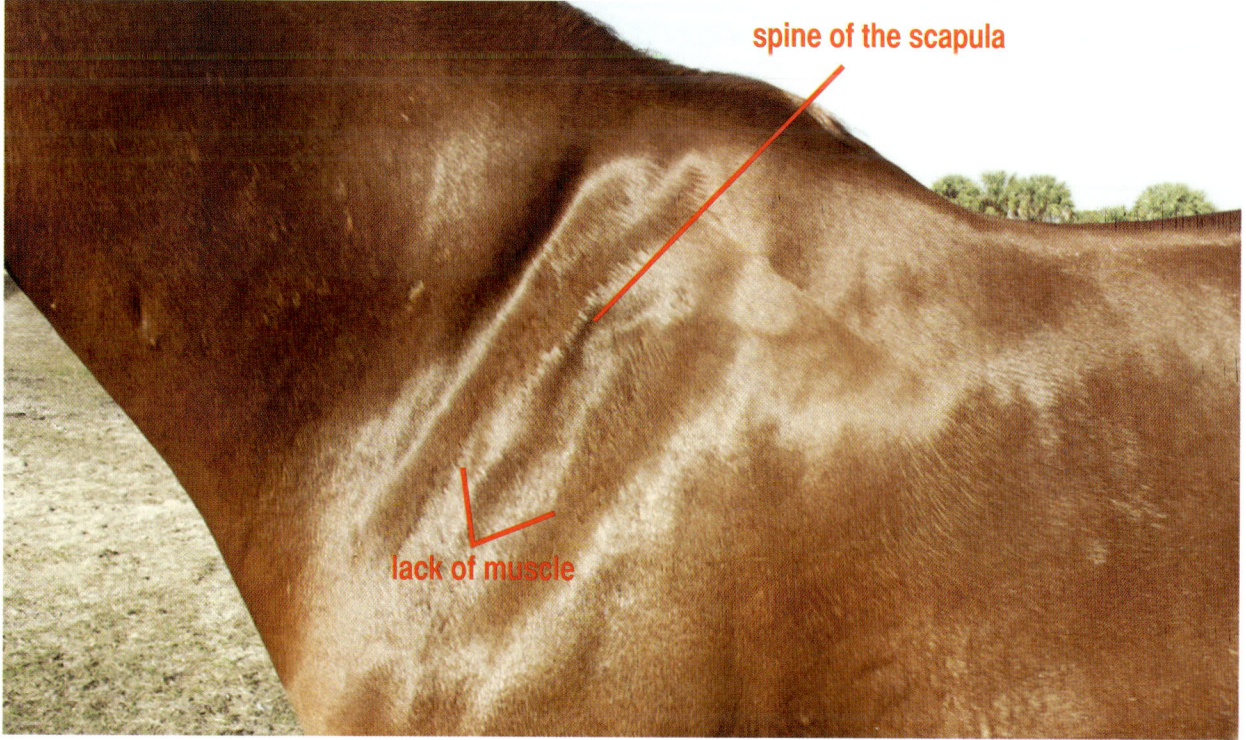

Your veterinarian palpates your horse's shoulder to look for any sign of pain or sensitivity to pressure and looks for symmetrical muscles as he compares both sides of your horse.

spine of the scapula

lack of muscle

When damaged, your horse's suprascapular nerve no longer sends messages to the attached shoulder muscles, and the muscles shrink, resulting in disuse atrophy. This horse has had shoulder trauma and nerve damage, and the concave areas to the left and right of the "spine of the scapula" depict muscle loss.

LAMENESS Q&A

What is muscle atrophy?

Inactive muscle cells shrink or diminish in size, resulting in loss of muscular mass. Muscular inactivity usually results from any chronic pain that causes the horse to avoid or limit the use of the affected muscles. Atrophy also occurs when the nerve that controls the specific muscular activity is damaged, and the proper nerve stimulus is absent.

What is a compensatory injury?

When one leg is injured and has Grade 4 or Grade 5 lameness, the opposite limb must take on a heavier load. Most often, the uninjured limb develops laminitis in the foot because of its increased load. Laminitis (discussed in Chapter 5) can be a serious and life-threatening complication. Young horses with developing support structures, such as joints, bones, ligaments, and tendons, can damage these tissues secondarily while avoiding support on the injured leg.

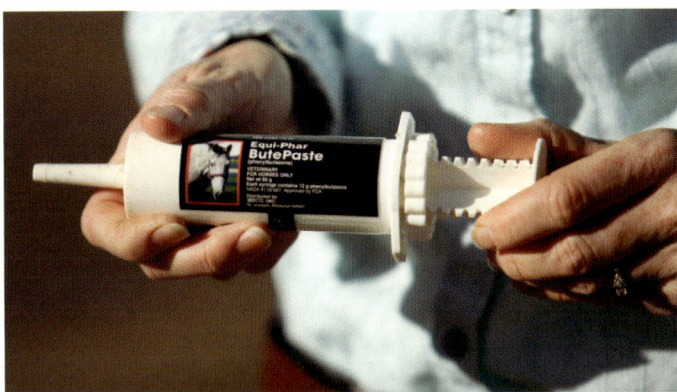

If your horse has axillary nerve damage, providing anti-inflammatory medication, important to his healing process, reduces swelling in and around the nerve, allowing for the return of proper nerve function.

mend rest, controlled exercise, anti-inflammatory medication and/or intra-articular or intrabursal injections to begin the healing process.

If your horse's injury isn't severe, and joint damage is minimal, your veterinarian recommends topical anti-inflammatory medications to reduce inflammation. Light exercise helps preserve the joint's range of motion and muscle tone. Shockwave treatment can help heal bursa and soft-tissue shoulder injuries. Your veterinarian also makes sure you know what to do at home to minimize swelling and limit further injury.

If a sweeny develops, your veterinarian might recommend decompression surgery to remove pressure on the nerves and allow the affected muscles to recover. If the muscle begins receiving nerve signals within

the year after the initial injury, your horse has a good chance at recovering successfully. In some cases, only a small portion of the horse's muscle is affected, and surgery isn't necessary.

The healing process: As with all injuries, the degree or extent of damage affects the success of recovery. If your horse has a severe shoulder injury, he might require extended rest time and a restricted workload for his shoulder to heal. A horse with permanent muscle loss requires a modified workload even after an initial healing time. All healing time depends on which structures are affected and to what degree.

If your horse's shoulder injury prompts secondary joint disease, he might require repetitive intra-articular medication in order to be serviceable or to live comfortably.

Down the road: If your veterinarian doesn't find fractures and your horse's joint suffers minimal or no nerve damage, your horse's prognosis should be favorable. A sweeny prognosis depends on the amount of nerve damage and your horse's response to treatment. Some horses with muscle damage have persistent low-grade lameness, and their shoulder joints move abnormally when viewed from the front. Still, with restricted workloads, these horses can continue to perform and even compete in some cases.

Axillary Nerve Damage

Your horse has just moved into his newly fenced pasture, but you decide to put him in his own run for the day with his usual pasture buddies in the adjacent fenced run. You're not sure if your horse tried to paw at the fence to get to his friends, or if he tried to reach grass on the other side. But somehow, he hung his right front leg over the highest fence board, then tried to pull his leg free. Instead, he pulled his leg sideways as his body moved away from the fence. When you arrive home, he's still caught in the fence. You and a barn buddy free your horse, only to see him stand without being able to put weight on his leg.

What might be happening: Your horse's axillary nerves, which provide functions to the entire front leg, originate from your horse's spinal cord in the area of the shoulder and travel from the spinal column to the front

Horseman's Dictionary

axillary nerves: the nerve bundle providing all nerve function for the forelimb. Originating from the spinal cord in the shoulder area, the axillary nerves travel from the spinal column to the front legs, where the bundle branches into the many nerves of the forelegs.

bursa: synovial-lined sac that provides lubrication for tendons and ligaments as they move over bone prominences.

disuse atrophy: muscle shrinkage due to a lack of use, often a result of regional pain or nerve damage.

point of the shoulder: the most prominent, forward portion of the shoulder visible from the horse's exterior.

scapula: the shoulder blade

sweeny shoulder: disuse muscle atrophy resulting in a visible ridge along the horse's shoulder blade or scapula.

legs. These nerves tolerate a long range of front-leg motion—when the leg moves from front to back—but become damaged if they're dramatically stretched laterally, or sideways. When a horse's leg is pushed or pulled to either side, for example, when he hangs a leg on a fence or is caught in a hole, the nerves can stretch and become temporarily damaged.

What you notice: Though only a temporary problem, you see a Grade 5 lameness as you also notice:

- Your horse can't bear any weight on the affected limb.

- Your horse can't move his affected leg forward.

- Your horse's injured leg can bear weight if manually moved forward by a handler.

What you do: Call your veterinarian to evaluate the damage and rule out a fracture.

What your veterinarian does: Your veterinarian examines your horse's leg and likely takes radiograph and ultrasound images to rule out bone and muscle damage. He might also fix your horse's leg in place with a splint, allowing your horse to support himself during further diagnostics and healing. After your veterinarian has ruled out bone and muscle trauma, he makes sure that your horse gets anti-inflammatory medication, cold therapy and confined rest. Many horses show signs of improvement within days.

The healing process: In most cases, this nerve damage is only a temporary condition, so no further management is required once the nerves heal. It's important to have your veterinarian perform a thorough evaluation of your horse's leg before the horse can safely return to performance work.

Down the road: Despite how serious the injury looks at first, the horse has a favorable prognosis. However, if the nerves are severely damaged or torn, the horse permanently loses use of the affected leg.

Case Study: The Shoulder

A 13-year-old Peruvian Paso gelding used for mountain pleasure riding exhibited swinging-leg lameness in his left front leg. Physical examination of the biceps muscle across the point of the shoulder demonstrated some loss in muscular mass and firmness, and sensitivity to hand pressure. The horse repeatedly showed signs of pain in the same area. Shoulder radiographs didn't show any bone pathology; however, ultrasounding the affected area showed muscle fiber disruption when compared with the unaffected right leg. The surface of the humerus and the bursa appeared normal.

Diagnosis was injury of the biceps muscle. The treatment program consisted of eight weeks of stall confinement with hand-walking. The horse also received three shock-wave treatments to the affected muscle area. After eight weeks, the horse returned to light work for one month and then returned to a regular workload.

11
THE HOCK

Your horse's hock, a complex combination of joints operating in an angled position, must endure significant stress whether he performs competitively or merely runs around your pasture.

The hock is made up of seven bones and numerous ligaments, all working together to keep the uniquely angled structure sound and moving with ease. The joints are under stress every time your horse pushes forward and reaches to take another high-impact step, for example, moving uphill or cantering. Your horse's hocks also are under stress during most any daily play he enjoys in your pasture.

These uniquely angled structures engage so many intricate parts that most any awkward motion can cause pressure to the hock bones, joints and ligaments. If your horse's hock causes lameness issues, it's most likely because of degenerative joint disease, developmental orthopedic disease (see Chapter 16 for more about DOD), or traumatic injuries. Read on to find out how secondary degenerative joint disease and trauma-related injuries can affect your horse and what to do if you see telling symptoms.

Degenerative Hock Joint Disease (Bone Spavin)

Your reining horse always has been a natural stopper that loves to dig into the ground and slides without fear. Lately, however, you've noticed that your horse doesn't slide quite as far or use his hindquarters as actively as usual. In your most recent run, he nickered as he stopped. Your horse wants to obey your cues, but you wonder if he's in pain when he works.

Observe the position of this horse's left hock as he pushes up a steep hill after passing through a creek. The hock must take the load of the horse's hindquarters in this angular position.

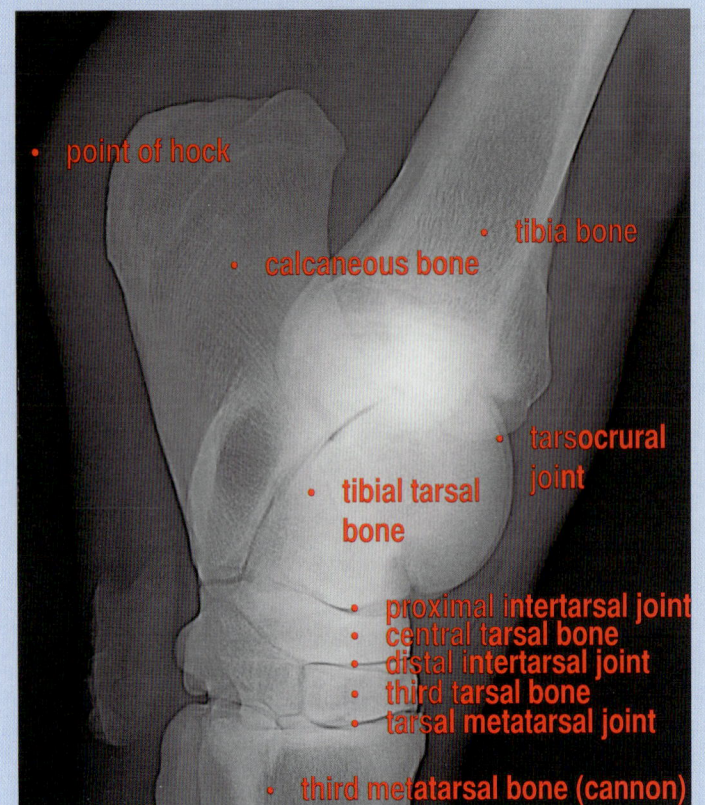

point of hock

tibia bone

calcaneous bone

tarsocrural joint

tibial tarsal bone

proximal intertarsal joint
central tarsal bone
distal intertarsal joint
third tarsal bone
tarsal metatarsal joint

third metatarsal bone (cannon)

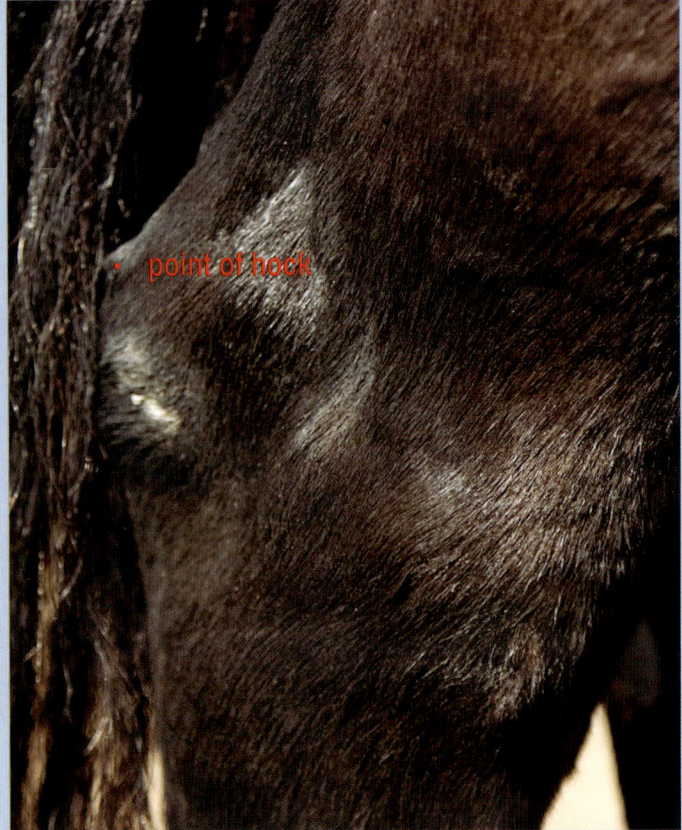

point of hock

The horse's hock, a complicated structure, involves seven bones and four notable joints.

What might be happening: If your horse's performance suddenly declines and he seems to be in pain when stopping or going uphill, he might have degenerative joint disease in the hock, commonly called a bone spavin. This condition affects the lower two hock joints, the distal intertarsal (DIT) and the tarsal metatarsal (TMT) joints. These joints have limited ranges of motion, yet if they develop a degenerative disease, your horse feels pain. The degeneration, commonly called arthritis, can develop from stress associated with work, poor conformation or, in some cases, poor bone quality.

Because a bone spavin develops slowly with time, your horse most likely continues to work and doesn't show signs of lameness until the condition reaches a clinical level. No matter a horse's job, when degenerative joint disease becomes a problem, the horse's performance level declines and causes subtle to significant lameness.

What you notice: You see a Grade 1 to Grade 3 lameness as you also notice:

- A decline in your horse's performance— with or without lameness symptoms. Your barrel-racing horse might run a slightly slower time, or your roping horse might nicker to express discomfort when he stops. Your trail-riding horse might lack drive when traveling uphill.

- Heat or slight swelling in your horse's hocks.

What you do: Consult your veterinarian as soon as you notice a change in your horse's performance. Call your veterinarian if you notice that your horse switches his tail and seems to be in pain during stops or seems to labor with his hindquarters as he pushes uphill on trails.

What your veterinarian does: Your veterinarian visually assesses the hock for swelling within the joint capsule or around the bones and feels for heat in the hock area. A 90-second flexion test frequently, but not always, makes your horse's lameness more pronounced. The affected leg might have a shortened stride and the leg's "push-off" motion might be exaggerated or labored after the flexion test. The veterinarian sees even more change in your horse's gait when the horse accelerates or moves uphill. The veterinarian also might note that your horse's back and croup are sore—back muscle soreness often is a sign of degenerative hock joint disease.

Radiographs usually confirm your veterinarian's joint degeneration diagnosis. However, your horse can show signs of lameness even when radiographs show little or no bone degeneration. In some cases, equine radiographs show dramatic bone change and obvious degeneration, but the horse moves smoothly and without lameness symptoms. Your horse is deemed asymptomatic when radiographs or other diagnostic tools show internal changes and damage without externally visible lameness signs.

Your horse's hock might be part of a larger lameness problem that also affects the foot or stifle. If your veterinarian thinks more than one body part is involved, he recommends diagnostic blocking to find out how much your horse's degenerative hock joint disease is contributing to the overall problem. Blocking also helps your veterinarian determine if your horse's hock is sore or becoming overworked because your horse is compensating for front-leg soreness. In many cases, horses have pain in their hocks when they attempt to avoid navicular pain in their front feet.

The healing process: Your veterinarian begins your horse's degenerative joint disease treatment by reducing inflammation in the hock joints. Anti-inflammatory medications, such as phenylbutazone, might allow your horse to perform at an acceptable level. Keep in mind that phenylbutazone's effects are temporary, but it can be used successfully for individual events. If your horse requires more anti-inflammatory and joint-healing medication, your veterinarian might recommend intravenous injections of sodium hyaluronate, as well as oral administration of pharmacy-grade glucosamine supplements. The treatments can be helpful for many cases, but their effects depend on the amount of joint damage already present. The treatments are most beneficial when your horse is first diagnosed with joint difficulties and help to maintain quality cartilage and joint fluid. Glucosamine supplements can help ward off future joint degeneration and can be given to prevent, as well as to help repair, damaged joints.

If these medications don't provide sufficient results, intra-articular injections of anti-inflammatory medication and sodium hyaluronate can help manage your horse's

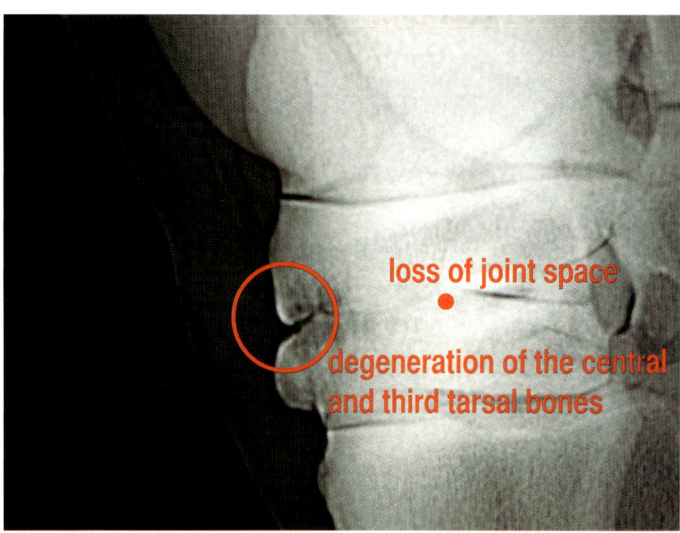

This horse's hock shows bone degeneration, noted by the darkened area of the central and third tarsal bones, and he also has a fused joint, as seen by the lack of joint space in the distal intertarsal joint.

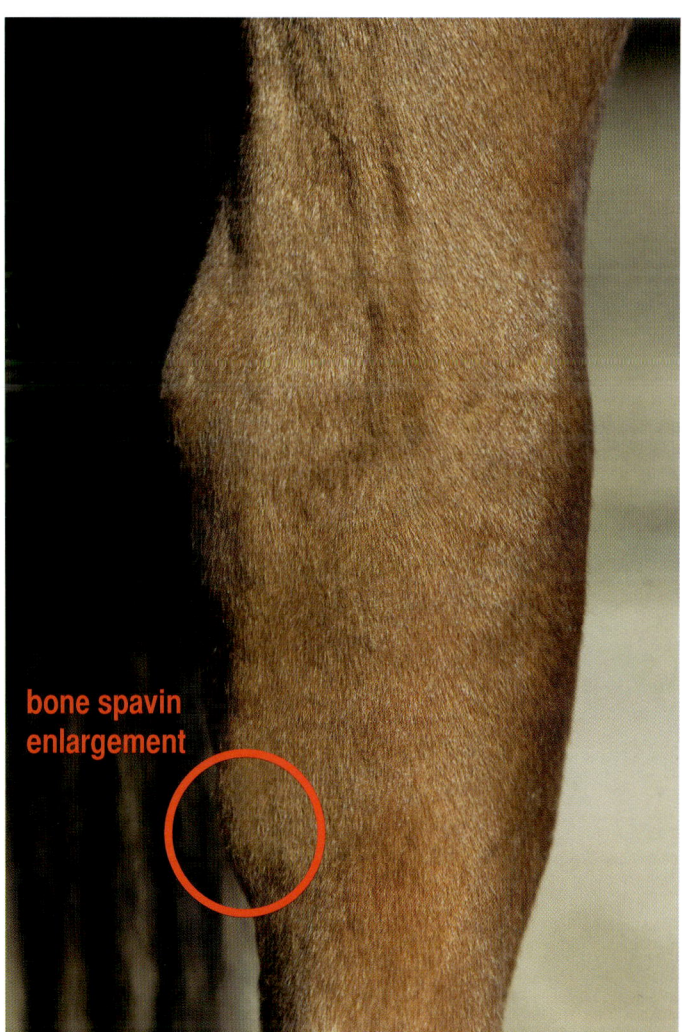

Some horses with bone spavin show a firm enlargement along the lower inside area of the hock. Looking from the front of this horse's hock, you see the enlargement.

joint problems. If your horse requires intra-articular injections, they often need to be repeated annually or semiannually. How often depends on the severity of your horse's joint degeneration, his work schedule and the workload. Shockwave treatments are a therapeutic alternative to intra-articular injections for refractory cases, which are more resistant to treatment.

If your horse's hock pain isn't managed easily with injections and supplements, your veterinarian can recommend cunean tenectomy surgery. During this surgery, your veterinarian removes a small section of the cunean tendon, which exerts a rotational pull on the hock and puts pressure on the lower joints. The surgery offers a significant success rate for managing degenerative hock joint disease. Veterinarians believe that the procedure eliminates the excess pressure without altering the leg's function.

If your horse's hock degeneration continues, the bones that make up the hock joints begin to fuse together. In most cases, the distal intertarsal joint closes, or fuses. With continued pathology, your horse's third tarsal bone fuses to the cannon bone, which closes the tarsal metatarsal joint. Fusion eliminates motion within the respective joint, and this actually minimizes pain and alleviates lameness unless the hock undergoes a more severe degenerative process, which is discussed later. The fusion process is unpredictable, and often it's a matter of if the joints fuse rather than when they do.

Three distinct veterinary procedures can be used to manually fuse the joints: instigating the process with a series of small holes drilled across the joints, by invading the joint with a medical laser beam or with chemical intra-articular injections. If your veterinarian believes that your horse suffers

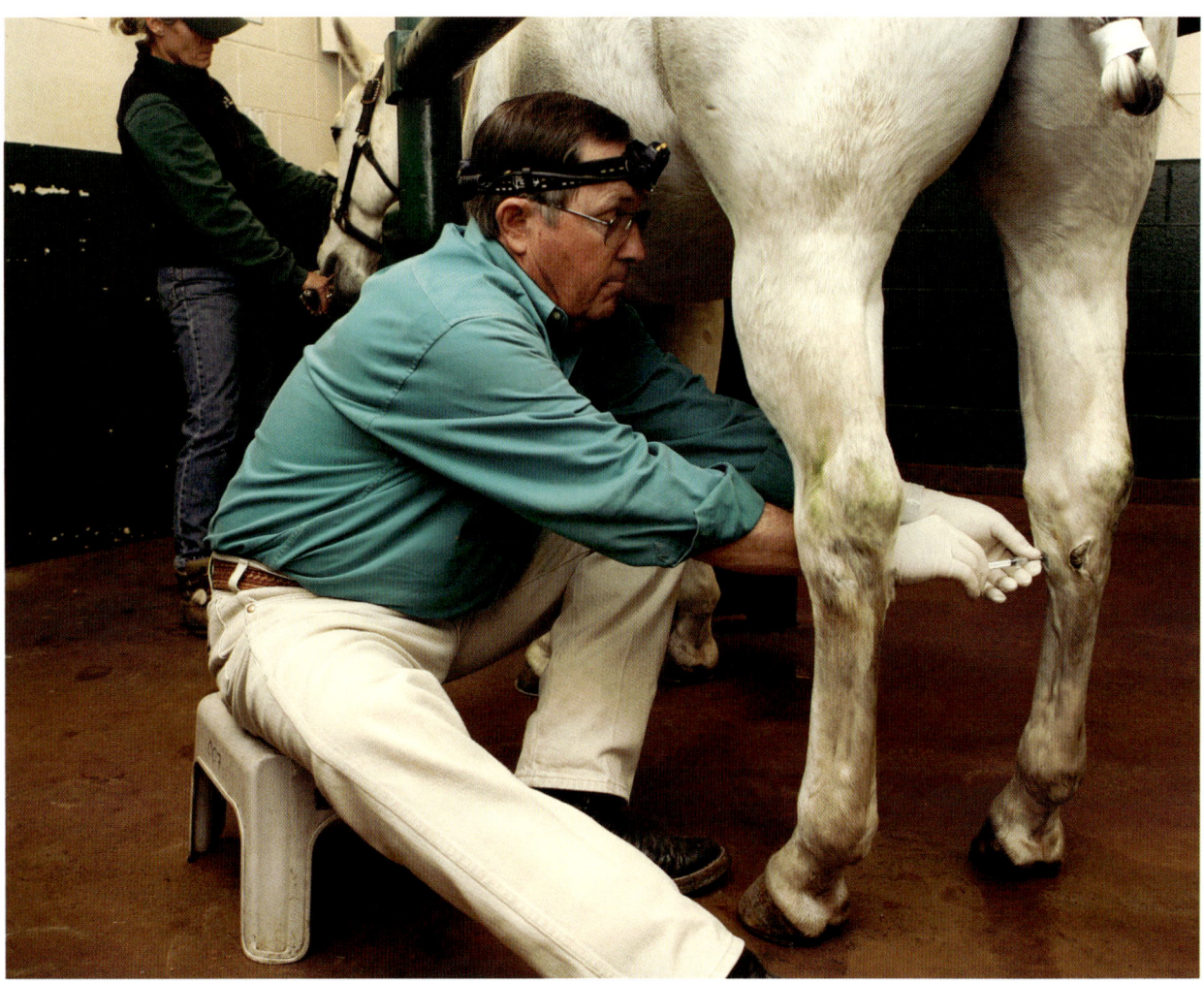

If your horse's hocks require constant anti-inflammatory and joint-healing medication to keep him in top performance form, your veterinarian might recommend intra-articular sodium hyaluronate and short-acting cortisone injections, commonly referred to as hock injections.

LAMENESS Q&A

Are there any complications associated with hock injections?

In the rare instance that complications arise with injections, three scenarios exist.

The most serious is the introduction of infectious material, or bacteria, into the joint. The horse's career and even his life might be threatened by this complication. The hock joint, like others, is a very hospitable environment for bacteria once they're introduced into the joint. This complication rarely develops if the injections are done in a clean environment using sterile surgical techniques and when the owner follows the veterinarian's after-care guidelines.

Second, the horse might have an adverse reaction to the injected medication. Following the injections, keep a close eye on the horse. Watch for abnormal swelling, heat and lameness. Call your veterinarian immediately if these symptoms arise.

Finally, the needle can lacerate a blood vessel within the joint capsule and cause hemorrhaging into the joint. Again, there's some heat and swelling in the joint.

It's important to be alert and recognize these conditions if they occur. Don't hesitate to call your veterinarian if there are any concerns after the horse has a joint injection. If there is an intra-articular infection, it's important to begin aggressive antibiotic therapy both intra-articularly and systemically. The second two conditions respond favorably to cold therapy and systemic anti-inflammatory medications.

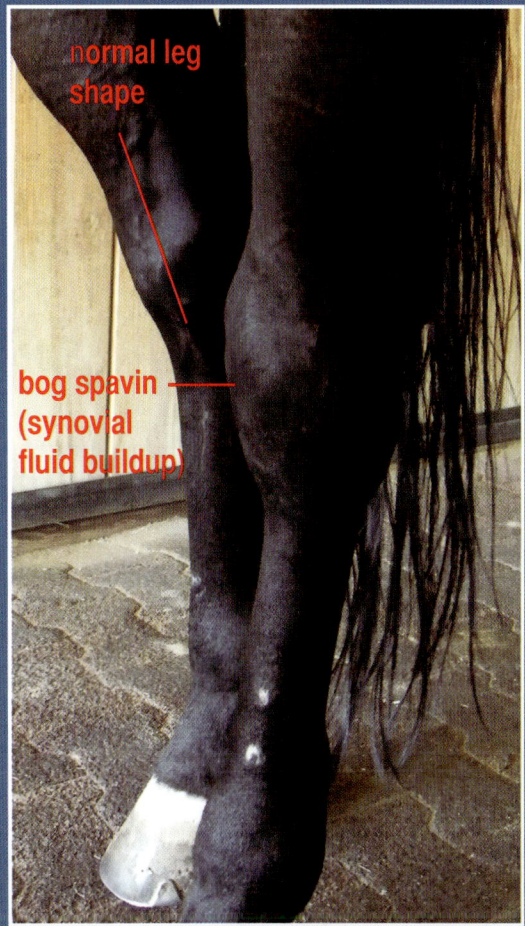

The swelling and change of shape in the front of this horse's left hock, as compared to the horse's opposite leg, is a result of synovial fluid buildup.

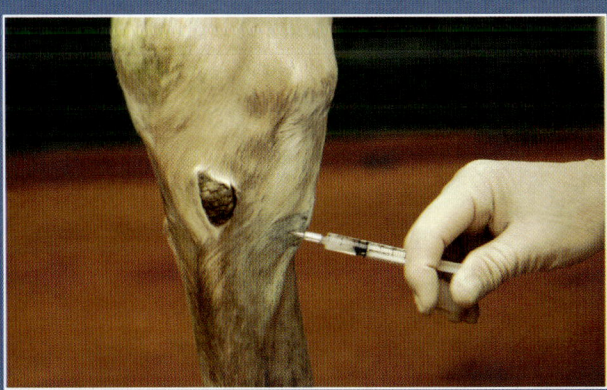

For safe hock injections, the veterinarian works in a clean environment and wears sterile gloves while providing intra-articular medication to a horse's distal intertarsal joint.

What is a bog spavin?

Bog spavin refers to a significant increase in the amount of synovial fluid found in the hock's top joint, the tarsocrural joint. Bog spavin is noticed as a large, fluid-filled pouch that's found on the front of the hock at its inside corner. When pressure is applied to the area, the fluid can be displaced into other pouches within the joint. A bog spavin develops in association with trauma to the tarsocrural joint or in some cases of developmental orthopedic disease (DOD).

How often can a horse's hocks be injected with corticosteroids, and for what portion of his career?

The hocks might be injected intra-articularly two or three times annually, depending on the horse's career, degree of pathology and length of his competitive season. Many horses require injections only once yearly. Assuming the joints are injected with high-quality medications, injections can be used to manage degenerative joint disease for a lengthy career. Each horse is different, and treatment schedules depend on the amount of pathology, the associated pain and the horse's occupation.

What role does conformation play in hock problems?

Use trauma is more detrimental in a sickle-hocked or cow-hocked horse. When viewed from the side, the sickle-hocked horse's cannon bone extends forward under the hock, rather than going straight to the ground. A cow-hocked horse, when viewed from behind, reveals hocks that are closer together than the fetlocks.

The negative effects of sickle-hocked conformation are less if the excess curvature originates in the upper hock joint, where the tibia meets the hock, rather than when excessive angulation occurs in the hock's body or lower joints.

Cow-hocked conformation always is a concern. Because the hock normally functions in an angular plane, the additional stress placed on the ligaments and joint surfaces due to this abnormal conformation predisposes a horse to degenerative joint disease.

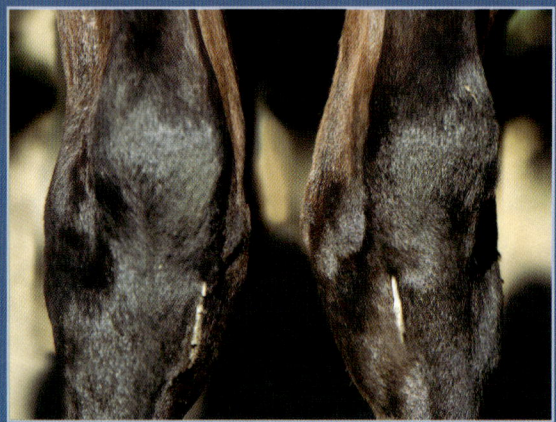

A cow-hocked horse's hocks are closer together than his fetlocks.

This horse shows a tendency toward sickle-hocked conformation.

What is bone spavin?

Bone spavin, a lay term, refers to degenerative joint disease or osteoarthritis that affects the hock's lower joints.

What's a curb?

Most common in racehorses, a curb involves injury to the hock joint's lower, backside or plantar ligaments. A curb appears as a bulging area on the hock's backside, below the point of the hock, when viewed from the side. A curb can require three to four months' rest and is managed with controlled exercise, anti-inflammatory medication and shockwave treatment. It's not a common problem for a performance horse, and can develop from local trauma, as well as stress.

less if the hock joints fuse, he can recommend that the joints be manually fused. Drilling involves a series of small holes placed across a small portion of the distal intertarsal and tarsal metatarsal joints to speed the natural fusion process. For the procedure, your horse is under general anesthesia, and after the drilling, the joints fuse in six to 12 months. Laser treatments across the joint surfaces also can complete the fusion process, again under general anesthesia. Chemical fusion introduces caustic medication into the appropriate hock joint and causes fusion, sometimes very quickly. However, chemical fusion introduces some concern as the chemical medication inadvertently can migrate into your horse's other joints and cause unwanted damage.

Treatments for degenerative joint disease of the hock usually don't cure the problem unless you catch the disease in the very early stages. Your horse always requires management. Pay attention to subtle performance changes that indicate that your horse might be in pain once again. Carefully evaluate your horse's work and performance schedule to properly time intra-articular and systemic injections. This condition isn't difficult to manage, and most horses have successful and rewarding careers.

Down the road: As discussed above, most horses have favorable prognoses. Note, however, that degenerative joint disease in the upper two hock joints—the tarsocrural and proximal intertarsal joints—have less favorable prognoses as compared with the lower two hock joints, the distal intertarsal and tarsal metatarsal joints. This is primarily because these two joints have different and more involved functions, and their joint capsules always communicate with each other.

Traumatic Hock Injury

You join your local riding club for a fall trail ride. As your group heads down a hill toward a water crossing, there's a bit of a traffic jam. A horse to your left spooks, spins out of control and bucks. His back hoof lands on your horse's back leg. You walk your horse away immediately and dismount. As you feel your horse's hock, you feel the instant swelling and tenderness.

What might be happening: When your horse receives a kick to his hock or moves in a way that causes a sprain or strain to his hock joints and ligaments, the pain can be acute and point to serious injury. Most hock trauma involves damage to the ligaments or the joint capsules. Some injuries cause avulsions, which means pieces of bone pull free at the ligament attachment site after the ligament encounters excessive stress. One of your horse's tarsal bones also can fracture and cause significant pain and lameness.

What you notice: Traumatic hock injuries can occur when a horse catches a leg in a panel or stall door, or is kicked by another horse. After a specific incident, you see a Grade 2 to Grade 4 lameness as you also notice:

- General swelling around an injured hock with heat surrounding the area.

- A bog spavin, or excessive fluid in the tarsocrural joint, which appears like a sudden soft, round bump on the inside front corner of the hock.

- Apparent lameness, especially on your horse's inside hind leg when he trots in a circle.

What you do: If you see an accident happen, examine your horse's hocks for signs of bog spavin, swelling and heat. Look closely for any drainage from wounds around the joint, which could indicate that trauma has opened the joint capsule. Lead your horse to watch his gaits; then contact your veterinarian if you see any signs of lameness.

What your veterinarian does: Your veterinarian palpates your horse's hock and evaluates the involved structures, including ligaments, tendons and joint capsules. He also looks for puncture wounds and takes radiographs to identify fractures and existing signs of joint disease. Imagery provided by an ultrasound examination demonstrates collateral ligament injury and insults within the joint capsule. In some cases, your veterinarian also collects and evaluates joint fluid to rule out infection.

Once your veterinarian discovers how the hock has been affected, he recommends cold-water therapy and gives your horse anti-inflammatory medications to reduce hemorrhaging and inflammation. Stall rest and controlled exercise allow the healing process to begin and play a major role during your horse's entire healing process. Your veterinarian also might apply a support bandage to help control swelling, support the area's vascular supply and protect any wounds. Bandaging a horse's hock takes special attention and training. Systemic antibiotics will be administered if there is a possibility of infection.

A horse with a collateral ligament rupture might require surgery to remove avulsion bone fragments, pieces of bone disrupted when the ligament pulls away from the bone. During recovery, the horse's leg is supported with a full-length cast to prevent the hock from dislocating. Intra-articular medication and shockwave therapy are important adjuncts to the therapy regimen, depending upon the structures damaged.

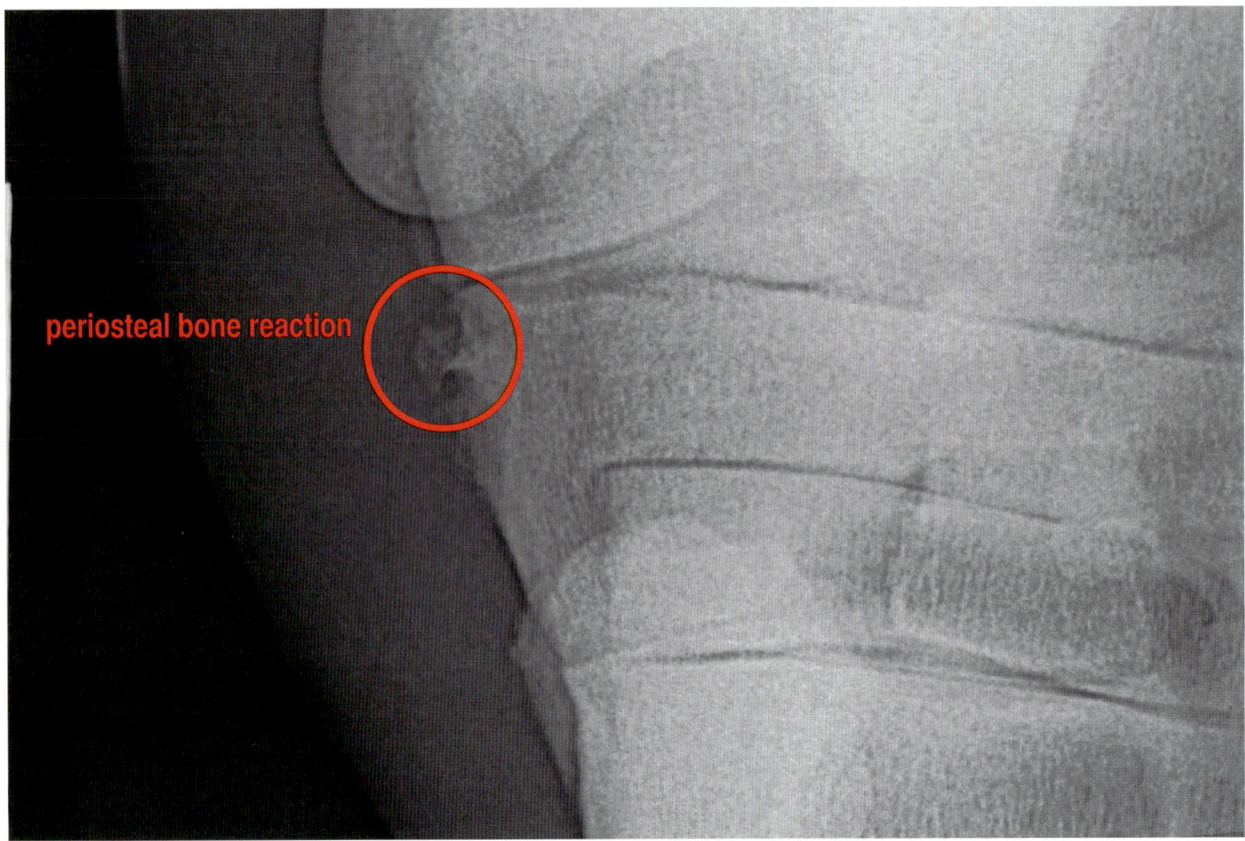

periosteal bone reaction

After this horse experienced traumatic injury to his hock's tarsocrural joint, new periosteal bone growth formed where the ligament had torn away from the bone.

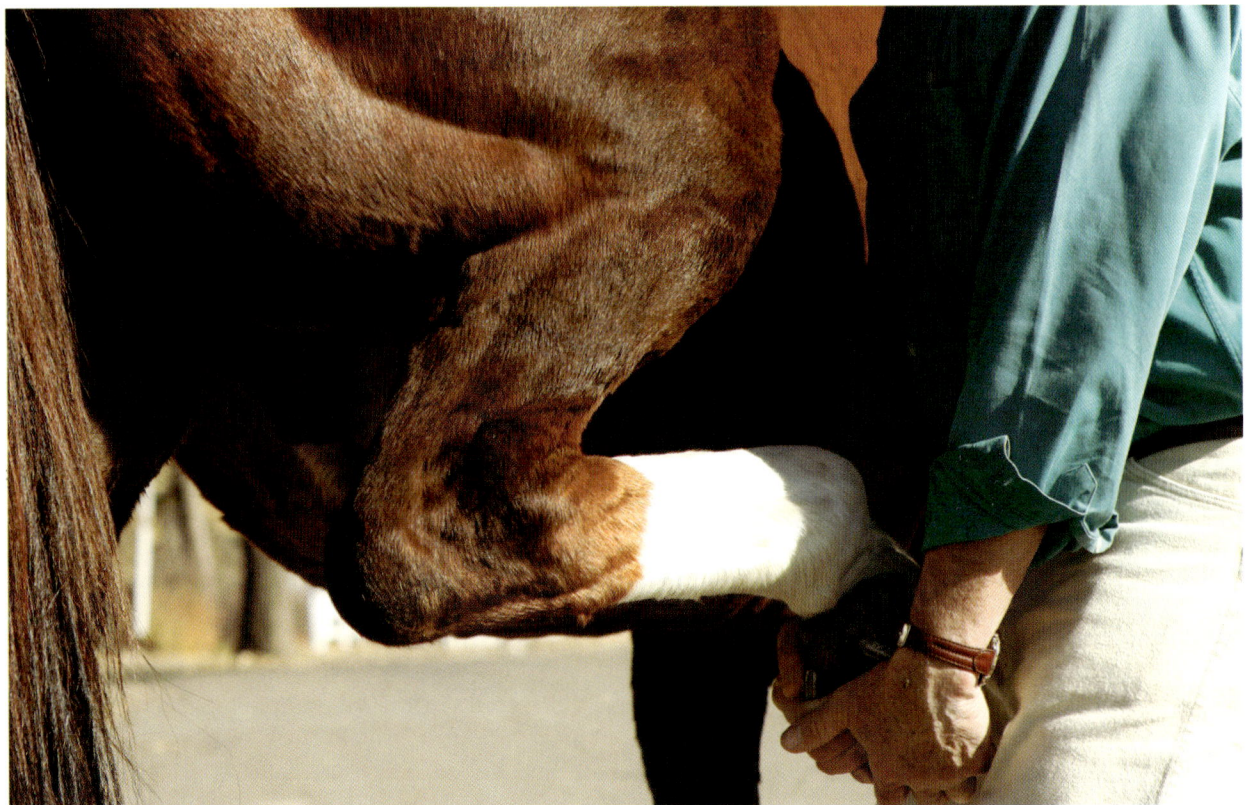

As part of the diagnostic procedures for hock lameness, your veterinarian performs a timed hock flexion test, which puts stress on the hock joint and temporarily enhances hock lameness.

The healing process: With any hock injury, rehabilitation is affected by and based on the injury's severity and status. Your horse requires some kind of activity to maintain his hock joint's range of motion. When a human rehabilitates from a similar injury, he can lie in bed and use a machine to maintain the injured leg's range of motion. A horse, however, must support all his body weight during the healing process, making it a much more strenuous process. Your veterinarian can offer specific exercise guidelines suitable to your horse's condition. The healing process might require several months or last as long as a year. It's important to give the horse an opportunity to heal if your veterinarian foresees a reasonable prognosis.

Down the road: Once a horse recovers, his future use depends on the extent of the original injury and the level of recovery attained. Your veterinarian might recommend regular intra-articular medication for long-term management. Assuming proper management, your horse should recover from most hock injuries. Keep in mind that serious degenerative joint disease can develop or worsen following a traumatic injury. It's important to continue an equine health management program with your veterinarian once your horse returns to work.

Stringhalt

Since you're expecting your first child this winter, you decide to board your horse at a friend's place for a few months—just to lighten your load. Her horses have done well grazing in the pasture throughout the summer. Soon after your horse moves to his new location, your friend calls to report that one of his back legs seems to be moving "strangely." You ask her to keep an eye on him. She calls back again to report he's now walking like a cartoon character. His hind hoof swings up and almost touches his abdomen when he walks. It's peculiar, she reports, that he seems to trot normally. You call your veterinarian right away.

What you notice: You see your horse walk with a leg-jerking stride. Stringhalt can result from a tendon injury and also can have a neurological or nerve component.

If your horse has stringhalt, he might have nerve damage within the connections between his leg and spine. As he moves forward at the walk, his hind leg sweeps forward, then jerks abnormally toward his abdomen—with the fetlock almost touching his belly. His hock flexes with exaggerated movement and rapidly pulls his leg from the ground. As he moves into a trot or lope, his gait becomes more normal. The abnormal movement isn't always present in each stride and often dissipates as he continues working. In severe stringhalt cases, the strange movement is seen in every step. Some rare cases involve both hind legs.

Stringhalt affects all breeds and horses of all ages. The problem is often associated with nerve degeneration, but the exact cause is unknown at this time. The degeneration might be linked to horses ingesting plants in specific pastures. Dandelions, sweet peas or flatweed—all plants that can contain nerve-damaging compounds—have been suspected. An injury to the lateral digital extensor tendon in the hock area also can cause stringhalt.

What you do: If the condition doesn't significantly hinder the horse's performance, stringhalt can go untreated. However, the longer your horse shows signs of the disease, the poorer his prognosis. If your horse's movements become pronounced and affect your horse's work and performance, consult the veterinarian.

What your veterinarian does: Therapy involves removing the lateral digital extensor tendon, which runs across the outside of the hock. The loss of this lateral tendon doesn't play a role in the horse's usability because it works in unison with the long digital extensor tendon. The surgery is 70 to 80 percent effective and requires a 30-day recovery period. Following this surgical procedure, your horse's surgery site must completely heal before he returns to work. Anti-inflammatory medication and a short period of antibiotics complement the healing process.

The healing process: Some horses continue to demonstrate stringhalt even after surgery, which indicates that the condition has a neurological component. If the horse can perform after healing from surgery, it's reasonable to continue work. Your veterinarian recommends a reduced workload during the healing process.

127

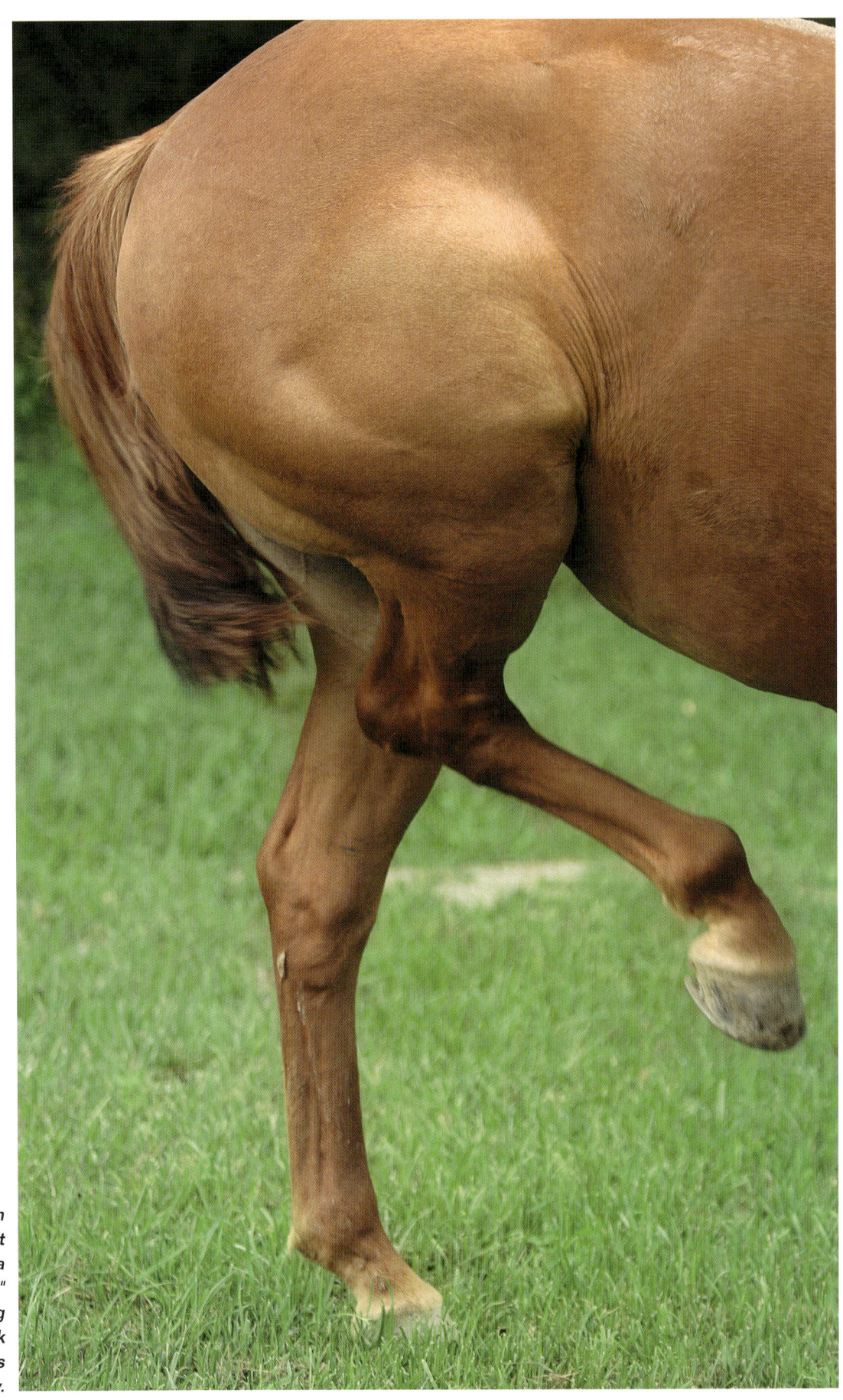

A horse with stringhalt walks with a "goose step," moving his fetlock toward his belly.

Horseman's Dictionary

asymptomatic: when radiographs or other diagnostic tools show internal changes and damage without externally visible signs of lameness.

avulsions: pieces of bone that pull free from the parent bone at the site of ligament attachments, usually as a result of excessive stress on the ligament.

bog spavin: excessive fluid in the tarsocrural joint, often noticed as a large, fluid-filled pouch that's found on the front of the hock at its inside corner.

bone spavin: a lay term that refers to degenerative joint disease or osteoarthritis that affects the hocks' lower joints, distal intertarsal and tarsal metatarsal joints.

cow-hocked: a conformation error; when viewing a horse from behind, the hocks are closer together than the fetlocks.

cunean tendon: the tendon that exerts rotational pull on the hock and puts pressure on the lower joints. In cunean tenectomy surgery, part of the cunean tendon is removed to help horses that suffer from degenerative hock joint disease.

curb: common in racehorses, an injury to the hock joint's lower, backside or plantar ligaments; viewed from the side, appears as a bulging area on the backside of the hock, below the point of the hock; can require three to four months' rest and is managed with controlled exercise, anti-inflammatory medication and shockwave treatment.

distal intertarsal joint: the lower of the two intertarsal joints; can close or fuse with advanced joint disease.

proximal intertarsal joint: the upper of the two intertarsal joints, which seldom close or fuse.

sickle-hocked: a conformation error; viewed from the side, a horse's cannon bone extends forward ahead of the hock rather than going straight to the ground.

tarsal metatarsal joint: the lowest joint in the hock, found between the hock and cannon bone; frequently associated with degenerative joint disease of the hock.

tarsocrural joint: the joint between the tibia and the upper section of the hock.

Down the road: If your horse's severe stringhalt is treated soon after the disease's onset, his prognosis should be favorable. Horses with mild stringhalt cases can continue to work without treatment, but should be closely monitored for worsening of signs.

Case Study: Hock

A show horse became cast in his stall and caught his leg in open bars at the top of the wall panel. The horse's hock sustained serious collateral ligament trauma and required extensive treatment. The horse was confined in a stall and hand-walked for a few minutes each day. The horse received daily anti-inflammatory medication for a period of time, oral glucosamine supplements, periodic intra-articular injections and shockwave treatment. It took a year for the horse to completely recover, and he's now back on the show circuit. However, pre-existing degenerative joint disease was worsened by the injury. The horse requires annual intra-articular medication in the lower hock joints for general maintenance.

129

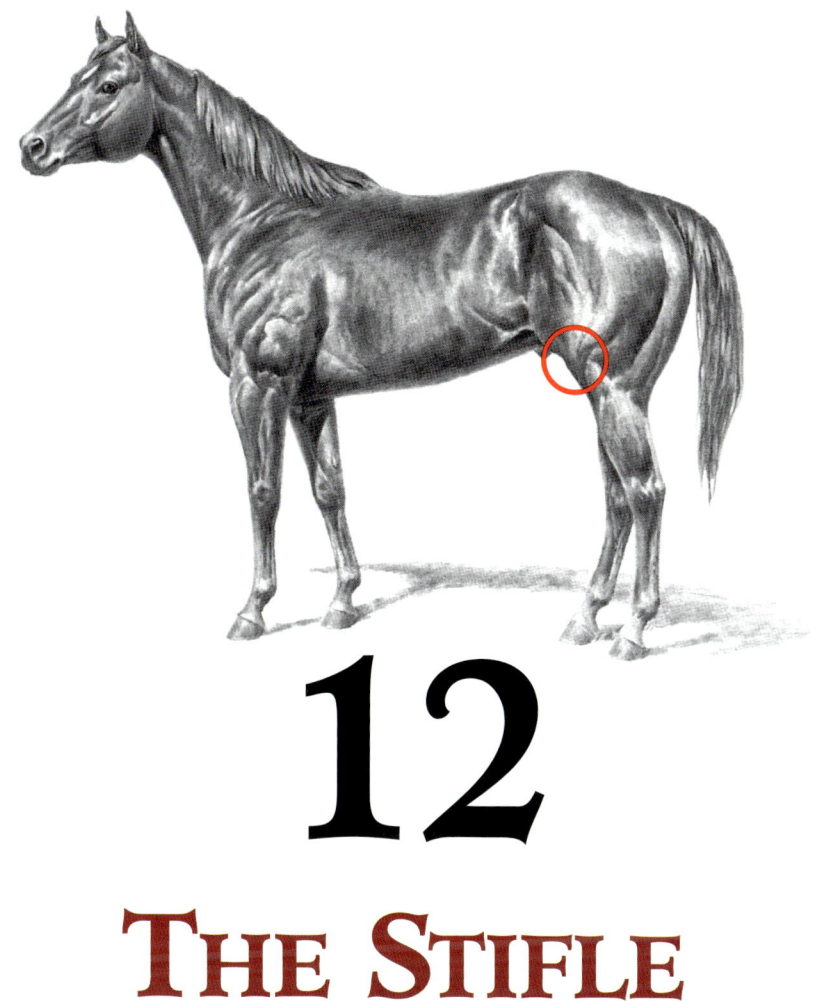

12

THE STIFLE

The equine stifle, which compares to the human knee joint, plays a key role in all hind-leg movement and weight-bearing activities.

The equine stifle compares to the human knee joint. The stifle includes 14 ligaments and three joint compartments: the patella (knee-cap), medial (inner) weight-bearing and lateral (outer) weight-bearing compartments. Two meniscal cartilages help the tibia and femur fit together, serving much the same function as the menisci in the human knee.

The stifle plays a key role in all hind-leg movement and weight-bearing activities. Stifle lameness generally stems from one of three conditions: delayed patellar release, a mechanical complication; stifle trauma, evident after a specific incident and resulting in degenerative joint disease; and developmental orthopedic disease, which is discussed in Chapter 16.

Delayed Patellar Release

You thought it was the footing. Maybe your horse kept slipping because weeds had grown in the arena. But you just trailered to your friend's freshly groomed facility, and you feel the same thing. When you ride at a trot, your horse stumbles with his left hind leg; it feels like his leg totally gives way. He immediately catches himself each time and trots on normally— without missing another step. Then your friend says that at the canter your horse looks heavy on his forehand. He also has trouble maintaining the correct lead with his hind end and cross-fires. It's almost impossible to keep him in a collected frame.

What might be happening: When a healthy horse canters, his hind leg fully extends as it reaches out

Your horse's stifle is active when he stands still, but especially active as he propels himself forward or through a turn, as shown here, while in a flexed position to support himself.

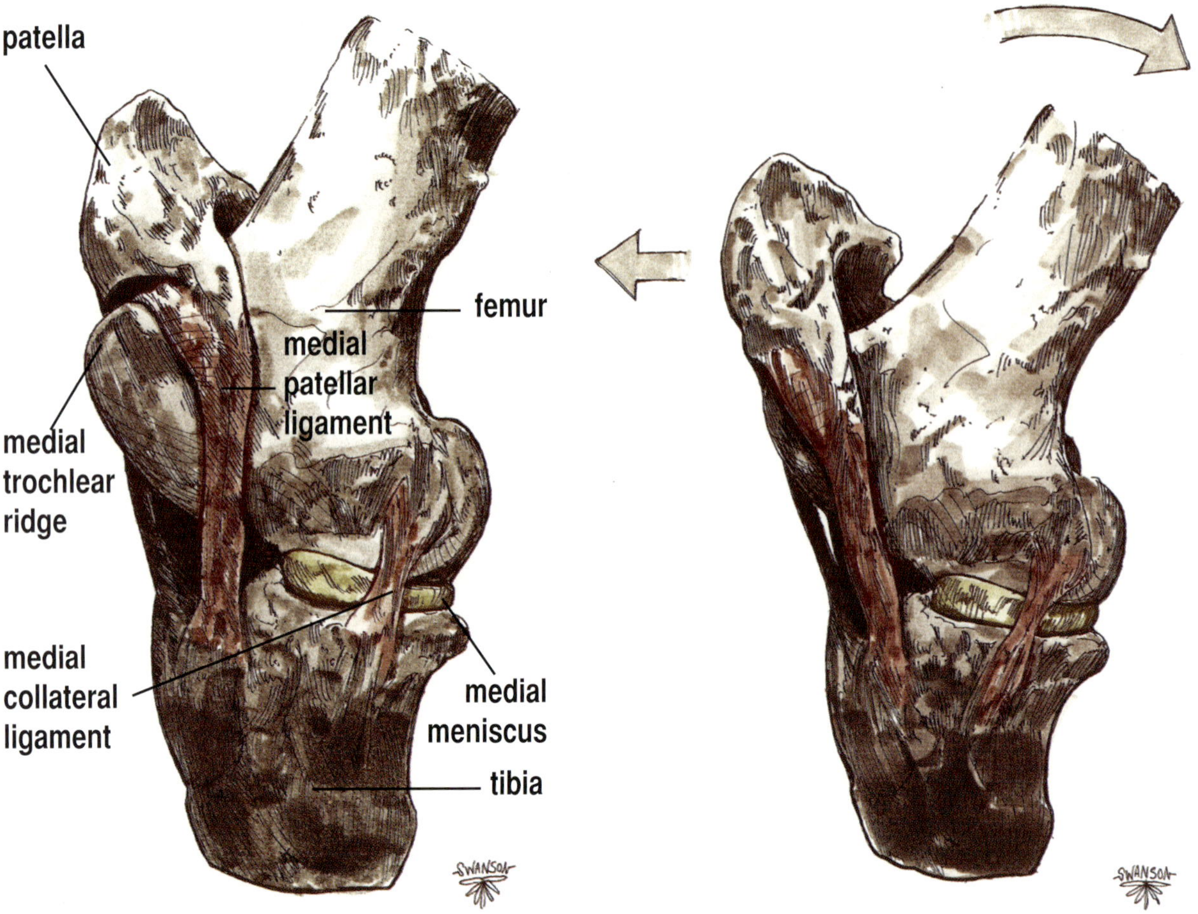

patella

femur

medial
patellar
ligament

medial
trochlear
ridge

medial
collateral
ligament

medial
meniscus

tibia

The left view shows a horse's right stifle from the inside or medial view. When the stifle flexes, as the curved arrow at right shows, the patella moves forward from its fixed position on the medial trochlear ridge, designated by the straight arrow.

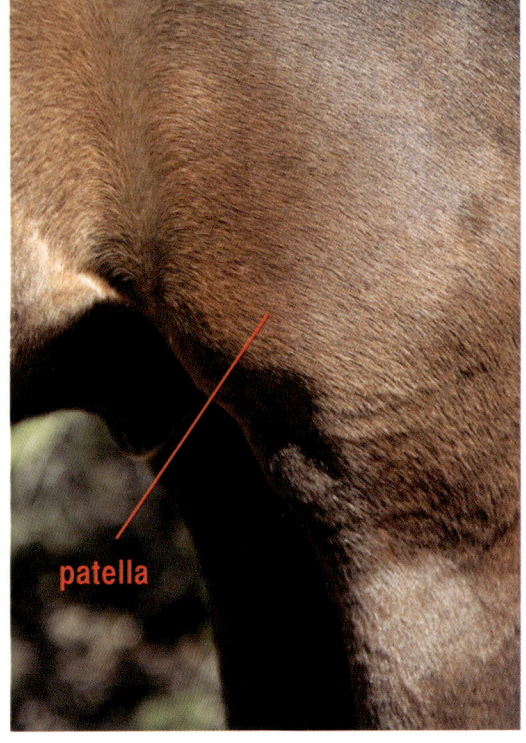

patella

Your horse's stifle is encased in muscle mass at the level of his flank.

behind him. In this extended position, the patella is arranged to "latch" over the medial trochlear ridge of the femur. The patella and medial patellar ligament must "unlatch" from the medial trochlear ridge to allow the leg to flex and begin moving forward. If the patella doesn't unlatch at the appropriate time, it can be fixed temporarily in its upward position. This temporary fixation can mean that your horse has a delayed patellar release or intermittent locking of the patella. Typically, the patella remains latched only instantaneously, causing some change of your horse's gait.

An extreme version of the latched condition is called a locked patella or complete upward fixation of the patella. In this severe case, your horse can't flex his leg and drags his toe on the ground. A horse with a less severe case might swing his leg to the side to minimize the amount he must flex.

As a rider, you notice your horse's subtle gait changes. When your horse raises his hindquarters excessively during upward

This healthy horse's right stifle is fully extended at the end of the cantering stride. With delayed patellar release, he might stumble as he moves forward from this extended position.

transitions, he suddenly feels heavy on the forehand. You also might notice that your horse refuses to travel in a straight line when moving downhill; the downward slope makes it difficult for his patella to unlatch. Instead, your horse prefers to travel downhill at an angle or in a zigzag pattern. You also notice that your horse stumbles behind more than usual, which is because your horse's foot doesn't land flat before his leg bears weight. His toe catches on the ground, causing him to stumble. You feel the dramatic stumble, and then your horse recovers and moves ahead normally with his next stride.

Because the unlatching problem stems from your horse's anatomy, you might feel your horse's delayed patellar release in both hind legs. Typically, though, the problem manifests primarily in one leg. Delayed patellar release occurs in horses of all ages. A young, immature horse, less than 4 or 5 years old, experiencing delayed patellar release likely improves with age. As your young horse

matures, he develops better muscle control, and the relationships between the bones change to allow normal function. In horses of any age, physical condition plays a large role in the problem's scope and severity. A well-muscled horse in good body condition is less likely to be bothered by the problem than a horse in poor physical shape.

Delayed patellar release can cause subtle changes that don't significantly affect a horse's performance, and that generally don't require veterinary intervention. However, the delayed patellar release can significantly alter your horse's ability to do his job, and he can require treatment.

What you notice: This condition generally is a mechanical issue and usually doesn't cause your horse constant pain. The following signs point to delayed patellar release:

- Your horse stumbles with his back legs, then recovers in the next stride.

133

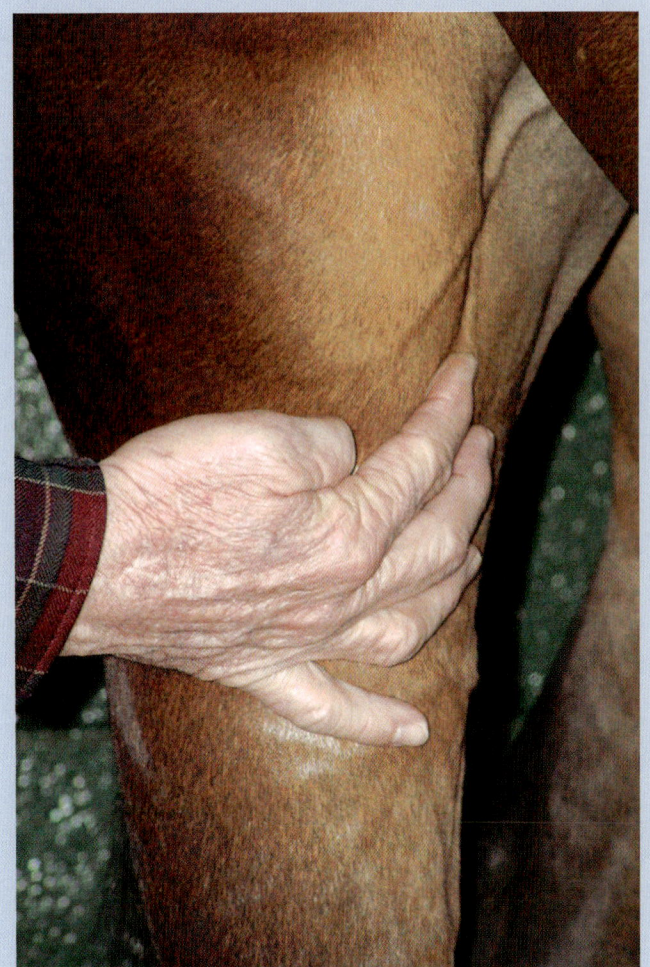

Careful palpation of the stifle joint is an important part of your horse's lameness exam.

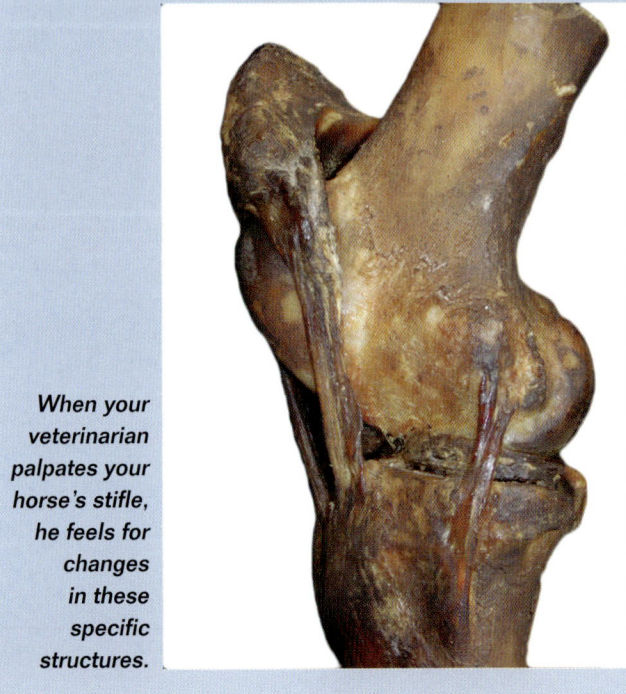

When your veterinarian palpates your horse's stifle, he feels for changes in these specific structures.

- Reluctant to travel straight downhill, your horse prefers to negotiate a slope at an angle or perhaps in a zig-zag pattern.

- Your horse has trouble maintaining the correct hind lead.

- Your horse travels heavily on the forehand.

- Your horse drags a toe on a hind leg.

- At a slow jog, your horse dramatically shortens his stride on one hind leg.

What you do: Call your veterinarian when you notice any change in your horse's movement.

What your veterinarian does: After gaining insight from you as the rider, the veterinarian examines the entire horse and watches your horse move on a circle and in a straight line, looking for any sign of stumbling in his hindquarters. The veterinarian might notice nothing or see slower and shorter forward movement on the outside hind leg when your horse travels on a circle.

Your veterinarian may not need further diagnostic tools unless symptoms indicate more than one possible cause for lameness. If your veterinarian believes that your horse's case is severe or that multiple issues might contribute to his lameness, radiographs could be used to evaluate involved bones, ultrasound to look for cartilage and ligament damage, and diagnostic blocking to localize any pain. Arthroscopy is helpful for examining the interior structures of the joint's three compartments.

To successfully treat delayed patellar release, you must keep your horse's muscles fit and toned. Consequently, unless your horse is lame for other reasons, continued exercise is a vital part of alleviating the problem. You must exercise your horse in good footing that isn't too deep and avoid steep downhill work.

Your veterinarian might opt for conservative treatment with injectable medication. Weekly systemic, intramuscular estrogen injections during the course of four to five weeks can offer your horse relief. The hormone is known to relax ligament tissue, but the scientific connection between estrogen and delayed patellar release hasn't been established. This treatment is mildly controversial for two reasons. First, there's no real science to support its efficacy. Second, previous treatments for delayed patellar release revolved around the theory of tightening the ligaments, not relaxing them. However, many veterinarians have experienced significant success with this treatment.

Another therapeutic option involves periarticular injections of medications in the quadriceps muscle, where it attaches to a horse's patella and along the patellar ligaments. These injections are generally administered three times at three-week intervals, but the regimen varies by case.

If your horse has a severe or unresponsive case, he might require medial patellar ligament splitting surgery. Your veterinarian cuts into the medial patellar ligament, making several small cuts parallel to the ligament's fibers. Again, with this treatment, the exact effect of the surgery is not understood, but the success rate is good.

Your veterinarian might recommend a second type of surgery instead. Doing a medial patellar ligament desmotomy, your veterinarian completely severs the ligament. When the ligament heals post-surgically, it's longer, so the patella no longer catches on the femur's medial trochlear ridge. Potential complications involving the patella make this procedure suitable only for extremely difficult-to-manage cases. Your veterinarian might not recommend this surgery if your horse has other stifle-related pathologies in addition to delayed patellar release. Thorough evaluation via radiographs and ultrasound is imperative before proceeding with this surgery.

The healing process: Shoeing plays an important role in alleviating delayed patellar release. Square-toed shoes or setting the shoes farther back on the hoof can ease hoof break-over and seems to reduce extension in the posterior (hind) stride. An egg-bar shoe might provide necessary stifle support, too. A wedge pad helps some cases, but might complicate lower-leg function in horses with longer sloping pasterns.

Keep your horse on a consistent exercise and conditioning program so that he stays in good physical shape. His fitness helps his overall prognosis. Closely monitor riding conditions to avoid those that exacerbate the problem, such as deep, heavy footing and steep downhill slopes.

Down the road: The outlook for a horse with delayed patellar release is generally favorable

LAMENESS Q&A

What does "stifled" mean?

"Stifled," a general term pertaining to hind-leg soreness, doesn't mean anything specific. Many injuries and lameness issues can develop in the stifle because of the numerous structures involved, including the patella, 14 ligaments and three joint compartments.

When someone says, "My horse is stifled," don't assume it's a specific lameness problem. That just means the horse experiences hind-leg soreness.

How can a horse lock his hind legs to sleep standing?

That's possible because of the patella's locked orientation and the reciprocal apparatus discussed below. When the patella is in its fixed position above the medial femoral ridge, the stifle can't flex. Hence the rest of the leg remains in a fixed extension position (because of the reciprocal apparatus), allowing your horse to sleep standing with minimal muscle effort.

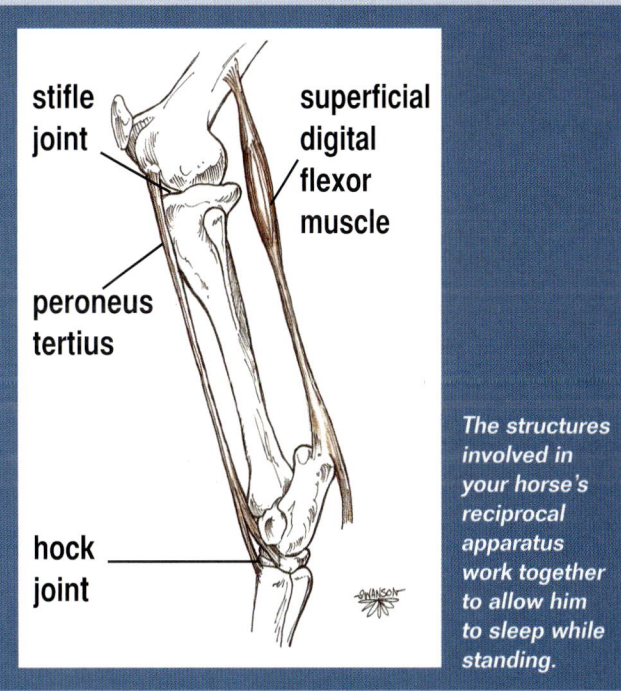

stifle joint

superficial digital flexor muscle

peroneus tertius

hock joint

The structures involved in your horse's reciprocal apparatus work together to allow him to sleep while standing.

What is the reciprocal apparatus?

One important hind-leg anatomical concept involves the reciprocal apparatus. This arrangement of tendons and ligaments on the front and back of the leg, from above the stifle to below the hock, causes the stifle, hock and fetlock to work in unison. When you pick up your horse's front leg, each joint can be manipulated individually. However, the hind leg joints all work in unison and can't move separately. The stifle, hock and, to some extent, the fetlock work together and depend on each other for movement. One of those joints can't flex or extend without the other two joints flexing or extending, too. This relationship complicates hind-leg lameness diagnosis because it's more difficult to isolate each joint to pinpoint the primary area of concern.

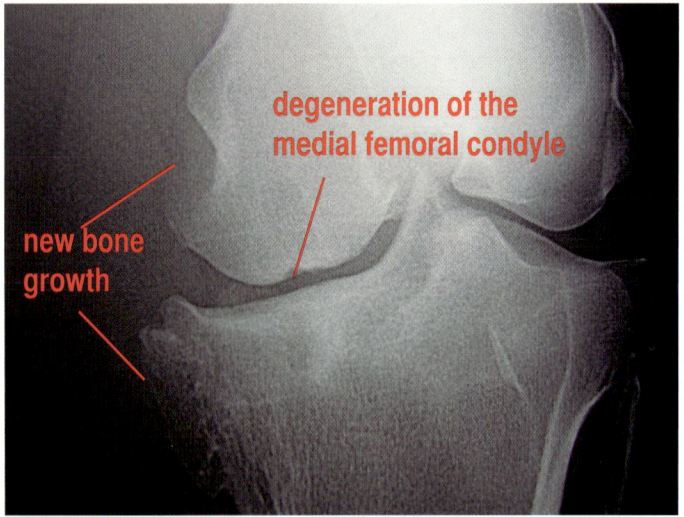

This radiograph shows the severe bony changes and new bone growth associated with stifle trauma.

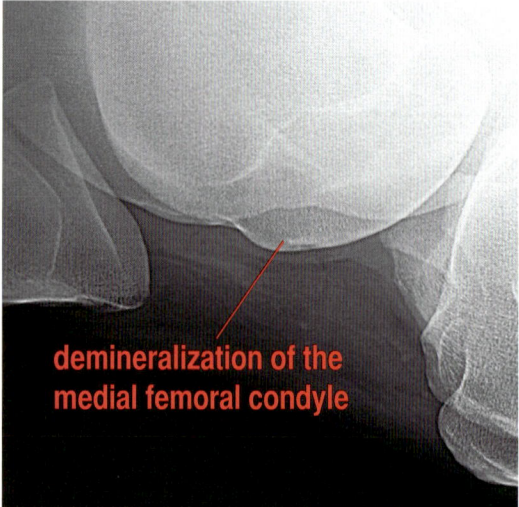

This subtle bone change can impact a horse's soundness.

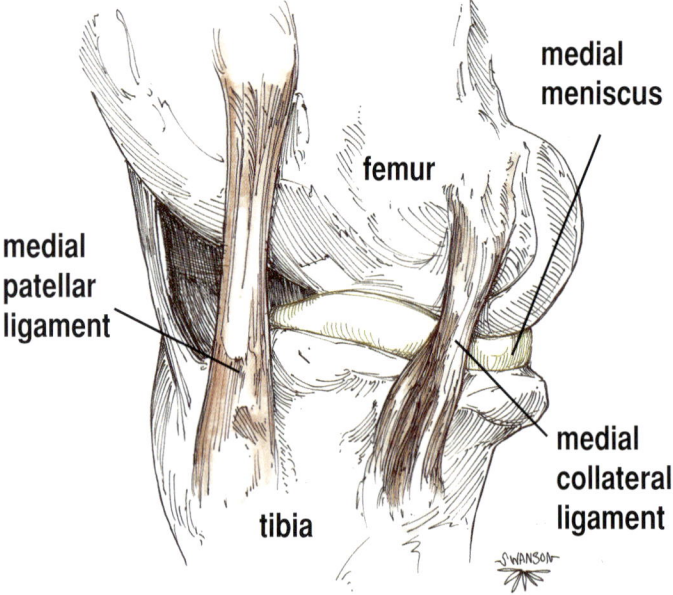

The inside, or medial, stifle structures, the medial collateral ligament and medial meniscus, or cartilage, often are involved in trauma.

with appropriate owner, rider and veterinary management. But it's important to remember: The problem might be only one component in a complicated hindquarter-lameness case.

Acute/Chronic Stifle Trauma

You're riding in the warm-up pen at a local schooling show when another rider loses control. Her horse bolts and heads straight toward you and your top-level mount. Time seems to slow down, but you can't get out of the way. All you can think: "I'm only here to practice for next week's big championship! Why is this happening?" The other rider attempts to stop her horse at the last possible moment, but all she can do is turn her horse's hind end toward your horse's right side. The other horse rams into your horse's stifle. You ask your horse to move forward, but he's reluctant to move. You hop off and slowly walk him to your trailer. There, you examine the impact area. There's muscle tenseness and firmness, and your horse also rests his right leg, avoiding placing his foot flat on the ground.

What might be happening: Your horse's stifle is complex and often unprotected from lateral or sideways bumping—a prime candidate for acute and chronic traumatic injury. As with all joints, the stifle is subject to progressive degenerative joint disease because the joint doesn't completely heal after trauma. The collateral ligaments, which run both inside and outside the stifle, stabilize the joint and prevent side-to-side movement. The most common trauma results from a blow to the stifle from the side, most often caused when one horse kicks or bumps into another horse, resulting in stretching damage to the medial collateral ligament.

The menisci also encounter horse-to-horse trauma and performance accidents. These C-shaped cartilages tend to tear along their thin, inner edges and endure stress at their ligament attachments deep within the stifle joint.

The equine cruciate ligaments also lie deep inside the joint and hold the tibia and femur together, along with the collateral ligaments, while allowing the stifle full range of flexion and extension motion. Cruciate ligaments

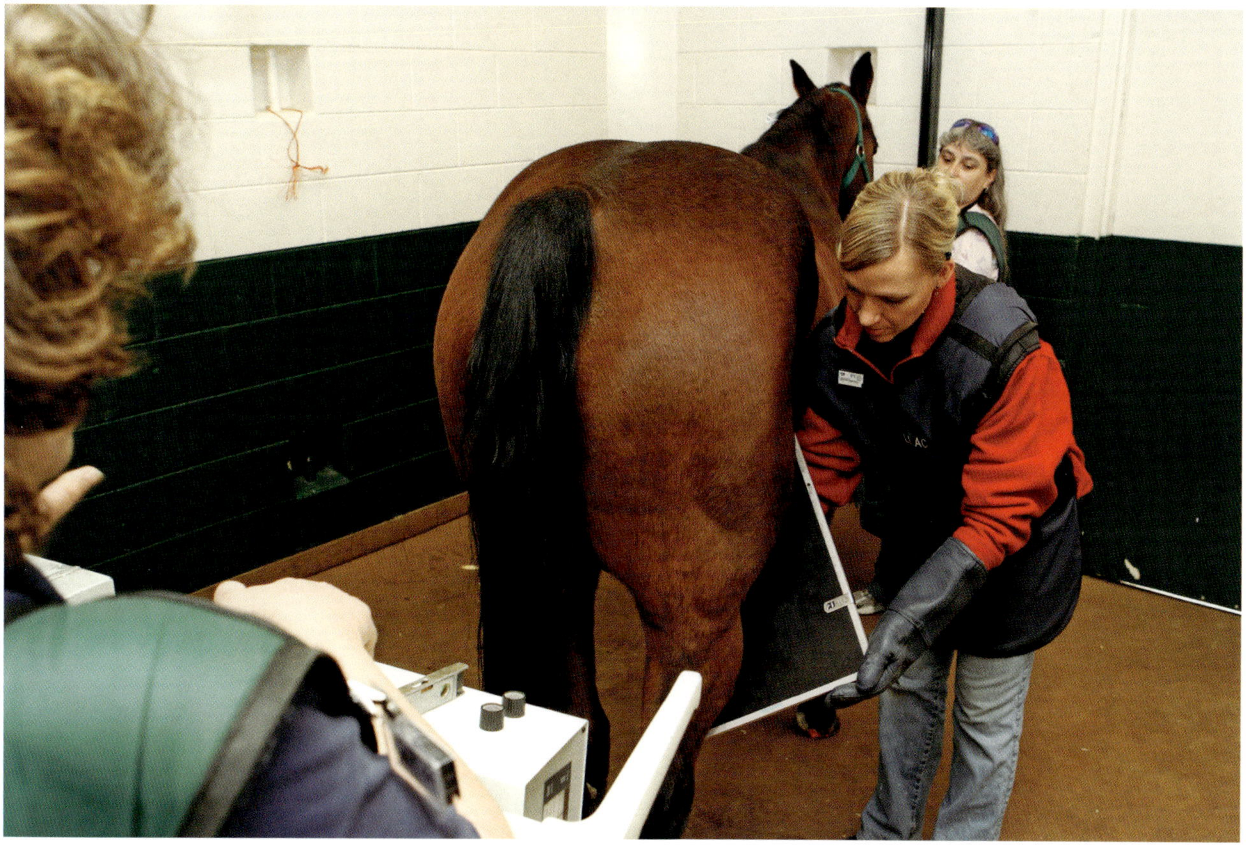

When your horse suffers a stifle injury, your veterinarian takes radiographs of the affected area.

Holding your horse's leg in this position flexes his stifle joint and often temporarily exacerbates stifle lameness.

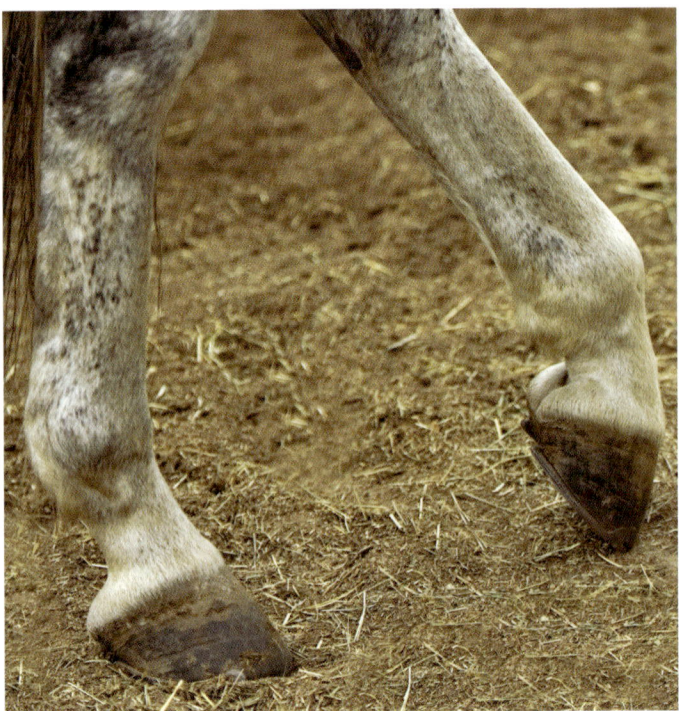

A horse with an acute stifle injury might stand with his toe touching, as shown.

also prevent excessive front-to-back movement or slippage within the joint. A torn cruciate or menisical ligament is difficult to diagnose and a very serious injury.

After a traumatic incident, the joint's degenerative process can progress in a smoldering manner as your horse continues to work. Acute and chronic stifle trauma leads to the most common stifle lameness.

The stifle is recognized as one of the most common sources of serious lameness issues for the performance horse. In addition to trauma, degenerative joint disease from varying degrees of developmental orthopedic disease (DOD) is a common cause of stifle lameness. The medial compartment of the stifle, the medial femoral patellar joint, is the most common source of stifle pain; however it is important to evaluate the entire joint.

What you notice: You see a Grade 1 to Grade 4 lameness as you also notice:

- Lameness when your horse's affected leg, in most cases, is on the outside of a circle.

- Problems maintaining hind leads.

- A tendency to rest the affected leg, letting it hang with the fetlock knuckled forward.

- Reluctance to stop hard during any performance move.

- Noticeable swelling in the stifle area.

- Reluctance to set the foot down flat.

What you do: Call your veterinarian as soon as possible after an acute injury.

What your veterinarian does: Your veterinarian's careful palpation helps him understand the extent of the stifle injury. It's normal for a horse to demonstrate sensitivity when his stifle is touched; therefore, it might take careful palpation by your veterinarian to assess the pain response. Your veterinarian feels for excess joint fluid and superficial anatomical changes.

The lameness, if mild or moderate, is often most noticeable when the afflicted limb is on the outside of a circle. Leg flexion tests can help identify the pain's source.

Radiographs demonstrate bony changes and soft-tissue mineralization. Ultrasound can assist in diagnosing menisci and ligament injuries and assess joint-fluid changes. Arthroscopic surgery provides direct visual access to stifle compartments, as well as an opportunity to correct damage. However, because of extensive muscling around the stifle, both ultrasound and arthroscopy have some limitations. Diagnostic blocking with intra-articular anesthesia can be a valuable aid to diagnosis in some cases.

Depending on the structures involved and degree of trauma, veterinary treatments might vary. Most treatment plans include providing the horse with extended rest and controlled exercise. Your veterinarian also might have you administer systemic anti-inflammatory medications. Intra-articular injections of anti-inflammatory medication will reduce inflammation in the joint capsule and in related soft tissues.

Intra-articular injections and systemic anti-inflammatory medication treatments also might be used as supplemental therapies prior to and after surgery. Arthroscopic surgery commonly is used to remove bone and soft-tissue fragments that can be left in the wake of an acute or chronic trauma. The surgery also provides the opportunity to clean ligament attachments and flush damaged tissue cells from the joint.

The healing process: Post-treatment manage-

Horseman's Dictionary

cruciate ligaments: ligaments in the horse's stifle that lie deep inside the joint, holding together the tibia and femur while allowing the stifle full range of motion. A torn cruciate ligament, a serious injury, is difficult to diagnose.

lateral condyle: the outside or lateral weight-bearing portion of the femur in the stifle joint.

medial condyle: the inside or medial weight-bearing portion of the femur in the stifle joint.

medial patellar ligament splitting surgery: small parallel cuts made in the medial patellar ligament to help reduce the incidence of delayed patellar release syndrome.

menisci: "C" cartilages that function as a bushing to help the tibia and femur fit together.

patella: the horse's kneecap, found in the front of the stifle joint. With the quadriceps muscle and its distal ligament attachment, the patella functions to extend the rear leg.

periarticular injections: injections made into the quadriceps muscle, where it attaches to the patella and along the patellar ligaments.

reciprocal apparatus: the arrangement of tendons and ligaments on the front and back of the leg, from above the stifle to below the hock, which causes the stifle, hock and fetlock to work in unison.

stifled: a general lay term pertaining to hind-leg soreness, but nothing specific. Many injuries and lameness issues can develop in the stifle because of the numerous structures involved: the patella, 14 ligaments and three joint compartments.

systemic: administered medication that affects the whole body, usually administered orally, intramuscularly, subcutaneously, or intravenously.

---

ment varies according to the injury severity. It's crucial to slowly reintroduce regular work to avoid reinjury. A consistent and cautiously increasing workload is essential to develop good muscle and ligament tone to support the stifle. Once the joint completely heals, your horse can resume regular work. Some horses might need to have their responsibilities scaled down with different jobs.

Shoeing for easy hoof break-over, by using square-toed shoes or setting regular shoes back on the foot, might be beneficial, too. Egg-bar shoes and wedge pads might help, as well, but some cases are worsened with wedge pads.

Down the road: The range of possible stifle injuries varies so greatly that your horse's prognosis depends on his personal injury, its severity and the quality of treatment he receives.

Case Study: The Stifle

A 4-year-old Western-pleasure horse performed well but had trouble with hind-end lead changes, especially when transitioning from the right to left lead. When the horse worked at a very slow jog, he appeared to take half-steps with his right hind leg. No other signs of lameness were evident to the rider or veterinarian. The horse didn't seem to be in pain or limp. The consulting veterinarian diagnosed delayed patellar release and gave the horse intramuscular injections of estrogen once a week for five weeks. The problem was controlled after the third injection, and no follow-up treatment was needed.

13

THE PELVIS

Your horse's pelvis is the upper portion of his hindquarters, created by the arrangement of the sacrum, ilium, pubis, ischium and coccygeal bones.

Reaching from your horse's spine to below his buttocks, the heavily muscled pelvis acts as a casing to protect many of his complex and intertwining ligaments and joints and connects his hind legs to his spinal column. Imagine a rectangle sitting at an angle in your horse's hind end. The rectangle's top two front corners represent his hipbones or "pin" bones, the tuber coxae, and the bottom rear two corners, or the tuber ischii, form the buttocks along each side of the tail. The hind legs attach at the hip joints, just in front of the buttock on each side. (See diagram on the following page.)

Your horse's spinal column travels through the rectangle's center—at the top of the croup—between the two tuber sacrale portions of the paired ilium bones. The spinal column is suspended within a pelvis by the short, broad sacroiliac ligaments of the sacroiliac joints. The pelvis and spinal column form a complete unit. With many complex structures in such close proximity, any disruptions, including ligament strains or bone fractures, cause the pelvis to shift. A shift and associated damages can lead to varying degrees of lameness.

Heavy musculature covers the pelvis, making it difficult to palpate much of the structure; however, the basic structure can be assessed by rectal examination. This musculature also is involved in hindquarter lameness, with topics addressed in Chapters 14 and 15.

Tuber Coxae Fracture (Knocked-Down Hip)

You call in your herd for the evening feeding. You watch as the crew gallops from the lower pasture and slows only slightly to file through the gate, a narrow passage that connects the pastures and allows you

When a horse pulls weight, his pelvis, as well as his lower leg, is heavily engaged.

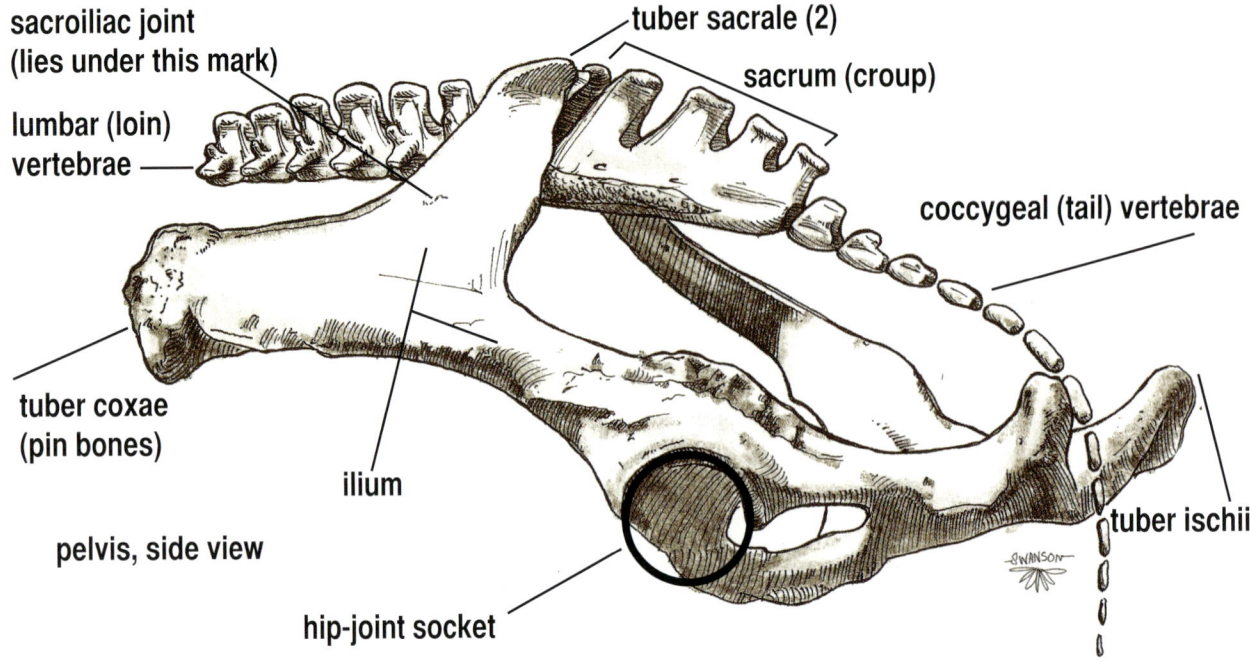

sacroiliac joint (lies under this mark)

lumbar (loin) vertebrae

tuber sacrale (2)

sacrum (croup)

coccygeal (tail) vertebrae

tuber coxae (pin bones)

ilium

pelvis, side view

hip-joint socket

tuber ischii

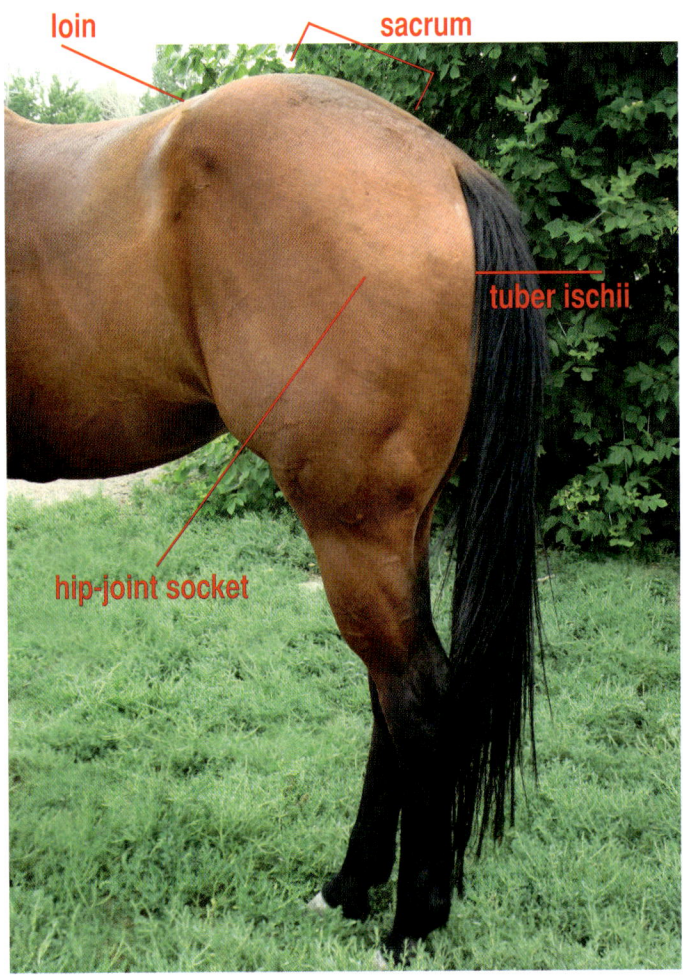

loin

sacrum

tuber ischii

hip-joint socket

The pelvis, as shown from the loin to the tail head, is the foundation for a horse's hindquarters and connects his spinal column to his hind legs.

to choose which grazing area the herd can access. Your gelding makes it to the barn without a problem. But when your mare reaches the gate, she doesn't slow enough. She starts through, but catches her hip on the gatepost. She slows to a walk and limps the rest of the way to the barn, where you look closely at her. She's more willing than usual to stand still. When you touch her hip, she's obviously sore, and the area around her hipbone is beginning to swell.

What might be happening: Anatomically, the tuber coxae, or pin bones, form the points of the pelvis on each side of your horse's hindquarters. A large cartilage cap on top of each pin bone serves as the origin of attachment for several major muscles that facilitate pelvic and hind-leg movement. If your horse fractures these bones, he shows varying degrees of lameness, depending on the trauma severity, the fracture's magnitude and any muscle and ligament damage. A blow can severely bruise the cartilage cap and the associated muscles. The injury also might fracture the cartilage cap loose from the pelvis or pin bone. In these cases, the the affected tuber coxa shifts downward, creating a tilted pelvis.

What you notice: You see a Grade 2 to Grade 5 lameness as you also notice:

- Evidence of pain during pelvis palpation or manipulation.

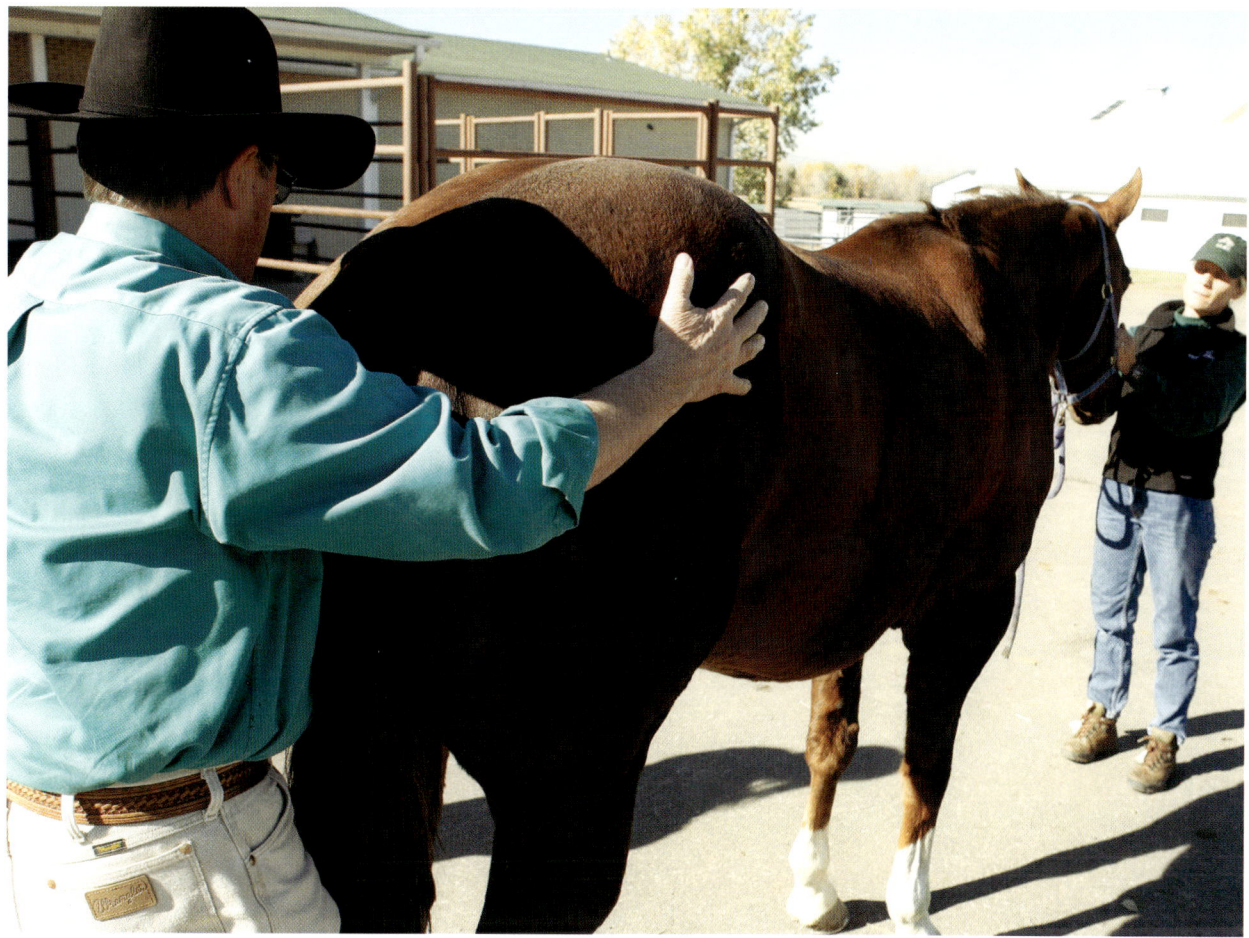

Common tuber coxae fractures occur when your horse hits a pin bone and the attached cartilage cap shifts down, creating a "knocked-down" hip, which your veterinarian can feel when comparing the bones on opposite sides.

- Swelling in the pin-bone (tuber coxae) area.

- Reluctance to move forward, but willingness to stand while appearing somewhat comfortable.

What you do: Call your veterinarian immediately after witnessing an impact injury or if you see pelvic area swelling.

What your veterinarian does: Your veterinarian begins his exam by palpating the pelvic area and looking for signs of pain and swelling. He stands squarely behind your horse and palpates the pelvis for symmetry and balance, and also might perform a rectal exam to further assess the difficult-to-reach internal pelvic bones.

Radiographs might be useful in some cases, but this area is difficult to assess radiographically because of so much attached muscling and the layered body structures. In some cases, ultrasound examination demonstrates pelvic fractures and helps assess soft-tissue damage. Nuclear scintigraphy often helps confirm the diagnosis in unclear cases.

After gathering as much information as possible, your veterinarian makes sure your horse is confined and has controlled exercise during the healing process. If your horse has a deep bruise and ligament injury, he requires up to four months of rest. A cartilage cap or pelvic fracture necessitates three to six months of confinement and controlled exercise.

The healing process: Once your horse heals, work with your veterinarian to evaluate your horse's future career. If your horse suffered bruising and ligament strain, he can return to his former job. However, if a displaced cartilage cap can't return to the normal position and your horse's affected muscles lack their usual natural leverage, performing some functions might be more difficult than in the past. Most horses compensate for the displacement and can perform satisfactorily. In

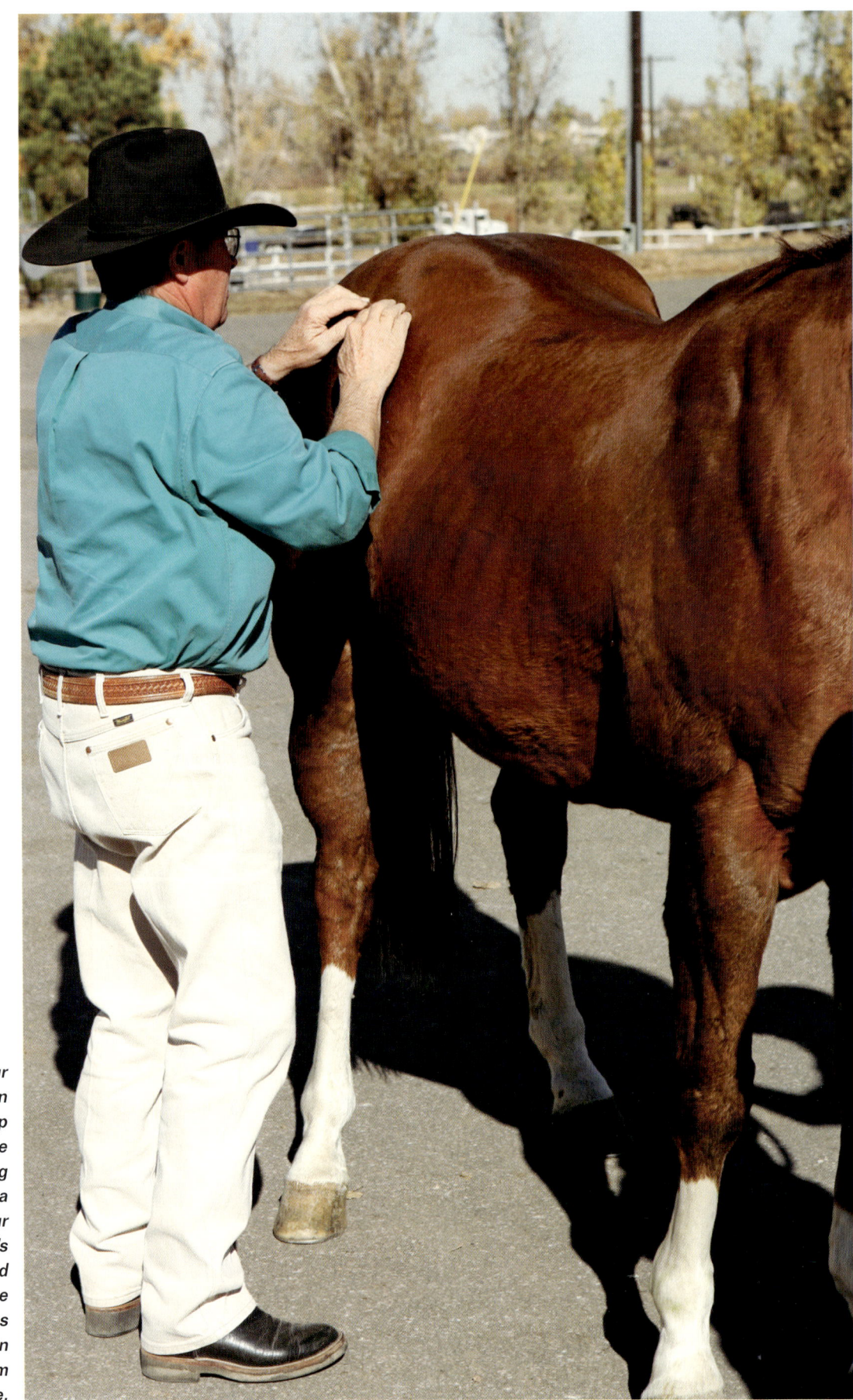

Your veterinarian uses deep pressure when feeling the area around your horse's affected tuber coxae and notes any pain reaction from your horse.

more endurance-type circumstances, some horses develop tying-up syndrome (discussed more in Chapter 14) because the hip muscles fatigue more quickly. Also, your horse might not have as much impulsion from behind because of his decreased muscle strength.

Down the road: Your horse should return to work with minor limitations.

Sacroiliac Subluxation (Hunter's Bump)

You've purchased a young team and are teaching them to pull. You'd love to enter them in the National Western Livestock Show's annual draft horse pull. You enter your youngsters in a local competition first—to see how their training stacks up to that of other teams, and to evaluate just how much your horses are able to pull. Halfway through the local competition, one of your youngsters quits pulling earlier than you expect. You know he's pulled more weight at home many times. His teammate is still trying, but can't do it alone. You're out of the competition—and also a bit worried about your tuckered-out horse. As you trot out of the ring, you notice he's "off" in his right hind. Back at the stalls, you check him and see that his pelvis—at the top of his croup—is higher on the right side than on the left.

What might be happening: The common name of this injury, "hunter's bump," implies that it develops only in English-type hunter horses, but the problem isn't limited to horses that propel themselves over stone walls during a fox hunt. Sacroiliac injury also is seen in horses that pull heavy loads, such as team-roping or cart-pulling horses.

Your horse injures his pelvis when he tears or stretches the sacroiliac ligaments found in the two sacroiliac joints. These ligaments and associated joints connect the pelvis to the spinal column. The joints lie six to eight inches below the tuber sacrale, deep in the pelvis mass. When the ligaments on one side tear, the affected side shifts upward, creating a bump atop the horse's croup, just off the midline on the affected side. The injury occurs when a horse stresses his pelvis while carrying or pulling a heavy load or propelling his body forward over a jump. The injury also could be a secondary lameness occurring when a horse compensates for an injury to the opposite rear leg because he can jar or stress his pelvis as he bears more weight on the healthy side.

Your horse also might appear to have a hunter's bump if he injures the dorsal sacrale ligament that travels over the top of the croup region. Injuring the dorsal sacrale ligament might cause your horse soreness for some time, but the injury heals sooner than a true sacroiliac injury and probably is a more common injury than luxation.

What you notice: You see a Grade 2 to Grade 3 lameness as you also notice:

- Your horse's hind end seems weak and lacking its usual impulsion.

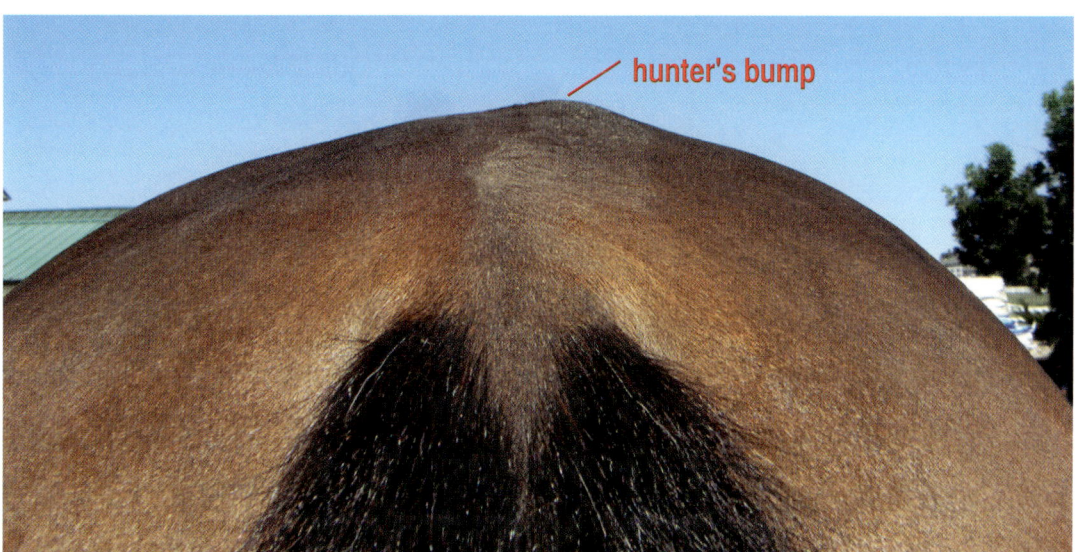

The "bump" just to the right of this horse's midline often represents an enlargement of the sacroiliac ligament.

LAMENESS Q&A

What is nuclear scintigraphy?

This diagnostic modality differs from radiographic technology and ultrasound in that those tools look at changes in anatomical structures. Nuclear scintigraphy measures physiology, in other words, active bone metabolic changes. For example, when examining a pastern bone, a radiograph doesn't show changes until the surface of the bone has changed. Nuclear scintigraphy examines the bone's activity and identifies changes within the bone and usually is done as an adjunct to other diagnostic procedures.

Your veterinarian intravenously injects a radioactive material with a short half-life and an affinity for areas of increased bone metabolic activity. He places a computerized Geiger counter over specific body sites, such as the back, pelvis and legs, for evaluation and measures the radioactive particles emitted from each site. A computer then composes an image to identify where the radioactive material congregates in the horse's body. The material has an affinity for areas where bone is repairing, where an injury has occurred. It's difficult for the process to identify muscle injuries, but when a muscle injury accompanies a skeletal injury, as is often the case with the back or pelvis, it's easy to gain information about the skeletal injury and relate it to the suspected muscle injury. Lower-leg soft-tissue injuries also can be identified with a special application of scintigraphy.

One caveat: Nuclear scintigraphy doesn't identify all lameness issues. If lameness stems from a soft-tissue injury, this procedure might not identify the problem. There also are a few chronic bone changes that can't be identified. What nuclear scintigraphy doesn't identify, however, can be just as helpful as what it does identify. For example, knowing that a horse doesn't have a pelvic stress fracture is valuable in terms of training and offering a prognosis for your horse's career.

What's a non-displaced fracture?

A non-displaced fracture refers to a crack in a bone that hasn't moved out of place. This type of fracture can become displaced if your horse continues to stress the injury.

- Atop his croup, one side of your horse's pelvis appears higher than the other.

- Your horse prefers working in one direction, or when pulling, favors one rear leg and moves crookedly.

What you do: Call your veterinarian when your horse's strength is "off" and when you see asymmetry at the top of the croup.

What your veterinarian does: Palpation isn't always helpful because your veterinarian can't reach the pelvis' key components through your horse's skin. Because the sacroiliac joint and ligaments lie deep within your horse's pelvis, you must rely on your veterinarian's visual skills. He visually evaluates your horse's conformation, looking for any signs of asymmetry, and might recommend nuclear scintigraphy to help locate and see the effects of the deep injury. He also recommends a rectal ultrasound to gain images of the sacroiliac joint area.

Your veterinarian might also choose diagnostic blocking to isolate the injury's precise location; however, the lumbrosacral joint isn't easy to block, requiring a special technique and a 10-inch needle. Injections should be done with care as significant nerves in the area can be damaged if proper techniques are not followed. In most cases your veterinarian considers injecting the affected joint with anti-inflammatory medications and monitoring your horse's response to the therapy. This procedure is both diagnostic and therapeutic. Your horse's response to treatment confirms the diagnosis and that healing has begun.

The healing process: Your veterinarian prescribes controlled exercise and confinement for your horse's sacroiliac injury. Direct injections of anti-inflammatory medication into the injured area also help. Your horse can require four to six months to heal depending on the injury's extent and how it responds to injections.

Once healed, a pelvis injury usually isn't a recurrent issue. However, if your horse's job involves jumping or pulling, he might be predisposed to re-injury. To keep your horse in top form, make sure he has careful conditioning and a precise workout schedule to help the muscles around the pelvis stay strong so he avoids future injury.

Down the road: The prognosis is favorable, and your horse usually returns to his job.

Pelvic Fracture

You and your top eventing horse enter a fall classic. It rained the night before the competition, but officials have cleared the courses and all is to begin on time. When it's your turn, you begin the cross-country course with power and precision. You're a bit worried about one upcoming obstacle—your horse must travel down a steep bank and into a pool of water. Others have completed the obstacle with style today. Now, it's your turn. Your horse, willing and listening, starts down the bank. Suddenly, he slips. His hind end spins and hits the large log support wall. Your worries became reality. He's down.

What might be happening: Your horse suffers a pelvic fracture if he breaks any of the bones composing the pelvis' rectangle-like structure. The pelvis supports a large percentage of your horse's hindquarter weight and acts as an anchor for the many muscles that operate his hind legs. Because so many muscles and ligaments are attached to the pelvis, a fracture can cause your horse great pain, especially when he tries to move.

Fractures can occur when a horse hits his pin bone on a doorjamb or gate, or when your horse runs backward into a wall or post. Many pelvis fractures occur when a horse falls forcibly to the ground or is broadsided by another horse.

With severe pelvic fractures there is a pos-sibility of sharp bone fragments severing major blood vessels, which can cause a horse to bleed to death internally.

Occasionally a horse experiences a non-displaced pelvis stress fracture; which often isn't as painful as a clean break. With a new stress fracture, your horse can perform, but you notice some hind-end lameness. If not recognized and treated, a stress fracture can progress to a complete fracture; both are diagnosed with nuclear scintigraphy.

What you notice: A horse with a pelvic fracture usually can stand quietly, but experiences great pain when he moves. You see a Grade 3 to Grade 5 lameness as you also notice:

- Reluctance to move and restlessness because your horse cannot move comfortably.

- Significant swelling and edema in one or both of your horse's rear legs.

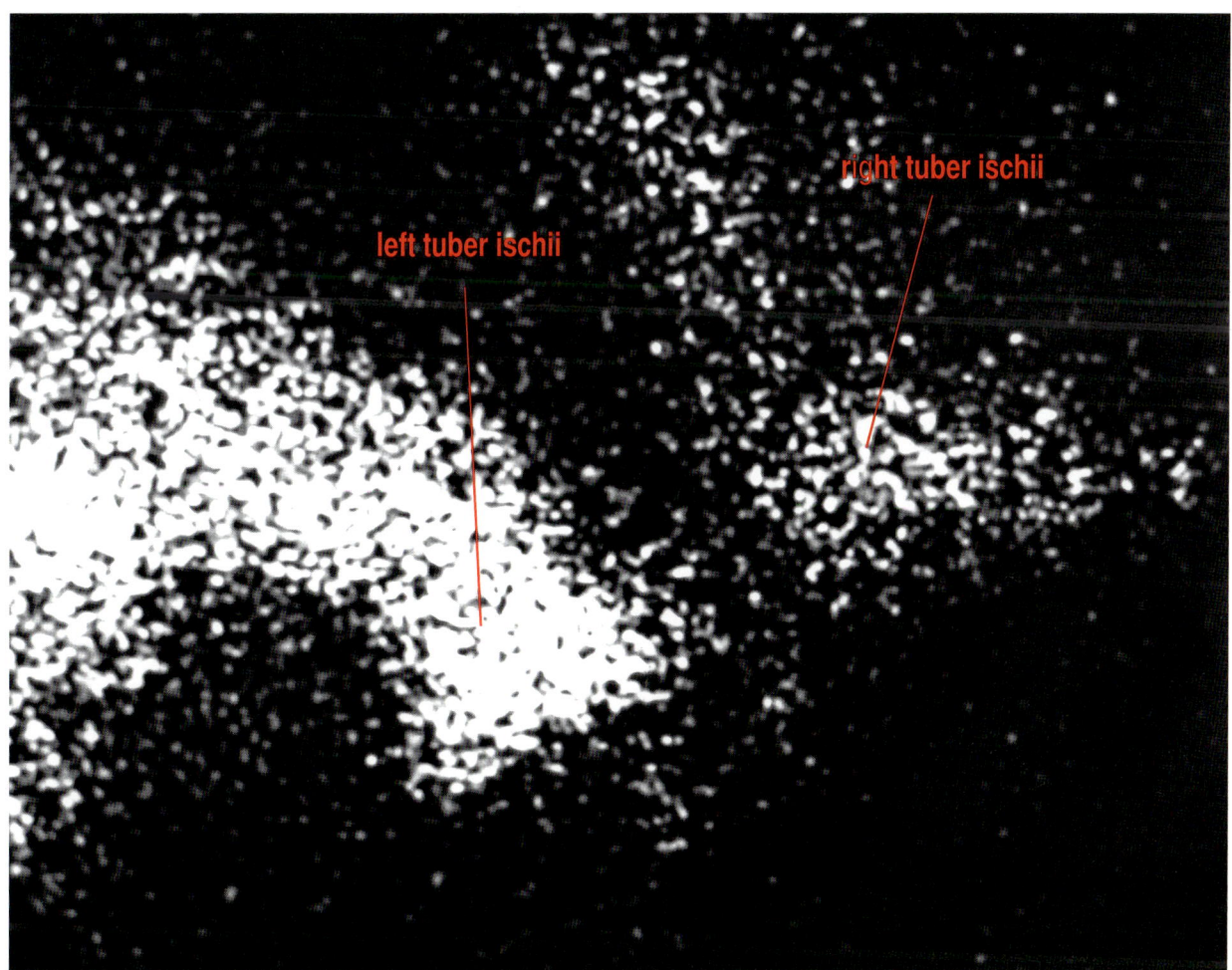

This nuclear scintigraph shows the right and left tuber ischii beside a horse's tail head. The left bone's brightness signifies an increased radioisotope uptake at a fracture site. Due to heavy pelvic muscling, a nuclear scintigraph is often the best way to see internal injuries.

147

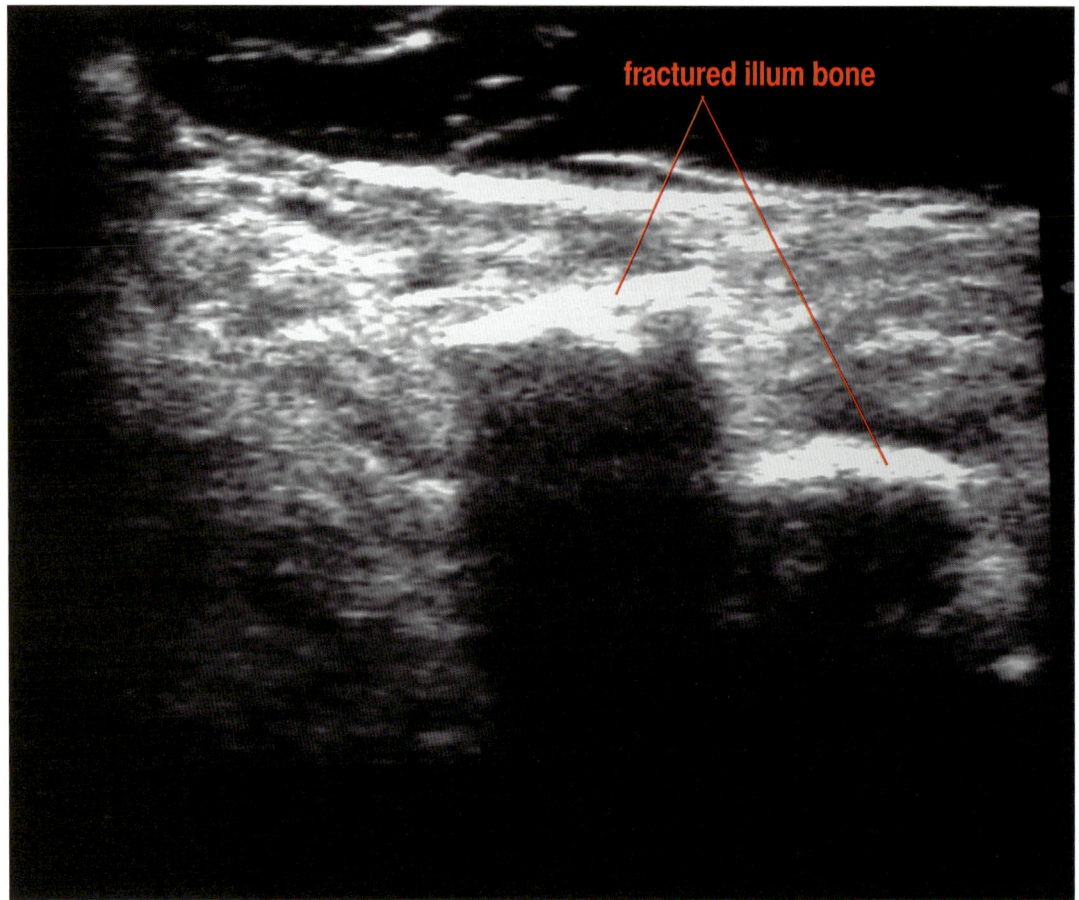

fractured illum bone

The bright white line in this ultrasound shows the horse's pelvic fracture. In a healthy horse, the bright line would be continuous.

- Signs of pain when your horse is forced to shift weight from side to side.

What you do: Call your veterinarian as soon as you notice your horse's hind-end pain and reluctance to move, a sign of a pelvic fracture, or if your horse suffers a fall and impacts his pelvic region.

What your veterinarian does: Your horse's heavy muscling makes a fracture difficult to diagnose from palpation and visual exams alone. Following external palpation, your veterinarian palpates your horse's pelvic region rectally for better access to the bony structure. That way your veterinarian also can identify a hematoma, swelling or crepitus, the characteristic vibration felt when two boney pieces move past each other, or bone rubbing on bone.

A radiograph reveals pelvic fractures, but the image is compromised because of the muscle mass surrounding the pelvis. Ultrasound displays some fractures and shows any damage to linked muscles or ligaments. Nuclear scintigraphy might demonstrate the fracture and is helpful when identifying a non-displaced stress fracture.

The healing process: Your horse must be totally confined for six to eight weeks after a pelvis fracture. Neither internal nor external pelvis-fracture fixation to aid the healing process is possible. You can begin controlled exercise, hand-walking your horse after eight weeks, depending on his progress. It's important to allow complete healing before your horse returns to work. Severe cases can take six to 12 months for total healing.

Down the road: Once healed, many horses resume some degree of performance, sometimes returning to their previous work levels. You must be aware of your horse's limitations and use cautious judgment as your horse returns to work. At any sign of pain or lameness, immediately limit work and consult your veterinarian.

If your horse's hip joint is involved in the fracture, his future performance is limited significantly. Systemic and intra-articular medication might improve his chance of returning to performance and avoiding future arthritis.

Fractures that don't involve the joint have a guarded prognosis with a reasonable chance of your horse returning to work and a favor-

Horseman's Dictionary

crepitus: the characteristic vibration felt when two boney pieces of a fracture move past each other; bone rubbing on bone.

dorsal sacrale ligaments: ligaments running from the tuber sacrale, two paired bones in the equine pelvis, to the top of the sacrum, another pelvic bone.

ilium bone: the largest of the three pairs of bones that fuse to create the horse's pelvis.

non-displaced fracture: a crack in the body of a bone without the pieces separating.

tuber coxae: "pin bones" that form the points of the

pelvis on each side of your horse's hindquarters.

tuber ischii: the lower rear two corners of the pelvis, which form the buttocks along either side of the horse's tail.

tuber sacrale: paired bones in the horse's pelvis, which "peak" at the rear end of the lumbar region and the top or front of the croup. These prominent peaks shift upward when a horse has a sacroiliac subluxation or "hunter's bump" injury.

tying-up syndrome: acute muscle degeneration, resulting in painful muscle cramping and reluctance to move. (See chapter 14 to learn more.)

able prognosis for pasture soundness. Keep in mind that a mare with this injury must have her pelvic canal evaluated before she can be considered a candidate as a natural-birth broodmare.

Case Study: The Pelvis

A 5-year-old jumping horse injured his left tuber coxae, the pin bone that forms the point of his pelvis, by hitting it on a stall door. The cartilage cap was displaced, and he showed Grade 3 lameness. The horse was rested for four months in a stall and hand-walked. The lameness resolved; however, the associated pelvis asymmetry didn't dissipate. In other words, the horse continues to have a knocked-down hip.

Once the lameness dissipated, the horse returned to training. He competed in open jumping events and performed very well, apparently up to his expected level.

14

MUSCLES AND BACK

Your horse's muscles are among the soft tissues that closely interact to control his body movement.

All skeletal movement depends on muscles contracting and relaxing. When your horse is in a relaxed, stationary pose and his muscles relax, they lengthen. With stimulation from nerve cells, when your horse reacts to your cues or is prompted to move, his muscles contract, shorten and move the connected joints. When a leg moves, the extensor muscles contract to pull the leg forward; when the leg impacts the ground, the flexor muscles contract to support your horse and then propel him forward.

Every muscle consists of thousands of muscle cells, each of which has a small range of contraction, but when combined as a group, they cause dramatic motion. At its origin, the muscle must attach to a bone by fascia, or fibrous tissue. Tendons connect the other end of the muscle to another bone beyond a joint, which allows the muscle to move that joint, which either the muscle or its tendon must bridge.

Soft-tissue injuries vary in severity. They usually result from working in slick or deep footing, or from intense training when a horse lacks physical condition or proper muscular preparation for the job.

Back Soreness

You want your competitive barrel-racing horse to have unstructured time to play in the arena, so you turn him out by himself to run, buck and play for more than an hour. The next morning, your horse is stiff, and his back seems a bit sore. You think he might "warm" out of it, so you mount up for a low-intensity ride. He's reluctant to flex and bend and turn around the barrels. He doesn't seem to favor any one leg, and there's no heat in his legs or noticeable injury. You

All performance horses use their backs to absorb shock as they stop and maneuver, much like this heading horse, whose back is stressed as he stops, turns, supports his rider, and takes on the dallied weight of the steer.

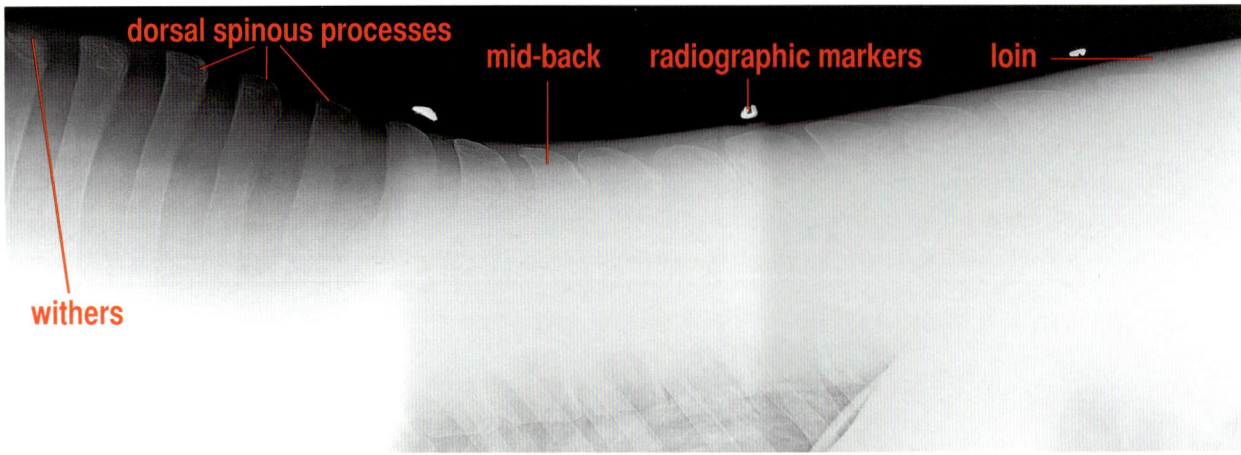

dorsal spinous processes mid-back radiographic markers loin

withers

This composite of three radiographs shows the contour of a horse's back created by each vertebrae's dorsal spinous process. Your veterinarian can see the top of your horse's spine—the portion above your horse's muscle mass.

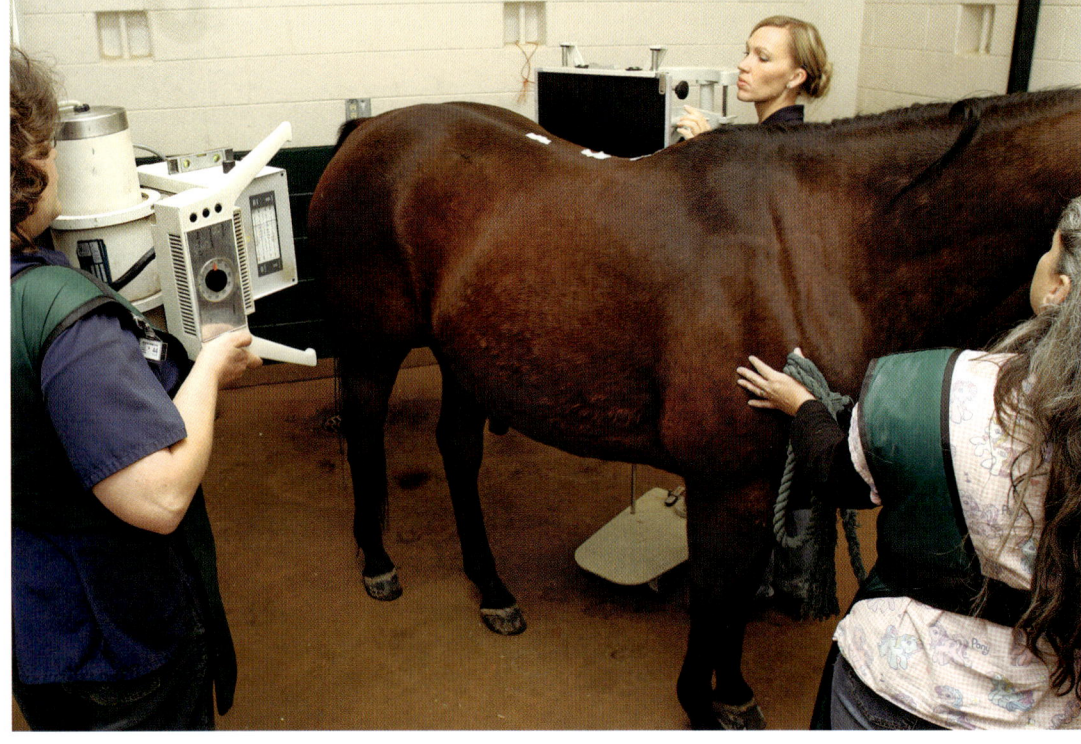

Radiographic markers taped along the horse's spine help your veterinarian know what part of the back corresponds with each radiograph.

need him ready to perform at a major rodeo in just a few weeks. You call your veterinarian right away.

What might be happening: Vertebrae, the bones making up the spinal column, run reasonably level through your horse's back and loin, and are all about the same size. Vertical vertebral spines, found atop each vertebra, are different lengths and create the back's topography. The spines are longest at the withers and shortest at the loin. In some cases, these spines interact with, override or bump into each other, which can be a source of back pain.

A tremendous amount of musculature surrounds the spinal column, allowing the horse to lift his forehand, kick up his hindquarters, support his massive abdomen and carry a rider. Muscular back soreness often is a secondary symptom of front-end or hindquarter lameness. The horse must protect himself from the primary pain, such as that from navicular syndrome, hence overuses the back muscles and becomes sore in that area.

Back soreness also can be a primary condition, such as the case with an ill-fitting saddle or a direct muscle trauma. Primary back soreness also might result from spinal-column injuries or malformations.

When a back injury is suspected, your veterinarian palpates your horse's entire back using smooth, firm pressure to check for muscle tension and pain reflexes.

Your veterinarian also uses his fingernails to push into your horse's back muscles, checking to see if your horse correctly extends or lowers his back in a reflexive response.

What you notice: Your horse might show varying grades of lameness and you see:

- An abrupt change in your horse's attitude or ability to work.

- An altered gait when your horse moves in a pasture, pen or under saddle, but no specific lameness.

- Lameness that's not associated with any specific leg.

- Reluctance to flex or bend under saddle.

- A rigid torso when your horse is at rest or in motion.

- Reluctance to take the bit for proper head-set or carriage.

- Pitting edema, a type of trauma in which fluid accumulates in and around the muscle mass. When you apply finger pressure, a dent develops in your horse's flesh and then gradually fills within a few minutes.

What you do: To identify back soreness, apply firm, even fingertip, not fingernail, pressure in specific areas, rather than running a hand or fingers down the back in one swift movement. If your horse jerks away or you notice that his muscles jerk at your touch, your horse might have muscle soreness. It is important to have your horse relaxed to make these assessments. Note: When examining your horse's hindquarter for muscle pain, work cautiously as he might kick or react abruptly when you touch the sore area. Call your veterinarian.

What your veterinarian does: Your veterinarian carefully palpates your horse's back to identify and assess the pain level. He continues the exam by evaluating the back's range of motion, noticing any limitations or pain intensification with movement. Next, your veterinarian watches the horse travel to ascertain any top-line rigidity. The horse might lack flexion as he moves in a circle or lack normal bounce in his torso because with back soreness a horse loses suppleness. Your veterinarian must discover whether the soreness is a secondary or primary issue before the diagnosis is complete.

Radiographs identify and confirm spinal-column injuries, especially in the dorsal spinous processes, the vertebral parts that extend above the spine and can override each other. However, the dense mass found in your horse's back and loin muscling can conceal bone-related problems. Ultrasound and nuclear scintigraphy also can help diagnose muscular- and skeletal-related back problems. If a separate primary lameness exists, that problem must be eliminated before your veterinarian can address any secondary back soreness.

No matter if the issue is primary or secondary, the use of anti-inflammatory medications is indicated, as well as methocarbamol to relieve pain. Furthermore, your veterinarian might inject medication into your horse's

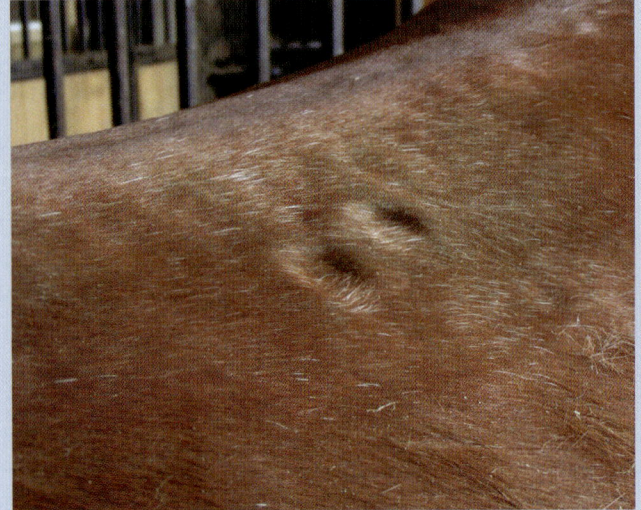

After some back traumas, fluid might collect between your horse's skin and muscle. Finger pressure can displace this fluid, creating dimples, or pitting edema, after you release the pressure.

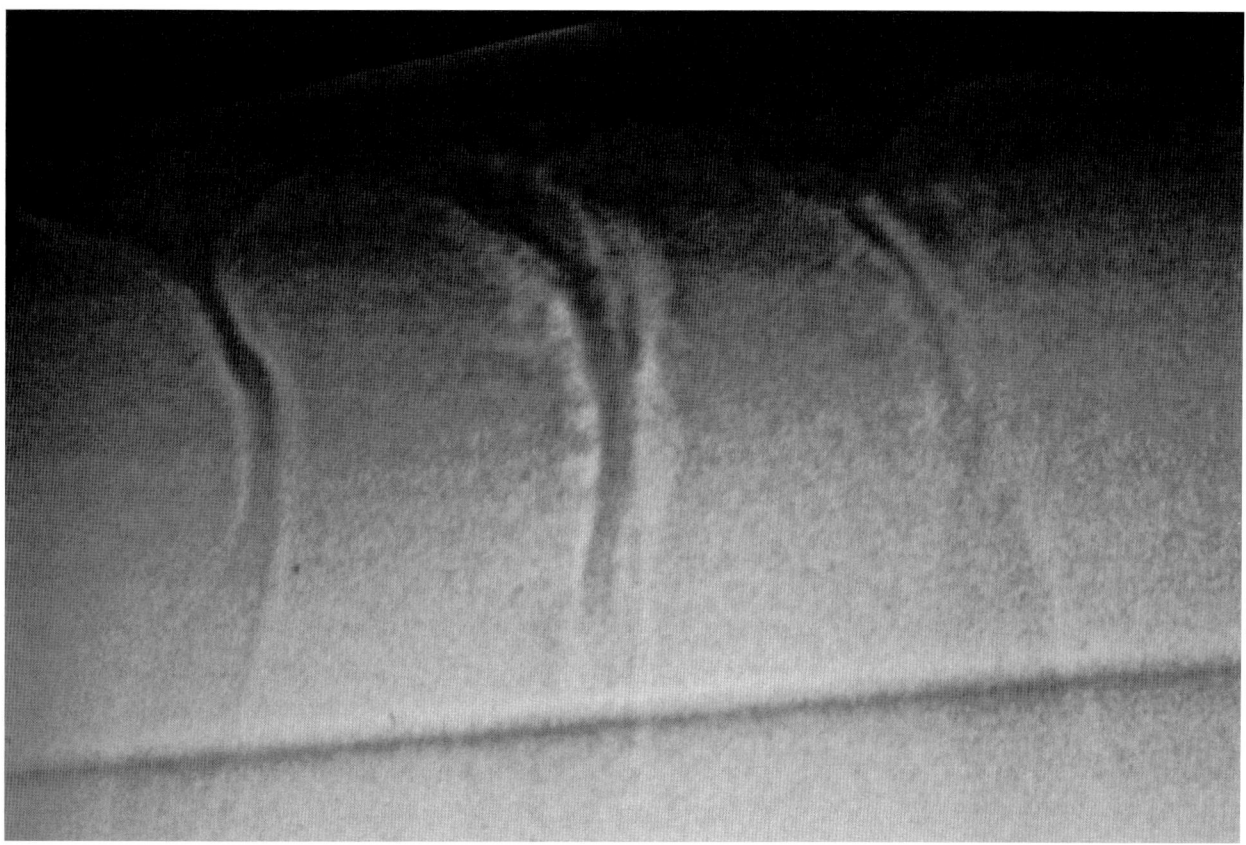

This radiograph of a horse's back shows reactive bone changes that occur when the dorsal spinous processes rub together, known as "kissing spines."

muscles and along the affected dorsal spinous processes to relieve inflammation. Cold therapy, massage and controlled exercise are warranted for some cases.

Extra corporeal shockwave therapy significantly enhances treatment of muscular and spinal-column injuries. Such treatment reduces inflammation and discomfort associated with back pain.

Surgical correction for overriding spines is possible. However, it's usually reserved for cases that don't respond to more conservative treatment because the procedure might cause some back or vertebral instability.

The healing process: Understanding the cause of the primary lameness is important to prevent its recurrence. Correction of the cause and tack adjustments obviously are important. Allowing the muscles to heal without continued trauma is a must, and the rider's equitation abilities, or lack thereof, must be considered.

Down the road: The prognosis is favorable for primary back-muscle soreness. If the dorsal processes override each other, the prognosis

is guarded, and therapy must be repeated on an as-needed basis. Back soreness secondary to other problems, such as navicular syndrome or hock soreness, usually is easily controlled once the primary issue is managed.

Specific Muscle Soreness

You hauled your favorite ranch mount more than 300 miles to have special veterinarians evaluate his right front leg. He's been sore for quite some time, and no one locally could find an answer. When you arrive at the clinic, you unload your prize horse to find he's lame on his right rear leg—a leg that has never before been a problem. Your horse doesn't want you to handle his back leg at all—a new behavior. When a veterinarian examines your horse's back leg, she finds the muscles of his right buttock are hard and tight—probably from leaning on the butt bar for the long trip to the veterinary hospital.

What might be happening: Most muscle injuries result from stress—during an event, while doing a job or even when playing in the pasture—when the muscle's elastic limits are

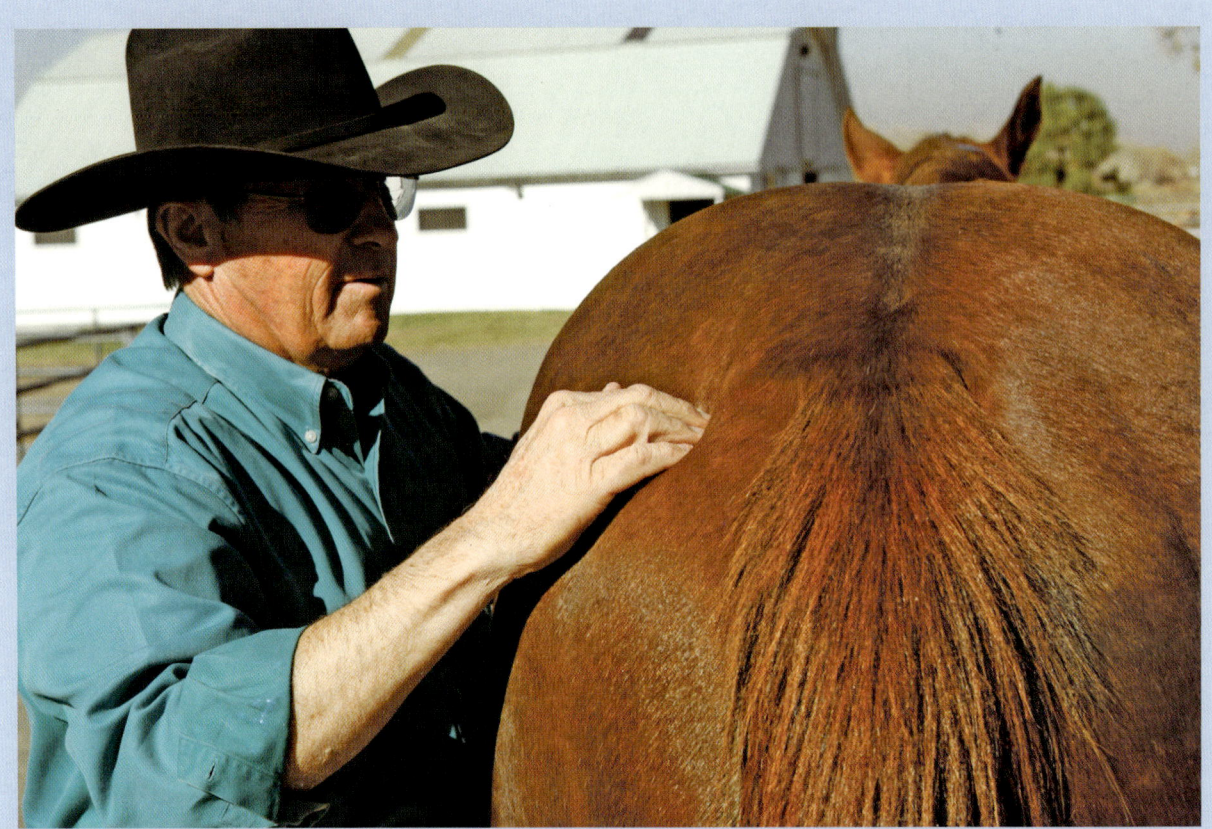

Your veterinarian detects specific muscle soreness by firmly pressing the pads of his fingers into each muscle section, but avoids quickly dragging his fingers along a muscle group—an action that creates a reflex response.

If a horse's saddle fits incorrectly and the gullet is too narrow, the muscles beside the withers become sore. By feeling them, your veterinarian detects any tension and notes if your horse flinches or moves.

exceeded. When muscle cells are bruised, damaged or torn, fluid and blood leak into the muscle tissue and release debris. The torn tissue, swelling and debris contribute to your horse's discomfort. Certainly a lot of muscle injuries result from horses playing and fighting among themselves.

What you notice: Depending upon the degree of injury, muscle soreness throughout your horse's body varies from no sign of lameness to slight stiffness to reluctance to move. However, the following symptoms are common with all levels of muscle pain.

- An abrupt change in your horse's attitude or ability to perform, especially following a hard workout.

- An altered gait when your horse moves in a pasture, pen or under saddle.

- Noticeable muscular knots or unusual firmness.

What you do: Palpate, or apply firm pressure with the pads of your fingers to feel your horse's anatomical structures, particularly the area around your horse's sore or injured muscle. Call your veterinarian if you notice edema or swelling. An injured area around a joint is of more concern.

What your veterinarian does: To diagnose muscle soreness, your veterinarian carefully palpates the horse, beginning at the neck, shoulder and front legs. He continues down the centerline to the croup, hip, hamstring and adductor muscles, the inner-thigh muscles that pull the legs toward the body. However, sometimes it's impossible to pinpoint a sore spot deep within a horse's muscle mass.

Your veterinarian also watches for gait alterations, including decreased range of motion in the front and rear quarters and top-line rigidity. A muscle-sore horse loses suppleness in affected areas and might appear tight or short-strided when he travels. Distinct muscle injuries can cause more specific lameness issues; for example, when a shoulder is bruised, the horse has difficulty moving his leg forward.

Ultrasound imaging can assess muscle damage. Serious cases might necessitate blood evaluation to quantify muscle-cell damage. Cold-water therapy with a hose is

LAMENESS Q&A

What is shockwave treatment?

Extra-corporeal shockwave treatment (ECSWT) concentrates ultra-high-energy sound waves into the body to help heal various body parts. At the highest energy levels, the sound waves are used to break apart kidney stones in humans. At lesser levels, the waves stimulate healing in soft tissues, joints and some bone conditions.

Much of the information regarding success with ECSWT is anecdotal, as opposed to scientific. However, recent research shows its significant healing effects on osteoarthritis cases. Ongoing veterinary research continues to provide further information regarding what the procedure does and for which conditions it's most effective.

Shockwave treatment, known as extra-corporeal shock wave therapy, sends high-frequency sound waves into your horse's muscle tissue, reducing inflammation and stimulating healing.

a commonly prescribed muscle-injury treatment. The cold water reduces inflammation, and the water vibration from the hose massages and helps mobilize tissue fluids.

With large areas of bruising and hematoma formation, your veterinarian needs to drain the collected serum in the bruised area.

Other treatments include anti-inflammatory medication, muscle relaxants, rest and controlled exercise. Your veterinarian prescribes the appropriate level of exercise, according to the amount of damage, unless the damage is extensive and requires complete rest. Deep-muscle massage also can aid in recovery. The goal is to prevent or minimize scar-tissue development, which reduces muscle elasticity.

The healing process: Consistent exercise is imperative for preventing reinjury. Carefully

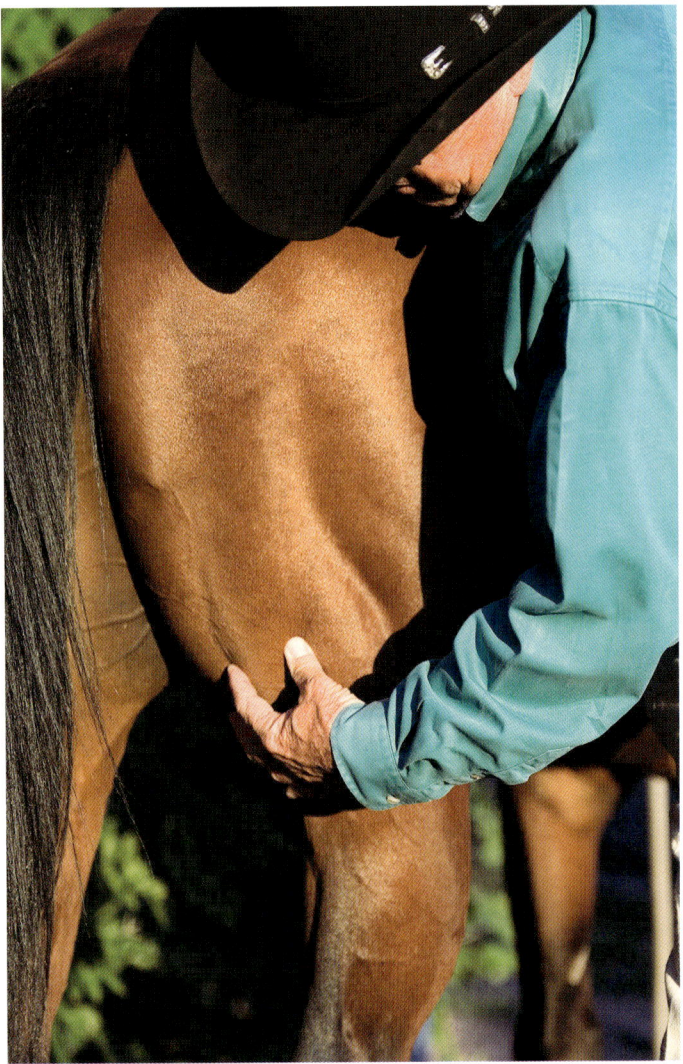

When the semitendinosis muscle is strained, it becomes encased in a fibrous—or even calcified—shell, a gross muscle change your veterinarian can feel.

consider your horse's fitness level when changing his job or returning him to work after downtime. Your horse's age also plays a role; an older horse requires a longer transitional period from a sedentary lifestyle to a working regimen than does a young horse.

Be aware that a fit horse can injure his muscles simply by playing too hard when he's turned out to pasture. The horse doesn't know his physical limits, which can lead to muscular and skeletal injuries. When turning out a fit horse to exercise, be sure to keep the turn-out time consistent and regular to avoid excessive pent-up energy. Not all horses in extremely fit condition can handle being turned out for uncontrolled exercise.

Down the road: Muscle injuries and soreness heal well, and in most situations the horse returns to normal activities. However, when major muscle bodies are injured, the associated scar tissue can cause mechanical lameness issues.

Fibrotic Myopathy

Your mare slipped while tied to the trailer, then pulled back in fear. As she did, her leather halter broke and she sat down, landing on her tail. She stood up and seemed all right. Nearly a month later, you notice a strange movement in her hindquarters.

What might be happening: Fibrotic myopathy involves injury of the semitendinosus muscle, which lies below the prominence of the buttocks alongside the tail. The condition is often associated with severe muscle injury caused by a horse pulling back or flipping over.

When the muscle is injured, it develops a scar, which reduces or limits the muscle's ability to stretch. This, in turn, causes the abnormal gait characteristic of fibrotic myopathy. The horse begins a normal stride with his hind leg, but when the hind foot moves forward and is a few inches from touching the ground, the muscle's decreased elasticity forces the foot to slide back and slap down on the ground, most evident at the walk.

The scarring process also causes an easy-to-feel mineralized "shell" to develop around the lower portion of the muscle.

What you notice: Many horses with fibrotic myopathy function well and continue working. Following are identifiable signs:

- A characteristic and unusual gait for your horse.

- Shell-like mineralization around your horse's affected muscle.

What you do: Watch your horse's movement and feel for any muscle change. If you notice changes, call your veterinarian.

What your veterinarian does: A veterinarian easily can identify fibrotic myopathy's characteristic gait. Furthermore, the muscle mineralization is very palpable. The condition is more mechanical than painful, so your horse might be able to continue performing.

If your horse can't perform at his usual level, surgical correction is possible and includes two approaches. The first involves cutting the attachment of the semitendinosus muscle to the tibia, just below the stifle on the inside of the leg. The second procedure requires removing a section of the scarred muscle mass at its tendon origin.

The healing process: If surgery isn't necessary, the horse might not require any special management. In this case, the condition doesn't significantly affect your horse's job. To continue using the horse, maintain his physical condition, keep him well-shod and establish a regular exercise program.

Post-surgery management depends on the surgical procedure prescribed by your veterinarian. A horse receiving the first previously discussed procedure usually returns to work after two weeks. The muscle-removal procedure usually requires six to eight weeks of confinement and controlled exercise for full recovery.

Down the road: A horse requiring surgery has a favorable prognosis if he has an uneventful recovery following the procedure. The procedure involving muscle and scar removal car-

ries a more favorable prognosis than that in which the tendon attachment is cut.

Myositis (Azoturia, Tying-Up or Monday Morning Syndrome, Rhabdomyolysis)

You rely on your Quarter Horse to help you work cattle on your big-scale Montana ranch. You trailer to a far pasture to look for strays, and leave the trailer at a long trot, moving over the higher ridges. Suddenly you notice your horse slowing down, as if he's tired, almost as if someone has stepped on his brakes—a feeling you have never noticed with him before. You pull him to a stop.

What might be happening: Myositis is a highly complicated condition of muscle physiology that results in abnormal glycogen metabolism; the affected muscles become very painful and are firm and tight in contraction. The affected horse is unable to move his muscles normally, due to simple mechanics, as well as the muscular pain. Research continues to provide new understanding of the syndrome, which is closely

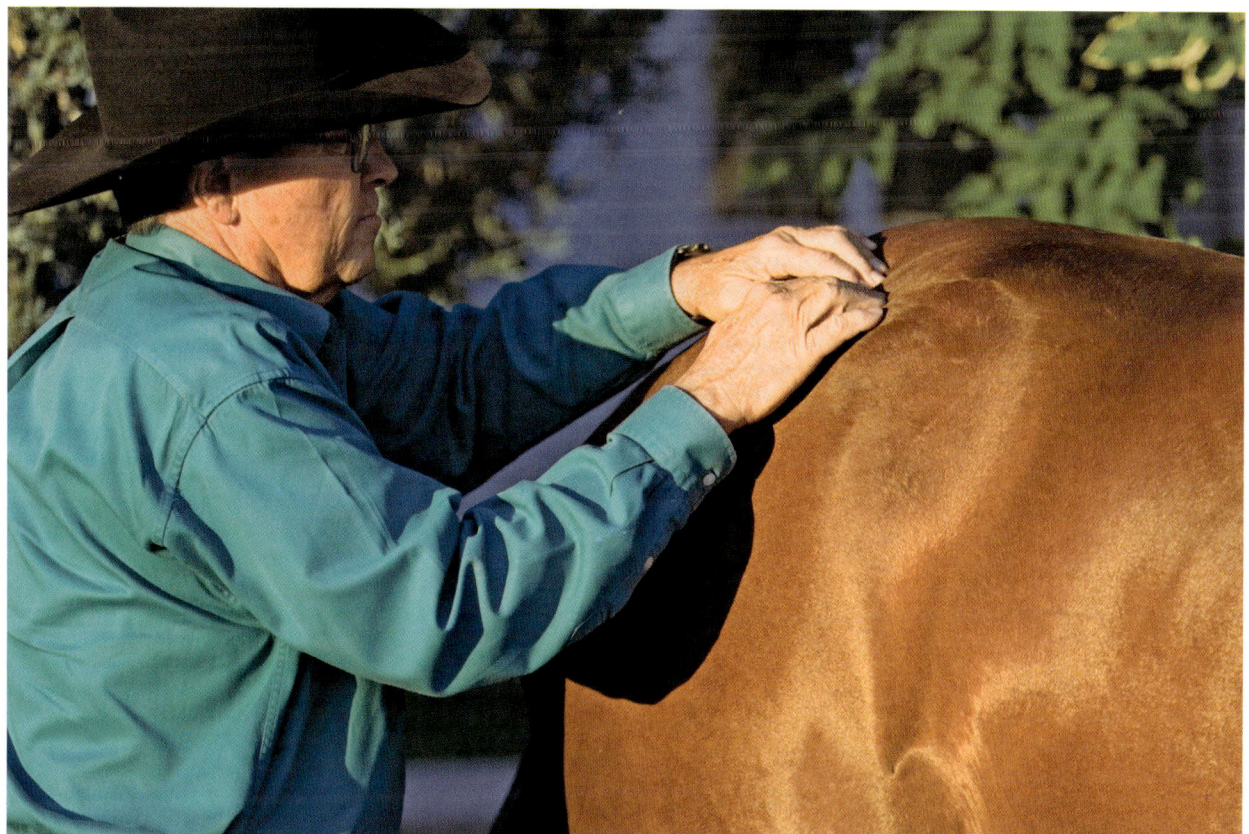

In most cases, your veterinarian can feel tense and hardened loin and croup muscles when your horse develops myositis. Other skeletal muscles also can be involved.

159

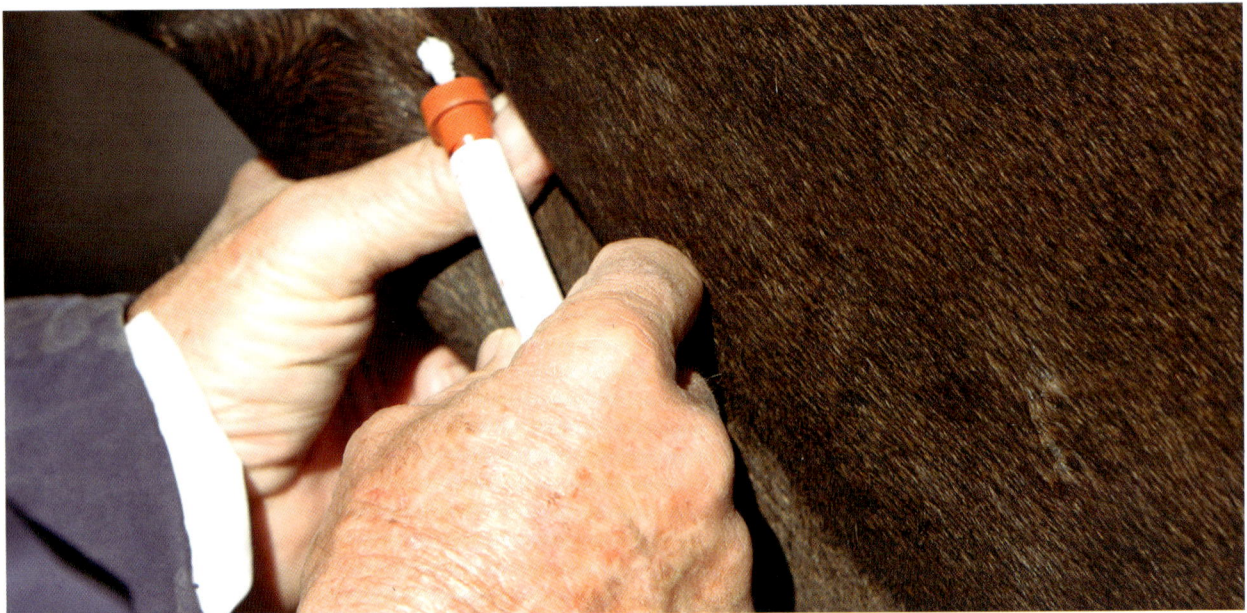

When a horse "ties up," muscle cells break down and proteins enter his bloodstream. Your veterinarian tests your horse's blood for excess creatine kinase (CK), a protein, to confirm a myositis diagnosis and quantify the amount of muscle damage.

related to polysaccharide storage myopathy (PSSM), affecting most all breeds and sometimes being caused by genetic mutation.

Myositis is generally brought on by exertion from riding or driving, though not always strenuous work. Damage occurs at the cellular level in the muscle. The affected muscle contracts, as if in spasm, making movement impossible. The involved muscle cells can burst, releasing cellular debris into the surrounding tissues, and your horse's body must metabolize the cellular debris and byproducts. Significant excesses of these byproducts have further negative effects on the body, especially the kidneys. The degree of the disease depends on the amount of affected muscle. Quick recognition and treatment are imperative to minimize muscle degeneration and significant kidney damage.

What you notice: This disease has affected performance and workhorses throughout history, causing enough pain that the horse completely quits working. Myositis generally surfaces in one of two situations: a horse that has just begun exercise or one that has just completed a period of extensive exertion. To have the horse effectively treated and prevent further muscle degeneration, you must quickly recognize the following specific symptoms:

- An apparent loss of energy within 10 to 15 minutes of beginning exercise or immediately following strenuous exertion, such as an endurance ride or race.

- Short-stepping with the hind legs.

- Overly firm muscle groups anywhere in your horse's body, but most likely in the loin or hindquarter. Note: Muscular firmness isn't always detectable, as the affected muscles might be far below the surface.

- Discolored, coffee-dark urine.

- Signs of pain and discomfort, including pawing, sweating and an anxious attitude.

- An inability to get up when your horse lies down.

What you do: Call your veterinarian at the first sign of tying-up. If your horse develops myositis when exercise begins, cease exercise and call your veterinarian. If the symptoms surface following heavy exertion, such as an endurance race, it's acceptable to continue walking the horse while awaiting veterinary assistance.

What your veterinarian does: Your veterinarian's diagnosis hinges on a physical exam and knowing your horse's history with myositis. Blood-chemistry tests measure the level of muscle-cell debris in the blood to confirm the diagnosis and quantify the damage.

Horseman's Dictionary

dorsal spinous processes: the spiny upward projections of the horse's vertebrae.

extra-corporeal shockwave treatment: applying ultra-high-energy sound waves into the body to help heal various body parts.

fascia: a sheet or band of fibrous tissue lying under the skin or encasing muscles.

palpate: feeling internal anatomy by careful touch and manipulation.

pitting edema: an area of trauma where fluid accumulates in and around the muscle mass. When you apply finger pressure, a dent develops in your horse's flesh and then gradually fills within a few minutes.

polysaccharide storage syndrome: a muscle disease that causes unusual storage of glycogen in the horse's muscle cells, resulting in painful muscle contraction. There is strong evidence this is caused by a genetic mutation.

vertebrae: bones that make up the spinal column.

Treatment focuses on reducing further muscle damage, pain and insult to your horse's body.

Your veterinarian administers medication to reduce pain and help relax your horse's muscles. Fluid therapy usually is required, either orally via stomach tube or intravenously. Fluid therapy reverses the shock created by the loss of body fluid and electrolytes, and dilutes the amount of muscle-cell debris, a product of muscle degeneration, dumped into the blood. This allows the kidneys to more efficiently handle the problem, which also minimizes kidney damage. The manner of administration, orally or intravenously, depends on the case's severity.

Sedation and analgesic medications are important to break the pain cycle occurring in the muscles. The medication dosage must be monitored closely in relationship to the horse's hydration.

Anti-inflammatory medications are used with caution to reduce pain and inflammation; however, excessive use can cause kidney damage.

Testing for PSSM, polysaccharide storage myopathy, involves a biopsy of the semitendinosus muscle, alongside the tail area, which is evaluated by a laboratory specializing in muscle pathology. Blood or hair testing can be used to screen the genetic cases.

The healing process: Following recovery from the initial insult, your horse can return to exercise depending upon the extent of the disease. Rest the horse for at least one day, and then begin a walking regimen determined by the case's severity. Muscle activity helps establish blood flow to the damaged area, which removes damaged cel-

lular tissue and other byproducts. In this stage, it's helpful to monitor the level of the muscle enzymes to evaluate the healing process, even though it's not necessary for the blood-enzyme levels to return to normal before the horse resumes work. Your veterinarian closely monitors your horse's progress to determine when the horse can return to work.

A horse that develops myositis is likely to encounter the problem again. Consequently, diet and exercise management are essential to decrease such incidents. A horse with a history of myositis requires daily exercise or at least extended daily turnout to manage the situation.

Reducing or completely eliminating your horse's carbohydrate intake—especially on non-exercise days—minimizes myositis episodes. If a horse requires more daily calories to maintain his body weight and energy level than are available in hay, feeding vegetable oil or another fat source helps. In areas where forage lacks vitamin E or selenium, supplementing these elements also can help alleviate myositis occurrences.

Electrolyte supplementation during exercise is very important. Some consistently recurring cases respond to rubella injections, or measles vaccinations.

Down the road: If myositis develops again, you instantly recognize the symptoms, end the workout and begin treatment, thereby minimizing the damage. With proper management, most bouts of myositis can be prevented. Adjustment to your horse's diet and exercise program and communication with a veterinarian are necessary for a favorable prognosis.

15

SOFT TISSUE: TENDONS AND LIGAMENTS

Tendons and ligaments, connecting muscle to bone and bone to bone respectively, help your horse's joints move within a typical range of motion.

Tendons and ligaments are two individual structure types that have similar roles in that they connect different parts of your horse's anatomy. Tendons are fibrous bands that hook muscles to bone. When muscles contract, the tendons move the attached bones. Ligaments also are fibrous bands, but they attach bones to bones—no muscles are involved.

You can picture how tendons and ligaments work by imagining industrial cables. Like cables, these structures combine many fibrous strands working together to provide optimum support. The strands have more strength when acting together than when alone. Tendon and ligament fiber strands tend to run parallel to one another. With this arrangement, tendons and ligaments have some give, an elastic quality that allows a horse's fetlock to extend toward the ground when landing from a jump or to help a horse absorb concussion when turning sharply. However, if a horse's tendons and ligaments are stressed beyond their elastic limits, the individual strands can begin to tear. There are many strands within the tendons and ligaments, and some or all might stretch or tear under stress. Tendons and ligaments also can become damaged from a direct blow, which causes a slight bruise or actually forces the tendon or ligament apart.

Speed-event horses can experience soft-tissue injury when running in deep footing, which stresses the flexor tendons and ligaments. Injuries also are possible when working on hard surfaces as the horse's joints absorb shock.

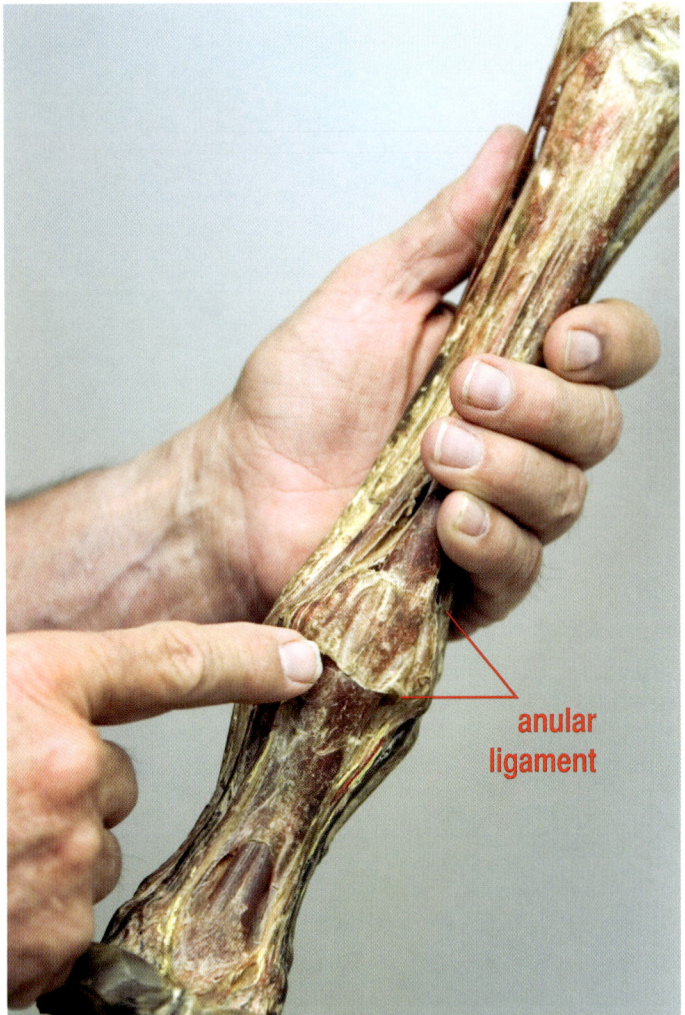

anular
ligament

The horizontal line is at the bottom of the anular ligament, a firm band of connective tissue that reaches across the back of the fetlock and covers the sesamoid bones and the flexor tendons.

Anular Ligament Injury

As you warm up your show hunter in the arena, he suddenly spooks at something along the rail. You feel him stumble, take a few lame steps and then seem better, but not okay. You notice a limp as you walk back to the stall. There is no obvious swelling, but you find tenderness on the back of his fetlock area.

What might be happening: The palmar anular ligament, a firm 2-inch band of connective tissue, cups around the back of the front fetlock, covering the sesamoid bones and the flexor tendons. Along with the sesamoid bones the ligament encases the superficial and deep flexor tendons and their sheath as they course down around the back of the fetlock joint. The anular ligament fibers are orientated parallel to the ground or perpendicular to the flexor tendon fibers, so the structure is firm and has minimal stretch or elasticity.

When your horse jumped, he hit the back of his front fetlock with a rear foot, bruising the anular ligament. Swelling within the ligament causes pain, as well as puts pressure on the flexor tendons as they course under the anular ligament. In addition, there also could be damage to the flexor tendons.

What you notice: You find heat and swelling associated with the back of the fetlock joint, the amount varying with the degree of injury. The lameness could range from Grade 2 to a Grade 4 in severity.

What you do: With a fresh injury you apply cold therapy, such as running cold water on the injury or packing it in an ice bandage for 30 minutes and then applying a support bandage. Be sure to have a discussion with your veterinarian to explain the degree of lameness, heat and swelling you've found, in order to establish the need for an examination.

What your veterinarian does: He performs a thorough evaluation of the involved structures, feeling for pain, disruption of tissue, pain with joint flexion, and the degree of lameness. To further assess the soft tissues, the anular ligament and flexor tendons, he performs an ultrasound exam and possibly radiographs to evaluate the sesamoid bones. The injury's extent determines further treatment.

The healing process: If the injury is limited to superficial bruising, your veterinarian has you continue the cold therapy and support bandages, as well as systemic anti-inflammatory medications. Applying a topical anti-inflammatory medication also can be helpful.

If the integrity of the anular ligament or the flexor tendons is damaged and they're swollen, surgical intervention can be required. In such surgery the ligament is severed longitudinally, which relieves pressure on the flexor tendons and also within the anular ligament if it is severely bruised.

A third scenario: The flexor tendons are injured within the digital tendon sheath, but the anular ligament is not injured. In this situation the tendons respond to the injury in normal inflammatory fashion by swelling. The anular ligament does not stretch and therefore puts binding pressure on the affected tendons as they travel under the anular ligament. This painful process interferes with healing and causes significant lameness. Even if the lameness improves, it's seldom resolved until the ligament is surgically severed to relieve pressure on the tendons, allowing the healing process to proceed. This is important to remember: Although there is significant relief after the ligament is cut, the tendon needs time to complete its healing process, often four to six months,

Down the road: With proper care and rest, there is reason to expect complete healing for most cases and for these horses to return to their regular work levels. Cases with repeated injuries and longer durations before surgery have poorer prognoses.

Suspensory Ligament Desmitis

Your cutting horse worked hard last night in the deep arena footing. Onlookers thought he might have taken a strange step during his work. Today, he doesn't seem to listen to your cues, not even as you walk slowly into the practice arena. You hop off to examine his legs and notice that his left rear leg is sensitive to deep pressure behind the lower area of his hock and behind the upper area of his cannon bone. His left leg is noticeably thicker than the right.

What might be happening: The suspensory ligament originates at the top of the cannon bone behind the knee in the front leg, and at the back of the hock on the hind leg. The ligament runs down the cannon bone's backside, between the two splint bones, and splits into two branches that attach to the respective sesamoid bones at the fetlock. The suspensory ligament's function is vital to fetlock support, along with the superficial and deep digital flexor tendons.

As with all ligament tissue, the suspensory ligament has some elasticity, but is susceptible to strain and tearing, which results in suspensory ligament desmitis, or ligament inflammation. Inflammation can result from sudden stress to the area, such as when a horse's foot lands incorrectly, which excessively stretches the structure. Hard work in deep, heavy footing or on hard, unforgiving surfaces predisposes a horse to suspensory ligament desmitis. Often an underlying lameness, such as foot soreness, seems to predispose a horse to suspensory injury. The ligament can completely rupture in some cases involving fatigue or chronic re-injury.

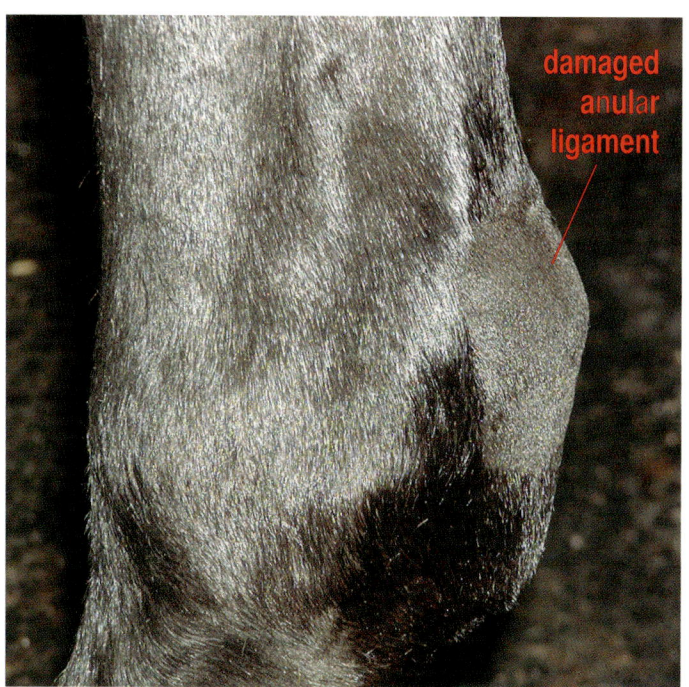

The bump on the back of this horse's fetlock is a damaged anular ligament.

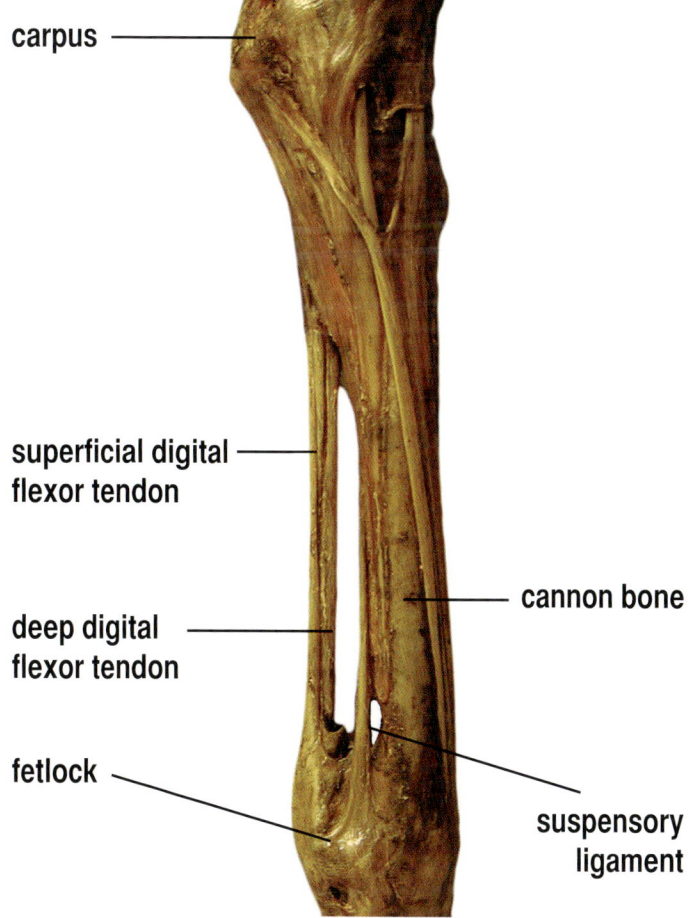

The flexor tendons and suspensory ligament provide support for your horse's fetlock and lower leg, and the flexor tendons with their respective muscles also help propel your horse forward.

165

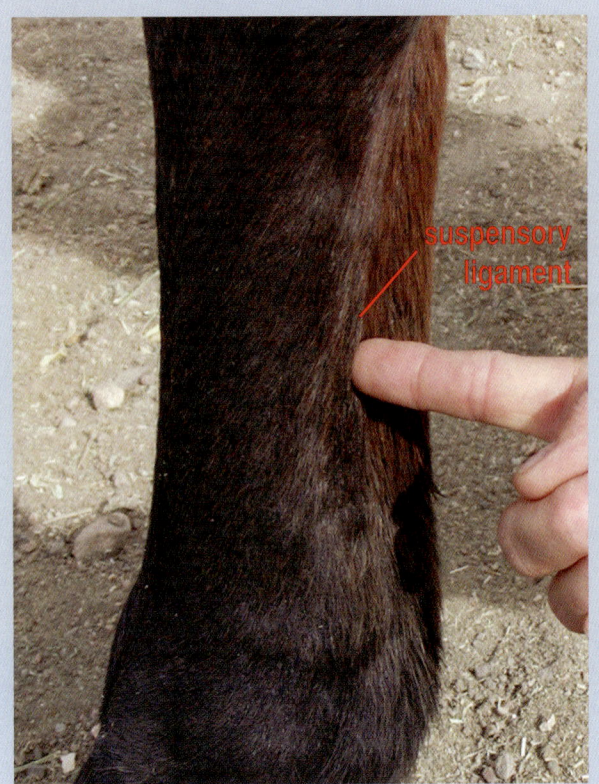
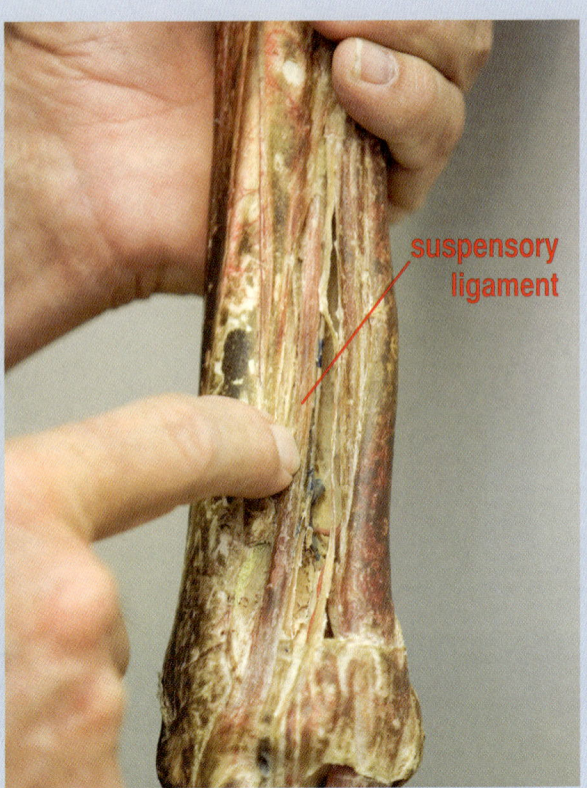

The suspensory ligament runs parallel to the flexor tendons and with the sesamoid bones and the distal sesamoidian ligaments forms the primary support for the fetlock joint.

Rear-leg suspensory ligament injuries are of greater concern than those in the front legs. The rear leg suspensory doesn't have as much auxiliary support, due to the lack of well-developed flexor tendon check ligaments. The ligament's upper portion is wrapped in a firm tissue sheath, which puts uncomfortable pressure on the ligament when it swells during the inflammatory process.

What you notice: You see a Grade 2 to Grade 4 lameness. The degree of suspensory-ligament damage significantly influences this problem's outward signs. Symptoms can range from minor and almost unnoticeable to severe and easily observable. You also notice:

- More lameness when the affected leg is on the outside of a circle as your horse trots.

- Soreness when pressure is applied just below your horse's knee and behind the cannon bone.

- Notable thickness behind the cannon bone and in front of the flexor tendons anywhere down to the sesamoid bones.

- The fetlock on the injured leg fails to settle well when compared to an unaffected leg.

- Usually more noticeable lameness after the horse has a short rest and when he moves in soft ground.

- In unusual cases, no weight-bearing on the injured limb.

- With severe suspensory injury, the fetlock drops lower than normal.

What you do: Treat the affected area with cold therapy and support bandage. Call your veterinarian any time you notice a change in your horse's gait and notice any swelling or thickness.

What your veterinarian does: Beginning with a visual and physical exam, your veterinarian looks for the above-listed symptoms. Diagnostic blocking often is required to isolate the lameness, especially in mild to moderate cases, and to identify any other sources of concurrent lameness.

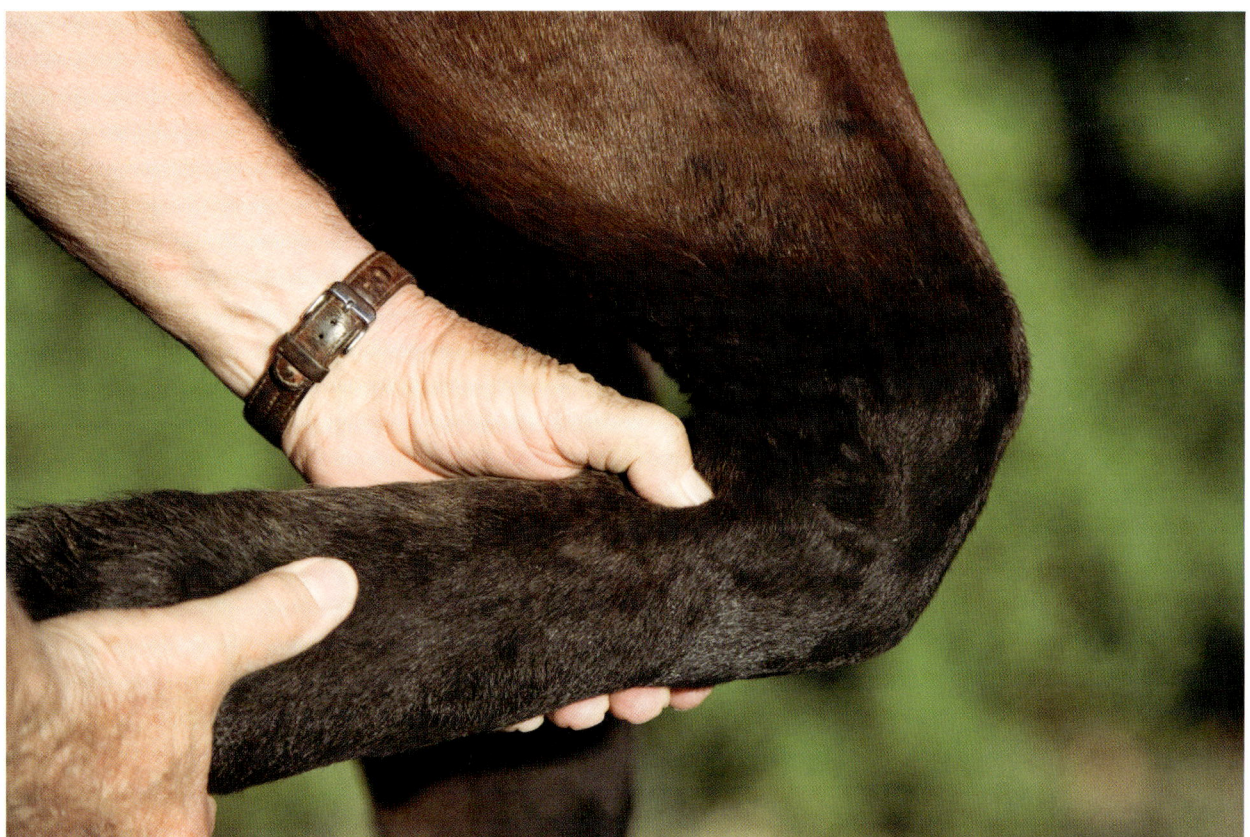

When your veterinarian palpates the origin of your horse's suspensory ligament, which originates at the upper end of the cannon bone, he checks for pain and swelling.

Ultrasound plays a major role in the diagnosis and prognosis. The imagery identifies and quantifies the injury's extent and also is useful for monitoring the healing process. However, in some cases, the lesion might not be easily identified with ultrasound.

Radiographs are necessary to rule out an avulsion fracture, which occurs if stress placed on the ligament causes it to pull a fragment from the cannon bone's back surface where the suspensory ligament originates.

Treatment is directed toward limiting suspensory ligament stress and reducing inflammation within the ligament. Immediately begin cold therapy and apply a support wrap. A minor strain or tear might be treated with support from a gel cast and support bandage.

Most injuries with some degree of ligament tearing require at least four months of confinement and controlled exercise. Hand-walking is the most suitable exercise, and the amount of exercise depends upon the degree of damage and the horse's temperament. The subtle stress placed on the suspensory ligament during controlled exercise helps the new fibers of scar tissue align in the direction of stress, which makes a more resilient scar, allowing for more complete and stronger healing.

Shockwave treatment begins in the first four weeks following the injury. Most cases receive three treatments on a two-week interval.

Intra-lesion injections of stem cells or platelet-enriched plasma have proven to be a valuable therapy for suspensory ligament injury.

More serious injuries to the area, including a complete suspensory rupture, require completely unloading the suspensory ligament by using an apparatus, such as a Kimzey splint, or a rigid lower leg cast for support during the initial four- to six-week healing process. Treatment then continues with confinement, controlled exercise and support bandages.

Shoeing usually doesn't change dramatically. A rolled-toe shoe without a wedge is ideal. Raising the heel puts slack in the deep flexor tendon, thus increasing the suspensory ligament's load and hindering the healing process.

The healing process: A suspensory-ligament injury can be a minor, nagging issue or career-ending and very frustrating to manage. Proper management is essential for your

167

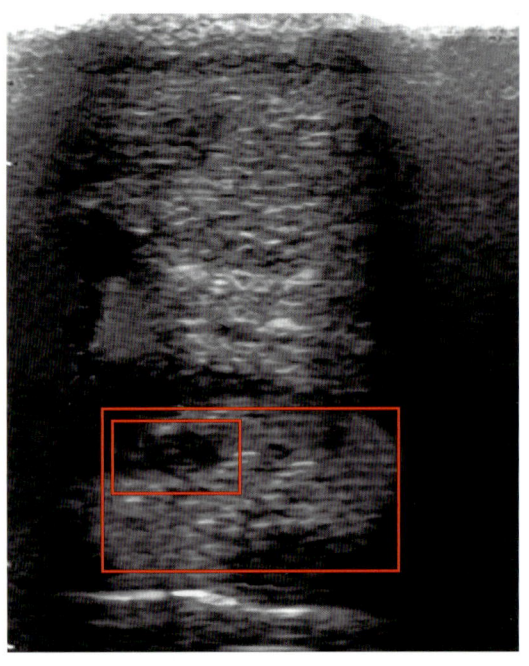

This ultrasound image shows the horse's suspensory ligament outlined by the larger rectangle and a tear or core lesion demonstrated by the dark coloring.

horse to return to his job and continue working after recovery. Avoid using the horse in deep ground, as well as letting the horse's feet get long at the toe. Furthermore, steer clear of fatigue-type work on hard ground, and your horse must be fit for his job. Finally, fully manage all other lower-leg lameness issues, as they can compound suspensory-ligament injuries.

Some horses with minor suspensory injuries can continue to perform, depending on the task to be performed, the ability to control the horse's efforts or exertion and knowledge of prior suspensory pain.

Down the road: The outlook ranges from favorable to unfavorable, depending on the injury's extent and the horse's job. Rear-leg suspensory ligament injuries are more career-limiting than those affecting the foreleg.

Tendon-Sheath Injury

Your horse always has had some extra fluid in the flexor tendon sheaths of his rear fetlocks, but no soreness or lameness has been associated with the structures. You participate in a two-day trail ride, which included going through deep boggy areas. Monday morning you notice additional tendon sheath enlargement in the right rear. With palpation and by applying pressure, you notice heat and soreness in the area. Your horse is noticeably short-strided at the trot.

What might be happening: A tendon sheath encases a tendon as it goes around a prominence, such as a joint or raised area in your horse's anatomy. The sheath has a slick synovial lining that reduces friction. Tendon sheath damage can be acute or due to chronic use-related insults.

The tendon sheath found in the rear fetlock frequently accumulates excess fluid due to use trauma resulting from normal work. This often represents only a blemish and doesn't cause lameness.

Wounds that puncture a tendon sheath might be very serious because of the possibility of infection within the sheath.

Sometimes a horse injures the tendon sheath along with the structures it protects, such as the digital flexor tendons, which can be very serious. Furthermore, a tendon sheath might adhere to the associated tendon, which results in chronic reinjury.

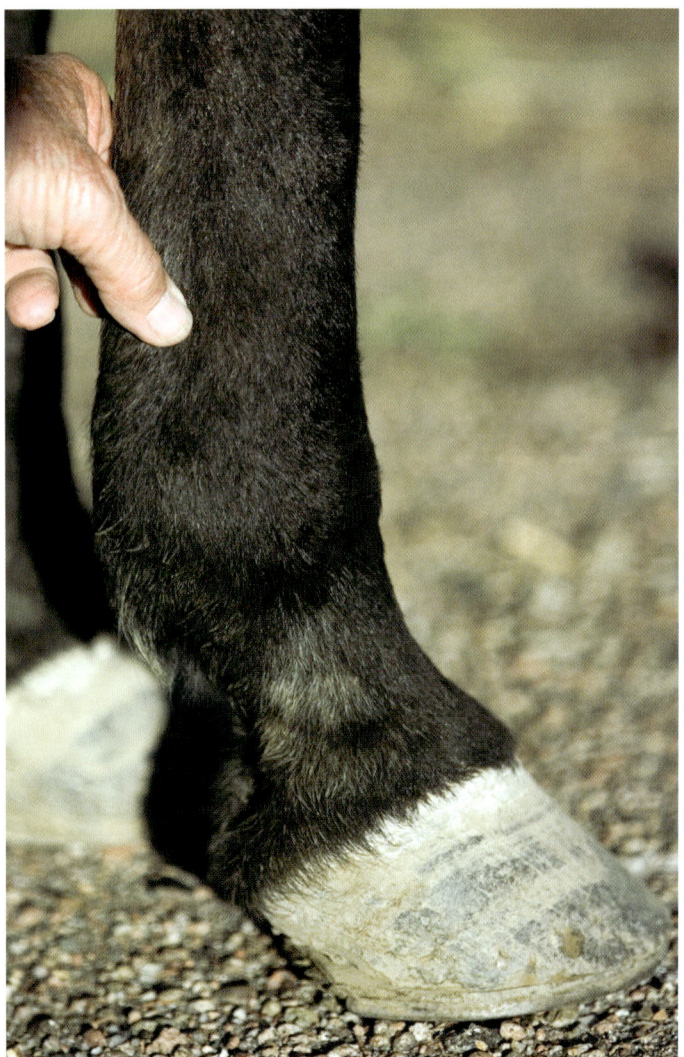

Your horse's digital flexor sheath encases the flexor tendons as they course down and around the fetlock.

Overall, a flexor tendon-sheath injury is more critical than one associated with an extensor tendon.

What you notice: You see a Grade 2 to Grade 4 lameness. Injured tendon sheaths throughout the horse's anatomy show the following signs:

• Soreness when palpated.

• Swelling confined to a specific area, with soft swelling that moves around within the sheath.

• Heat in the affected area.

• Pain when the joint is flexed.

What you do: Call your veterinarian when you notice a new wind puff, especially if there is lameness. While on his way to do a formal evaluation, your veterinarian might recommend that you treat your horse with 30 minutes of cold therapy and a bandage.

What your veterinarian does: Your veterinarian notes the above symptoms, and then uses ultrasound to assess the tendon sheath's and tendons' condition and evaluate the type of fluid in the sheath. If he suspects an infection, your veterinarian removes some fluid for laboratory evaluation. He also takes radiographs to ensure that the bony structures aren't compromised.

A more involved procedure entails arthroscopy, or intra-synovial surgery using instruments passed through small portals to assess internal damage and perform any necessary surgical cleanup in the area. This is done for cases involving tendon injury within the sheath, for chronic cases having tendon adhesions or in some cases of infection.

Cold-water therapy and support bandages are important for first-aid. Confinement, controlled exercise and administration of anti-inflammatory medication are indicated according to the extent of the injury. Shockwave therapy might help speed the recovery process.

As mentioned, arthroscopy can play a role in more severe cases, whether it begins during the diagnostic process or as a treatment measure. Using arthroscopy, your veterinarian can break down adhesions and wash blood from the area.

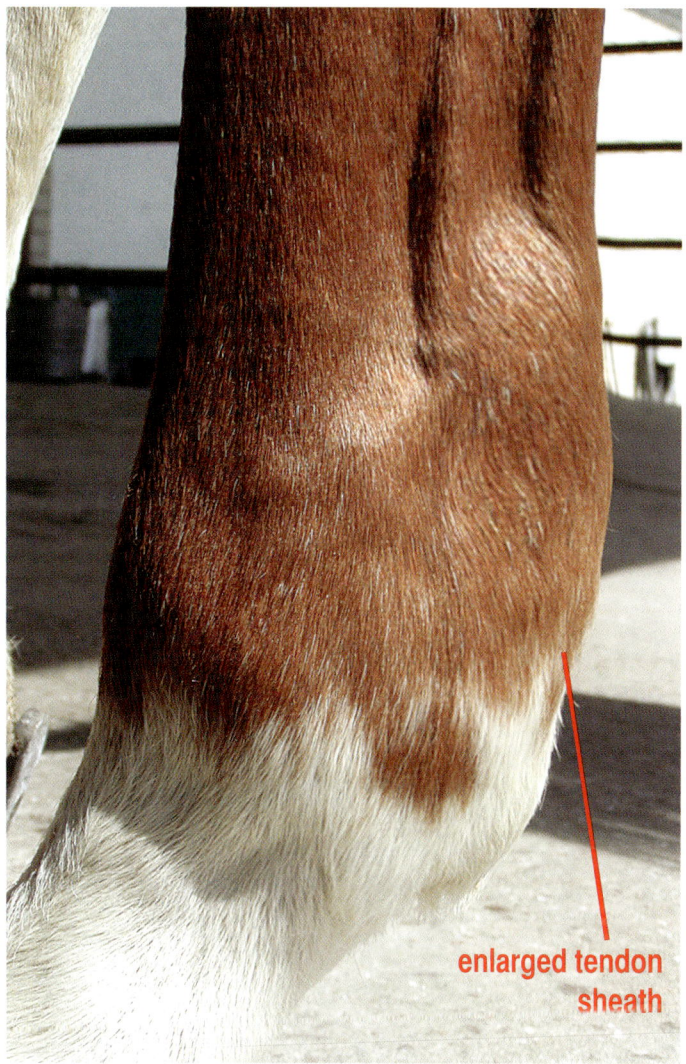

enlarged tendon sheath

This horse has an enlarged tendon sheath, filled with fluid and fibrous tissue, which is evident from the outside and dramatic when compared with his healthy leg.

Furthermore, the sheath and tendon can be restricted by the anular ligament, a fibrous band with little elasticity that holds the tendons and sheath in place behind the fetlock. It's difficult to heal a tendon injured along with the sheath because the anular ligament restricts the normal phases of healing—swelling and increased blood supply. (See Chapter 7.) If necessary, the anular ligament can be transected, or cut, to relieve the tension, allow necessary swelling to develop and the healing process to continue.

Recovery time hinges on the injury's extent, from three weeks to six months.

The healing process: A sports-medicine boot might help protect and support the affected sheath and tendon during work to prevent re-injury.

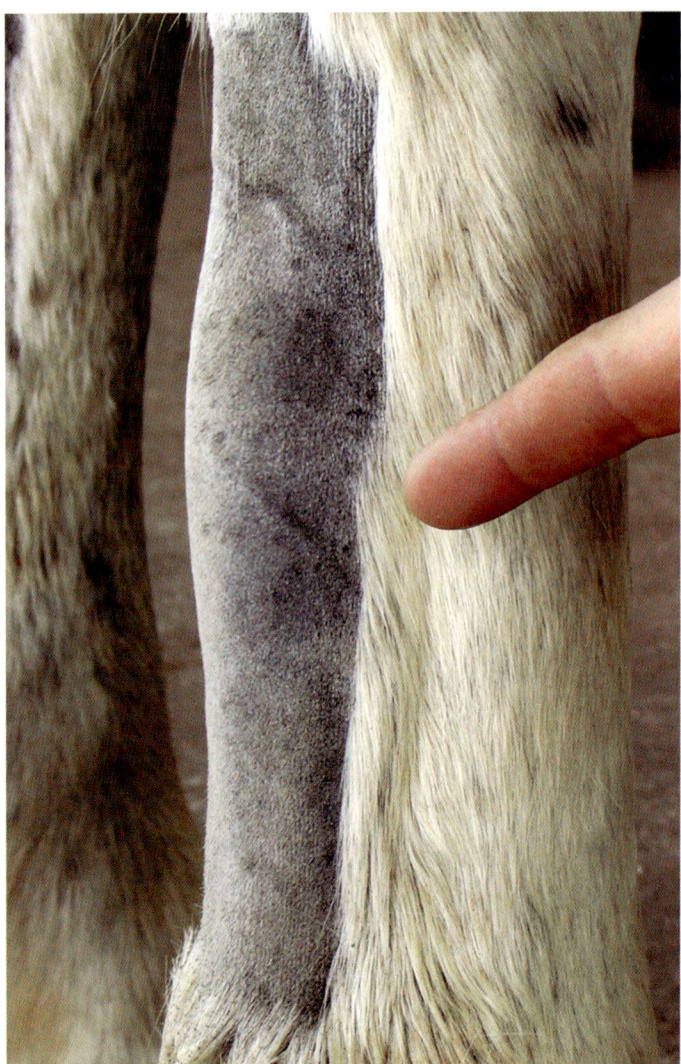

When tendon fibers tear, blood and fluid collect, creating an enlargement as seen in this photograph.

Down the road: In most situations, a favorable prognosis exists, assuming the injury is quickly and completely treated. If tendons also are involved, the prognosis can be less favorable, depending on the damage.

Bowed Tendon

On a recent trail ride, you and your barn buddy decide to race as you approach a wide, flat field. You stay in the lead for nearly 50 yards—your horse at a full gallop. Suddenly, you feel a change in his gait and pull him to a stop, dismount and check his legs. There is no specific change or lesion and really not much lameness. You walk back to the barn, remove the tack and groom your horse. When you walk him to his lot, you notice a distinct lameness of his left front leg. A quick exam shows swelling along the tendons behind the cannon

bone, and palpation of this area results in a definite pain response from your horse.

What might be happening: A bowed tendon, one of the most common soft-tissue injuries, can occur alone or possibly in concert with a tendon-sheath problem. The classic bowed tendon refers to injury of the superficial digital flexor tendon in the cannon-bone region. Most use the term to indicate damage to either the superficial or deep flexor tendons. In some cases, both structures are involved. Both tendons originate above the knee or hock and continue down the backside of the leg. The superficial digital flexor tendon ends below the fetlock at the pastern, and the deep flexor tendon attaches to the bottom of the coffin bone. Along with the suspensory ligament, these tendons provide primary front- and rear-leg support.

Both the superficial digital flexor tendon and the deep digital flexor tendon have heavy auxiliary attachments in the knee area, which act as accessory support structures when their respective muscles become fatigued. These attachments are the superior check ligament, which connects to the superficial digital flexor tendon, and inferior check ligament, connecting to the deep digital flexor tendon. The superior check ligament originates on your horse's radius bone above the knee. The inferior check ligament originates at the back of the knee and attaches to the deep digital flexor tendon in the cannon-bone area and might be involved in an injury to that tendon, but can incur primary damage.

The following discussion of diagnosis, treatment, management and prognosis refers to injury of the superficial digital flexor tendon, deep digital flexor tendon or inferior check ligament.

This injury occurs most often when a horse works to fatigue, such as when racing or competing in cross-country speed events. The injury also can develop in any performance horse due to unexpected stress placed on his body structures. An injury results from pulling the structure beyond its normal elasticity, causing a portion or all of the fibers to rupture, and the injury's extent is relative to the percent of structural damage.

What you notice: You see Grade 2 to Grade 5 lameness as you also notice your horse's symptoms in a period of time after a workout:

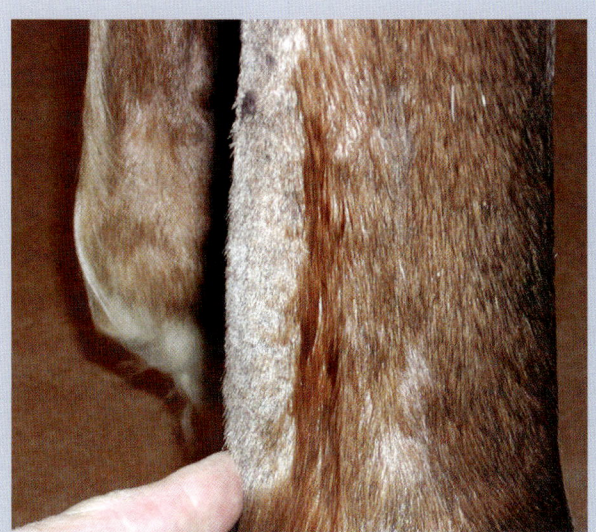

Not all bowed tendons are conspicuous. This moderately bowed tendon still needs rest and treatment.

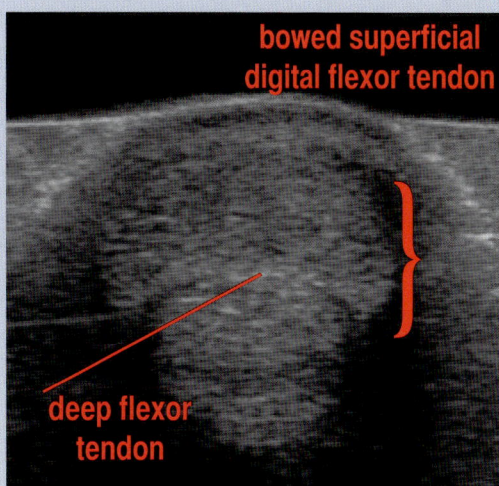

bowed superficial digital flexor tendon

deep flexor tendon

This ultrasound image of the same horse's bowed tendon shows the enlarged, cup-shaped superficial digital flexor tendon and the normal deep flexor tendon.

- Noticeable swelling and heat between the knee and fetlock, behind the cannon bone.

- A pain response to firm digital pressure in the above-noted area.

- Possibly failure to completely load the fetlock when it's in a weight-bearing position.

What you do: Limit your horse's activity, begin ice therapy and apply a support bandage. Ask your veterinarian to see your horse as soon as possible, but note that this isn't an emergency. However, prompt attention is a real asset to the healing process.

What your veterinarian does: Your veterinarian looks for the above symptoms and evaluates the damage by using ultrasound imaging.

Treatment focuses on preventing further damage, reducing inflammation and controlling the horse's exercise during recovery. At the first signs of injury, cease exercise, begin cold therapy and apply dimethyl sulfoxide, also known as DMSO, an anti-inflammatory and antibacterial topical agent, under a dry support bandage. Anti-inflammatory medication helps control swelling and offers pain relief. Remember that even though pain is reduced, your horse still has an injury, and his exercise regimen must be controlled. The injury's continued management depends on the damage, which is assessed by using ultrasound.

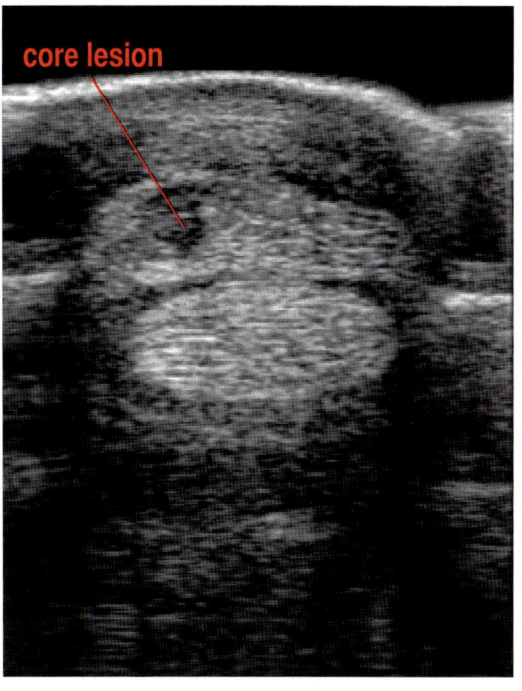

core lesion

A horse's bowed tendon and a significant tear or core lesion are obvious in this ultrasound and will require extended healing time.

Cold therapy should be continued twice daily for at least the first two weeks following the injury.

After the horse has rested for two weeks, your veterinarian usually begins shockwave treatment, which facilitates quicker, more solid healing.

Your horse's controlled exercise program varies according to the extent of damage. It's believed that some stress placed on the healing tendon helps align the scar's fibers along the lines of stress, resulting in a stronger scar.

LAMENESS Q&A

Why does cold therapy play such a major role when treating soft-tissue injuries? Are there any variables to consider?

The goal of cold therapy is to reduce inflammation at the site of a fresh injury. The total physiological influence of cold therapy isn't completely understood, but the effects can be quite dramatic.

Cold therapy constricts blood vessels, which minimizes fluid leaking into the tissues, and thus limits swelling. Such therapy is most effective in the first 48 hours following an injury.

In most situations, the water can't be too cold. Water from a hose is usually sufficient, and its massaging capabilities offer an additional asset. Turbulator boots with ice water work well, as do commercially produced ice packs that can be bandaged to the leg. Standing a horse in a cold stream can be adequate, too.

Most often, veterinarians recommend 20-minute intervals of cold therapy several times a day for optimal results. To avoid skin irritation, it's best not to apply ice directly to the horse's skin. Commercially available cryo-cuff machines are very effective.

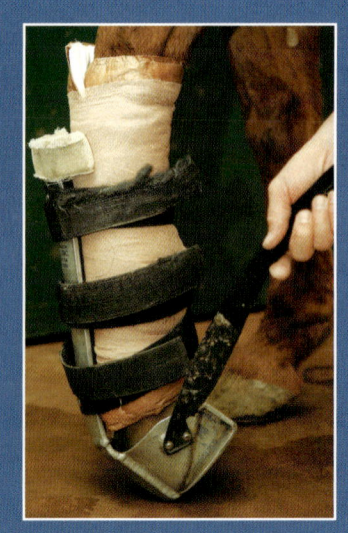

A Kimzey splint holds the horse's foot and pastern at a steep enough angle to unweight the flexor tendons and suspensory ligament.

leakage into the injured area. Once the bleeding or leaking of fluid is under control, usually after 48 hours, heat therapy can begin.

What is heat therapy, and can heat therapy be used too soon in the healing process?

The goal of heat therapy is to increase circulation, thereby reducing swelling or edema. Heat dilates blood vessels and, in theory, facilitates greater blood flow to assist in removing fluid and cellular debris from an injury. This therapy can consist of a horse standing in a bucket of hot water, running hot water from a hose over the injury or using a sweat bandage. Adding hydroscopic agents, such as Epsom salts, can further enhance edema removal.

When an injury first occurs, heat therapy isn't a good choice because it might promote excess bleeding or fluid

What's a Kimzey splint?

It's an aluminum apparatus with a foot cup and a vertical brace that runs up the front of the leg to just below the knee or hock. Wide hook-and-loop closure straps hold the splint in place. Properly used, the splint holds the foot, pastern and fetlock in vertical alignment, which unloads the suspensory ligament and flexor tendons.

The Kimzey splint was developed as a first-aid tool for racehorses whose fetlock support structures break down during a race. The splint also has important applications for management of performance horses with other lower-leg injuries.

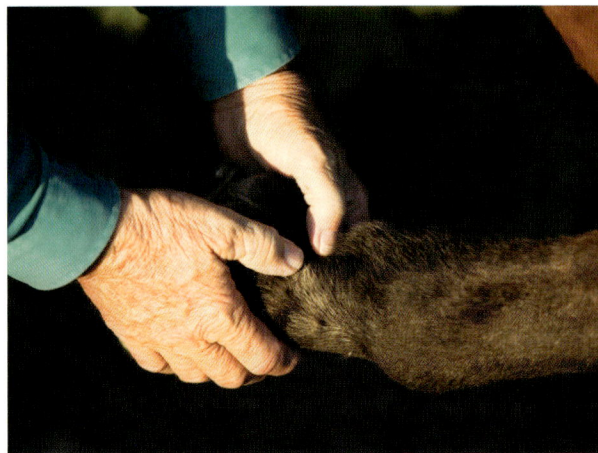

Your veterinarian can feel the deep flexor tendon as it courses through the back of your horse's pastern and reaches your horse's foot.

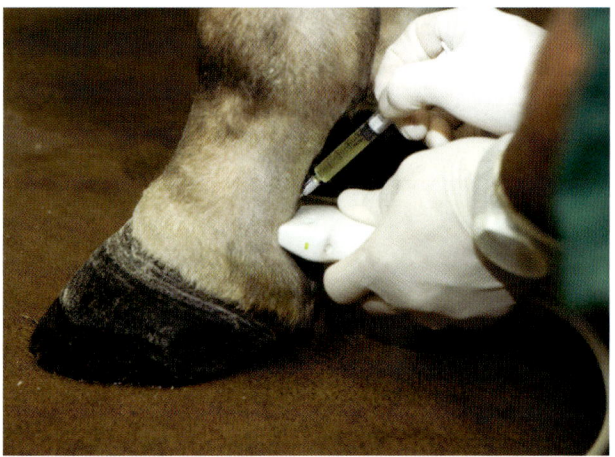

Ultrasound-guided injection of cultured stem cells into a torn deep flexor tendon allows the formation of new tendon cells and reduces the amount of fibrous scar cells.

How do you wrap a leg to avoid causing a bandage bow?

Careful wrapping technique can alleviate the problem of a horse developing a bandage bow. Follow these step-by-step instructions and photos to properly wrap a horse's leg.

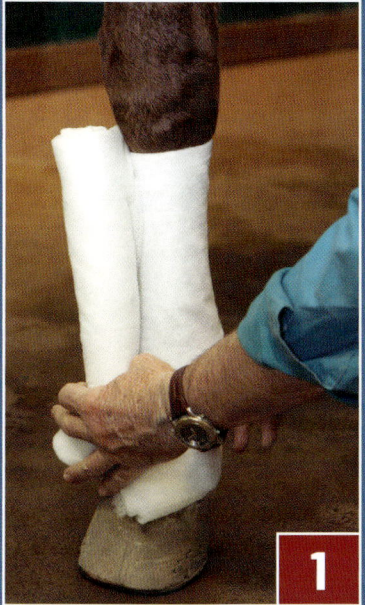
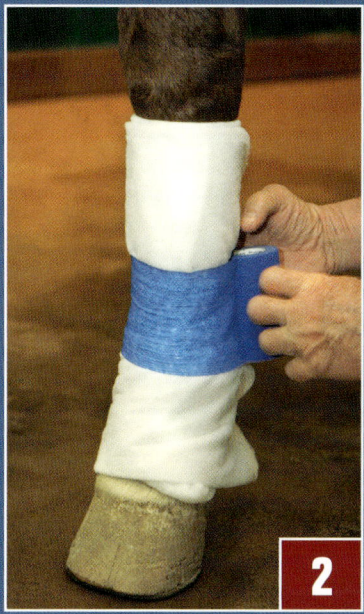
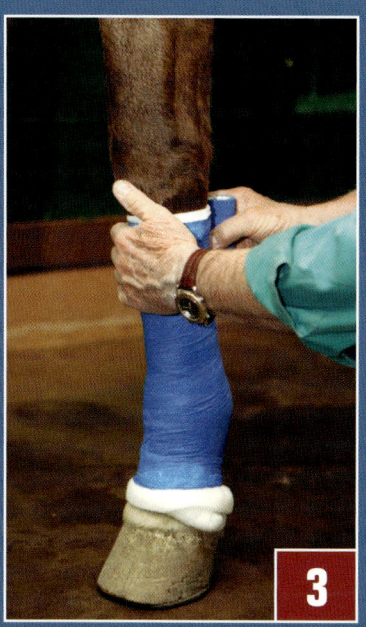

1. Begin wrapping the leg with a soft padding material that conforms to the horse's leg. Looking at the outside of the leg, wrap from front to back around the horse's leg. 2. Place the starting end of the elastic top wrap just above your horse's fetlock. Begin wrapping from the inside of the horse's leg outward. Place enough tension on the top wrap to remove half of its stretch when wrapping. Never pull out all of the wrap's stretch, or your horse's leg is wrapped too tightly. 3. Continue wrapping the leg with even tension, pulling the bandage from the roll by unwrapping one section at a time. Be sure wrinkles don't develop in the wrap because that can lead to a bandage bow. The completed leg wrap is smooth and supportive.

Work with your veterinarian to critically evaluate your horse's improvement and to ensure that your horse doesn't regress with exercise.

Stem-cell or platelet-enriched plasma injections into the tendon tear help the quality of the healing process. Stem cells have the ability to mature into the same cell type as those in the surrounding area. Injecting stem cells into a tendon-core lesion results in the development of new tendon cells to heal the injury, rather than only fibrous scar cells, which lack the elasticity of normal tendon cells.

A surgical procedure called tendon splitting also is used to aid healing of the injured tendon. A series of small incisions or cuts is made into the tendon's core lesion. This allows the accumulated fluid to escape and aids the development of blood supply to the lesion.

For injuries to the superficial flexor tendon, surgical severing of the superior check ligament is used. In performance horses this procedure is more widely used for cases of repeated injuries.

Hyperbaric oxygen therapy also helps serious cases by increasing the oxygen supplied to the injury.

Bimonthly ultrasounds evaluate the horse's progress. Recovery time depends on the stress of the horse's job, the degree of injury and the horse's response to treatment, which usually requires four months to a year.

If the injury involves the carpal canal or anular ligament, arthroscopy is necessary and dictates the proper treatment procedure.

The healing process: Once the structure heals, closely and regularly survey your horse's injured area and palpate for swelling, pain and heat after each workout. If there's any

173

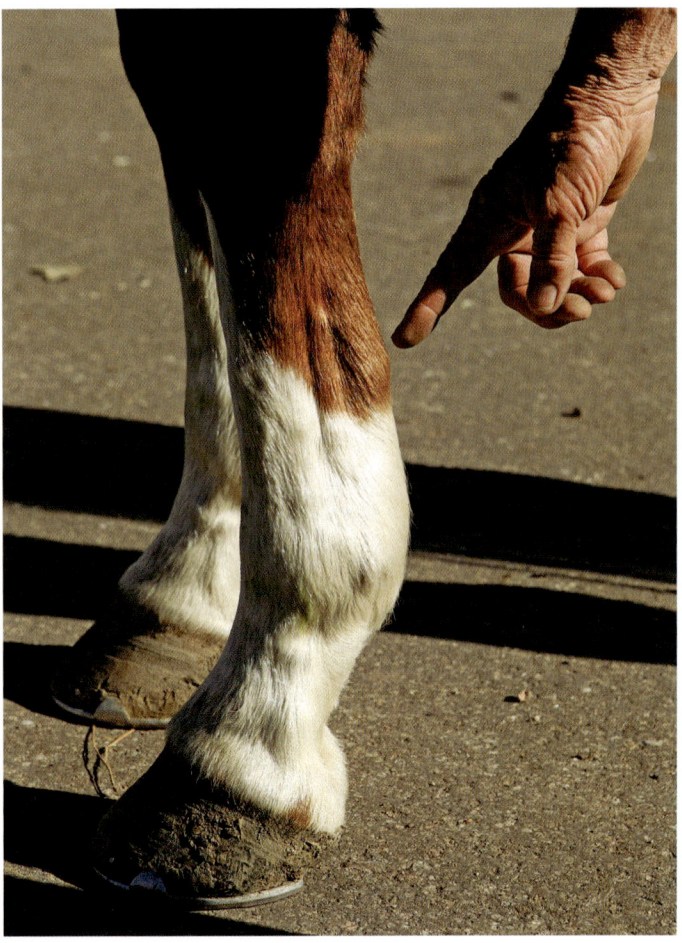

A bandage bow occurs when a too-tight bandage irritates a nerve that crosses the superficial flexor tendon in the mid-cannon area, and the tissue around the tendon becomes thickened and enlarged.

fresh swelling or heat, or if your horse seems to be in pain, cold therapy is necessary. The regular use of sports-medicine boots is a good practice. However, because they loosen as the horse works, reset the boots after each performance.

Down the road: As with most soft-tissue injuries, the degree of damage influences the prognosis. Most arena performance horses have good prognoses with good management.

Bandage Bow

You misplaced your usual sports-medicine boots just before your team-penning practice. Instead of allowing your horse to go without leg gear, you decide to wrap his legs with a set of polo wraps your friend keeps in your mutual tack room. You haven't used polo wraps often and realize too late that your wraps were too tight. When you remove the wraps, your horse's legs look normal, but after the wraps are off for a few minutes, you notice swelling along the backside of the flexor tendons and also some pain response to palpation.

What might be happening: When you apply a bandage too tightly, it places pressure on the peritendon tissue surrounding the tendon and on the nerve bundle that crosses the backside of the superficial digital flexor tendon midway between the knee and fetlock. This pressure damages the tissue, and the body responds with swelling. In most cases, the tendon isn't involved, and there's no great risk for lameness with careful management.

Splint boots that attach with hook-and-loop closure straps also can create the same injury if the straps thread through flat dee-rings and pull back to secure the boot. With the straps pulled too tightly, these boots can place excessive pressure on the tendons without the rider's knowledge.

What you notice: The following symptoms of a bandage bow are noticeable after removing a support wrap or bandage. You see up to a Grade 2 lameness as you also notice:

- Heat and swelling along the back surface of your horse's superficial digital flexor tendon.

- A classical bowed shape when viewed from the side.

- Soreness in response to digital pressure in the affected area.

- Damage usually centered at the site of the anastomotic nerve branch, which crosses the backside of the superficial digital flexor tendon.

- In chronic cases, pressure sores with scabs developing along the back of the tendons and on the front of the cannon bone.

What you do: As soon as you notice a problem, limit your horse's activity, begin cold or ice therapy and use DMSO ointment when you wrap your horse's leg. Ask your veterinarian to see your horse soon.

What your veterinarian does: It's important that your veterinarian evaluate the swell-

Horseman's Dictionary

arthroscopy: intra-articular surgery using instruments inserted through small portals; used for both diagnostic and treatment procedures.

core lesion: a significant tear in a ligament or tendon and diagnosed by ultrasound.

desmitis: ligament inflammation.

DMSO: dimethyl sulfoxide, an anti-inflammatory, antibacterial and analgesic topical agent.

inferior check ligament: located along the upper half of the deep digital flexor tendon, this check ligament originates at the back of the knee and attaches to the deep digital flexor tendon in the cannon-bone area. It supports the tendon when the muscles become fatigued.

ligaments: fibrous bands that attach bones to bones.

peritendon tissue: tissue surrounding the tendon.

superior check ligament: originating from the radius bone and connecting to the superficial digital flexor tendon, this ligament supports the tendon when the muscle becomes fatigued.

suspensory ligament: a large ligament that originates at the top of the cannon bone, behind the knee in the front leg, and at the back of the hock on the hind leg; the primary support of the fetlock along with the sesamoids, distal sesamoidian ligaments and the digital flexor tendons.

sweat bandage: a bandage in which a compound, such as DMSO and furacin, is applied beneath plastic wrap to create heat, dilating your horse's blood vessels, increasing blood supply and promoting healing.

tendons: fibrous bands that connect your horse's muscles to bone.

---

ing and tendon with an ultrasound to ensure that the tendon isn't compromised before your horse resumes hard work. Even though a bandage bow seems less significant than other soft-tissue injuries, it is important to determine the extent of the damage.

Use cold-water therapy for the first 48 to 72 hours to stop the hemorrhaging within the tissue. Apply DMSO under a dry wrap, making sure the wrap isn't too tight but is snug enough to prevent slipping, to help dissipate swelling. In some cases, the swelling is somewhat chronic, and some owners and riders might forego the bandage and alternate heat and cold-water therapies. Providing heat therapy increases your horse's circulation. When you alternate hot and cold therapies, swelling reduces more quickly than with either option alone. Your veterinarian can teach you to make a sweat bandage by applying a compound, such as DMSO and furacin, beneath plastic wrap and a bandage. The resulting heat dilates your horse's blood vessels, increasing blood supply and promoting healing.

The healing process: Once healed, there's little risk for reinjury. Pay close attention to bandaging and wrapping practices. If you closely monitor your horse, he can continue working with a bandage bow.

Down the road: The prognosis is favorable. A bandage bow that is not managed well can develop into a more serious bowed tendon.

Case Study: Tendons & Ligaments

A show hunter went over a jump, stumbled and took another bad step. He pulled up, showing Grade 4 lameness. The owner noticed swelling on the back of the horse's fetlock, and the area was sore to firm palpation. The veterinarian isolated the lameness to the anular ligament area, and an ultrasound demonstrated a tear or hole in the anular ligament structure. The associated swelling within the anular ligament and the digital flexor sheath lining was pushing out through the ligament.

Conservative therapy consisting of rest, support bandages and anti-inflammatory medications was not effective. The horse was referred for surgery to longitudinally sever the anular ligament. With rest and careful exercise management, the horse made a complete recovery.

16

DEVELOPMENTAL ORTHOPEDIC DISEASE

Bone and joint problems result from improper maturation of cartilage into bone.

As with all mammals, young horse bones begin as cartilage structures basically in the shape of the bones they will become. As a young horse matures, the cartilage turns into bone. This process can result in defects developing in the newly formed bone ends, where joints form. Two abnormal changes can occur with developmental orthopedic disease, or DOD.

First, small islands or sites of bone develop as fragments adjacent to the parent bone, rather than as part of the main bone. These bone fragments, poorly attached to the main bone, create an irregular joint surface that can inhibit normal joint function. Additionally, the fragment can dislodge from the main bone, creating a loose foreign body within the joint that causes irritation. This lesion is called osteochondritis dessicans, or OCD.

The second type of DOD lesion occurs when an area within the bone's body, near the joint surface, fails to develop true bone matrix. This area is referred to as a subchondral, or below the cartilage, bone cyst and on a radiograph appears as a hole or dark area in the main bone. The joint cartilage surface that lies over the cyst can be unstable, resulting in joint irritation.

The exact cause of DOD is debatable among experts who study the disease because many factors could contribute to its development, and all those components aren't completely understood. Joint trauma

A horse needs four sound legs to make extremely athletic moves, and any sign of DOD likely could make this maneuver difficult.

177

at a certain point in development could cause DOD. Poor nutrition and mineral imbalances in the pregnant mare or young horse are predisposing factors. Specifically, a lack of quality protein, imbalances of calcium, phosphorous, copper and zinc and excess calories are considered predisposing factors. Finally, DOD is more prevalent in some equine family lines and could be genetically related. This disease more often affects rapidly growing young horses that appear clinically healthy, and DOD appears in all equine breeds.

DOD affects many joints, so this chapter first discusses DOD in general and then addresses the most common, specific areas of DOD.

General DOD Information

DOD often surfaces clinically by the time your horse is 8 or 9 months old, with most

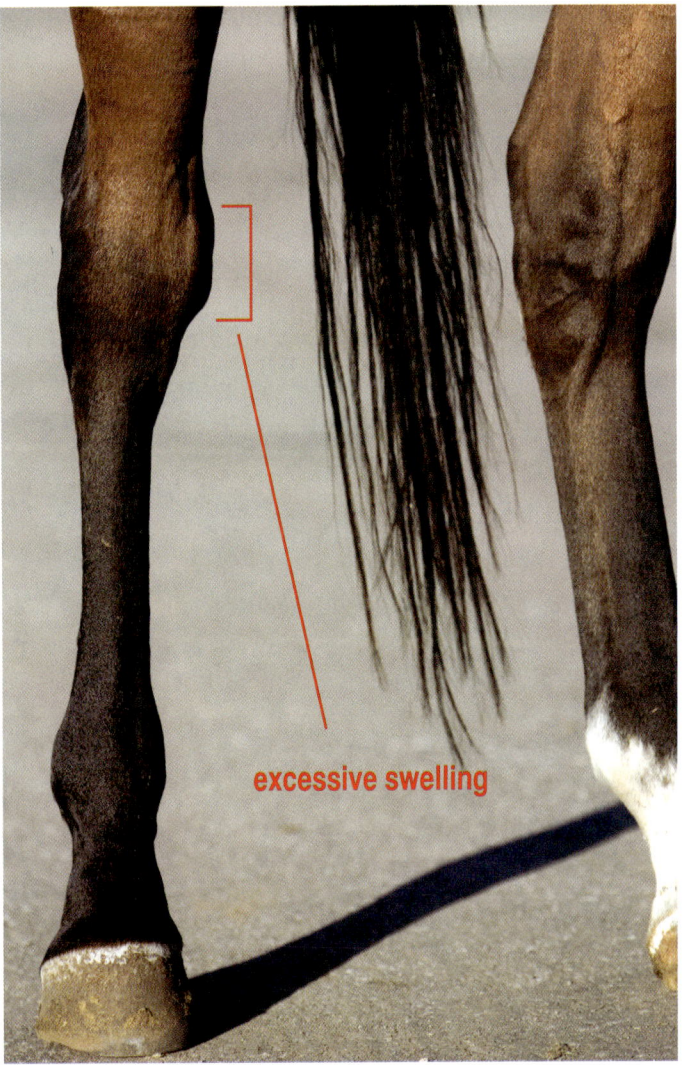

excessive swelling

This horse's upper hock joint is filled with excessive fluid. In a horse unaffected by DOD, this same area would be flat.

cases becoming clinically evident when your horse begins training, usually around age 2. The increased use of the affected joint when working causes irritation, which surfaces as lameness or swelling due to the presence of excess joint fluid. Or your horse might never show any clinical signs immediately, and the issue doesn't surface until your horse undergoes a routine exam, such as a prepurchase exam, later in life.

Radiographs offer the only consistent manner in which to diagnose DOD-related lesions. MRI, or magnetic resonance imaging, can play a role in the future for cases that aren't identified with radiographs. Ultrasound imaging can identify OCD fragments or irregular joint surfaces in some cases, but can't demonstrate cysts within the bone.

DOD treatment is fairly straightforward. A clinically visible fragment that is floating or creating excessive joint fluid within the joint should be removed. Attached fragments that are not clinically active often can be left alone. Arthroscopic surgery is the preferred method for removal.

Subchondral bone cyst treatment varies according to the lesion's location, the extent of the affected joint surface, and the degree of joint inflammation. Some procedures require surgical removal of cellular debris within the cyst and the loose cartilage covering the cyst. Currently, direct injections into the cyst's wall, guided via arthroscopy or ultrasound, show promise for successful treatment of cysts that have a reasonable cartilage surface. Some cases can be managed with intra-articular anti-inflammatory medication; however, success is usually limited unless the case is surgically corrected.

Since good bone matrix doesn't support the joint cartilage over the cyst, the horse is subject to further damage as his workload increases. Small bone and/or cartilage fragments can become free to irritate the joint. If the cartilage layer is disrupted, it leaks the cyst's contents, known as cellular debris, into the joint, causing significant irritation there.

If your horse's performance isn't affected by the DOD condition, the lesion can be left alone. In that situation, it's important that you closely watch for signs of lameness associated with the fragment or cyst, because immediate treatment upon recognizing lameness provides the most favorable prognosis. If your horse competes on a strict schedule or is destined for sale, it's usually a good idea to consider treating DOD issues upon diagnosis.

DOD most often develops in the hock, stifle or fetlock joints, which are discussed individually below.

DOD in the Hock

Your young reining prospect has just started in training for the futurities. Not long after you drop him off at the trainer's, he calls with a concern. Despite starting your horse slowly, the trainer notices that your horse seems off in the hindquarters, especially when being longed in a small circle. The trainer feels your horse's hocks and finds fluid build-up in the right hock. The trainer's giving your horse a break until your veterinarian can come.

What might be happening: In comparing all the joints in your horse's body, DOD most commonly affects the hock joint. In most instances, an OCD fragment is loosely attached to the end of the tibia, the distal intermediate ridge, which causes irritation in the tibial-tarsal joint. In response to the irritation, the joint produces extra fluid, which stretches the joint capsule and makes it bulge, especially on the joint's inside front corner. A second type of hock lesion occurs when an OCD fragment is loosely attached to a trochlear ridge surface in the joint, which acts as a grooved track within your horse's stifles and hocks.

Complications can arise with a fragment. If the joint is forcibly overflexed or sustains rotational stress, the fragment might be knocked free from the parent bone or shattered into many smaller pieces, causing further irritation.

What you notice: You see Grade 1 to Grade 3 lameness as you also notice:

- Increased fluid, also called a bog spavin, in the hock's main tibial-tarsal joint.

- Possible swelling around the joint due to twisting of the joint.

What you do: Closely feel the joint to access the swelling and look for evidence of a puncture wound. Call your veterinarian and request a thorough evaluation of the hock.

What your veterinarian does: Upon visual examination, your veterinarian identifies a bog spavin due to increased joint fluid.

Radiographs are taken to identify the irritation's source and locate the bone fragment if it is present.

In most cases the fragment can be identified, but your veterinarian must ascertain if that's the primary cause of lameness. He relies on a complete leg examination, performing flexion tests and possibly diagnostic blocks to help pinpoint the problem.

Arthroscopic surgery is a very successful way to remove the fragment. Following removal, your horse usually requires a 60-day rest period before returning to work. If the fragment has broken into many pieces, during the surgery your veterinarian flushes or irrigates the joint to remove as much of the debris as possible.

Joint supplementation with products such as glucosamine or systemic injections of

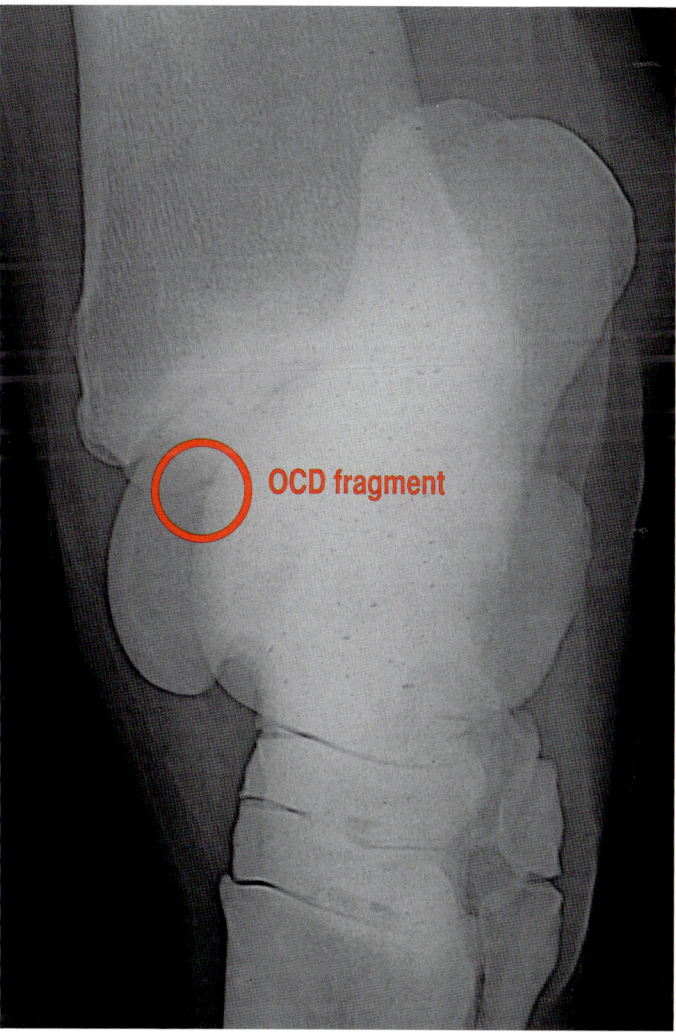

OCD fragment

The unstable OCD fragment in this radiograph creates joint irritation when the horse moves. In response to that irritation, excessive joint fluid develops, and a bog spavin forms.

hyaluronate can prolong your horse's career.

The healing process: Depending on the amount of swelling caused by the bog spavin, your horse might have a permanent hock blemish. Early removal of the irritant source increases the chance of not having a blemish.

If the lesion isn't treated—possibly because your horse is moving without lameness—you must carefully watch him. At any lameness signs or irritation in the hock, your veterinarian must begin treatments.

Down the road: If the lesion lies in the upper third of the hock's trochlear ridge, your horse has a guarded prognosis because the problem involves the weight-bearing area of the joint. If the fragment lies in the lower area of the trochlear ridge or is associated with the distal intermediate ridge of the tibia and is removed, your horse has a favorable prognosis for any use.

DOD in the Stifle

You're watching your weanlings play together in the back pasture. Out of the corner of your eye, you see a strange movement. At first, you think the baby is just playing. As you watch more, you see that he always pushes off with both feet at the same time when he canters to keep up with his buddies. This is the weanling from the other side of the county, a neglect case you saved. He's in "foster care" with you and your larger herd until he finds a permanent home. When the group moves on or starts to play, he's happy to stay put.

What might be happening: DOD of the stifle most often manifests as OCD lesions of the trochlear ridges or subchondral bone cysts of the femur, or upper leg bone. Subchondral cysts of the tibia, the lower bone in the stifle, or the patella, or kneecap, also can occur.

The lateral trochlear ridge is one of the most common sites for OCD. If the defect lies in the upper portion of the ridge, the condition has a more pronounced effect on your horse's soundness because this part of the joint bears more weight than the other areas.

The lower end of the femur, or thigh, bone has two weight-bearing surfaces in the stifle joint that meet with the top of the tibia, or

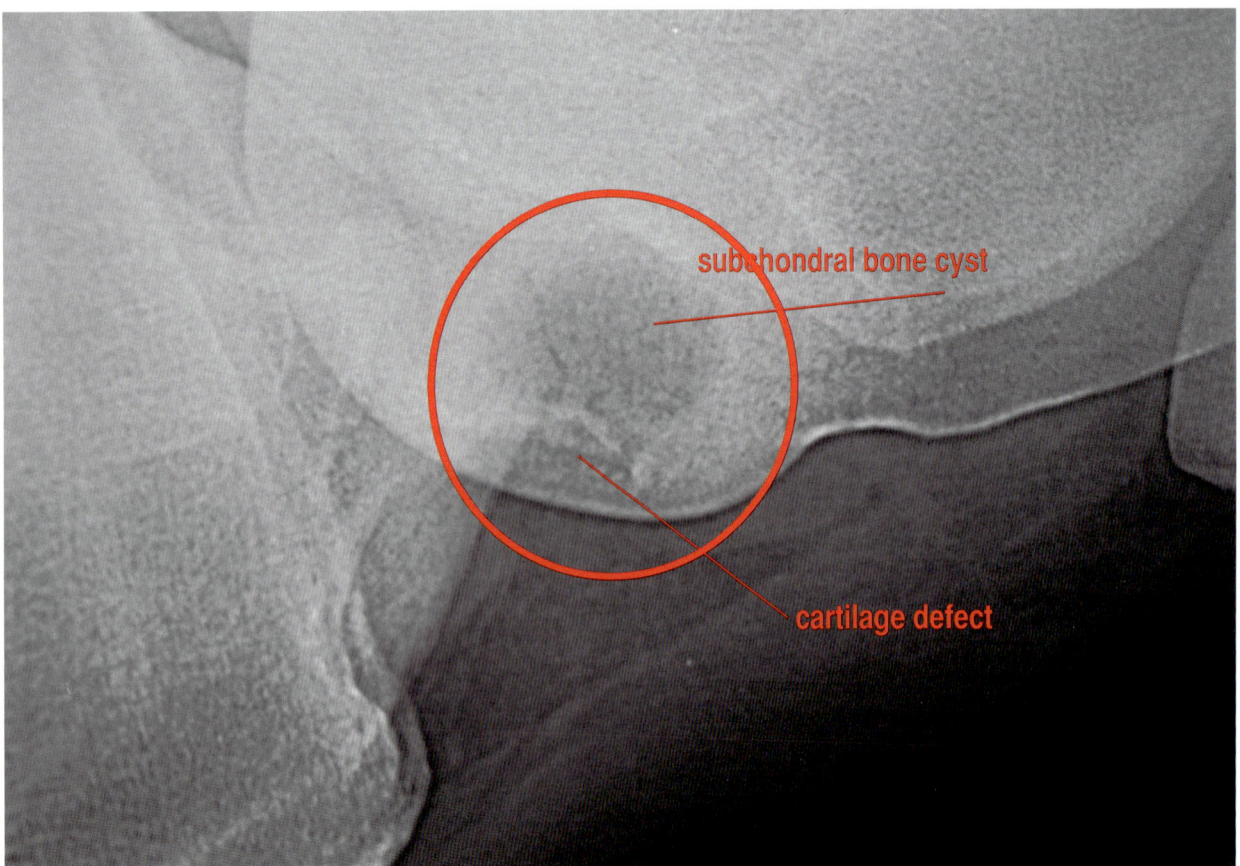

The large subchondral bone cyst and a cartilage defect in the stifle irritate this horse's joint.

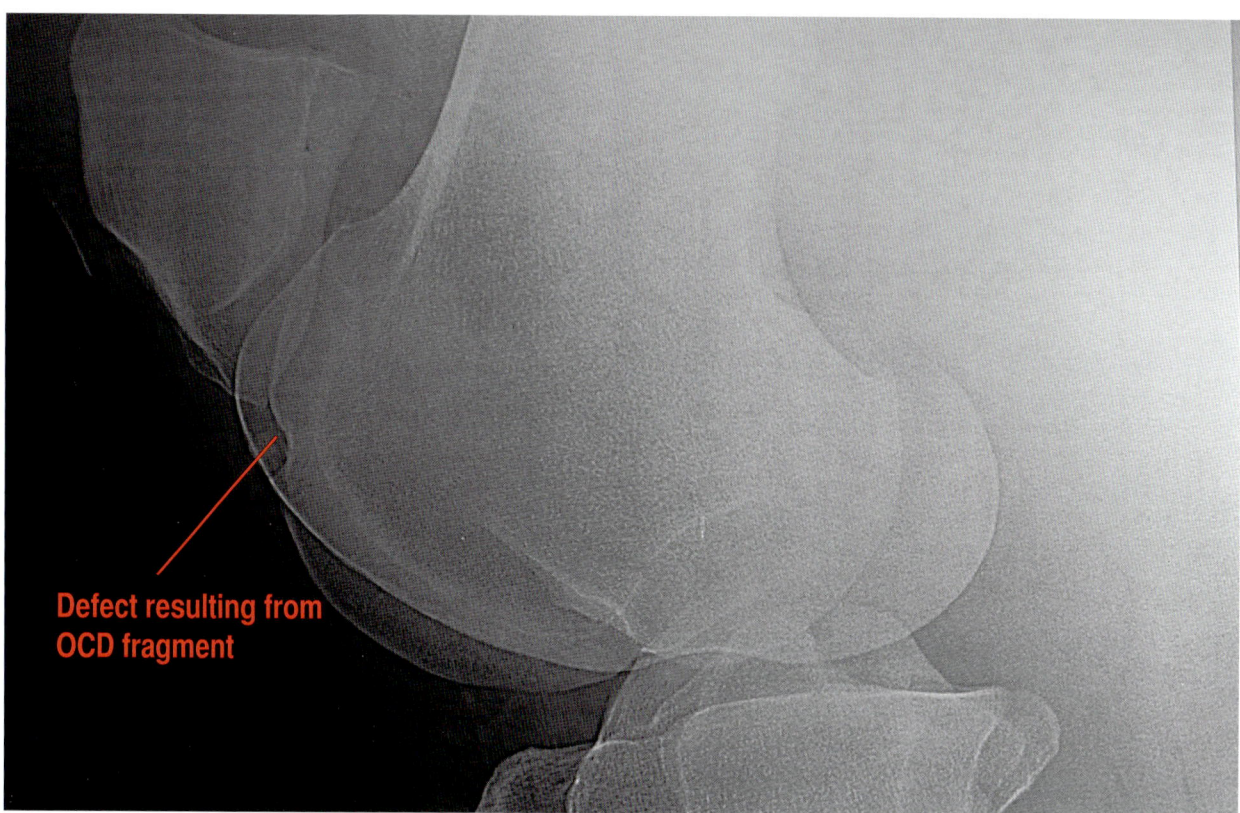

Defect resulting from
OCD fragment

When an OCD fragment dislodged, it left a crater or defect in the stifle trochlear ridge. The crater, the darkened area, irritates the horse when he moves.

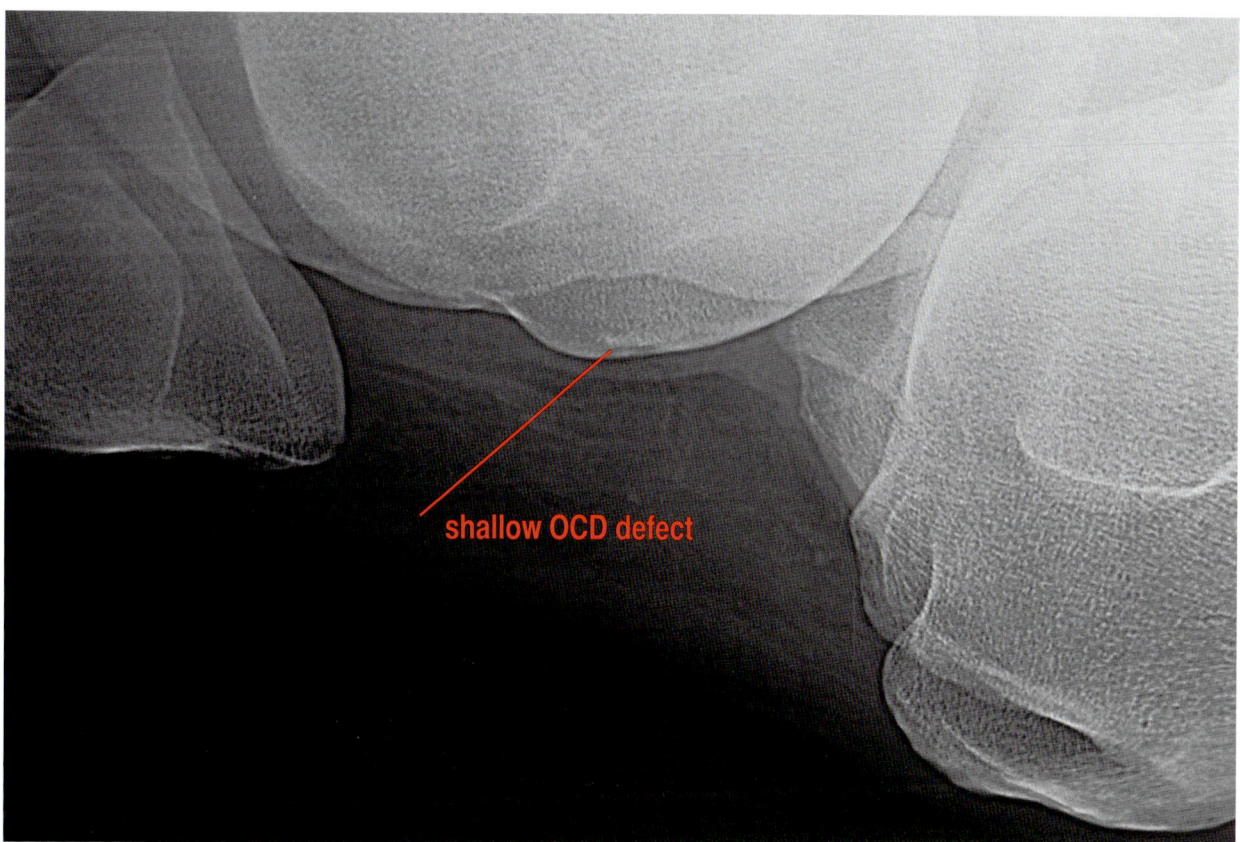

shallow OCD defect

The shallow defect in this stifle's femoral condyle, which can be seen in the radiograph, might or might not cause lameness.

gaskin, bone. These surfaces are the lateral and medial condyles, and cysts most often develop in the medial condyle, which is more often affected by DOD. These cysts have great lameness-causing potential, even though some cases show only a small dimple in the bone-joint surface.

DOD on the backside of the patella isn't common, but is serious because the defect interferes with the joint's mechanical action, causing pain and lameness.

What you notice: You see Grade 1 to Grade 3 lameness, and sometimes even worse, as you also notice:

- Increased joint fluid in the stifle, but not as noticeable as in the hock.

- Your horse's reluctance to move forward, as opposed to limping when moving.

- Your horse pushing with both hind legs at the same time, or bunny-hopping as he lopes.

What you do: Once you notice the altered gait or lameness, contact your veterinarian and discuss your findings. Limit your horse's exercise.

What your veterinarian does: Your veterinarian notes the above clinical signs; radiographs confirm the lesion's location and severity, though not all lesions are seen on radiographs. Ultrasound imaging can demonstrate some fragments, but that depends on their locations. Diagnostic blocking might be necessary to isolate stifle DOD as the primary lameness issue. Arthroscopy can play a diagnostic role, as well as provide access to treat or clean the joint.

Each case is considered individually in terms of treatment considerations. Therapeutic measures vary according to the lesion's location, degree of lameness, and your horse's use.

A lesion that causes no clinical problems can be treated conservatively, with or without intra-articular injections. Oral joint supplements, glucosamine, MSM and omega-3 fatty acids are helpful.

An OCD fragment of the stifle's trochlear ridge, which causes the patellar pouch to swell, as well as lameness, requires arthroscopic removal. Lesions on the backside of the patella are also treated via arthroscopy.

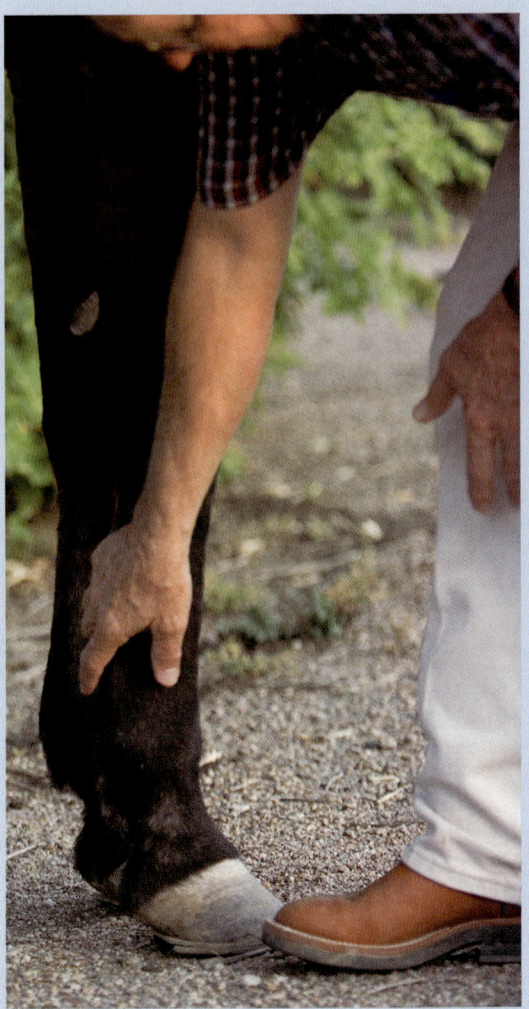

Before calling your veterinarian about fetlock DOD, evaluate your horse's fetlock. Begin by picking up your horse's hoof as if you were going to clean it.

A medial condyle cyst might be medicated with intra-articular injections or intra-lesion injections, surgical cleaning and debridment of the cyst. Extracorporeal shockwave therapy is used to treat some young horses.

Many treatments are followed by a series of intra-articular injections of hyaluronate or glucosamine or IRAP solutions.

The healing process: If the fragment isn't removed, you must closely watch your horse to notice any stifle irritation or lameness.

If an OCD fragment is removed, your horse's healing process and ability to return to performance depend on the lesion's extent. Most cases do very well.

A horse with a subchondral bone cyst has more serious disease process, and each case is

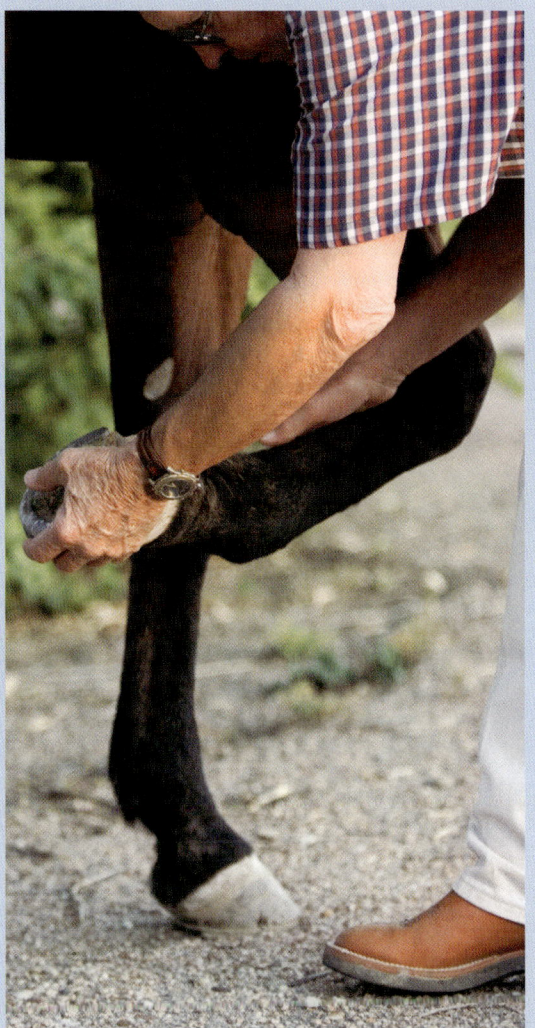

Then hold up your horse's leg, bending his knee. Switch hands so that you can hold your horse's cannon bone and toe.

Flex up your horse's toe as your opposite hand holds his cannon bone steady Gradually increase the pressure and notice if your horse flinches or pulls away.

considered on its own signs and response to treatment, but all require long-term management programs.

Down the road: Your horse has two trochlear ridges in each stifle. The structures act as grooved tracks for your horse's patella as it moves. If the OCD lesion lies in the lower two-thirds of the stifle's trochlear ridge, your horse has a favorable prognosis for use. A lesion in the stifle's upper third or behind the patella has a guarded-to-unfavorable prognosis for athletic performance. A horse with a subchondral bone cyst has a wide range for prognoses, depending on the amount of affected joint surface and any existing secondary degenerative joint disease.

DOD in the Fetlock

You've decided to purchase one of your friend's horses. You trust her not to lie about the horse's condition, but you feel strongly about doing a prepurchase evaluation. Your dad's voice in your head tells you to be safe, no matter with whom you're dealing. You've ridden the horse, and he seems sound—it was a great ride. When your veterinarian arrives to look at him, he at first thinks the horse looks great. But when he does the usual flexion tests, he says the horse feels pain in the fetlock joint on his left front leg. Your veterinarian also notices excess fluid in the joint—something he calls a wind puff. When you report to your friend, she tells you the horse had an injury to that same leg a few years back, but he's never shown signs of lameness.

LAMENESS Q&A

What might be happening: The most common causes of fetlock-related DOD include fragments from the cannon bone's saggital ridge that aren't attached to the parent bone. Subchondral bone cysts also can develop in the medial or lateral condyles of your horse's cannon bone.

What you notice: You see no lameness or lameness up to Grade 3 as you also notice:

- Slight heat around the fetlock joint.

- Increased joint fluid, called a wind puff.

- A fluid increase the more the horse is worked.

- Lameness when the horse works hard.

- A pain response when you pick up the horse's foot and flex his fetlock.

What you do: Examine your horse's fetlock by feeling it—noticing if your horse is in pain when you flex the fetlock. To flex it, pick up your horse's affected leg as if you are going to pick out his hoof. Once his leg is bent, move your hands to hold the cannon bone in one hand and his toe in the other hand. Gradually increase the pressure you use to push up your horse's toe, toward your opposite hand. Be careful not to spook your horse or use torque, but notice if he pulls or flinches his leg away from your pressure. If he pulls away or flinches—and doesn't have the same reaction on the opposite, unaffected leg—it's time to call your veterinarian and ask for a full examination.

What your veterinarian does: Your veterinarian notes the above signs and relies on radiographs to assess the lesion's extent and location. MRI can be helpful for cases that don't

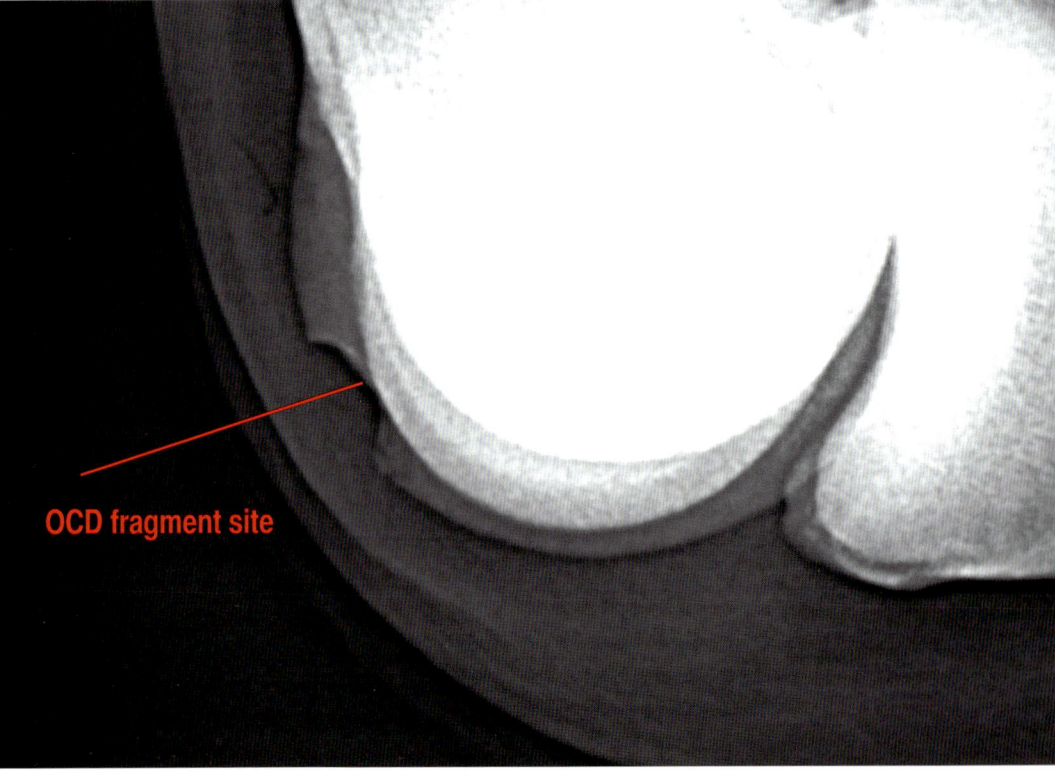

This radiograph shows a crater-shaped area that was the site of an OCD fragment. Once the fragment was surgically removed, the horse was sound.

OCD fragment site

Horseman's Dictionary

cervical: of the neck.

DOD: developmental orthopedic disease.

OCD: osteochondritis dessicans; the fragment next to the parent bone that causes joint irritation.

subchondral: below the cartilage.

trochlear ridge: structures that act as grooved tracks within your horse's stifles and hocks.

show in radiographs. Diagnostic blocking also might play a role in isolating fetlock DOD as the primary cause of lameness.

Fragments are most often removed using arthroscopic surgery if clinical signs warrant that. Subchondral bone cysts are treated with many of the same considerations as when they're found in the stifle, including intra-articular medication, intra-lesion injections and surgical cleaning and debridement of the cyst. If the lesion onsets acutely, flushing the joint to remove cellular debris that's escaped from the cyst into the joint is very helpful. Extracorporeal shockwave therapy has proven beneficial in some cases, and some cases can be managed conservatively with oral supplements and intra-articular medication. A horse without any clinical signs might not require treatment. As with all joint diseases, your veterinarian will recommend good oral supplements of glucosamine and MSM, or methylsulfonylmethane.

The healing process: Post-treatment use requires monitoring the fetlock's progress as your horse's workload increases.

Down the road: The prognosis for OCD depends on the lesion's size and location. Removing OCD fragments has a favorable prognosis in most cases. The prognosis for a subchondral bone cyst depends on its location in relation to the joint's weight-bearing surface and the amount of the joint surface involved. Your horse's level of use also affects the prognosis.

Case Study: Developmental Orthopedic Disease

A 4-year-old Warmblood stallion intended for grand prix jumping was presented for purchase exam. The exam uncovered increased synovial fluid in both femoral patellar joints and, with palpation, some irregularity along the lateral trochlear ridges. No lameness was detected, and flexion tests of the stifles weren't significant. Radiographs of the stifles showed OCD fragments along both lateral trochlear ridges. The lesions were close to the patella when the horse was in the standing position. The horse received a guarded prognosis if the fragments weren't removed surgically and a guarded-to-favorable prognosis with surgery. The buyer elected not to buy the horse, and the seller decided to take the horse off the market and continue training him for jumping. The horse had a successful career as a grand prix jumper and appeared to reach his athletic peak without the stifles being a concern.

185

17

NEUROLOGY AND LAMENESS

When your horse's brain and spine don't send correct information to the attached muscles, ligaments and tendons, your horse can't move properly.

L ameness doesn't always root itself in a horse's bone, joint or muscle. Your horse's lameness might be linked to a neurological origin or be a combination of musculo-skeletal and neurological problems.

Here, we discuss two common neurological diseases—equine protozoal myeloencephalitis, commonly known as EPM, and vertebral instability, or "wobbler syndrome." In their more subtle states, these two diseases are difficult to differentiate from musculo-skeletal lameness.

If your veterinarian suspects a neurological disease is causing your horse's lameness, he includes a neurological evaluation in addition to a typical equine lameness exam. He might perform a hop test by holding your horse's front leg and leaning into him until the horse hops to the side. If your horse doesn't hop sideways to catch his own weight, but instead leans into the pressure, he might have a neurological deficit and need further, specialized testing. If your veterinarian suspects a neurological problem, he also might do a blindfold test. A horse with a neurological deficit might use his sight to compensate, helping to correct his movements and limb placement. With a blindfold in place, a neurologically affected horse might walk tentatively or show an

When you depend on your horse's surefootedness on steep trails, it's important to know he's free of neurological defects that can jeopardize your safety.

A blindfold limits your horse's ability to visually compensate if he suffers from a balance-affecting neurological disease.

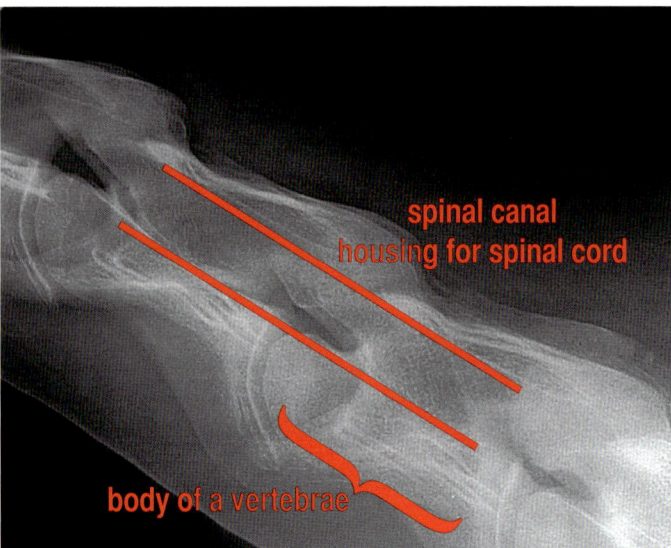

spinal canal
housing for spinal cord

body of a vertebrae

This radiograph shows two of the neck's seven vertebrae; the lines down the center show where the spinal cord lies. If the vertebrae pinch the spinal cord, your horse might experience a motor deficiency.

altered gait. A horse with subtle neurological problems might appear lame, begin to trip, or just move in a stiff and undesirable fashion.

Depending on the neurological evaluation results, your veterinarian might consult a neurological specialist. Once such diseases progress, horses often show obvious neurological problems that aren't related to lameness. Because the diseases often begin with lameness symptoms, it's important to know the early lameness-related signs.

The onset of neurologically related lameness can be abrupt or a slowly developing process. Furthermore, the issue might go unnoticed until your horse experiences an accident or incident that makes the problem surface.

Equine Protozoal Myeloencephalitis (EPM)

Your champion stallion is a smooth mover and a celebrated winner with titles in trail, Western pleasure and hunter under saddle. At a local breed show, he trips as he heads out of the show pen. The show is over, and he's worked hard, so you don't think much of it. But two days later, he moves weakly on his left hind leg. You call your veterinarian immediately. Your horse has had no signs of lameness or any health problems before this. By the time your veterinarian arrives, your stallion is sore in both back legs and has difficulty standing.

What might be happening: Microscopic organisms called protozoa cause EPM in horses. The organisms invade your horse's nervous system and destroy a local area of nerve cells, preventing normal neurological function. Your horse's outward signs and symptoms depend on which areas of the nervous system the protozoa invade, as well as the extent of the invasion. For these reasons, clinical signs of EPM vary in severity, from a horse with almost no clinical signs to a horse that can't walk. For the same reasons, the symptoms can worsen as this disease progresses.

Most scientists agree that EPM protozoa enter your horse's body when he ingests feed contaminated with infested opossum, raccoon or armadillo feces, and scientists are finding that more and more animals can act as carriers for the organism. Providing clean feed is an important part of EPM prevention and management. Most common along the Eastern seaboard, throughout the South and in the Midwest, EPM can be found anywhere. It's

A hop test can help evaluate a horse's neurological functions.

especially important to consider EPM when a horse originating from these areas shows any sign of lameness or neurological disease.

What you notice: You see Grade 1 to Grade 4 lameness as you also notice the following symptoms seen in EPM's early stages:

- A slight decline in performance, with your horse not doing as well as expected.

- Stumbling or a lack of coordination.

- Tripping or falling, even when your horse moves across a well-groomed arena.

- Apparent lameness on a specific leg.

- Stiffness or soreness in your horse's neck.

What you do: Call your veterinarian if you notice that your horse is suddenly prone to stumbling or at any time your horse is suddenly "off."

Horses can contract EPM by ingesting hay, grass, grain or water contaminated by infected opossum feces.

What your veterinarian does: Clinical EPM symptoms run the whole gamut. Any abnormal neurological activity could signify EPM. A complete neurological exam involves a physical exam, radiographs, a spinal tap and laboratory tests. All four elements must be

Palpating the neck is part of any lameness exam where neurological deficiencies might be present. Your veterinarian feels for vertebrae placement and notes any swelling and tenderness.

considered to make an informed diagnosis.

Currently two medications specifically kill the protozoa associated with EPM. Treatment must be initiated as soon as EPM is diagnosed in order to minimize damage. However, once a nerve cell is destroyed, as occurs with EPM, the cell can't regenerate, so early diagnosis and treatment are imperative for the drugs to effectively minimize cellular damage. Once the treatment begins, the death of the protozoal organisms can create a transient inflammatory response. Afterward, it's reasonable to expect some improvement in your horse's clinical signs. The amount of improvement is relative to each individual case.

The healing process: An inflammatory process accompanies nervous-system cell destruction. After the protozoa are eradicated, the inflammation dissipates, which allows some improvement of your horse's clinical condition. The damaged nervous tissue, however, cannot regenerate. After a few months, it's apparent on what level your horse can perform—as a breeding animal, a companion animal or, in some fortunate cases, as a performance horse.

Down the road: A positive prognosis hinges on diagnosing EPM in its earliest stages. As the disease progresses, it causes irreparable damage, leading to an unfavorable prognosis.

Cervical Vertebral Instability (Wobbler Syndrome)

Your classic-style barn has split doors that open at the top or the bottom, but your new boarder forgot to latch the bottom half of a stall door. When the wind blew the bottom half open, the top stayed secured with its own latch. One of your mares saw the opening and attempted to sneak through—skidding her neck and spine along the stationary top. When she realized she couldn't fit through the opening, she panicked, hitting her neck and head again as she backed out of the stall entrance. Though she's always been healthy before, your mare now walks strangely, seems uncoordinated and continuously stumbles.

What might be happening: Malformed vertebral articular processes allow slack to develop between the neck's vertebrae. This instability exposes your horse's spinal cord to pinching

When your veterinarian suspects wobbler syndrome, he applies pressure to the neck joints as he turns your horse's head, watching for a pain response and range of motion.

and bruising. This condition might be static, meaning the malformation is fixed and doesn't change, or dynamic, which means the malformation is changing or can change when the neck moves. Pinching damages the spinal cord nerve bundles that operate the limbs, so the brain loses its propreoception, or the ability to know where the feet are at all times. This deficit leads to erratic foot placement when your horse moves, hence the term "wobbler." The condition doesn't cause noticeable pain or even induce fear in your horse. In some cases, the affected limbs develop secondary lameness conditions, and in more severe instances your horse has difficulty moving at all.

Your horse might be clinically normal until a precipitating accident occurs, such as a fall that puts excess pressure on a specific area of the spinal cord. One insult can cause enough damage for an acute onset of the syndrome, or it can result from the repetitive damage of minor events.

In cases with minimal signs, the condition might be confused with mild stifle problems. Or, as mentioned above, your horse's stifles might develop soreness secondary to the neurological problem.

What you notice: You see Grade 1 to Grade 3 lameness and notice lameness-like symptoms such as:

- A slight decline in performance.

- Stumbling or falling.

- Your horse's apparent inability to know where his feet are, especially when changing gaits or moving in small circles. He might place them out and to the side or in an abnormal fashion.

What you do: Confine your horse away from other horses so he isn't bumped and has less chance of falling. Call your veterinarian.

What your veterinarian does: A complete neurological exam identifies the place or places where your horse's spinal cord has been pinched and which nerves are affected. In many cases, radiographs identify vertebral abnormalities in the neck. If needed, a spinal tap to examine and test the cerebral spinal fluid completes the exam.

191

LAMENESS Q&A

What's a spinal tap and what does it do?

A spinal tap involves drawing a sample of the cerebral spinal fluid from the spinal column. It's an invasive procedure, but involves little risk. A needle is inserted, on the midline of the back and 5 to 6 inches deep, into the spinal canal at the loin-pelvis (lumbosacral) juncture. This must be a sterile procedure to avoid introducing infection.

Cerebral-spinal-fluid examination involves three elements. First, your veterinarian makes a visual assessment. Is the fluid clear? A laboratory then evaluates the fluid for increased protein levels and the presence of abnormal blood cells, such as red ones, which indicate trauma to the area, or white blood cells indicating infection. Another sample goes to a serology lab to test for antibodies against diseases, such as EPM and rhino-pneumonitis.

Your veterinarian recommends a myelogram, a radiograph of the spinal cord after injecting it with radio-opaque material, if your horse's symptoms are mild and difficult to detect. The procedure requires general anesthesia before your veterinarian injects radio-opaque liquid into the cerebral spinal fluid chamber surrounding the spinal column. Following the injection, your horse's neck radiograph clearly shows the spinal fluid, which lies above and below the spinal cord. When the affected neck is flexed and radiographed, bands representing the cerebral spinal fluid are pinched dramatically to demonstrate abnormal spinal-column pressure.

The healing process: Wobbler syndrome raises a safety concern regarding your horse's continued use, relative to the degree of neurological compromise. Your horse might not be safe to ride, even though he runs, plays, bucks and experiences no pain.

Wobbler syndrome is considered a type of developmental orthopedic disease (further discussed in Chapter 16), so if your horse is a mare, her health and diet during gestation and lactation have a large influence on preventing the problem in her foal. Also, carefully managing a newborn foal's diet during maturation decreases the odds of wobbler syndrome developing.

Unfortunately, the syndrome can develop in spite of careful management practices. As with most neurological diseases, the concern for and the risk to those handling your horse must be considered when planning your horse's future.

Down the road: Your horse might continue to perform following surgical stabilization, especially if the condition is subtle. Generally, the prognosis is guarded-to-unfavorable. Left untreated, a wobbler has an unfavorable prognosis for a return to performance.

Case Study: Neurology & Lameness

A 2-year-old gelding showed promise as a successful Western-riding mount. The horse reached a training plateau and began having trouble changing leads. The trainer reasoned that the horse had stifle problems, potentially caused by delayed patellar release.

The veterinary exam didn't reveal any stifle problems relative to the patella. But the trainer recalled an incident in which the horse jumped the paddock fence and landed on his head and neck. At the time, the horse appeared to recover completely.

With that information in mind, the veterinarian performed a neurological exam. Clinical neurological signs were present, but subtle. Radiographs of the horse's neck showed an area of dynamic vertebral instability between two cervical vertebrae. A myelogram confirmed this diagnosis.

The owner elected to humanely euthanize the horse based on an unfavorable prognosis for performance. Surgical stabilization was an option; however, costs and an uncertainty of complete recovery led the owner to determine this was a poor financial risk. The owner also was reluctant to give away the horse for fear that the condition could worsen and that the new owners might become discouraged and not provide the level of care required.

Horseman's Dictionary

blindfold test: walking your horse after applying a blindfold. A horse with mild neurological signs can worsen if he is using his sight to compensate for the neurological deficit.

cerebral spinal fluid: the fluid within the spinal column chamber surrounding the spinal cord.

cervical vertebral stabilization: surgically placing a basket or bone insert across the joint between two vertebrae to fuse them together and correct dynamic compression of the spinal cord.

dynamic: changing or having the ability to change.

EPM: equine protozoal myeloencephalitis, an equine neurological disease caused by protozoa attacking the nerve cells.

hop test: holding a horse's front leg and leaning into the horse until the horse hops to the side. If the horse doesn't hop sideways to catch his own weight, he might have a neurological deficit.

myelogram: a radiograph of the spinal cord after it has been injected with radio-opaque material.

propreoception: the brain's ability to know where the feet are at all times.

static: fixed and unchanging.

wobbler syndrome: a problem that occurs when horse's spinal cord is exposed to pinching and bruising.

18

AT-HOME HEALING

**Once your horse is diagnosed and treated, you are his primary caregiver.
Find out how to keep your horse healing safely at home.**

You've tracked your horse's lameness symptoms and consulted your veterinarian. After your horse is diagnosed, you and your veterinarian have a treatment plan in place. Your horse needs special care as he recuperates. Whether he had a sudden lameness-causing injury or has a chronic or conformation-based lameness, you most likely are his primary care provider as he heals.

After a lameness diagnosis, many horses require confinement and controlled exercise, as well as daily medications. Your veterinarian also might ask you to wrap your horse's leg or treat him with cold-water therapy. Here, we discuss the common "take home" medications and healing techniques your veterinarian is likely to recommend.

Confinement

Once your horse is on medications or has had some therapy, he might feel better, but he still needs healing time. Because your horse doesn't understand that soreness after playing hard is associated with the overexertion, he can't self-regulate his turnout time. Consequently, it's your responsibility to control the exertion level and limit trauma to his already-injured structures. When your horse is confined, you can closely monitor his healing process. You also limit your horse's chances for re-injury.

Confining your horse can be difficult on him and you. He might seem unhappy and restless. Plus, you have more stall-cleaning chores and might need to fortify your horse's living conditions to ensure that

Your horse needs controlled exercise and confinement as he heals. Take time to monitor and work with your horse during his recovery.

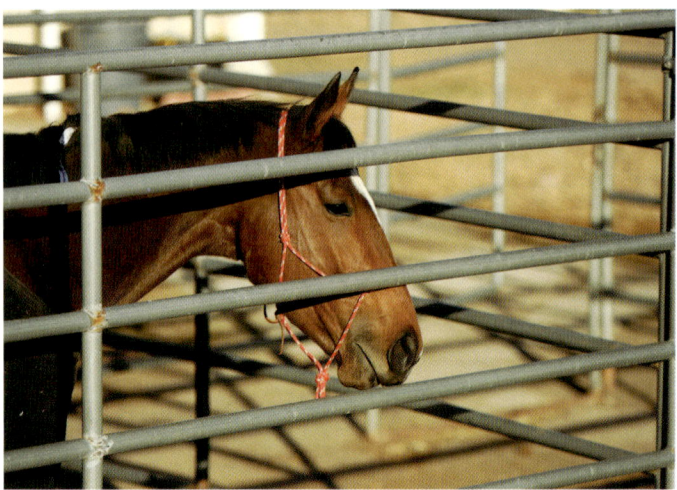

Hand-grazing your horse helps him see new surroundings without the risk of re-injury.

Studies show that horses are the most calm and content when confined in open-paneled stalls that allow them to see the horizon.

he—and your barn—are safe during his confinement for healing. A bored horse might pace, kick or chew.

To present the best situation for your horse, consider your horse's living conditions, his diet, how to prevent boredom and when to compromise.

A 12-by-12-foot or 12-by-16-foot box stall is generally the safest environment for an injured horse—especially if your horse has a bandage, splint or cast that must be kept dry. Ask your veterinarian how much confinement is necessary. If your horse is allowed a little more room to roam, you might keep him in a paneled pen with a shed or roof to provide shade and protection from the elements.

Research about horse confinement following injury shows that horses often are more comfortable and relaxed in stalls where they can see beyond the stall walls. Horses are naturally calm when they can see the horizon—a natural link to their prey instinct and need to see what, if anything, is coming. Therefore, a stall with many open windows or composed of open panels helps calm a horse and should reduce your horse's pacing and nervousness. Panels with solid pieces on the lower portion are safer than panels with openings near the ground. The solid-bottomed panels help limit a horse from stepping through the panel or becoming tangled as he stands or lies down.

Outfit your horse's confinement area with cushioned footing to help your horse's body absorb impact. Make sure the pen ground beneath the cushioned mat or footing is flat. If there are holes or uneven areas, your horse

Your horse wants to be near other horses during his confinement. Make sure that he can see other horses and has a buddy nearby.

can twist and re-injure a sore leg. Place a 1-inch thick rubber mat or other specially designed stall liner over the dirt or concrete for support and cushion.

Wood shavings, paper, straw and sand are suitable for bedding. Wood shavings offer cushion and absorption and are easy to clean and replace. Paper bedding is absorbent and is an approach to recycling. Straw can be difficult to properly clean and is not nearly as absorbent as shavings or paper. Keep in mind that your horse will be in this confined area for an extended time. Be sure to ask about the bedding's dust content to avoid respiratory ailments and limit the use of any bedding that your horse might ingest. Caution: Don't use walnut shavings; just standing on walnut can cause laminitis.

Diet

Your veterinarian can advise you about your horse's new dietary needs. If he has suffered from laminitis or is at risk for laminitis during the healing process, it's important that he have the proper nutrition. Consider that when your horse is confined, he doesn't

Provide your recovering horse with grass hay instead of high-calorie alfalfa, which has excess calories your horse won't burn while confined.

197

To help avoid spooks and the possibility of re-injury, introduce boredom-relieving toys to your horse gradually before hanging them in a stall.

chart at the chapter's end for which medications can be administered orally.)

Boredom

It's not easy to keep a horse happy and entertained during confinement, especially if your horse isn't accustomed to stall life. To make the transition to confinement easier, be sure your horse gets lots of attention and provide him with toys and interaction. Install a hanging ball or rolling lick toy. However, your horse must be accustomed to such toys to prevent spooking and causing further injury. You also can turn on the radio to mix up the sounds that your horse hears during the day.

Make sure your horse can see another horse at all times, so that he doesn't feel alone and anxious. His equine herd instincts can kick in, and he feels agitated and paces if he perceives he's totally alone. You also can help by interacting with your horse daily by grooming him and taking time to examine your horse's healing progress.

Also make sure that your horse has a brief change of scenery whenever possible. Move him to another stall or pen when you clean his stall. He has new surroundings to explore, and you're safe as you clean. With your veterinarian's approval, your horse might be moved to an outside pen during the day—depending on the extent of his injury and if bandages must be kept dry. You also can allow your horse to graze while you lead him—allowing him time to be outside without the risk of him moving too quickly in an open field.

Some horses simply can't tolerate confinement and become too agitated when kept inside and alone. Allow your horse time to settle into his new environment before deciding confinement doesn't work. If your horse is agitated and anxious after a few days, consult your veterinarian about medical sedation. Medical sedation might be used on a limited basis to help your horse tolerate confinement. In appropriate cases, your veterinarian might prescribe medication to help your horse relax and limit his movement.

Controlled Exercise

When your veterinarian prescribes controlled exercise, he explains what type of movement and how much your horse can handle. Plan your horse's daily routine and

spend his usual caloric intake. He can't burn as many calories without his usual turnouts or workouts.

Provide high-quality grass hay. Grass hay doesn't have as many calories per pound as alfalfa; horses usually don't consume the grass as fast as alfalfa. Providing enough free-choice grass hay throughout the day to allow your horse to "graze" when he wants can help eliminate boredom and help your horse retain his usual grazing patterns. Give grain only as a treat or as a carrier for necessary medications, vitamins and supplements. Providing excess carbohydrates can lead to your horse's heightened energy level. If your horse is confined, unnecessary energy can cause behavior problems. Excess grain intake and reduced exercise also predispose your horse to digestive-tract problems and laminitis. (See the

Work with your veterinarian to develop a controlled exercise plan, progressing from walking on the lead line to groundwork and later a full workload. Use caution if trotting your horse in hand; following confinement, it's easy for a horse to jump beyond his handler and then kick.

chart when your horse can begin moving more. Controlled exercise plays an important role in your horse's recovery and helps eliminate his boredom. Many times, limited exercise can help your horse heal faster and more fully than stall-rest alone.

Your horse's controlled exercise program depends on his temperament and the type of lameness he's experienced. If you're fearful of your horse or worried that he has too much energy, employ a knowledgeable horse person or trainer to help you safely handle and exercise your horse. Be aware that after a period of confinement, even a quiet, gentle horse can be dangerous to his handler.

Generally, you begin by walking your horse with a halter and lead. Before you begin, outfit your horse in his usual protective boots or any gear that your veterinarian recommends during the healing process. Splint boots help your horse avoid nicking himself as you exercise at increasing speeds. A bandage or boot might help your horse move comfortably as he heals from a hoof wound.

Your veterinarian specifies if your horse should walk on a specific surface, such as an arena with soft footing, or if hard ground conditions might be appropriate. Ask your veterinarian if you should maintain a pace, at first, or simply allow your horse to meander and see new surroundings. When it's time for

Your veterinarian might wrap your horse's hoof, more smoothly than shown here, and ask that you outfit him with a therapeutic boot to keep an injury site clean as your horse recovers and returns to work.

your horse to regain muscle, you need to walk the horse in straight lines and at a constant pace and controlled speed. As your horse continues to recover, you might be asked to move him at a trot on a longe line or to do other groundwork. Ponying your horse while

199

Feel your horse's legs and hooves regularly and visually examine your horse so that you can report any changes during his healing process.

when he feels sore. If he's sore after a rehab workout, his tissues might be stretching with exercise. The soreness can be a normal part of the healing process. In any case, it's imperative to completely and precisely follow your veterinarian's instructions and modify the program only after veterinary consultation.

At-Home Checks and Treatment

Throughout your horse's healing process, watch for any significant changes in his movement or how the wound is healing. Your veterinarian might recommend cold-water therapy, soaking, or basic health checks to help make sure your horse continues to heal.

Regularly monitor your horse's injury. Check for heat in and around his symptomatic leg and hoof. Make sure to feel your horse's legs to check for any bumps or swelling. Immediately report any changes to your veterinarian. Only by checking your horse often can you notice changes and understand what's typical and what's unusual.

If your veterinarian suggests cold-water therapy—often recommended when a horse has swelling or soreness—you need a water source, hose and area with proper drainage. Avoid tying your horse if he's not accustomed to cold-water baths; he might spook and pull back. Ask a friend to hold your horse as you hose his injury for up to 15 to 20 minutes.

To soak your horse's hoof, a common treatment when your horse has a sole or wall abscess, fill a tub with a sturdy bottom with water before ever asking your horse to step forward. Use caution and make sure your horse is used to the sound of the tub and sloshing water before asking him to place his foot in the tub. Your veterinarian recommends how long to soak your horse's hoof and if you should add anything to the water.

If your veterinarian sends your horse home with with prescription medication, follow precise directions and administer the medication as directed. Find out more about the commonly given equine drugs in the chart at the end of the chapter. Certain medications are sold only with a veterinarian's prescription. Prescriptions ensure that medications are dosed appropriately for your horse's size and are used for the proper conditions, all the while considering animal and handler safety.

Before your veterinarian can write a prescription or dispense prescription medications for your horse, he must have a client-patient

you ride a well-trained horse is an option if your horse is accustomed to the activity and an experienced pony-horse is available. When it's time for your horse to exercise at faster speeds, your veterinarian might ask that you ride rather than turn out your horse to run freely on his own. Under saddle, you often can control his movements and limit his speed, thus limiting his chances of re-injury. Simply riding at a walk might be your horse's best therapeutic workout.

Some horses can be turned out to pasture. Before considering pasture turnout, consult your veterinarian to be sure that any lesions are healed and that re-injury is unlikely. Remember: A rested, confined, fit horse is at high risk to injure himself when turned out to pasture because he's ready to run.

In some cases, your horse might seem to regress, showing worsened signs of lameness or pain. Watch your horse closely and note

Your veterinarian might ask you to soak your horse's hoof during the healing process. Some horses will need confinement to allow this procedure.

LAMENESS Q&A

When do you recommend a professional rehabilitation center?

Professional rehabilitation centers aren't necessary for every horse, but they're advantageous for some horses with complex diagnoses or for horses with tough-to-manage temperaments. A rehabilitation center's staff should be trained and experienced in handling injured horses and carrying out treatment programs. The staff knows important veterinary language and when to consult your horse's veterinarian for further treatment advice. Also, some horses might be more content with other horses confined nearby. These horses are more at ease and stay calm when they have constant companions and interaction. The centers provide low-stress environments and often have access to necessary therapy equipment to promote fast recovery. Rehabilitation centers also are good options for horse owners who're unable to complete the recovery program, don't have confinement facilities or don't have the time to fulfill their horses' needs.

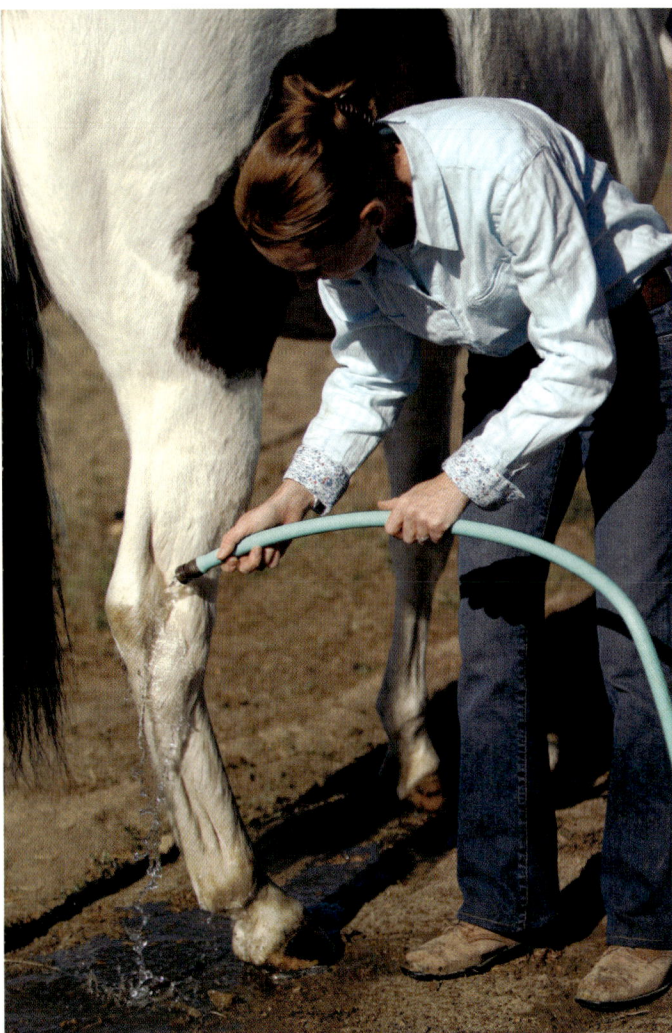

Cold-water therapy can help reduce your horse's swelling during recovery. Other options include ice boots, turbolator boots, commercial cooling cuffs or the creek.

relationship. Your veterinarian must see the animal for whom he's dispensing medication or must have a working knowledge of the horse. The Federal Drug Administration establishes these guidelines, and each state has additional drug-dispensing regulations.

Here are a few more medication-related terms your veterinarian might mention. If your horse's medications don't require prescriptions, they're referred to as "over the counter" or OTC. Additionally, some medications haven't been tested and approved for use in horses. If your veterinarian suggests these non-approved medications, it's called "off-label use." Many medications used in equine veterinary medicine fall into this use category.

Once your veterinarian recommends or prescribes a medication, you need to know how to administer it to continue treating your horse at home during his recovery. For "orally" given medications, use the medication as a top dressing on your horse's feed. Your horse ingests the feed and the medication. Watch closely to make sure your horse eats the full dose soon after it's given. Eating all the medication at once allows your horse to take in the proper amount so that the medicine reaches his blood level in the right doses. If your horse doesn't like the medication's taste, add flavoring to it, such as honey, molasses or other supplements that your horse likes.

If you must "drench" your horse's medication, you squirt the substance into your horse's mouth with a dosing syringe. If the medication comes in the form of a powder or tablet, you must suspend that in a small amount of liquid (water, molasses or honey) before placing it in the syringe.

Intramuscular or "IM" dispensing calls for injection by needle and syringe into one of your horse's large muscle masses. Before administering your horse's medication, you must learn the proper injection technique from your veterinarian and be sure you are familiar with potential complications and how to deal with them. When your horse is insured, the primary permission for or regulation regarding an owner treating his own horse comes from the insurance company holding the policy for that horse. Once injected, the medication then absorbs into the horse's bloodstream and circulates throughout his body. The most common injection sites are the flat muscles on your horse's neck just in front of his shoulder. Another common injection site is in the hamstring muscle on the back of your horse's leg, alongside the tail. Avoid using the large muscle of the croup as an injection site because this area is more prone to serious complications.

Shake the medication to make sure its ingredients haven't settled, and then wait for the bubbles in the bottle to dissipate. Load the syringe. After you insert the needle into the muscle, you pull back on the syringe plunger to see if any blood is sucked back into the syringe; if not, inject the medication in the muscle. You usually don't inject more than 10 milliliters per site. After the injection is completed, massage the muscle to spread the medication. Your horse might become sore at injection sites. If so, massage his muscles after administering the injection and ask your veterinarian about injecting a small distance away from the first site when dosing your horse for multiple days. Each successive dose should be administered in a different body location.

For "intravenous" or IV medications, you inject a prescription by hypodermic needle and syringe into the horse's jugular vein. Again, check with your veterinarian to make sure you know precisely how to complete the injection and to make sure your insurance company allows you to perform the injection without a veterinarian present. The medication travels to the horse's heart and circulates throughout the body.

Cautions: You must make sure that the medication is injected only into a vein. Some substances can cause severe injury if injected into a muscle and not a vein. You also must make sure that medication isn't injected into the carotid artery, which lies near the jugular vein. If medication goes into your horse's carotid artery, it immediately travels to the brain. Your horse can suffer severe conse-

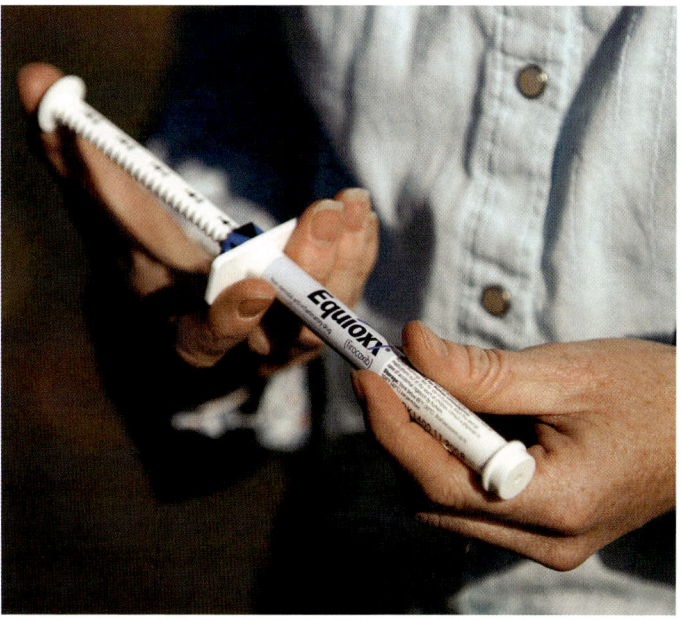

Several anti-inflammatory medications are available to help your horse during his healing process. Some are easier on your horse's digestive system than others.

quences and even die if the medication isn't administered correctly.

Some horses react negatively to intramuscular and intravenous drugs. Be prepared for a violent neurological reaction after the administration of drugs such as the antimicrobial known as procaine penicillin G, or PPG. If your horse has a reaction, it happens within seconds of the intramuscular injection. Your horse becomes excitable, backing up, kicking out, bouncing his head, even acting blind. Prepare your horse by housing him in a stall or have an experienced horse person hold him. The reaction might last for two to five minutes. These reactions aren't common, and injecting the horse's rear leg muscles seems to minimize the reactions. If your horse becomes excited or anxious, and appears to cramp or sweat after you administer any drug, consult your veterinarian immediately.

Take-Home Medications

Here's a look at some of the medications that might be used to treat your horse's lameness and how they are administered.

Drug Name	Drug Type	Category
trimethoprim/sulfadiazine	antimicrobial, or a medication used to fight bacterial infection anywhere in the horse's body	prescription
procaine penicillin G	antimicrobial	prescription
gentamicin	antimicrobial	prescription
ceftiofur	antimicrobial	prescription
phenylbutazone	nonsteroidal anti-inflammatory medication, or NSAID; an anti-inflammatory medication not in the corticosteroid family and which has few side effects on the body's physiology	prescription
flunixin	nonsteroidal anti-inflammatory medication (NSAID)	prescription
ketoprofen	nonsteroidal anti-inflammatory medication (NSAID)	prescription
firocoxib	nonsteroidal anti-inflammatory medication (NSAID)	prescription
diclofenac	nonsteroidal anti-inflammatory medication (NSAID)	prescription
acepromazine	tranquilizer	prescription

Your veterinarian can prescribe medications suited for your horse's particular ailment.

Why Given	Administration	Concerns
treats bacterial infections, but doesn't affect viruses or influenza; commonly dispensed for respiratory infections or contaminated wounds	oral or drench; usually given for 7 days	rare, but can include digestive upset, diarrhea
aids in respiratory infections, such as streptococcus, and infected or contaminated wounds; can aid digestive-tract infections	intramuscular, usually for a 5-day minimum	muscle soreness at injection site, anxious reaction, anaphylactic shock
aids digestive-tract or any effectiveness; used in conjunction with penicillin for wide-spectrum infections	intramuscular or intravenous; once daily for total of 5 days	few; can cause kidney damage with high doses for extended time or in a dehydrated horse
helpful against many types of bacteria	intramuscular or intravenous for up to 13 days	rarely associated with severe diarrhea
to minimize inflammation for acute or chronic musculoskeletal injuries; peak therapeutic effect in 12 hours and lasts 18 to 24 hours	oral or intravenous; not to exceed 4 grams daily for more than 5 days	digestive-tract ulcers and kidney damage with overdosage or long-term dosage; oral mucus membrane irritant in some horses; excess salivation; tissue damage when vein is missed while injecting intravenously
as an anti-inflammatory for musculoskeletal injuries; as an analgesic for mild colic and to combat toxicity; therapeutic effect within 3 to 4 hours and lasting about 12 hours	intravenous or oral for maximum of 5 days	digestive-tract ulcers and kidney disease with high or long-term dosage
therapeutic anti-inflammatory medication for acute and chronic musculoskeletal injuries; therapeutic effect within 3 to 4 hours lasting for 12 to 16 hours	intravenous	digestive-tract ulcers and kidney damage with high or long-term dosage
anti-inflammatory therapy for musculoskeletal injuries	oral for up to 14 days	minimal compared to other NSAIDs.
anti-inflammatory therapy for joint injuries; remains in the local tissues with little systemic effect	topical	minimal, but not to be combined with other NSAIDs; lower systemic risk than with oral medications
to reduce anxiety	intramuscular or intravenous	fainting and hypotension, or lowblood pressure; avoid in cases of blood loss or other shock situations

Take-Home Medications (cont.)

Here's a look at some of the medications that might be used to treat your horse's lameness and how they are administered.

Drug Name	Drug Type	Category
zylazine	sedative and analgesic	prescription
detomidine	sedative and analgesic	prescription
romifidine	sedative and analgesic	prescription
fluphenazine decanoate	behavior modifier	off-label prescription
hyaluronate	joint therapy	prescription for intravenous;
polysulfated glycosaminoglycan	joint therapy	prescription
glucosamine	joint therapy	over-the-counter (OTC)
methylsulfonylmethane (MSM)	joint therapy	over-the-counter (OTC)
Omega 3 fatty acids	joint therapy	over-the-counter (OTC)

Your veterinarian can prescribe medications suited for your horse's particular ailment.

Why Given	Administration	Concerns
sedative for restraint	intramuscular or intravenous	shock in hypotensive horses with low blood pressure; unsteady horses whose defensive reflexes can be sudden and violent
as a restraint for body clipping, sedation for shoeing, or for violent colic; longer therapeutic effect than with zylazine	intramuscular or intravenous	can cause shock in hypotensive horses; unsteady horses whose defensive reflexes can be sudden and violent
restraint for body clipping, shoeing, etc.	intravenous	hypotension; unsteady horses with sudden and violent defensive reflexes; horses more steady than with zylazine or dormosodan
to calm nervous horses during confinement for healing	intramuscular, lasting up to four weeks	possible serious excitable reaction; unpredictable results; prohibited in most show and racing jurisdictions
to reduce joint-capsule inflammation and to protect and maintain joint health	intravenous once a week for three weeks	minimal
to reduce joint inflammation and aid cartilage healing	intramuscular once every four days for total of seven injections	minimal
to increase joint lubrication; as joint anti-inflammatory	oral	minimal
to reduce inflammatory free radicals within inflamed joints	oral	minimal
for joint protection	oral	minimal

GLOSSARY

abscess: a pus-filled cavity formed during the inflammtion process, often caused by bacterial infection.

acute: sudden onset often sparked by an injury.

adhesions: scarring that causes structures to adhere together.

arthroscopy: intra-articular surgery using instruments inserted through small portals; used for both diagnostic and treatment procedures.

asymptomatic: when radiographs or other diagnostic tools show internal changes and damage without externally visible signs of lameness.

avulsion fracture: when the ligament pulls away from its attachment and a piece of bone pulls away, as well.

avulsions: pieces of bone that pull free from the parent bone at the site of ligament attachments, usually as a result of excessive stress on the ligament.

axillary nerves: the nerve bundle providing all nerve function for the forelimb. Originating from the spinal cord in the shoulder area, the axillary nerves travel from the spinal column to the front legs, where the bundle branches into the many nerves of the forelegs.

blindfold test: walking your horse after applying a blindfold. A horse with mild neurological signs can worsen if he is using his sight to compensate for the neurological deficit.

blocking: injecting anesthetic along a horse's nerve or into a joint to block pain in an attempt to locate the lameness source.

bog spavin: excessive fluid in the tarsocrural joint, often noticed as a large, fluid-filled pouch that's found on the front of the hock at its inside corner.

bone spavin: a lay term that refers to degenerative joint disease or osteoarthritis that affects the hocks' lower joints, distal intertarsal and tarsal metatarsal joints.

bone-lipping: with chronic joint inflammation, the extra bone the body produces along the bone edge; often called bone-modeling; common in horses with osteoarthritis.

break-over point: the most forward place on the ground surface of your horse's foot or shoe, which acts as a fulcrum as he moves forward and his heel leaves the ground.

bursa: synovial-lined sac that provides lubrication for tendons and ligaments as they move over bone prominences.

carpitis: inflammation of the carpus, or knee.

carpus: the knee, or joint between the forearm and the cannon bone.

cerebral spinal fluid: the fluid within the spinal column chamber surrounding the spinal cord.

cervical: of the neck.

cervical vertebral stabilization: surgically placing a basket or bone insert across the joint between two vertebrae to fuse them together and correct dynamic compression of the spinal cord.

core lesion: a significant tear in a ligament or tendon and diagnosed by ultrasound.

corn: a bruise to deep, sensitive structures at the angle of the sole, the triangular area between the bar and the hoof wall.

corticosteroids: manmade drugs that closely resemble cortisol, a hormone naturally produced by your horse's adrenal glands. Given for a short period of time, steroids reduce inflammation and pain and can minimize tissue damage. Administering in excessive amounts intra-articularly can result in cartilage damage. Excessive systemic administration can result in reduced immune function and other physiological changes, including laminitis.

cow-hocked: a conformation error; when viewing a horse from behind, the hocks are closer together than the fetlocks.

crepitus: the characteristic vibration felt when two boney pieces of a fracture move past each other; bone rubbing on bone.

cruciate ligaments: ligaments in the horse's stifle that lie deep inside the joint, holding together the tibia and femur while allowing the stifle full range of motion. A torn cruciate ligament, a serious injury, is difficult to diagnose.

cunean tendon: the tendon that exerts rotational pull on the hock and puts pressure on the lower joints. In cunean tenectomy surgery, part of the cunean tendon is removed to help horses that suffer from degenerative hock joint disease.

curb: common in racehorses, an injury to the hock joint's lower, backside or plantar ligaments; viewed from the side, appears as a bulging area on the backside of the hock, below the point of the hock; can require three to four months' rest and is managed with controlled exercise, anti-inflammatory medication and shockwave treatment.

Cushing's disease: a hormonal disorder caused by a benign pituitary gland tumor that causes horses to store fat and keep from shedding. The disease also is linked to horses that are predisposed to laminitis.

degeneration: a disease process causing gradual deterioration of a body part's structure, to the point the structure might lose ability to function.

desmitis: ligament inflammation.

digital pulse: a pronounced pulse in an area where a horse's pulse isn't usually easy to detect—just above the heel bulb, along the tendon sides in the pastern area.

distal intertarsal joint: the lower of the two intertarsal joints; can close or fuse with advanced joint disease.

disuse atrophy: muscle shrinkage due to a lack of use, often a result of regional pain or nerve damage.

DMSO: dimethyl sulfoxide, an anti-inflammatory, antibacterial and analgesic topical agent.

DOD: developmental orthopedic disease.

dorsal sacrale ligaments: ligaments running from the tuber sacrale, two paired bones in the equine pelvis, to the top of the sacrum, another pelvic bone.

dorsal spinous processes: the spiny upward projections of the horse's vertebrae.

dynamic: changing or having the ability to change.

edema: swelling caused by fluid in the horse's body tissues, outside of the blood vessels.

EPM: equine protozoal myeloencephalitis, an equine neurological disease caused by protozoa attacking the nerve cells.

extra-corporeal shockwave treatment: applying ultra-high-energy sound waves into the body to help heal various body parts.

fascia: a sheet or band of fibrous tissue lying under the skin or encasing muscles.

fissure fracture: a bone crack that extends only partway through the bone with no displacement of the parts; also known as a hairline fracture.

fructan: a carbohydrate found in grass and hay that, in excess, can cause physiological changes in a horse's gut and trigger effects in the hoof's laminae.

hematoma: a collection of blood resulting from a hemorrhage or bleeding into tissue.

hitch: a descriptive word for lameness having different meanings, depending upon geographic region. Avoid using.

hoof capsule: the cornified portion of the foot that encases the foot's sensitive structures. The hoof capsule includes the hoof wall, sole, bars, heel buttress and frog.

hoof-testers: a clamp-like device used to evaluate your horse's foot. A horse pulls away when sensitive to pressure from the metal testers.

hop test: holding a horse's front leg and leaning into the horse until the horse hops to the side. If the horse doesn't hop sideways to catch his own weight, he might have a neurological deficit.

ilium bone: the largest of the three pairs of bones that fuse to create the horse's pelvis.

implant: a screw or plate positioned to hold your horse's bones together for proper healing.

inferior check ligament: located along the upper half of the deep digital flexor tendon, this check ligament originates at the back of the knee and attaches to the deep digital flexor tendon in the cannon-bone area. It supports the tendon when the muscles become fatigued.

insulin resistance: failure of tissues to respond appropriately to insulin, which results in high insulin levels and contributes to the metabolic causes of laminitis. Insulin levels in the blood can be tested.

intra-articular: administered via injection into a horse's joint.

intra-synovial injections: medication injected into the tendon sheath or joint.

IRAP: scientifically known as interleukin-1 receptor antagonist protein, IRAP is a collection of blood factors that combats osteoarthritis.

keratinized: becoming horn-like in consistency.

Kimzey splint: a large aluminum brace that keeps your horse's hoof angled down so the ligaments and flexor tendons of the lower leg aren't weighted.

knee chip fractures: fragments along the edges of the carpal bone.

lameness: a deviation from the horse's normal gait or posture due to pain or mechanical dysfunction.

laminae: vertical, leaf-like projections between the coffin bone and the hoof wall.

lateral: outside or away from your horse's midline.

lateral condyle: the outside or lateral weight-bearing portion of the femur in the stifle joint.

ligaments: fibrous bands that attach bones to bones.

long pastern bone: also known as the first phalanx, or P1.

medial: inside, closest to your horse's midline.

medial condyle: the inside or medial weight-bearing portion of the femur in the stifle joint.

menisci: "C" cartilages that function as a bushing to help the tibia and femur fit together.

micro-picking: a process performed via arthroscopy that can help heal damaged joint cartilage.

myelogram: a radiograph of the spinal cord after it has been injected with radio-opaque material.

non-displaced fracture: a crack in the body of a bone without the pieces separating.

OCD: osteochondritis dessicans; the fragment next to the parent bone that causes joint irritation.

orthopedic: relating to the bones, joints, ligaments or muscles.

palmar: describing the backside of a horse's front leg.

palmar carpal ligaments: strong ligaments that aid in motion and provide stability for your horse's knee, whether the structure is bent or straight.

palpate: feeling internal anatomy by careful touch and manipulation.

pastern joint: also known as the proximal interphalangeal joint, or PIP joint, the joint between P1 and P2.

patella: the horse's kneecap, found in the front of the stifle joint. With the quadriceps muscle and its distal ligament attachment, the patella functions to extend the rear leg.

Patton shoe: a shoe that raises your horse's heel dramatically.

periosteum: the tough, thin tissue layer that covers each bone in your horse's body.

periarticular injections: injections made into the quadriceps muscle, where it attaches to the patella and along the patellar ligaments.

peritendon tissue: tissue surrounding the tendon.

pitting edema: an area of trauma where fluid accumulates in and around the muscle mass. When you apply finger pressure, a dent develops in your horse's flesh and then gradually fills within a few minutes.

plantar: describing the backside of a horse's hind leg.

pointing: a horse's stance when he places one front foot forward to relieve pressure from his body weight.

point of the shoulder: the most prominent, forward portion of the shoulder visible from the horse's exterior.

polysaccharide storage syndrome: a muscle disease that causes unusual storage of glycogen in the horse's muscle cells, resulting in painful muscle contraction. There is strong evidence this is caused by a genetic mutation.

posterior digital neurectomy: commonly referred to as nerving; permanently removing a portion of the posterior digital nerves to relieve pain in a portion of the horse's foot.

poultice: a moist, hydroscopic dressing applied to painful and swollen body parts.

propreoception: the brain's ability to know where the feet are at all times.

proximal intertarsal joint: the upper of the two intertarsal joints, which seldom close or fuse.

radiopaque: anything that doesn't allow radiation to penetrate; can be a liquid or metal.

reciprocal apparatus: the arrangement of tendons and ligaments on the front and back of the leg, from above the stifle to below the hock, which causes the stifle, hock and fetlock to work in unison.

red zone: the most critical hoof area because it includes vital structures: the central portion of the frog, the deep flexor tendon, the navicular bone, the impar ligament and the coffin joint.

ringbone: osteoarthritis in the horse's pastern joint.

road founder: a breakdown in a horse's laminae following work on hard surfaces. Such constant pounding can initiate the complex set of events that causes laminitis or founder.

scapula: the shoulder blade

serviceably sound: a horse's ability to complete a suitable job willingly as asked.

short pastern bone: also known as the second phalanx, or P2.

sickle-hocked: a conformation error; viewed from the side, a horse's cannon bone extends forward ahead of the hock rather than going straight to the ground.

sodium hyaluronate: a long chain protein, which reduces joint inflammation, and an important part of a horse's synovial fluid.

splint: anatomically, the common name for the small, slender bones that lie on either side of your horse's cannon bone. In the front leg these are the metacarpal bones, and in the rear leg they are the metatarsal bones. "Splint" also can refer to the firm, soft-tissue enlargement or mineral deposit that forms when the splint-to-cannon bone attachment is challenged by trauma or stress, or as a result of the periosteal tissue that covers the splint bone being traumatized

static: fixed and unchanging.

stifled: a general lay term pertaining to hind-leg soreness, but nothing specific. Many injuries and lameness issues can develop in the stifle because of the numerous structures involved: the patella, 14 ligaments and three joint compartments.

stress fracture: a break caused by continuous repetitive stress or an acute incident. The bone break is not evident from the outside, creating a narrow fracture line within nondisplaced bone fragments. Scintigraphy, MRI or CT can be the only diagnostic tools to demonstrate this pathology.

subchondral: below the cartilage.

subchondral bone: supportive bone lying directly under the cartilage.

sulci: depressions alongside the frog and in the frog's centerline.

superior check ligament: originating from the radius bone and connecting to the superficial digital flexor tendon, this ligament supports the tendon when the muscle becomes fatigued.

surgical joint fusion: a surgical process to end joint pain by stopping the joint's ability to move and wear. After removing the joint cartilage, the joint bones are screwed together, causing them to fuse in the healing process, much as a fracture heals.

suspensory ligament: a large ligament that originates at the top of the cannon bone, behind the knee in the front leg, and at the back of the hock on the hind leg; the primary support of the fetlock along with the sesamoids, distal sesamoidian ligaments and the digital flexor tendons.

sweat bandage: a bandage in which a compound, such as DMSO and furacin, is applied beneath plastic wrap to create heat, dilating your horse's blood vessels, increasing blood supply and promoting healing.

sweeny shoulder: disuse muscle atrophy resulting in a visible ridge along the horse's shoulder blade or scapula.

swinging-leg lameness: the action in which a horse swings his entire limb in a labored movement, as opposed to limping when weight is placed on the affected leg.

syndrome: a group of signs and symptoms that together characterize a specific disease or disorder.

synovial fluid: fluid inside the joint that lubricates and protects, and also provides nutrition to the joint cartilage. Excess fluid creates a soft swelling called a wind puff.

systemic: administered medication that affects the whole body, usually administered orally, intramuscularly, subcutaneously, or intravenously.

tarsal metatarsal joint: the lowest joint in the hock, found between the hock and cannon bone; frequently associated with degenerative joint disease of the hock.

tarsocrural joint: the joint between the tibia and the upper section of the hock.

tendons: fibrous bands that connect your horse's muscles to bone.

thrush: frog degeneration caused by anaerobic bacteria that thrive when trapped in the area. Untreated, the bacteria can eat away the frog and expose the foot's soft tissue.

toed-in: a conformational fault causing a horse's hooves to angle toward one another at the toe and thus appear pigeon-toed.

tracking: moving a horse, usually in hand, in straight lines or circles to the right or left to observe his way of going.

trochlear ridge: structures that act as grooved tracks within your horse's stifles and hocks.

tuber coxae: "pin bones" that form the points of the pelvis on each side of your horse's hindquarters.

tuber ischii: the lower rear two corners of the pelvis, which form the buttocks along either side of the horse's tail.

tuber sacrale: paired bones in the horse's pelvis, which "peak" at the rear end of the lumbar region and the top or front of the croup. These prominent peaks shift upward when a horse has a sacroiliac subluxation or "hunter's bump" injury.

tying-up syndrome: acute muscle degeneration, resulting in painful muscle cramping and reluctance to move.

unsound: injured or unsuited to perform a task because of lameness.

use trauma: a progressive and accumulative trauma occurring to an anatomical structure, such as a joint, with normal work. Use trauma might be enhanced due to conformational problems, some types of work and the work environment.

vertebrae: bones that make up the spinal column.

wind puff: A soft-to-the-touch bump near a horse's joint and filled with joint fluid.

wobbler syndrome: a problem that occurs when horse's spinal cord is exposed to pinching and bruising.

PROFILE
TERRY SWANSON, DVM

Terry Swanson, DVM

Terry Swanson, DVM, and the practice where he's a partner, Littleton Equine Medical Center, based in Littleton, Colo., have made a significant impact diagnosing and treating equine lameness. Swanson always has been dedicated to horses and interested in their care. Growing up on a ranch in Wyoming, Swanson learned to appreciate horses and learned the importance of keeping them sound. He team ropes with his family and works to keep his competition mounts safe and feeling great.

After graduating from Colorado State University in 1967, Swanson interned at Littleton Equine Medical Center—then known as Littleton Large Animal Clinic. Demonstrating a work ethic that equaled his knowledge of horses, Swanson worked up through the ranks from intern to partner. Now, Swanson is a respected and nationally known lameness expert.

Founded in 1950, Littleton Equine Medical Center has provided the Denver area and surrounding suburbs with professional veterinary care for decades. Dr. Harry W. Johnson established the clinic as a large-animal veterinary clinic, treating horses, cattle, pigs, sheep, and goats. But horses always have been a passion at Littleton Equine Medical Center. It wasn't by chance that Littleton Equine Medical Center's original location was but a mile from Centennial Race Track.

Doctors Marvin Beeman, Charles Vail, and Swanson partnered with Johnson to build a practice unmatched for dedication and quality of care. Today, Littleton Equine Medical Center exclusively treats horses. Including veterinarians, interns, technicians, and support personnel, Littleton Equine Medical Center has grown to a staff of more than 60, providing Colorado and the region with a referral center for specialized horse care. (Visit www.littletonequine.com for more information.)

Demonstrating an interest in helping in ways beyond just his own practice, Swanson also has served as the president of the American Association of Equine Practitioners and the Colorado Veterinary Medical Association, and has been named Colorado Veterinarian of the Year. Swanson is a strong advocate of using new digital imaging technology as a means for better diagnoses of equine health-care problems and suggesting corrective procedures.

PROFILE
HEIDI NYLAND, MS

Heidi Nyland, MS

Heidi Nyland has ridden since age 5. Growing up in the suburbs of Columbus, Ohio, she began riding Ponies of the Americas at Smiley "R" Ranch with mentors W.E. Richardson and Janet Hedman. When her legs grew longer than the ponies' barrels, she moved "up" to ride American Quarter Horses throughout high school.

In college at Ohio Wesleyan University, Nyland studied English and journalism by day and practiced for the school's Intercollegiate Horse Show Association team in the evenings. She rode with well-known Paint Horse trainer Terry Myers, who coached the school's team. Nyland served as team president and, later, as assistant coach, helping at Western and English competitions throughout Ohio and Michigan.

During graduate school at the E.W. Scripps School of Journalism at Ohio University, Nyland met visiting journalism professor and former Iranian hostage Terry Anderson, who then was building his large-scale Tennessee Walking Horse breeding barn and riding facility. Nyland helped Anderson with several of his first horses—working with them to make steady trail mounts. At the same time, Nyland began writing for several online horse publications, focusing her journalism on the equine world.

Nyland headed west to Colorado in 2001—pursuing horse and horse press country. Her work has been published in *Western Horseman, Horse & Rider, Equine Veterinary Management, The Trail Rider, America's Horse, American Cowboy* and many more publications. Nyland was an author of *Western Horseman's Legends 6*, contributing chapters about several famous American Quarter Horse stallions. Her photography has won numerous awards including a prestigious AIM Award, presented by the Western-English Trade Association. Nyland also is the producer for Julie Goodnight's *Horse Master* television show and handles Goodnight's photography and marketing.

When not writing or taking pictures, Nyland is often riding, working with her Australian Shepherds, or teaching riding lessons. She's a North American Riding for the Handicapped Association therapeutic riding instructor and a licensed Brain Gym instructor. (Visit www.wholepicture.org for more information.)